INTERNATIONAL
POLITICAL
ECONOMY:
PERSPECTIVES ON
GLOBAL POWER
AND WEALTH

International Political Economy: Perspectives on Global Power and Wealth

Jeffry A. Frieden
University of California, Los Angeles

David A. Lake
University of California, Los Angeles

St. Martin's Press   New York

Acknowledgments

George W. Ball, "Cosmocorp: The Importance of Being Stateless," from *The Columbia Journal of World Business*, November–December 1967. Reprinted with permission.

David P. Calleo and Benjamin M. Rowland, "Free Trade and the Atlantic Community," from *America and the World Political Economy*. Reprinted with permission from Indiana University Press.

A. W. Clausen, President of the World Bank, "Poverty in the Developing Countries," Address given at the Martin Luther King Jr. Center, Atlanta, Georgia, January 11, 1985 (Washington: The World Bank, 1985). Abridged.

Benjamin J. Cohen, from *Organizing the World's Money: The Political Economy of International Monetary Relations*. Copyright © 1977 by Basic Books, Inc., Publishers. Reprinted by permission of the publisher.

Richard N. Cooper, "Economic Interdependence and Foreign Policy in the Seventies," *World Politics* 24, no. 2 (January 1972). Copyright © 1972 by Princeton University Press. Reprinted with permission of Princeton University Press. (Portions of the text have been omitted.)

Richard E. Feinberg, "LDC Debt and the Public-Sector Rescue," © Overseas Development Council. Adapted from the author's article originally published in *U.S. Foreign Policy and the Third World: Agenda 1985–86* (Transaction Books, 1985), pp. 51–71.

Jeffry Frieden, "Third World Indebted Industrialization: International Finance and State Capitalism in Mexico, Brazil, Algeria, and South Korea," *International Organization* 35, 1 (1981). Reprinted by permission of The MIT Press, Cambridge, Massachusetts.

John Gallagher and Ronald Robinson, "The Imperialism of Free Trade," *Economic History Review* 2nd Series, 6, 1 (1953). Reprinted with permission.

James Hawley, "The Internationalization of Capital: Banks, Euro-Currency, and the Instability of the World Monetary System," *Review of Radical Political Economics* (Winter 1979). Copyright *Review of Radical Political Economics*. Reprinted by permission of the Union for Radical Political Economics.

G. K. Helleiner, "Transnational Enterprises and the New Political Economy of US Trade Policy," from *Oxford Economic Papers*, 29, Number 1 (1977). Reprinted by permission of Oxford University Press.

Stephen D. Hymer, "International Politics and International Economics," Copyright © 1978 by Monthly Review Inc. Reprinted by permission of Monthly Review Foundation.

Charles P. Kindleberger, "The Rise of Free Trade in Western Europe," *The Journal of Economic History* 35, 1 (1975). Reprinted by permission of The Economic History Association and the author.

Stephen D. Krasner, "State Power and the Structure of International Trade," *World Politics* 28, no. 3 (April 1976). Copyright © 1976 by Princeton University Press. Reprinted with permission of Princeton University Press. (Footnotes have been omitted.)

Stephen D. Krasner, "The Tokyo Round: Particularistic Interests and Prospects for Stability in the Global Trading System," Reprinted from *The International Studies Quarterly* Volume 23, No. 4,

Acknowledgments and copyrights continue at the back of the book on page 410, which constitutes an extension of the copyright page.

Preface

The readings in *International Political Economy: Perspectives on Global Power and Wealth* are primarily intended to introduce the study of International Political Economy to those with little or no prior knowledge of it. The book is designed for use in courses in International Political Economy, International Relations, and International Economics. The selections present both clear and identifiable theoretical arguments and important substantive material.

Although the twenty-seven selections can be used in any order, they are grouped in four parts that reflect some of the more common organizing principles used in International Political Economy courses. Each part begins with an introduction by the editors that provides background information and highlights issues raised in the readings. Each reading is preceded by an abstract summarizing its specific arguments and contributions. The readings were edited to eliminate extraneous or dated information, and most footnotes were removed.

The Introduction defines the study of International Political Economy, summarizes the three major theoretical perspectives on the field, and identifies several current debates. Part I then presents examples of the three perspectives on International Political Economy: Liberalism, Marxism, and Realism. The three readings in this part are intended to suggest the underlying logic and types of arguments used by proponents of each approach. Although they are representative of their respective schools, they do not necessarily capture the wide range of opinion *within* each approach.

Part II, which reviews the history of the international economy since the seventeenth century, provides the background and perspective necessary to understand the contemporary international political economy. The selections describe the major developments in the history of the modern international economy from a variety of different theoretical viewpoints. The post-1945 *Pax Americana* is surveyed in Part III, the largest section of the book. Following an overview of the postwar era, the readings in Part III are organized into three subsections on production, money and finance, and trade. Finally, Part IV examines current problems in the politics of international economics.

The selections in this volume have been used successfully in our respective versions of Political Science 124, International Political Economy, at the University of California, Los Angeles. In our own research, we approach the study of International Political Economy from very different perspectives. Yet, we find that this set of readings accommodates our individual approaches to the subject matter while simultaneously covering the major questions of the field.

The students of Political Science 124 experimented with several versions of this text as it was being "fine-tuned." David Dollar, of the University of California, Los Angeles, Department of Economics, made helpful suggestions on the editors' introductions, as did Ronald A. Francisco and several anonymous reviewers. Peter Dougherty and Larry Swanson of St. Martin's Press helped us shepherd the project through the publication process. We would also like to acknowledge Cynthia Tournat and Mark Brawley, who assisted in the editing. Finally, we want to thank our respective spouses, Anabela Costa and Wendy K. Lake, for their encouragement.

JEFFRY A. FRIEDEN
DAVID A. LAKE

Contents

INTERNATIONAL
POLITICAL
ECONOMY:
PERSPECTIVES ON
GLOBAL POWER
AND WEALTH

INTRODUCTION

INTERNATIONAL POLITICS AND INTERNATIONAL ECONOMICS

Over the past fifteen years, the study of International Political Economy has gone through a remarkable resurgence. Virtually nonexistent before 1970 as a field of study, International Political Economy is now one of the most popular areas of specialization for both undergraduates and graduate students, as well as the source of some of the most innovative and influential work by modern social scientists. The revival of International Political Economy after nearly forty years of dormancy has enriched both social science and public debate, and promises to continue to do both.

International Political Economy is the study of the interplay of economics and politics in the world arena. In the most general sense, the economy can be defined as the system of producing, distributing, and using wealth; politics is the set of institutions and rules by which social and economic interactions are governed. Political economy has a variety of meanings; for some, it refers primarily to the study of the political basis of economic actions, the ways in which government policies affect market operations. For others, the principal preoccupation is the economic basis of political action, the ways in which economic forces mold government policies. The two focuses are in a sense complementary, for politics and markets are in a constant state of mutual interaction.

It should come as no surprise to inhabitants of capitalist societies that markets exist and are governed by certain fundamental laws that operate more or less independently of the will of firms and individuals. Any shopkeeper knows that an attempt to raise the price of a readily available and standardized product—a daily newspaper, for example—above that charged by nearby and competing shopkeepers will very rapidly cause customers to stop buying newspapers at the higher price. Unless the shopkeeper wants to be left with stacks of unsold newspapers, he or she will have to bring the price back into line with "what the market will bear." The shopkeeper will have learned a microcosmic lesson in what economists call the market-clearing equilibrium point, the price at which the number of goods supplied equals the number demanded or the point at which supply-and-demand curves intersect. At the base of all modern economics is the general assertion that, within certain carefully specified parameters, markets operate in and of themselves to maintain balance between supply and demand. Other things being equal, if the supply of a good increases far beyond the demand for it, the good's price will be driven down until demand rises to meet supply, supply falls to meet demand, and the market-clearing equilibrium is restored. By the same token, if demand exceeds supply, the good's price will rise, thus causing demand to decline and supply to increase until the two are in balance.

If the international and domestic economies functioned like perfectly competitive markets, they would be relatively easy to describe and comprehend. Fortunately or unfortunately, however, the freely functioning market is only a highly stylized or abstract picture that is rarely reproduced in the real world. A variety of factors influence the workings of domestic and international markets in ways that a focus on purely economic forces does not fully capture. Consumer tastes can change—how large is the American market for spats or sarsparilla today?—as can the technology needed to make products more cheaply, or even to make entirely new goods that displace others (stick shifts for horsewhips, calculators for slide rules). Producers, sellers, or buyers of goods can band together to try to raise or lower prices unilaterally, as OPEC did with petroleum in 1974 and 1979. And governments can act, consciously or inadvertently, to alter patterns of consumption, supply, demand, prices, and virtually all other economic variables.

It is this last fact, political "interference" with economic trends, that is the most visible, and probably the most important, reason to go beyond market-based, purely economic explanations of social behavior. Indeed, many market-oriented economists are continually surprised by the ability of governments—or of powerful groups pressuring governments—to contravene economic tendencies. When OPEC first raised oil prices in December 1973, some market-minded pundits, and even a few naive economists, predicted that such naked manipulation of the forces of supply and demand could last only a matter of months. What has emerged from the past fifteen years' experience with oil prices is that they are a function of *both* market forces *and* the ability of OPEC's member states to organize concerted intervention in the oil market. Somewhat less dramatic are the everyday operations of local and national governments that affect prices, production, profits, wages, and almost all other aspects of the economy. Wage, price, and rent controls; taxation; incentives and subsidies; tariffs; government spending—all serve to mold modern economies and the functioning of markets themselves. Who could understand the suburbanization of the United States after World War II without taking into account government tax incentives to home mortgage-holders, government-financed highway construction, politically driven patterns of local educational expenditures? How many American (or Japanese or European) farmers would be left if agricultural subsidies were eliminated? How many Americans would have college educations were it not for public universities and government scholarships? Who could explain the proliferation of nonprofit groups in the United States without knowing the tax incentives given to charitable donations?

In these instances, and many more, political pressure groups, politicians, and government bureaucrats have at least as much effect on economic outcomes as do the fundamental laws of the marketplace. Social scientists, especially political scientists, have spent decades trying to understand how these political pressures interact to produce government policy. Many of the results provide as elegant and stylized a view of politics as the economics profession has developed of markets; as in economics, however, social science models of political behavior are little more than didactic devices whose accuracy depends on a wide variety of unpredictable factors, including underlying economic trends. If only a foolish economist would dismiss the possibilities of intergovernmental producers' cartels (such as OPEC) out of hand, only a foolish political scientist would not realize that the economic realities of modern international commodity markets ensure that successful producers' cartels will be few and far between.

It is thus no surprise that political economy is far from new. Indeed, until a century ago, virtually all thinkers concerned with understanding human society wrote about political economy. For individuals as diverse as Adam Smith, John Stuart Mill, and Karl Marx, the economy was eminently political and politics was obviously tied to economic phenomena. Few scholars before 1900 would have taken seriously any attempt to describe and analyze politics and economics separately.

In the last years of the nineteenth century and the first years of the twentieth century, however, professional studies of economics and politics became more and more divorced from one another. Economic investigation began to focus on understanding more fully the operation of specific markets and their interaction; the development of new mathematical techniques permitted the formalization of, for example, laws of supply and demand. By the time of World War I, an economics profession per se was in existence, and its attention focused on understanding the operation of economic activities in and of themselves. At the same time, other scholars were looking increasingly at the political realm in isolation from the economy. The rise of modern representative political institutions, mass political parties, more politically informed populations, and modern bureaucracies all seemed to justify the study of politics as an activity that had a logic of its own.

With the exception of a few isolated individuals and an upsurge of interest during the politically and economically troubled Depression years, the twentieth century saw an increasing separation of the study of economics and politics. Economists developed ever more elaborate and sophisticated models of how economies work; similarly, other social scientists spun out ever more complex theories of political development and activity.

The resurgence of Political Economy since 1970 has had two interrelated sources. The first was dissatisfaction among academics with the gap between abstract models of political and economic behavior on the one hand, and the actual behavior of polities and economies on the other. As theory became more ethereal, it also seemed to become less realistic. Many scholars began to question the intellectual justifications for a strict analytical division between politics and economics. Second, as the stability and prosperity of the first twenty-five postwar years started to disintegrate in the early 1970s, economic issues became politicized, and political systems became increasingly preoccupied with economic affairs. In August 1971, Richard Nixon ended the gold-dollar standard that had formed the basis for postwar monetary relations; two-and-a-half years later, a previously little-known group, the Organization of Petroleum Exporting Countries (OPEC), succeeded in substantially raising the price of oil. In 1974 and 1975, the industrial nations of Western Europe, North America, and Japan fell into the first worldwide economic recession since the 1930s; unemployment and inflation were soon widespread realities and explosive political issues. In the world arena, the underdeveloped countries—most of them recently independent— burst onto center stage as the Third World, demanding a fairer division of global wealth and power. If in the 1950s and 1960s economic growth was taken for granted and politics occupied itself with other matters, in the 1970s and 1980s economic stagnation fed political strife while political conflict exacerbated economic uncertainty.

For both intellectual and practical reasons, then, social scientists began seeking, once more, to understand how politics and economics interact in modern society. As interest in political economy grew, a series of fundamental questions were posed, and an even broader variety of contending approaches arose.

To be sure, today's political economists have not simply reproduced the studies of earlier (and perhaps neglected) generations of political economists. The professionalization of both Economics and Political Science led to major advances in both fields, and scholars now understand both economic and political phenomena far better than they did a generation ago. It is on this improved basis that the new political economy is being constructed, albeit with some long-standing issues in mind.

Just as in the real world, where politicians must pay close attention to economic trends and economic actors must keep track of political tendencies, those who would understand the political process must take the economy into account and vice versa. A much richer picture of social processes emerges from an integrated understanding of both political and economic affairs than from the isolated study of politics and economics as separate realms. This much is by now hardly controversial; it is in application that disagreements arise. Government actions may color economic trends, but government actions themselves may simply reflect the pressures of economic interest groups. Economic interest groups may be central in determining government policy, yet the political system—democratic or totalitarian, two-party or multiparty, parliamentary or presidential—may crucially color the outlooks and influence of economic interests. In the attempt to arrive at an integrated view of how politics and economics interact, we must disentangle economic and political causes and effects. In this effort, different scholars have different approaches, with different implications for the resulting view of the world.

THREE PERSPECTIVES ON INTERNATIONAL POLITICAL ECONOMY

Nearly all studies in International Political Economy can be classified into one of three mutually exclusive perspectives: Liberalism, Marxism, and Realism. Each of the three perspectives has a unique set of simplifying assumptions used to render the world less complex and more readily understandable. Assumptions are assertions accepted as true for purposes of further investigations. The value of an assumption lies in the ability of the theory built upon it to explain observed phenomena. Thus, assumptions are neither true nor false, only useful or not useful.

The assumptions upon which each of these three perspectives is based lead international political economists to view the world in very different ways. Many Liberals regard foreign direct investment in less developed countries, for instance, as a mutually rewarding exchange between entrepreneurs. Many Marxists, on the other hand, see the foreign firm as exploiting the less developed country. Consequently, a first step in studying International Political Economy is to understand the assumptions made by each of the three perspectives.

Liberalism

The Liberal perspective is drawn primarily from the field of economics and can be traced to the writings of Adam Smith (1723–1790) and David Ricardo (1772–1823). Smith and Ricardo were reacting to the pervasive economic controls that existed under mercantilism between the six-teenth and nineteenth centuries (see Viner, Reading 4). In this period, the domestic and international economies were tightly regulated by governments in order to expand national power and wealth. Smith, Ricardo, and their followers argued that the philosophy underlying this practice was mistaken. Rather, these Liberals asserted that national wealth was best increased by allowing free and unrestricted exchange between individuals in both the domestic and international economies. As their ideas gained adherents in the early nineteenth century, many of the mercantilist trade restrictions were dismantled (see Kindleberger, Reading 5).

Smith and the nineteenth-century Liberals were the economic reform-ers of their era. In International Political Economy, advocates of free trade and free markets are still referred to as Liberals. In twentieth-century American domestic politics, on the other hand, the term has come to mean just the opposite. In the United States today, "Conserva-tives" generally support free markets and less government intervention, while "Liberals" advocate greater governmental intervention in the market to stimulate growth and mitigate inequalities. These contradic-tory usages of the term *Liberal* may seem confusing, but in the readings below and elsewhere the context usually makes the author's meaning clear.

Three assumptions are central to the Liberal perspective. First, Liberals assume that individuals are the principal actors within the political economy and the proper unit of analysis. While this may seem obvious, as all social activity can ultimately be traced back to individuals, this first assumption gains its importance by comparison with Marxism and Realism, each of which makes alternative assumptions (see below).

Second, Liberals assume that individuals are rational, utility-maximiz-ing actors. Rational action means that individuals make cost-benefit calculations across a wide range of possible options. Actors are utility maximizers when, given a calculated range of benefits, they choose the option which yields the highest level of subjective satisfaction. This does not imply that individuals actually gain from every utility-maximizing choice. In some circumstances, utility maximization implies that the individual will choose the option that makes him or her least worse off.

Third, Liberals assume that individuals maximize utility by making trade-offs between goods. Consider the trade-off between clothing and BMWs. At high levels of clothing and low levels of BMWs, some individuals—depending upon their desires for these two goods—might be willing to trade some of their wearing apparel for a fancy automobile. Likewise, if an individual possesses a large number of BMWs but little clothing, he or she might be willing to trade automobiles for apparel. Individuals thus increase their utility, according to Liberals, by exchanging goods with others. Those who desire cars more strongly than clothing will trade the latter for the former. Others who prefer BMWs over clothing will trade apparel for automobiles. This process of exchange will occur until each individual, given the existing quantities of BMWs and clothing, is as well off as possible without making someone else worse off. At this point, all individuals in society will have maximized their uniquely defined utilities. Some will possess BMWs but no clothing. Others will possess only clothing. The vast majority of us, on the other hand, will possess varying mixes of both.

These three assumptions imply that there is no basis for conflict within the political economy. If markets are open and no impediments to trade between individuals exist, everyone can be made as well off as possible given existing stocks of goods and services. Everyone, in other words, will be at his or her highest possible level of utility.

According to Liberals, the role of government is and should be quite limited. Many forms of government intervention in the economy, they argue, intentionally or unintentionally constrict the market and thereby prevent potentially rewarding trades from occurring. The government does have a legitimate and necessary role, however, in creating and subsequently maintaining the existence of a free and competitive market. Governments must provide for the defense of the country, protect property rights, and prevent unfair collusions or concentrations of power within the market. The government should also, according to most Liberals, educate its citizens, build infrastructure, and provide and regulate a common currency. The proper role of government, in other words, is to provide the necessary foundation for the market.

At the level of the international economy, Liberals assert that a fundamental harmony of interests exists between as well as within countries. As Richard Cobden argued in the fight against trade protection in Great Britain during the early nineteenth century, all countries are best off when goods and services move freely across national borders in mutually rewarding exchanges. If universal free trade were to exist, Cobden reasoned, all countries would enjoy the highest level of utility and there would be no economic basis for international conflict and war.

Liberals also believe that governments should manage the international economy in much the same way as they manage their domestic economies. They should establish rules and regulations—often referred to as "international regimes"—to govern exchanges between different national currencies and ensure that no country or domestic group is damaged by "unfair" international competition.

For Liberals, then, economics and politics are largely separate realms. The role of government is limited to managing the market to ensure that all potentially profitable trades can occur. Where markets are functioning well, no economic basis for political conflict exists; everyone is as well off as he or she can be.

Marxism

Marxism originated with the writings of Karl Marx, a nineteenth-century political economist and perhaps capitalism's severest critic. Just as Liberalism emerged in reaction to mercantilism, Marxism was a response to the spread of Liberalism in the nineteenth century. Where for Liberals the market allows individuals to maximize their utility, Marx saw capitalism and the market creating extremes of wealth for capitalists and poverty for workers. While everyone may have been better off than before, the capitalists were clearly expanding their wealth more rapidly than all others. Marx rejected the assertion that exchange between individuals necessarily maximizes the welfare of the whole society. Accordingly, Marx perceived capitalism as an inherently conflictual system that both should and will be inevitably overthrown and replaced by socialism.

Marxism makes three essential assumptions. First, Marxists assume that classes are the dominant actors in the political economy and are the appropriate unit of analysis. Marxists identify two economically determined aggregations of individuals, or classes, as central: capital, or the owners of the means of production, and labor, or workers.

Second, Marxists assume that classes act in their material economic interests. Just as Liberals assume that individuals act rationally to maximize their utility, Marxists assume that each class acts to maximize the economic well-being of the class as a whole.

Third, Marxists assume that the basis of the capitalist economy is the exploitation of labor by capital. Marx's analysis began with the labor theory of value, which holds that the value of any product is determined by the amount of past and present labor used to produce it. Marx believed that under capitalism the value of any product could be broken down into three components: constant capital, or past labor as embodied in plant and equipment or the raw materials necessary to produce the good; variable capital, the wages paid to present labor to produce the item; and surplus value—defined as profits, rents, and interest—which was expropriated by or paid to the capitalist. The capitalists' expropriation of surplus value, according to Marx, denies labor the full return for its efforts.

This third assumption leads Marxists to see the political economy as necessarily conflictual, because the relationship between capitalists and workers is essentially antagonistic. Surplus value is not the capitalist's "reward" for investment, but something that is taken away from labor. Because the means of production are controlled by a minority within society—the capitalists—labor does not receive its full return; conflict between the classes will thus occur because of this exploitation. For Marx, the relationship between capital and labor is zero-sum; any gain for the capitalist must come at the expense of labor, and vice versa.

Starting with these three assumptions, Marx constructed a sophisticated theory of capitalist crisis. Such crises would, Marx believed, ultimately lead to the overthrow of capitalism by labor and the erection of a socialist society in which the means of production would be owned jointly by all members of society and no surplus value would be expropriated.

While Marx wrote primarily about domestic political economy, or the dynamics and form of economic change within a single country, Lenin extended Marx's ideas to the international political economy to explain imperialism and war (see selections from *Imperialism*, Reading 6). Imperialism, Lenin argued, was endemic to modern capitalism. As capitalism decayed in the most developed nations, they would attempt to solve their problems by exporting capital abroad. As this capital required protection from both local and foreign challengers, governments would colonize regions to safeguard the interests of their foreign investors. When the area available for colonization began to shrink, capitalist countries would compete for control over these areas and intracapitalist wars would eventually occur.

Today, some Marxists believe that capitalists have become cosmopolitan or "transnational," interested in global trends and having few ties to their home governments (see Hymer, Reading 2). As a result, they argue, a single international capitalist class is emerging. According to this perspective, relations between capitalists of whatever national origin are now increasingly harmonious. Where Lenin believed conflict between capitalists of different countries, and between capital and labor, would both persist, "transnational" Marxists think that disputes among capitalists of different nationalities are fading, leaving only the labor-capital division in world politics.

While Liberals perceive the political economy as inherently harmonious, Marxists believe conflict is endemic. Marxists adopt different assumptions and derive a very different understanding of the world. For Marxists, economics determines politics. The nature of politics and the fundamental cleavages within and between societies, in other words, are rooted in economics.

Realism

Realism has perhaps the longest pedigree of the three principal perspectives in International Political Economy, starting with Thucydides's writings in 400 B.C. and including Niccolo Machiavelli, Thomas Hobbes, and the mercantilists Jean-Baptiste Colbert and Friedrich List. Discredited with the rise of Liberalism in the nineteenth century, Realism reemerged as an important perspective only in the aftermath of the Great Depression of the 1930s as scholars sought to understand the causes of the widespread economic warfare or "beggar-thy-neighbor" policies initiated in 1929. Realists believe that nation-states pursue power and shape the economy to this end. Unlike Liberals and Marxists, Realists perceive politics as determining economics.

Realism is based upon three assumptions. First, Realists assume that nation-states are the dominant actors within the international political economy and the proper unit of analysis. According to Realists, the international system is anarchical, a condition under which nation-states are sovereign, the sole judge of their own behaviors, and subject to no higher authority. If no authority is higher than the nation-state, Realists also believe that all other actors are subordinate to the nation-state. While private citizens can interact with their counterparts in other countries, Realists assert that the basis for this interaction is legislated by the nation-state. Thus, where Liberals focus on individuals and Marxists on classes, Realists concentrate on nation-states.

Second, Realists assume that nation-states are power maximizers. Because the international system is based upon anarchy, the use of force or coercion by other nation-states is always a possibility and no other country or higher authority is obligated to come to the aid of a nation-state under attack. Nation-states are thus ultimately dependent upon their own resources for protection. For Realists, then, each nation-state must always be prepared to defend itself to the best of its ability. It must always seek to maximize its power; the failure to do so threatens the very existence of the nation-state and may make it vulnerable to others. Power is a relative concept. If one nation-state (or any other actor) expands its power over another, it can do so only at the expense of the second. Thus, for Realists, politics is zero-sum and by necessity conflictual. If one nation-state wins, another must lose.

Third, Realists assume that nation-states are rational actors in the same sense that Liberals assume individuals are rational. Nation-states are assumed to perform cost-benefit analyses and choose the option which yields the greatest value, in this case, the one which maximizes power.

It is the assumption of power maximization that gives Realism its distinctive approach to International Political Economy. While economic considerations may often complement power concerns, the former are—

in the Realist view—subordinate to the latter. Liberals and Marxists see individuals and classes, respectively, as always seeking to maximize their economic well-being. Realists, on the other hand, allow for circumstances in which nation-states sacrifice economic gain to weaken their opponents or strengthen themselves in military or diplomatic terms. Thus, trade protection—which might reduce a country's overall income by restricting the market—may be adopted for reasons of national political power. — U.S. —日本 — Congressional Politics

Given its assumptions, Realist political economy is primarily concerned with how changes in the distribution of international power affect the form and type of international economy. The best known Realist approach to this question is the "Theory of Hegemonic Stability," which holds that an open international economy—that is, one characterized by the free exchange of goods, capital, and services—is most likely to exist when a single dominant or hegemonic power is present to stabilize the system and construct a strong regime (see Krasner, Reading 3, and Lake, Reading 9). For Realists, then, politics underlies economics. In the pursuit of power, nation-states shape the international economy to best serve their desired ends.

Each of these three perspectives adopts different assumptions to simplify reality and render it more explicable. Liberals assume that individuals are the proper unit of analysis, while Marxists and Realists make similar assumptions for classes and nation-states, respectively. The three perspectives also differ on the inevitability of conflict within the political economy. Liberals believe the political economy to be essentially harmonious, while Marxists and Realists see it as inherently conflictual. Finally, Liberals believe economics and politics are largely autonomous spheres, Marxists maintain that economics determines politics, and Realists argue that politics determines economics.

These three perspectives lead to widely different explanations of specific events and general processes within the international political economy. Their differences have generated numerous debates in the field, many of which are contained in the readings herein. Overlaying these perspectives are two additional debates on the relative importance of international or domestic factors, and social or state forces, in determining economic policy. We now turn to this second set of issues.

ANALYTICAL ISSUES IN INTERNATIONAL POLITICAL ECONOMY

Within International Political Economy, two sets of important analytical issues serve to define many of the debates that divide scholars. To an extent, these debates cut across the three perspectives outlined above; on some issues, there is more agreement between some Realists and some Marxists than there is amongst Realists or Marxists themselves. The first set of problems that divides the discipline has to do with the relationship between the international and domestic political economies; the second set concerns the relationship between the state and social forces.

It should surprise no one that American tariff policy, German international financial goals, and South Korean foreign debt strategies are important to the world's political economy. Disagreements arise, however, over how best to explain the sources of the foreign economic policies of individual nations, or of nation-states in general. At one end of the international-domestic spectrum, some scholars believe that national foreign economic policies are essentially determined by the global environment. The actual room for national maneuver of even the most powerful of states, these scholars believe, is limited by the inherent nature of the international system. At the other end of the spectrum are scholars who see foreign economic policies primarily as the outgrowth of national, domestic-level political and economic processes; for them, the international system exists only as a jumble of independent nation-states, each with its own political and economic peculiarities.

The international-domestic division is at the base of many debates within International Political Economy, as in the world at large. While some argue, for example, that the cause of Third World poverty is in the unequal global economic order, others blame domestic politics and economics within developing nations. Many see multinational corporations as a powerful independent force in the world—whether for good or for evil—while others see international firms as tools and products of their home countries.

The distinctions between the two approaches can be seen quite clearly, for example, in explanations of American trade policy. To take a specific instance, in 1982, the United States government negotiated limitations with Japan on the number of Japanese automobiles that would be imported by the United States. The initiative arose from the complaints of American automakers, and the trade unions that represented their employees, over stiff Japanese competition that was causing a major decline in profits and employment. From this, the most self-evident analytical conclusion would be that American domestic political and economic pressures—the electoral importance of the midwestern states where the auto industry is concentrated, the economic centrality of the sector to the rest of the American economy, the political clout of the United Auto Workers within the labor movement—led to an important foreign economic policy measure, the negotiation of auto import quotas. And, indeed, many scholars saw the decision as a confirmation of the primacy of domestic concerns in the making of foreign economic policy.

Yet, analysts who search for the causes of national foreign economic policies in the international, rather than the domestic, arena, could also find support in the 1982 auto import quota. After all, the quota responded to the rise of Japan as a major manufacturer and exporter of automobiles, a fact which had little to do with the American domestic scene. Much of United States industry has been losing competitive ground to rapidly growing overseas manufacturers, a process that is complex in origin but clearly one of worldwide proportions. Realists have thus argued that trade policy is a function of realities inherent to the international system, such as the existence of a leading, hegemonic, economic power and the eventual decline of that power (see Krasner, Reading 3). On the other hand, the internationally minded scholar might also argue that it is also important to understand why the American measures took the relatively mild form they did, simply limiting the Japanese to an established (and very appreciable) share of the American market. If the measure had been simply to respond to the distress of the American auto industry, the logical step would have been to exclude foreign cars from the market. Yet, the position of the United States in the global economic and political system—and here we could include everything from world finance to national defense—dictated that American policy be cooperative.

More generally, scholars have explained long-term changes in United States trade policy in very different ways. From the Civil War until the 1930s, the United States was highly protectionist; its borders were all but closed to most foreign-made products. Since World War II, on the other hand, the American market has essentially been open to overseas producers. Scholars whose theoretical bent is international point out that American domestic politics has not changed enough to explain such a radical shift. The United States' role in the international political and economic system, however, has indeed been different since World War II than it was before 1930. Systemic-level analysts, such as proponents of the Theory of Hegemonic Stability (see Lake, Reading 9), would argue that the causes of modern American foreign economic policy can be found in the dramatic changes in the American international position— the decline of Europe, the Soviet challenge, the rise of the Third World.

Domestic-level explanations take the opposite tack. For them, the postwar system was itself largely a creation of the United States. To cite the modern international political economy as a source of American foreign economic policy, domestically oriented scholars argue, is to put the cart before the horse, since it was United States foreign economic policy itself—the Marshall Plan, the Bretton Woods Agreements, the Alliance for Progress—that essentially molded today's international political economy. The true roots of the shift in American trade policy must therefore be searched for within the United States.

The example of American trade policy illustrates that serious scholars can arrive at strikingly different analytical conclusions on the basis of the same information. For some, domestic political and economic pressures caused the adoption of auto import quotas. For others, trends in the international environment explain this same action.

It should be pointed out that, to a certain extent, the distinction drawn between international and domestic sources of foreign economic policy is an artificial one. Most scholars recognize that *both* systemic *and* domestic pressures are important in explaining why governments choose the policies they do. Yet, there are fundamental disagreements over the relative weight that should be placed on each set of causes; for some, international sources are primary, for others, domestic causes predominate. And the division cuts across ideological lines: some Marxists, for example, are "systemic-level theorists" and believe that the international capitalist system is the primary cause of national policies, while other Marxists downplay international aspects and focus on the national development of capitalism. Similar divisions exist among Realists and Liberals as well.

The interaction between state and society, or between national governments and the social forces they represent, rule, or ignore serves as a second dividing line within International Political Economy. In the study of the politics of the world economy, questions continually arise about the relative importance of independent government action versus a variety of societal pressures on the policymaking process.

The role of the state is at the center of all of Political Science; International Political Economy is no exception. Foreign economic policy is made, of course, by foreign economic policymakers; this much is trivial. But just as scholars debate the relative importance of overseas and domestic sources of foreign economic policies, so too do they disagree over whether policymakers represent a logic of their own, or reflect domestic lobbies and interest groups. In one vision, the national state is relatively insulated or autonomous from the multitude of social, political, and economic pressures that emanate from society. The most that pluralistic interest groups can produce is a confused cacophony of complaints and demands, but coherent national policy comes from the conscious actions of national leaders and those who occupy positions of political power. The state, in this view, molds society, and foreign economic policy is one part of this larger mold. For the opposing school of thought, policymakers are little more than the reflectors of underlying societal demands. At best, the political system can organize and regularize these demands, but the state is simply a tool in the hands of socioeconomic and political interests. Foreign economic policy, like other state actions, evolves in response to social demands; it is society that molds the state, and not the other way around.

Once again, it should be noted that this simplistic dichotomy hardly describes actual theoretical approaches; nearly all scholars recognize that both state actors and sociopolitical forces are important determinants of foreign economic policies. The disagreements are over relative weights to be assigned to each set of causes. Once more, the state-society division cuts across other theoretical differences: pluralist Liberals and some Marxists assign primacy to social forces, while statist Realists and structuralist Marxists give pride of place to autonomous state action.

We can illustrate the difference in focus with the previously discussed example of American trade policy before and since World War II. Many of those who look first and foremost at state actors would emphasize the dramatic change in the United States government's overall foreign policy after World War II, starting with American responsibility for European reconstruction and the demands of the Cold War, all of which required that the American market be opened to foreign goods in order to stimulate the economies of the country's allies. Trade liberalization arose out of national-security concerns, understood and articulated by a very small number of individuals in American government, who then went about "selling" the policies to American public opinion. Other scholars, for whom society is determinant, emphasize the major socio-economic and political changes that had been gaining force within the United States after World War I. American corporations were more international, and had come to fear overseas competition less. For important groups, trade protection was counterproductive, because it limited American access to the rest of the world economy; freer trade and investment opened broad and profitable new horizons for major portions of the United States economy.

A wide variety of theoretical and analytical differences separate scholars interested in International Political Economy. The selections in this reader serve both to provide information on broad trends in the politics of international economic relations, and to give an overview of the contending approaches to be found within the discipline.

I. CONTENDING PERSPECTIVES ON INTERNATIONAL POLITICAL ECONOMY

Three contending perspectives dominate the study of international political economy: Liberalism, Marxism, and Realism. In the Introduction, we have discussed the principal assumptions underlying each of these perspectives. Part I contains three selections, one representative of each approach, as applied to a specific issue. Richard N. Cooper, from the Liberal perspective, examines how the rapid growth of international economic transactions, or interdependence, has increasingly constrained government policy in the post-1945 era. He suggests a market solution—floating exchange rates (discussed further in our essay on Money and Finance in Part III)—to relax these constraints. Stephen Hymer presents a Marxist analysis of the changing relations of production within the international capitalist system stimulated by the rise of the multinational corporation. Finally, Stephen D. Krasner discusses the relationship between the distribution of power and international economic openness and closure, a question at the center of Realist inquiry. Each selection reflects the assumptions, research agenda, and types of arguments developed in its respective school. These schools, in turn, are essential for understanding current issues in the field of international political economy.

1. Economic Interdependence and Foreign Policy in the Seventies

RICHARD N. COOPER

In this 1972 article, Richard N. Cooper, a Liberal economist, examines the increasing "sensitivity of economic transactions between two or more countries to economic developments within those nations," or interdependence. Noting that interdependence has increased since World War II, Cooper argues that it weakens the ability of states to pursue autonomous domestic policies. Fearful that governmental attempts to cope with interdependence may undermine the economic liberalization upon which it is based, Cooper suggests that floating exchange rates will ease the tensions created by increased national sensitivity. Cooper reflects the Liberal perspective in two ways. First, he recognizes that governments play a necessary role in regulating and stabilizing both domestic and international markets. Second, Cooper advocates that governments fulfill this economic management role not by restricting market forces but by enhancing the market through floating exchange rates.

A casual reading of contemporary news reports suggests that during the past decade economic issues have taken on growing importance in the relations of non-Communist developed countries. The disputes between the United States and Japan over textiles, between the United States and the European Economic Community over agricultural trade, and between France and Germany over currency alignments come readily to mind. It is perhaps symbolic of the enormous success of early postwar foreign policy that issues no graver than these play such a prominent part in relations among countries that, earlier in the century, were sporadically at each other's throats. But I contend that economic issues are becoming, and will continue to become, more problematic in relations among advanced non-Communist countries, and that their relative prominence today is not merely due to the fact that other, more fundamental issues have been resolved. Indeed, the trend toward greater economic interdependence among countries will require substantial changes in their approach to foreign policy in the next decade or so. . . .

"Economic interdependence" normally refers to the dollar value of economic transactions among regions or countries, either in absolute terms, or relative to their transactions. I shall use it in a more restricted sense: to refer to the *sensitivity* of economic transactions between two or more nations to economic developments within those nations. This approach means that two countries with much mutual trade would still experience a low degree of interdependence if the value of that trade were not sensitive to price and income developments in the two countries; on the other hand, two countries would be highly interdependent if their transactions were greatly sensitive to economic developments, even if their mutual trade were initially at a low level. *Inter*dependence implies two-way sensitivity; one-way sensitivity leads to a dependent economy. The reason for this focus on sensitivity rather than on level will become clearer as the argument proceeds; for the moment I will simply observe that the economy of the United States is becoming highly interdependent with that of Europe and Japan, even though total U.S. exports to those areas account for only about 3 per cent of total output and (so far as we can tell) international financial transactions are a similarly small proportion of the total financial transactions in the United States. . . .

GROWING ECONOMIC INTERDEPENDENCE

The extraordinary and unprecedented growth in international trade has frequently been mentioned. The increase in international travel has been even faster, and is equally unprecedented. It is not clear whether international trade has grown in relation to total economic output (GNP); the relative growth of "services" would argue against this. But, in any case, that is less important than the sensitivity of international transactions to domestic economic developments such as taxation, inflation, and interest rates. There is no question that this sensitivity has increased in certain dimensions. Although merchandise imports account for only 4 per cent of total U.S. expenditure, for example, imports account for a much larger share of the increment during periods of rapidly rising expenditure (17 per cent in 1968, in real terms). When demand runs ahead of output, the rest of the world fills the gap. This process has long been more operative in other countries than in the

United States, but even there the response has become more rapid and more complete.

It is less clear whether the *price* sensitivity of international demand has increased. Improved transportation and communications, wider acceptability of foreign styling, and narrowed cost and quality differences among nations suggest that it has; but growing product differentiation, with each major firm trying to establish its secure niche in the market, cuts the other way. So does the growing importance of the multinational firm wherever market-sharing conventions prevail among its various components. But these firms have also contributed to the convergence of cost and design and to the wider acceptability of "foreign" products. On balance, price sensitivity for international trade has probably increased as well.

This increased sensitivity has extended even to labor, an area in which the integrative forces of policy and technology are undoubtedly weaker than in any other. In 1967, when Germany slumped into its first post-war recession, one-third of the unemployed workers who lost jobs were foreigners on short-term contracts. On returning to their homelands they raised unemployment there and reduced it in Germany, literally representing an exportation of unemployment. The reverse occurred once Germany expanded again. When reductions in federal funding, the stock market slump, and rising prices combined to bring about a sharp reduction in new hiring of university teachers in the United States, graduate students in Britain—whose higher educational establishment continues to grow at a rapid pace—nonetheless also felt the pinch: Britons and Commonwealth students studying in the United States started to look for jobs in Britain to replace those they could not find in the United States.

Finally, the greatest growth in interdependence has undoubtedly been in investment, both real and financial. The great growth in direct foreign business investment in the sixties testifies to the new search for earning opportunities everywhere, not merely in the national market. Barriers of language and law have gradually been broken down or surmounted by large and even non-so-large American firms, who have flocked to Europe to exploit new or newly perceived market opportunities and tax advantages. Financial capital has also become much more sensitive to yield differentials among major financial markets, and an increasing number of both borrowers and lenders scan a world horizon for sources of funds and investment opportunities; in doing so, they tie national markets more closely together. German firms can borrow from Arabian sheiks and Iowa farmers in London's Eurodollar market. Even national stock markets, although they are subject to diverse influences, have shown increasing parallelism of movement during the past decade.

As in other areas of economics, it is the marginal transaction that counts in linking markets together.

This growing interdependence may be confidently projected into the future, in the absence of strong government action to retard the process, because it is based on the technological advances in transportation and communication which increase both the speed and the reliability of moving goods, funds, persons, information, and ideas across national boundaries—in short, the same forces that are producing the much-touted shrinking world, in terms of both economic and psychological distance.

Although this process is world-wide, it is much further advanced among the industrial countries of the non-Communist world—Western Europe, North America, and, increasingly, Japan—countries that, in the last few decades, have converged remarkably in their objectives of social and economic policy and in their political processes for reconciling differences and for executing policies. Although these countries will continue to be concerned about the second and third worlds, their concerns will derive largely from considerations other than growing economic interdependence. (Economic interdependence must, in this context, be distinguished from the growing psychological interdependence brought about by increasing direct exposure through television and other media.) The remarks that follow will largely concern relations among the Western industrial countries.

A second kind of growing economic interdependence, institutional rather than structural, can be discerned among industrial nations. This institutional interdependence occurs when these countries must, by prior agreement, confer, and even reach joint decisions, on matters of economic policy. The two outstanding examples of this, neither of them present a decade ago, are the periodic decisions leading to the creation of Special Drawing Rights (paper gold) at the International Monetary Fund, and the decisions concerning the formation of commercial and agricultural policies within the European Economic Community. Both involve truly supranational decision-making, although of course only after prior negotiations among nations. Less dramatic instances are the attempts by donors to coordinate foreign aid to particular countries in "consortia" under the general direction of the World Bank, and the attempts, so far largely unsuccessful, to coordinate trade policies of the developed countries with respect to the products of the less developed countries. This kind of institutional interdependence is in some measure a response to the growing structural interdependence, but it often also has a quite different, more strictly political origin, and thus is a separately identifiable factor in the economic area. It will therefore be ignored in my argument, as will British accession to the EEC.

THE CHALLENGE OF GROWING INTERDEPENDENCE TO NATIONAL ECONOMIC POLICIES

Domestic Policies

Most national economic policies rely for their effectiveness on the separation of markets. This is true of monetary policy, of income taxation, of regulatory policies, and of redistributive policies (whether the last be through differential taxation or through direct transfers). Increased economic interdependence, by joining national markets, erodes the effectiveness of these policies and hence threatens national autonomy in the determination and pursuit of economic objectives. The term "threaten" is used nonpejoratively; there are also economic advantages to the joining of markets, and in some—but not all—cases these outweigh the resultant loss of economic autonomy; indeed, that is what creates the predicament. It is aggravated by the fact that during the past few decades the peoples of all industrial countries have substantially raised their expectations of governmental activity in managing the economy with respect to employment, inflation, growth, income distribution, and a host of other objectives, leading to the emergence of what is sometimes called the welfare state.

The loss of autonomy has been most prominently discussed in the area of monetary policy. As national money and capital markets are joined by international flows of funds, interest rates in various markets are drawn together. Subsequently, if an individual country wishes to pursue a contractionary monetary policy in order to discourage a domestic boom, it will find, in the course of trying to tighten monetary conditions, that it is merely drawing funds from abroad; the more its central bank tightens, the more its would-be domestic borrowers will satisfy their needs by borrowing abroad rather than at home. Under these circumstances, monetary policy becomes an effective tool for influencing the short-term balance-of-payments position of a country, since it can attract or repel short-term funds; but it has become an ineffective tool for its customary objective of influencing the course of domestic economic activity.

The international mobility of firms and funds also erodes the tax policies of nations. It is no secret that the nascent international bond market has thrived on funds that engage in tax evasion. Host countries such as Luxembourg have a disincentive to police carefully the taxation of interest earnings on foreign funds: they thereby attract financial business. Without the full cooperation of countries where the earnings take place, the difficulty of enforcing tax laws on residents holding funds abroad will enable the wealthy and astute residents of all nations to maintain a tax-free source of interest income; as more people become aware of the possibilities open to them, this will, in turn, increasingly erode both the revenue and the redistributive objectives of many countries.

For operating business firms it is more difficult to avoid an accurate declaration of earnings. But by adjusting the prices at which transactions take place among branches in different countries, they may sharply reduce their total tax liabilities and thereby thwart the fiscal objectives of countries with high tax rates.

In both of these cases—tax evasion and transfer pricing for tax avoidance—national authorities are not without countervailing courses of action. But, as will be made clear, in some respects these courses of action either infringe on the sovereignty of other nations or place their own international firms in a difficult competitive position. So a dilemma remains.

The same is true of regulatory policies of business, such as antitrust regulations, capitalization requirements, disclosure requirements, trading regulations, and the like. In each case the international mobility of funds and firms erodes the national capacity to impose and enforce limitations on business behavior. A Swiss corporation, faced with local requirements to give initial rights to new equity to existing stockholders, found it convenient to establish a subsidiary in Curaçao instead; and to raise its new equity from that base, drawing on international (including Swiss) sources of funds. If it were not for laws extending the jurisdiction of the United States to its citizens everywhere—a powerful irritant to some countries—American firms could escape U.S. proscriptions on trade with Cuba simply by locating in countries more sympathetic to such trade.

Although labor is still far less mobile than capital, the mobility of certain groups of people is sufficiently high to limit policies designed toward redistribution, whether through taxation or, as in the case of the British Health Service, through imposed conditions of work. This force can be seen most clearly within the United States, where states and municipalities with generous welfare programs have been swamped by immigrants from elsewhere in the country; in the end this requires a fiscal bale-out by the federal government.

Mobility unites previously fragmented markets, and in so doing threatens policies that, for their feasibility, depended on the fragmentation of markets. As nations become increasingly interdependent, as capital and skilled labor become less exclusively national in their orientations, countries desiring to pursue tax or regulatory policies that deviate widely from those policies in other countries will find themselves stimulating large inflows or outflows of funds, firms, or persons; these induced movements will in turn weaken the intended effects of the policies, or make them more costly. Economic policies that have hitherto been regarded as exclusively domestic will come under increasing influence from the international environment. . . .

RESPONSES TO THE CHALLENGE TO NATIONAL AUTONOMY IN ECONOMIC POLICY

Domestic Policies

The intrusions of growing interdependence into domestic economic policy, which are already visible but are likely to become much more intense in the next decade, have elicited five quite different, but not mutually exclusive, types of response by national governments: passive, exploitative, defensive, aggressive, and constructive. These designations are meant to be descriptive, not normative.

A *passive* response involves acceptance of the loss of domestic economic autonomy and virtual abandonment of any attempt to pursue courses independent of those determined by the countries to which the passive country is closely linked with ties of trade and finance. It is largely a resort of small countries who have become aware of their dependence on others and for whom the costs of independent action (i.e., of foregoing the benefits of linked markets) are likely to be high.

Some of these countries also pursue an *exploitative* course, which attempts to take advantage of the growing interdependence in ways which are successful if pursued by only a few countries, but which cannot be generalized for the world economy. Thus, we observe countries offering flags of convenience on ocean shipping, light registration and disclosure requirements for securities, nominal taxation on certain forms of business activity (tax havens), and generous subsidies to foreign investment. So long as only a few countries create especially favorable conditions for certain forms of economic activity, they will succeed in attracting that kind of activity from elsewhere; if many countries begin to compete for the same activities in similar ways, international location will be little influenced, and net benefits will accrue to the favored activities at the general expense of governments, consumers, or labor. This kind of policy competition is already noticeable in the tax concessions, and even direct subsidies, given by many less developed countries to foreign investors; as the practice spreads, revenue bases will be eroded while the effect in attracting investment will diminish. Competition can also be observed in the export credit terms given by the industrialized countries, in subsidies to hotel-building and other aspects of tourism in Europe, and in the use, by municipalities *within* the United States, of tax-free industrial development bonds to attract industry. (This development has recently been restrained by Congressional action.) Success in exploiting the new mobility is therefore limited to those countries who *begin* the process, and continues only so long as other countries do not follow or retaliate.

A *defensive* response involves attempts to reduce economic interdependence by preserving or restoring the fragmentation of markets in order to retain some economic autonomy. An early example was the imposition of restrictions on immigration into the United States. This was done, among other reasons, in order to protect the distribution of income then prevailing and to reduce the flow of new immigrants to a level which might reasonably be assimilated. More recently, Britain, Denmark, and Switzerland have all imposed limits on the number of foreign workers. The reasons are both political (on the assumption that certain minimum requirements of homogeneity in the population must be met in a functioning democracy) and economic (concerning in particular the distribution of income between relatively unskilled labor and other factors of production). The United States has long maintained an escape clause on its commitments to lower tariffs that can be invoked if foreign competition creates insuperable adjustment problems for domestic firms and labor. Some countries have for years imposed impediments to the movement of financial capital across their boundaries. Others have started to do so more recently. The United States has its interest equalization tax on purchases of foreign stocks and bonds, and its mandatory restrictions on foreign lending by U.S. firms and banks. Britain and France have even more stringent controls. These restrictions are often imposed under the heading of balance-of-payments measures, but they are more correctly viewed, I think, as devices to insulate national capital and money markets from one another in order to preserve some degree of national monetary control. This view is supported by the fact that countries such as Germany and Switzerland, with strong or neutral payments positions, have also resorted to such measures.

Some countries have engaged in *aggressive* as well as defensive actions to preserve national autonomy. Rather than reduce mobility, these actions attempt to extend national control to the mobile factors wherever they be. Thus, the United States (which because of its size and relative importance is in the best position to engage in extraterritorial extension of its laws and regulations) has from time to time extended its antitrust laws to the foreign subsidiaries of U.S. firms and even to the foreign parents of foreign subsidiaries operating in the United States. For example, it has demanded the disclosure of financial information by foreign firms whose securities are traded informally in the United States, prevented foreign subsidiaries of U.S. corporations from selling to certain Communist countries, imposed minimum limits on repatriation of earnings by American firms operating abroad, and attempted (unsuccessfully) to compel submission of certain business information by foreign sea and air carriers. These various actions invariably provoke cries of outrage from other countries, for they attempt to extend U.S. regulatory jurisdiction to economic agents that are the legal entities of other countries and hence under their jurisdiction, despite their American ownership. On the other hand, failure to subject these foreign entities to U.S. regulations or their equivalent invites circumvention of the regulatory intent through movement abroad. If the records of American-owned firms outside the United States are not subject to subpoena, for example, firms which are prevented by law from conspiring to fix prices or share markets within the United States may do so abroad, with impunity. Or, if United States firms operating from foreign bases are not affected by the U.S. proscription on exports to Cuba, the restrictive policy can be vitiated simply by locating abroad. (This observation is not meant to imply approval of this proscription—only that a national policy can be undercut by international mobility of its firms.) In other words, while the response of the United States in these cases has been aggressive, it has not been capricious; it is addressed to a real problem in which the decision-making domain of businesses covers a wider geographic area than the jurisdiction of government.

A fifth type of response involves the *constructive* attempt by governments to frame their policies jointly, so that mobility among the cooperating countries ceases to offer an escape from governmental jurisdiction. Examples of true coordination of policies are rare, although in the area of monetary management there have been several faint signs of coordinated action, notably in the general lowering of interest rates in 1967. There have also been attempts, partially successful, to limit export credit concessions by government-sponsored export credit institutions. Bilateral tax treaties have, of course, for years been used to reconcile the conflicting claims of tax jurisdiction over business income. But this approach through coordination could go much further, and encompass a wide range of policies concerning taxation, the regulation of business structure and activity, the framing of monetary policy, and other "domestic" policies. It is an approach that requires considerable patience, however, for joint regulation can proceed only as rapidly as the most laggard participant; since some potential participants have successfully exploited the new mobility, they will be reluctant to give up their gains. . . .

ECONOMIC INTERDEPENDENCE: IMPLICATIONS FOR FOREIGN POLICY

The foregoing excursion into the challenge that increased interdependence constitutes to domestic economic policies, and the possible national responses, sets the stage for an examination of the implications for foreign policy.

Obviously, the impact on domestic politics is one route whereby economic interdependence can influence a nation's foreign policy, hence the problems facing the foreign policy of the United States. The shift from De Gaulle to Pompidou and from Labour to Tory may not basically alter the shape of world affairs, but it can affect them in important details. For example, France's willingness to consider Britain's entry into the European Economic Community blunted Britain's general foreign policy role as long as negotiations were in process, and will divert British and European official attention and energy from other matters for some time. Another example is the restoration of Britain's military commitment east of Suez before the withdrawal had proceeded so far as to become irreversible. The important influence of domestic politics on foreign policy is also demonstrated by the election of a Communist as President of Chile. It has been alleged that the very rapid growth of foreign ownership in Chilean manufacturing in the late sixties, much of it in the form of takeovers, played a significant role in the public appeal of Sr. Allende, who during his campaign raised the spectre of foreign domination of Chile's infant manufacturing sector.

The impact on political leadership may possibly lead to the most important effect of interdependence on foreign policy, but it is too subtle and too uncertain in direction to be analyzed with any confidence. More direct and clearly identifiable effects arise from the challenges to national autonomy in the realms of economic policy. These challenges take foreign policy right into the thicket of domestic politics. On the whole, foreign policy, in the narrower sense of national security and military-strategic considerations, has in all countries been elitist—the interest and province of a relatively small group of persons. Strategic considerations do become political issues, but generally in a rather abstract fashion, as broad issues and postures. Even the foreign policy budget—largely military—has until recently been relatively immune from domestic political considerations. (This is equally true of foreign aid, where one small group is pitted against another, and the public remains passive and uninterested.)

With the advent of increased economic interdependence, however, foreign developments will intrude on a whole range of policies that are traditionally domestic, and these bread-and-butter domestic political issues will in turn influence and greatly complicate the management of foreign policy. It follows that foreign policy in the sense of all official relations between countries will become more intricate both in the range of issues and the frequency with which they arise. National reaction in the seventies will undoubtedly blend all five types of response. Many of these responses will create frictions between countries, and diplomats will be kept busy at their traditional task of smoothing ruffled feathers. If foreign policy is to be regarded as successful, it will have the additional task of channeling and controlling the reactions to greater interdependence in order to prevent the dominance of those exploitative, defensive, and aggressive responses that, if generalized, are detrimental to international order and hence to all participants. This means, in particular, confining the exploitative responses to *de minimus* cases and introducing some kind of order into the defensive and aggressive responses so that they will not provoke retaliation that is damaging to all parties.

To say this, however, is to say little more than that in times of tension and conflicting objectives it is in the interest of all to avoid outcomes that are detrimental to all. It is far more difficult to define the maximal task for foreign policy (even in an area limited to economics), for that depends, among other things, on our basic objectives and in particular on the value we attach to the preservation of *national* autonomy as such. We must sooner or later face in a global context the issue of centralization-decentralization that is so prominent within the United States. In thinking about these issues, I find it helpful to consider three extreme cases—Weberian "ideal types." None of them will be realized during the next ten years, but each may serve as a model, or general guideline, toward which we might move; all of them accept as given the fact of extensive government influence on the operation of market forces.

The first is a regime of nation-states, each successfully pursuing its own objectives that have been determined in its own way, democratically or otherwise. As noted above, successful pursuit of economic objectives at the national level requires markets that are fragmented at least to the national level, and this in turn implies that each nation is sufficiently insulated from other nations to pursue its independent course (although groupings of like-minded nations need not be excluded). This does not rule out trade and capital movements, but it does presuppose some instrument of policy (tariffs, quotas, taxes on international transactions, flexible exchange rates, or other defensive measures) that will permit the country to prevent emaciation of its domestic policies by international transactions that are highly sensitive to them. It is the sensitivity of international transactions that must be reduced, and that objective does not require autarky.

The second regime involves a supranational state that will take over many of the functions that are now performed by the nation—an extreme form of "constructive" response. In the area of economic policy this would mean economic stabilization, taxation of mobile factors, regulatory policies concerning businesses and unions, and even, up to a point, redistributional policies. In other words, the span of government control would be brought into correspondence with the decision-making domain of mobile businesses and individuals. Such a superstate need not be global in scope. Businesses, funds, and labor are not free to move globally, and they will not be for some time. The Communist countries and many less developed countries are effectively insulated from the main economic centers of the industrial world, either by policy or by uncertainty inherent in the absence of policy under politically unsettled circumstances.

There is a natural historical analogy here. It is the gradual passage of responsibility for increasing areas of economic management from the American states to the federal government. As American business became truly national rather than regional or local in character, the states found it increasingly difficult, in a country within which free trade prevailed and contracts made in one state had to be honored in others, to regulate business activity effectively. Businesses simply left the states that imposed onerous restrictions on their activities; or at least the head offices migrated. Consequently, the federal government gradually took over regulatory responsibilities.

The third regime involves American hegemony, an extreme form of "aggressive" response. Rather than turn responsibility over to a superstate, the United States would gradually extend its regulations to cover U.S. citizens abroad and foreigners residing in, or dealing with, the United States. By a combination of persuasion and (nonmilitary) threat, it would either bring other countries into line or drive them into the first regime, thereby insulating them from such contact with the United States as they find offensive to their sovereignty. The world would be on a dollar standard, and many nations would adopt systems of regulation and taxation similar to those of the United States in order to avert punitive reactions from it, and to avoid internal embarrassments arising from differential treatment favoring American over domestic enterprises. This state of affairs could not be brought about, of course, without overcoming a certain amount of domestic American opposition, concerning, for instance, the taxation of income from foreign sources even when it is not repatriated.

None of these regimes is immediately foreseeable, for none is politically feasible. But the model regime which we implicitly use at present—autonomous and purposeful nation-states in harmonious and unrestricted economic intercourse, through the competitive market place, at fixed exchange rates, governed by occasional treaties and conventions to assure good conduct and to iron out modest problems of overlapping jurisdiction, leaving virtually all economic decisions to national governments—is simply not viable in the long run, for the reasons already given. Unless we develop some new conception of world economic order, the search for specific solutions to specific problems will run a substantial risk of slipping into practices that are detrimental to all. We will enjoy neither the full benefits of economic integration on a "global" scale nor the full benefits of national autonomy in the establishment and pursuit of economic and social objectives. In short, it is the . . . grand conception of a world economic order, which will be profoundly affected by the impact of increased economic interdependence, for greater interdependence will inevitably compel a basic re-examination of the kind of world we ultimately want.

Various viable compromises among these three regimes are of course possible, and we should no doubt work toward one of them in the near future rather than toward the ideal types. Three come to mind. The first leans toward preservation of national autonomy by reducing the degree of interdependence through action by individual governments; such actions would be governed by international conventions to assure that they were mutually consistent and that they went no further than necessary to achieve their purposes. Thus, agreement might be reached, and controls instituted, to limit movements of financial capital between countries. The blockage would not have to be complete to preserve some degree of national autonomy in monetary policy, but it would have to cover the major sources of flows. Similarly, taxes could be imposed on the outflow of business capital to prevent modest national differences in taxation and regulation of business from influencing the location of industry. Tariff quotas might be used to inhibit any rapid growth of imports that would greatly disturb domestic industries; the quotas could be allowed to grow automatically so that loss of competitiveness would be reflected in a relative but controlled decline in the domestic industry.

A second, preferable approach accomplishes much the same objective by introducing somewhat greater flexibility in exchange rates, with international rules governing the changes in rates and surveillance of adherence to the rules. This approach would, I believe, help enormously with respect to balance-of-payments adjustment, and considerably with respect to the movement of yield-sensitive funds and price-sensitive goods from country to country, but it would still leave the whole area of business regulation untouched. It might therefore be combined with a third approach, involving intensive efforts to discover areas of potentially overlapping jurisdiction with a view to reaching common tax and regulatory policies among countries—preferably while the process of extensive foreign investment is still at a relatively early stage, so that a reasonably firm framework of expectations regarding corporate practices is available. . . .

2. International Politics and International Economics: A Radical Approach

STEPHEN D. HYMER

Stephen Hymer presents a Marxist analysis of the spread of capitalist relations of production, and therefore of class conflict, to a global level. In this essay, written before his death in 1974 and published in 1978, Hymer charts the development of capitalism at the national level. He then discusses the internationalization of capital and the changing role of the state in capitalism. Hymer argues that class conflict, which previously took place primarily within national economies, is becoming global as capital is internationalized. In this essay, Hymer demonstrates the characteristic Marxist view that economics lies at the basis of politics, and that politics is fundamentally a struggle between classes. He also illustrates the tendency of many Marxists since World War II to emphasize the reduction of antagonisms between national capitalists and the emergence of a global bourgeoisie—to which a global proletarian socialist movement is the only adequate response.

To be radical, or to be a scientist, is the same thing; it is a question of trying to go to the root of the matter. For Marx, this meant trying to uncover the "economic laws of motion of modern society," that is, first of all, seeing society as an organism in motion constantly changing and developing as it moves from its beginning to its end, and second of all, searching in the economy, i.e., in changing conditions of production and exchange, for the underlying basis of this motion.

In this essay, I wish to follow Marx's approach by viewing the present conjuncture of international politics and economics in terms of the long-term growth and spread of capitalist social relations of production to a world level. More concretely, I want to try to relate the current crises in national and international politics to the world market created during the last twenty-five years by the American Empire, first by examining

Keynes' 1933 warnings of the difficulties and dangers for the development of modern society posed by the world market, and second, by using Marx's analysis of the general law of capitalist accumulation, and, in particular, his theory of the reserve army to go deeper into the roots of our present difficulties.

The basic text for this analysis is a provocative statement Marx wrote to Engels in October 1858:

> We cannot deny that bourgeois society has experienced its Sixteenth Century a second time—a Sixteenth Century which will, I hope, sound the death-knell of bourgeois society just as the first one thrust it into existence. The specific task of bourgeois society is the establishment of a world market, at least in outline, and of production based upon this world market. As the world is round, this seems to have been completed by the colonization of California and Australia and the opening up of China and Japan. The difficult question for us is this: on the Continent the revolution is imminent and will immediately assume a socialist character. Is it not bound to be crushed in this little corner, considering that in a far greater territory the movement of bourgeois society is still in the ascendent?[1]

THE BEGINNINGS OF INDUSTRIAL CAPITALISM

Capitalism began as a world market system in the Mercantilist age of the sixteenth and seventeenth centuries when the discovery of America and the rounding of the Cape led to an explosion of maritime commerce and the creation of the first international economy. The epoch-making significance of this great burst of international trade, however, did not lie in the world market itself, but in the transformation of the home market that it unwittingly brought about.

The merchants, adventurers, financiers, and sovereigns of this age set out on an international quest for gold, spices, and new lands, but the really important discoveries were made at home. Specifically, the expansion of foreign trade and the growth of merchant and finance capital resulted, along with other factors, in the disintegration of the traditional non-market domestic economy and the setting free of labor from its precapitalist forms of production. This newly created wage-labor force, when harnessed by industrial capital first into manufacturing and then into modern industry, unleashed an explosion in productivity that provided society with an entirely new material basis for its existence and ushered in the modern world.

The state's roles flowed from this process of development. The first focus of the new industrial state was primitive accumulation, i.e., a conscious political effort to establish the conditions of modern capitalist production by setting free a wage-labor force to work and fostering a national industrial class to organize it. Those countries which did not effect such a transformation of the domestic economy soon fell prey to one imperial power or another and became underdeveloped.

Once industrial capitalism got going, a second task emerged, namely, that of keeping it going by mediating the contradictions it inevitably produced. These contradictions stemmed from two basic interconnected conditions: (1) the anarchic relations between capitalists which produced great waste and resulted in periodic crises, and (2) the concentration of people into factories and cities and their growing politicization. With the accumulation of capital, these contradictions intensified and a large and elaborate superstructure was formed to contain them.

Thus we find during the late nineteenth and twentieth centuries that the growth and spread of industrial capitalism was accompanied by a strengthening and not a declining nation-state and an intensification of national rivalry rather than its withering away. Internally, the visible hand of the state operated continuously alongside the invisible hand of the market. Internationally, one by one, countries erected national barriers against trade and in the late nineteenth century a scramble began to divide the underdeveloped countries into exclusive spheres of interest and into a new colonial system. The end result of *laissez-faire, Pax Britannica*, and free trade was the "welfare state," the First World War, and the complete breakdown of the international economy during the depression.

THE WORLD MARKET VERSUS NATIONAL WELFARE

It is at this point that our story begins. We find in 1930 a world economy in which:

1. The industrial revolution has more or less spread to Western Europe, America, Russia, and Japan, but is far from complete, in the sense that to varying degrees large pockets of non-industrial, non-capitalist sectors remain in each country. Although certain beginnings toward industrial capitalism have been made in isolated spots in Latin America, Asia, and Africa, the vast majority of the world's population lives outside these enclaves.
2. There is a strong disenchantment with capitalism and internationalism, and a belief that the nation-state and not the invisible hand will play the dominant role in economic development. (Even the Fascists call themselves National Socialists.) On the other hand, thinking still remains one-dimensionally capitalist as far as production is concerned since no alternative has emerged to the alienated work process of the capitalist factory. Marx had felt that the working class would organize itself in revolt against the dominance of capital and create a new system of production, but in the 1930s

an international revolutionary working class to lead us beyond capitalism still had not emerged.

It is in this context that we turn to Keynes' analysis of the conflict between a world market and national welfare as presented in his 1933 article on "National Self-Sufficiency." In this article Keynes argues that a restoration of the world market would unnecessarily prolong capitalism with its inherent evils and interfere with our progress toward the good society.

Describing himself as a man "who in the last resort prefers anything on earth to what the financial reports are wont to call 'the best opinion of Wall Street,' " he argues that world peace, prosperity, and freedom could best be achieved by emphasizing non-capitalist national self-sufficiency rather than international market capitalism.[2] In stronger language than almost any other economist would dare use, he came to the following conclusion:

> I sympathize, therefore, with those who would minimize, rather than with those who would maximize, economic entanglement among nations. Ideas, knowledge, science, hospitality, travel—these are the things which should of their nature be international. But let goods be homespun whenever it is reasonably and conveniently possible, and above all, let finance be primarily national.[3]

He supports his case with three basic arguments. First, he notes that contrary to the belief of the nineteenth-century free traders, the world market created in the Golden Age of *Pax Britannica* did not ensure peace but ended in war and a depression. In his words:

> To begin with the question of peace. We are pacifist today with so much strength of conviction that, if the economic internationalist could win this point, he would soon recapture our support. But it does not now seem obvious that a great concentration of national effort on the capture of foreign trade, that the penetration of a country's economic structure by the resources and the influence of foreign capitalists, and that a close dependence of our own economic life on the fluctuating economic policies of foreign countries are safeguards and assurances of international peace. It is easier, in the light of experience and foresight, to argue quite the contrary. The protection of a country's existing foreign interests, the capture of new markets, the progress of economic imperialism—these are a scarcely avoidable part of a scheme of things which aims at the maximum of international specialization and at the maximum geographical diffusion of capital wherever its seat of ownership.[4]

Second, he deals with the question of economic efficiency. He argues that the spread of modern technology makes it easier to produce locally the basic needs of a community and makes the argument for international specialization and export-oriented growth less compelling.

Third, and I think this is the most important part of his case, he argues that the free trader's economic internationalism assumes the whole world was, or would be, organized on the basis of private competitive capitalism. In contrast, Keynes felt that we had to go beyond capitalism if the fruits of the industrial revolution were to be realized in a humane and rational way. But a world market would prevent experimentation in socio-economic organization and thus inhibit the free and full development of our potential.

Expressing a view that is not very popular today except among socialists, Keynes argues:

> The decadent international but individualistic capitalism, in the hands of which we found ourselves after the war, is not a success. It is not intelligent, it is not beautiful, it is not just, it is not virtuous—and it doesn't deliver the goods. In short, we dislike it, and we are beginning to despise it. . . .
>
> We each have our own fancy. Not believing that we are saved already, we each should like to have a try at working out our own salvation. We do not wish, therefore, to be at the mercy of world forces working out, or trying to work out, some uniform equilibrium according to the ideal principles, if they can be called such, of *laissez-faire* capitalism. . . . We wish—for the time at least and so long as the present transitional, experimental phase endures—to be our own masters, and to be as free as we can make ourselves from the interferences of the outside world.[5]

THE INTERNATIONALIZATION OF CAPITAL

Keynes' view, as expressed in this article, had little effect on the policies which governed the post-Second World War reconstruction and development plans for the world economy. Instead, the best opinion of Wall Street and the City prevailed. "Let there be no mistake about it," wrote *The Economist* in 1942 in an article on "The American Challenge," the policy put forward by the American Administration is revolutionary. It is a genuinely new conception of world order."[6] In this way *The Economist*, reflecting the policy discussions taking place in London during the war, welcomed the plan to create a post-war world economy based on international capitalism under American hegemony.

The goal of this plan was " 'a new frontier, a frontier of limitless expanse, the frontier of human welfare,' " and " 'the instrument will be industrial capitalism, operating, broadly speaking, under conditions of private enterprise.' "[7] Or, as *The Economist* put it, "the idealism of an international New Deal will have to be implemented by the unrivalled technical achievements of American business. The New Frontier will then become a reality."[8] Or as *Fortune* expressed it with regard to underdeveloped countries, "American imperialism can afford to complete the work the British started; instead of salesmen and planters, its representatives can be brains and bulldozers, technicians and machine tools."[9]

As we now know, this plan was highly successful. The world experienced a twenty-five-year secular boom in which employment, capital, and technology grew rapidly and even the socialist countries began to be drawn away from autarky into the whirlpool of the international market.

Ironically, Keynes' theory of state policy, which he himself believed to be a tool for bringing about the end of capitalism, was used to preserve it. In his *General Theory*, Keynes argued that by restoring full employment through government intervention, we could in a reasonable time destroy capital's monopoly and free ourselves from its grip. He judged that "it might be comparatively easy to make capital goods so abundant that the marginal efficiency of capital is zero," and that this peaceful evolution might "be the most sensible way of gradually getting rid of many of the objectionable features of capitalism."[10] In his view technological change could rather quickly (one or two generations) reduce the rate of profit and thus bring about "the euthanasia of the rentier, and, consequently, the euthanasia of the cumulative oppressive power of the capitalists to exploit the scarcity-value of capital."[11] And at the same time we could save money on management through "a scheme of direct taxation which allows the intelligence and determination and executive skill of the financier, the entrepreneur *et hoc genus omne* (who are certainly so fond of their craft that their labour could be obtained much cheaper than at present), to be harnessed to the service of the community on reasonable terms of reward."[12]

Keynes was as far off the mark here as he was in his call for national self-sufficiency. One generation has already passed. The rate of profit has not fallen; instead, the state has been harnessed to shore it up and ensure the continued growth of private wealth nationally and internationally. Neither have managers' salaries been reduced. Rather, the techno-structure has gained in status and income as it has become an even more crucial element in supporting the expansion of capital and preventing its euthanasia.

Thus, contrary to Marx and Keynes, the world market and the welfare state have not sounded the death-knell of capitalism. At least not yet. Instead capitalism revived from the interwar crisis and flourished in the quarter century following the war.

Now, however, there are signs of strain in the system and a wave of re-examination and reconsideration of its basic framework is taking place in the light of emerging contradictions and crises, national and international. The tightening of the web of interdependence, to use a now popular phrase, seems to be becoming increasingly uncomfortable as we progress into the 1970s. There is a certain unease in many quarters (dramatized by the oil crisis) that we may be too much at the "mercy of world forces" and too little "our own masters." And there are signs of an outbreak of the national rivalry that Keynes thought was scarcely avoidable if we placed too much emphasis on the world market.

I have argued elsewhere[13] that due to the internationalization of capital, competition between national capitalists is becoming less and less a source of rivalry between nations. Using the instrument of *direct investment*, large corporations are able to penetrate foreign markets and detach their interests from their home markets. At the same time, capitalists from all nations, including underdeveloped countries, are able to diversify their portfolios internationally through the international capital market. Given these tendencies, an international capitalist class is emerging whose interests lie in the world economy as a whole and a system of international private property which allows free movement of capital between countries. The process is contradictory and may break down, but for the present there is a strong tendency for the most powerful segments of the capitalist class increasingly to see their future in the further growth of the world market rather than its curtailment.

In the next section of this essay, I would like to turn to the other side of the coin and examine the interests of labor in the world market. The main theme is that labor will tend to become more nationalistic and possibly more socialistic as the continued growth of the world market undermines its traditional strategy.

Labor and the World-Market Stage of Capitalism

"Accumulation of capital is, therefore, increase of the proletariat."[14] This is the key concept in Marx's analysis of the general law of motion of capitalist society. Capitalist competition leads, at one level, to the concentration and centralization of capital in large corporations tied together by a capital market and unified at the political level by the state. At another level, it draws an ever-increasing portion of the population into the wage-laboring class, concentrates them into large factories and urban centers, and develops in them a group cohesiveness which makes them a political force in opposition to capital. In this way, capitalism, which is based on the competitive wage-labor system, creates within itself forms of social organization which are antithetical to competition and the market system and which, in Marx's view, serve as the embryo of a new society beyond capitalism.

The trend toward class consciousness is, however, a long drawn-out process that proceeds dialectically out of competition between workers.

On the one hand, the continuous expansion of capital and extension of the market unifies wage workers into larger and larger groupings as they strive to eliminate competition between themselves; on the other hand, it also introduces new elements of competition which divide workers into antagonistic groups and inhibit their realizing the latent potential of their unity.

Marx identified two major forces in the development of capitalism (in addition to the ideological superstructure of the corporation and the state) which continually create competition between workers and allow capitalism to reproduce itself on an expanded scale and to survive even its worst crises. First, technological change substitutes machinery for labor: by throwing, or threatening to throw, the worker out of the factory and into the market, it breaks up the cohesiveness of labor organization and reduces workers to individuals or small groups competing with each other instead of cooperating. Secondly, capitalism continuously breaks down pre-capitalist areas—what Marx calls the latent surplus population—thus forming a fresh supply of non-class-conscious workers to compete in the labor market.

These two dynamic forces create a stratified labor force which keeps the pretensions of the working class in check. Above the proletariat stands a vast officer class of managers, technicians, and bureaucrats to organize it and to overcome its resistance by keeping it divided. Below it is a pool of unemployed, underemployed, and badly paid strata continuously fed by technological change and the opening up of new hinterlands, which undercut its position and inhibit its development toward class consciousness. This reserve army drives the labor aristocracy to keep on working and keeps it loyal to the capitalist system from fear of falling from its superior position. By the nature of things, these different strata often come from different regions within a country, different racial or ethnic groups, and different age and sex classes. Thus, the competitive cleavages between workers often reflect lines of race, creed, color, age, sex, and national origin, which make working-class consciousness more difficult.

The significance of the world-market stage of capitalism into which we have now entered is that this competitive process, which both brings labor together and separates it, has not taken on an international dimension. The growth of world trade brings labor of different countries into closer contact and competition; the internationalization of production via the multinational corporate system was a reaction on the part of capital to this fact. American firms, for example, found that the recovery of Europe and the development of labor surplus economies in the Third World, made it possible to produce certain things more cheaply abroad than in the United States; and competitive pressure from emerging non-American capitalists forced them to invest abroad or enter into licensing and management contracts in order to preserve their position and maintain their growth. More generally, the emergence of a unified world commodity market, which in effect is the emergence of a unified world labor market, switched the domain of competition and its accompanying tendencies toward concentration and centralization from the national to the international plane. But this quest for profit, which led capital to shed its national character and escape the narrow confines of the nation-state, has also intensified competitive pressure on labor and undermined its traditional organization and strategy. This, I suggest, is bound to bring about a new stage of development of labor organization, and it is here we must search for the root of the matter if we wish to understand our present predicament and the development track we are on.

The Political Role of Labor

From a Marxist perspective, the main theoretical shortcoming of Keynes' analysis is that he paid no attention to the conditions of production and the political role of labor. He viewed the market system, based on greed and selfishness, with considerable disdain and wanted to go beyond the profit motive toward a society managed by a society-oriented elite, operating in a loose framework that combined state planning and large quasi-public operations. He did not believe that either the capitalists or the "boorish proletariat" could or would lead us to this higher form of organization, but felt that the process of capital accumulation and technological progress would achieve this end naturally, despite the wrong-headed interferences by capital and labor. Thus, neither in his political nor his economic writings, did he pay attention to class struggle as a moving force in capitalist development.

Ironically, this limited perspective was also in one sense his genius, for in fact during the post-war period, the issue of class struggle was highly subdued and labor did not form a serious challenge to capitalism as a system, but instead cooperated within its framework. This was one of the reasons capitalism grew so rapidly and one of the reasons Keynes' theory of monetary and fiscal policy could work.

In the *General Theory*, Keynes shifted the focus of discussion away from the labor market to the capital market. Classical economists saw unemployment and stagnation as the result of too high a level of wages. (In Marxian terms, too low a rate of surplus value.) Keynes instead postulated an elastic supply of labor at the going wage and sought the breakdown of the system in the contradictions between savers and investors, i.e., the rentier class and the entrepreneurial/managerial class. Keynes' preferred way out of this dilemma seemed to be through an expansion of the state and public consumption at the expense of the rentier class, but the alternative preferred by the capitalist was an expansion of the state to promote the growth of private wealth through the stimulation of private investment and private consumption. It was this path that finally predominated.

This strategy was possible because of specific conditions emerging from the great depression and the war which restored the workings of the labor market. In Marxist theory, the functioning of the wage-labor market, upon which capitalist expansion depends, is maintained in the first instance through the institutions of the reserve army.

> The industrial reserve army, during the periods of stagnation and average prosperity, weights down the active labour army; during the periods of over-production and paroxysm, it holds its pretensions in check. Relative surplus-population is therefore the pivot upon which the law of demand and supply of labour works. It confines the field of this law within the limits absolutely convenient to the activity of exploitation and to the domination of capital.[15]

In this sense, the long period of large-scale unemployment of the thirties served as a disciplinary action to make labor ready, willing, and anxious to work again in the post-war period. But action at the political level was needed as well. . . .

The New Deal, the World War, and the Cold War made it possible in the United States to purge the labor movement of its radical elements and create a system of collective bargaining within the framework of the welfare state. This system left the basic capitalist institutions of private wealth and wage labor largely untouched, and channeled labor protest into narrowly-defined trade unionism, which concentrated on selling labor at a more advantageous price without challenging the prerogatives of management and capital, either inside the plant or out of it.

A major factor in making the system work was the existence of a latent surplus-population in the underdeveloped countries and backward sectors of advanced countries which could be broken down to form a constantly flowing surplus-population to work at the bottom of the ladder. In the United States the replacement of southern sharecropping agriculture by modern capitalist methods created a flow of black labor to the northern cities, just as the "development" of Puerto Rico led to large-scale immigration into the eastern United States. Similarly, in Europe modernization of agriculture and the importation of labor from foreign countries played a major role in creating the labor supply needed for capitalist expansion. In addition, the advanced countries benefited from cheap prices for raw materials made possible by the creation of a labor-surplus economy in the underdeveloped countries.

Thus, during this twenty-five year period, labor was able to enjoy prosperity and growth as it concentrated on working harder for steadily rising standards of living and refrained from challenging the system politically. By and large the major source of rebellion and protest did not come from the established proletariat during the fifties and sixties, but from the new strata being incorporated into the wage-labor force from their previous position in the latent surplus-population. These groups were highly critical of the conditions of capitalist production, as they found themselves caught between the breakdown of the old system and the unfulfilled expectations of the new one. They were acutely aware of the coercive nature of the capitalist work relationship, since, unlike the traditional working class, they were "disadvantaged," i.e., they had not yet internalized the capitalist values of alienated work. And they were also extremely bitter at the inequality of their position and the discrimination they suffered.

These factors, which gave such great force to their reaction, also limited the scope of their challenge to capitalism. Because they were outside production and at odds with the privileged strata, they were relatively powerless actually to transform the capitalist system. Their programs often tended to be backward-looking, harking after a return to older forms of community production, and/or anarchistically radical, seeking to burn, destroy, and sabotage the system which oppressed them, rather than to seize it for their own. They were caught in a dilemma. On the one hand, they were antagonistic to capitalism, but on the other hand, they also wanted to get into it and share its benefits and privileges. The result of this dualism was a tendency for their group to split as some entered the labor force and became part of the system, while others fell down into the stagnant part of the reserve army with extremely irregular employment, well below average conditions of life, and into the lowest sediments which dwell in the sphere of pauperism, thus forming an incredible pool of wasted human beings in the slums, ghettos, and rural hinterlands of the capitalist economy.

The Seeds of a New Class Conflict

The success of the "American Challenge" and the "New Frontier," we have argued, rested on a particular set of initial conditions arising out of the great depression and the World War. These wore down the resistance of labor, destroyed its radical wing, and made organized labor into a willing participant in a strategy based on strong state action to promote growth and international expansionism. But the very success of the plan has tended to undermine these initial conditions, and lead us to a stage marked by crisis and reorientation of basic strategies.

In the first place, memories of the thirties and forties have faded in this period of affluence, while the New Frontier has turned out to be less rewarding than it promised. The growth of national income satisfied some of the pent-up needs of previous decades and created new needs which the market system cannot fulfill. The consumer durables revolution provided most families with a car, a television set, and a refrigerator, but also resulted in overcrowding, pollution, and an energy crisis. The middle-class standard of living, toward which the working class aspired, is predicated in large part on only a few people having it. When everybody has a car, the result is not freedom to escape from overcrowded cities into the countryside, but a crowded countryside. Similarly, when everybody has access to higher education, its elite qualities and privileges are destroyed, and a college degree no longer means a ticket to the top of the hierarchy, but an upgraded job at the lower level. Thus, many of the promises of capitalistic consumption tend to be illusory, while alienation and exploitation in the work process remain an ever-present reality. Therefore, job dissatisfaction and a decreased motivation to work has increased steadily over the last twenty-five years, and resulted in the productivity crisis that is causing so much discussion and concern in business circles.

In the second place, the latent surplus-population has been steadily drying up, thus exhausting national pools of cheap labor and lessening the competitive pressure on the work force. Moreover, as more and more people from the non-wage sector are drawn into the wage-labor force, the locus of their struggle against discrimination, alienation, and exploitation shifts from outside to inside, thus infusing the labor movement with new dimensions of protest and militancy. At the same time, the demands for welfare and other support programs by those who are non-incorporated into the wage-labor force eat up the surplus and limit the scope for expanding wages.

These two trends have seriously threatened the collective-bargaining strategy which dominated the trade-union movement over the last twenty-five years. Trade unions can obtain higher wages within capitalist expansion only to the extent that they are matched by increased productivity or passed on to lower strata of the labor force. However, the tightening of the labor market that accompanies capitalist expansion increases the pretensions of the working class, both with regard to wages and relief from work, at the same time that it diminishes the possibility of placing the burden on disadvantaged sectors. Hence, wage demands result in inflation and a crisis in labor organization.

These tendencies in the labor market, which are occurring throughout the advanced capitalist world as capital expansions occur, have led to the widespread adoption of wage and price controls, thus signaling the de facto end, or at least the beginning of the end, of the era of collective bargaining. Trade unions can no longer confine their horizons to the struggle between their membership and its employers, but must bargain politically at the national level over the share of wages in national income. In Marxian terms, the material conditions of trade-union consciousness are coming to an end in advanced capitalism since the trade unions can no longer confine themselves to wages, but must deal directly with the problem of the aggregate rate of surplus value, which is a class phenomenon. At this point of development, they soon find out that there is very little that can be done about the rate of surplus value within a capitalist framework, since increases in the share of wages cut down on investment and result in unemployment and a slackening of growth. A socialist alternative, under which the working class seizes control of the investment process, could open new possibilities of organizing production and promoting the growth and development of the potential of social labor. Failing this radical break, the working class is a hostage to the capitalist class on whom they depend for capital accumulation and to whom they must provide incentives in the form of profit and accumulation of capital, that is, more work.

Thus, labor organizations must shift their horizons from the industrial to the national level, that is, they must shift from economic to political action. At the same time, the growth of the world market and the internationalization of capital implies they must also shift their horizons to the world level. Once again, they discover how limited their options are if they do not challenge the capitalist system. If, for example, they adopt a protectionist policy, they can lessen the competition from imports, but they cannot ensure a high rate of national investment if capitalists can escape their national demands by investing abroad. If they try to control capital flight, they then discover that the size and complexity of multinational corporations and the international financial market provide capitalists with numerous escape valves and that unless they take over the whole system, they can only achieve partial control.

Therefore, on both counts—the internal reserve army and the external reserve army—labor is in an objective crisis where its old institutions and policies no longer work, and, what amounts to the same thing, so is capitalism. This is what I believe to be the radical view of international economics and international politics at this juncture in history.

The Next Twenty-Five Years

Work in the Marxist framework is a political relationship. In the market, where workers sell their labor in exchange for wages, it seems to be only an economic phenomenon, but this is an illusion. What the workers sell is not labor but labor power, that is, their life activity. How this labor power will be used, its duration and intensity, is not settled by competition but by struggle and force. Hence there arises within the business enterprise a political superstructure whose function is in part to coordinate work and in part to overcome the resistance of workers arising out of the antagonistic social relations of production. Similarly, the struggle over work leads to the capitalist state whose function in the last instance is to ensure the reproduction of the basic structural elements of the work relationship—capital and labor. The rise and spread of the market system is thus closely connected to a political struggle to create and maintain the wage-labor force, divided by competition, upon which capitalism rests.

Politics—the getting, keeping, and using of power—is mainly a question of uniting your allies and dividing your enemies. Marx's analysis of the general laws of capitalist accumulation is an attempt to uncover the tendencies toward concentration and class consciousness that develop in the two main contending parties as capitalism progresses.

The peculiar feature of capitalism is that it obtained power and in some sense maintains it with an inherently limited degree of class consciousness. Capitalism is a system based on the mutual indifference of its participants, operating in a structure of competition and the pursuit of selfish interests. In economists' terms, it is a highly decentralized system based on private profit maximization and united through the invisible hand of the market, that is, the law of value. The great strength of this system, which differentiates it from all previous modes of production, is that the competition between capitalists, and between capital and labor, forces a continuous revolution in technology and an epoch-making expansion of material production. But this competitive market nexus is also its chief limit, for it prevents the development of a total view of society commensurate with the increasingly interdependent social division of labor that it is creating. The capitalist state attempts to provide some sort of total view, but is sharply limited by the divisions in capitalist society between capital and labor and between capitalists themselves. As capitalism progresses, this contradiction intensifies. The problems of "externalities," to use economists' language, and "socialization" and "legitimization" become more important as more and more problems arise which cannot be managed by the invisible hand of the market. The world market, created since the Second World War, has brought things to a critical point. Capital has expanded to global dimensions, but still maintains a consciousness based on narrow private calculation. The structure of the American Empire, which kept some sort of order on this process in the past, is dissolving and a Hobbesian-like struggle of all against all seems to be emerging at the world level. As the anarchy of competition asserts itself, we find ourselves facing numerous crises, with even greater ones looming in the background.

Labor, in contrast to capital, though it too is divided by competition, steadily struggles to eliminate this competition at higher and higher levels until it reaches a world historic perspective far more total than capital and replaces capitalism by socialism. This unification, however, is a long-drawn-out process, requiring a high development of material forces, i.e., a long expansion of capitalist production. . . .

In this [selection] we have tried to suggest that the world market, by expanding the edge of competition, has created a critical juncture in the labor movement which will force a change in its strategy and structure. During the last twenty-five years, capital has been able to expand and internationalize, first by strengthening and then by eroding the powers of the nation state. During the next twenty-five years we can expect a counter-response by labor and other groups to erode the power of capital. This response will take a political form, i.e., a struggle over state power around the central issue of capitalism and its continuance. Since states are territorial, the locus of the struggle will be largely national, or at least regional, even though the context is international. In the United States, it will probably tend to the formation of some sort of labor party. In Europe, it will probably lead to unification and a closer union between social democratic and communist parties. In the underdeveloped countries, it will lead to an increased role of labor in politics as the new proletariat emerges. And so on.

In this [selection] we cannot even begin to examine the complexity of the struggle and the numerous paths it can take between the following two extremes

1. A privileged part of the new working class in the advanced countries joins with capital in a new imperialistic alliance to get higher benefits in return for suppressing blacks, Third World people, foreign workers, women, the aged, etc. I personally think that this extreme is unlikely, due to the large numbers and strength of the disadvantaged groups and the enormous brutality it would take to contain them.
2. At the other extreme, we can imagine a socialist consciousness which unites the disparate elements of labor to effect the transition from capitalism to socialism. Since socialism implies that communities obtain control over their own work and consumption, it would probably have to be based on national or regional self-sufficiency, as Keynes suggested; though with a great deal of international cooperation to permit the free flow of ideas, hospitality, etc.

Much research needs to be done on both labor and non-labor political groups before we can sort out the possible sets of intermediate alliances that might emerge, and analyze their implications for the balance between capitalism and socialism, internationalism and nationalism. This paper merely attempts to point to the crucial role of the capital-labor struggle that we can expect in the future. We might end by noting that whatever the outcome—international fascism, socialism, or mixed free enterprise—a great deal of conflict and struggle domestically and internationally is in store for us, especially in the Third World, as the powerful forces unleashed by advanced capitalism come to a head. Our main problem as social scientists and human beings is not only to analyze what is happening, but also to decide which side we want to be on. That is why I spent so much time on Keynes, who asked the right questions, even though he was sharply limited in his answers—because he tried to think history without Marx.

NOTES

1. "Marx to Engels in Manchester, London, October 8, 1858," in Karl Marx and Frederick Engels, *Selected Correspondence* (Moscow: Progress Publishers, 1965), p. 111.

2. John Maynard Keynes, "National Self-Sufficiency," *The Yale Review*, vol. 22 (Summer 1933), p 766.

3. *Ibid.*, p. 758.

4. *Ibid.*, p. 757.

5. *Ibid.*, pp. 760–762.

6. "The American Challenge," *The Economist*, July 18, 1942, p. 67.

7. Sumner Wells, quoted in "The New Frontier," *The Economist* (June 13, 1942), p. 824.

8. "The New Frontier," p. 825.

9. "An American Proposal," *Fortune* (May 1942), p. 63.

10. John Maynard Keynes, *The General Theory of Employment, Interest and Money* (London: Macmillan & Co., Ltd., 1964), p. 221.

11. *Ibid.*, p. 376.

12. *Ibid.*, 276–377.

13. Stephen Hymer, "The Internationalization of Capital," *Journal of Economic Issues*, vol. 6, no. 1 (1972), pp. 91–111.

14. Karl Marx, *Capital*, 3 vols. (New York: International Publishers, 1976), I:614.

15. *Ibid.*, p. 639.

3. State Power and the Structure of International Trade

STEPHEN D. KRASNER

In this essay, Stephen Krasner applies a Realist analysis to the relationship between the interests and power of major states and the trade openness of the international economy. He identifies four principal goals of state action: political power, aggregate national income, economic growth, and social stability. He then combines the goals with different national abilities to pursue them, relating the international distribution of potential economic power to alternative trade regimes. Krasner maintains, most significantly, that the hegemony of a leading power is necessary for the creation and continuance of free trade. He applies his model to six periods. While the argument works well for three of the periods, it works less well for the other three and requires an amendment. Krasner's analysis in this 1976 article is a well-known attempt to use Realist ideas to explain international economic affairs. The theory he propounds, which has been dubbed the "Theory of Hegemonic Stability," has influenced most other Realist and neo-Realist writing on the subject.

INTRODUCTION

In recent years, students of international relations have multinational-ized, transnationalized, bureaucratized, and transgovernmentalized the state until it has virtually ceased to exist as an analytic construct. Nowhere is that trend more apparent than in the study of the politics of international economic relations. The basic conventional assumptions have been undermined by assertions that the state is trapped by a transnational society created not by sovereigns, but by nonstate actors. Interdependence is not seen as a reflection of state policies and state choices (the perspective of balance-of-power theory), but as the result of elements beyond the control of any state or a system created by states.

This perspective is at best profoundly misleading. It may explain developments within a particular international economic structure, but it cannot explain the structure itself. That structure has many institutional and behavioral manifestations. The central continuum along which it can be described is openness. International economic structures may range from complete autarky (if all states prevent movements across their borders), to complete openness (if no restrictions exist). In this paper I will present an analysis of one aspect of the international economy—the structure of international trade; that is, the degree of openness for the movement of goods as opposed to capital, labor, technology, or other factors of production.

Since the beginning of the nineteenth century, this structure has gone through several changes. These can be explained, albeit imperfectly, by a state-power theory: an approach that begins with the assumption that the structure of international trade is determined by the interests and power of states acting to maximize national goals. The first step in this argument is to relate four basic state interests—aggregate national income, social stability, political power, and economic growth—to the degree of openness for the movement of goods. The relationship between these interests and openness depends upon the potential economic power of any given state. Potential economic power is operationalized in terms of the relative size and level of economic development of the state. The second step in the argument is to relate different distributions of potential power, such as multipolar and hegemonic, to different international trading structures. The most important conclusion of this theoretical analysis is that a hegemonic distribution of potential economic power is likely to result in an open trading structure. That argument is largely, although not completely, substantiated by empirical data. For a fully adequate analysis it is necessary to amend a state-power argument to take account of the impact of past state decisions on domestic social structures as well as on international economic ones. The two major organizers of the structure of trade since the beginning of the nineteenth century, Great Britain and the United States, have both been prevented from making policy amendments in line with state interests by particular societal groups whose power had been enhanced by earlier state policies.

THE CAUSAL ARGUMENT: STATE INTERESTS, STATE POWER, AND INTERNATIONAL TRADING STRUCTURES

Neoclassical trade theory is based upon the assumption that states act to maximize their aggregate economic utility. This leads to the conclusion that maximum global welfare and Pareto optimality are achieved under free trade. While particular countries might better their situations through protectionism, economic theory has generally looked askance at such policies. . . . Neoclassical theory recognizes that trade regulations can . . . be used to correct domestic distortions and to promote infant industries, but these are exceptions or temporary departures from policy conclusions that lead logically to the support of free trade.

State Preferences

Historical experience suggests that policy makers are dense, or that the assumptions of the conventional argument are wrong. Free trade has hardly been the norm. Stupidity is not a very interesting analytic category. An alternative approach to explaining international trading structures is to assume that states seek a broad range of goals. At least four major state interests affected by the structure of international trade can be identified. They are: political power, aggregate national income, economic growth, and social stability. The way in which each of these goals is affected by the degree of openness depends upon the potential economic power of the state as defined by its relative size and level of development.

Let us begin with aggregate national income because it is most straightforward. Given the exceptions noted above, conventional neoclassical theory demonstrates that the greater the degree of openness in the international trading system, the greater the level of aggregate economic income. This conclusion applies to all states regardless of their size or relative level of development. The static economic benefits of openness are, however, generally inversely related to size. Trade gives small states relatively more welfare benefits than it gives large ones. Empirically, small states have higher ratios of trade to national product. They do not have the generous factor endowments or potential for national economies of scale that are enjoyed by larger—particularly continental—states.

The impact of openness on social stability runs in the opposite direction. Greater openness exposes the domestic economy to the exigencies of the world market. That implies a higher level of factor movements than in a closed economy, because domestic production patterns must adjust to changes in international prices. Social instability is thereby increased, since there is friction in moving factors, particularly labor, from one sector to another. The impact will be stronger in small states than in large, and in relatively less developed than in more developed ones. Large states are less involved in the international economy: a smaller percentage of their total factor endowment is affected by the international market at any given level of openness. More developed states are better able to adjust factors: skilled workers can more easily be moved from one kind of production to another than can unskilled laborers or peasants. Hence social stability is, *ceteris paribus*, inversely related to openness, but the deleterious consequences of exposure to the international trading system are mitigated by larger size and greater economic development.

The relationship between political power and the international trading structure can be analyzed in terms of the relative opportunity costs of closure for trading partners. The higher the relative cost of closure, the weaker the political position of the state. Hirschman has argued that this cost can be measured in terms of direct income losses and the adjustment costs of reallocating factors. These will be smaller for large states and for relatively more developed states. Other things being equal, utility costs will be less for large states because they generally have a smaller proportion of their economy engaged in the international economic system. Reallocation costs will be less for more advanced states because their factors are more mobile. Hence a state that is relatively large and more developed will find its political power enhanced by an open system because its opportunity costs of closure are less. The large state can use the threat to alter the system to secure economic or noneconomic objectives. Historically, there is one important exception to this generalization—the oil-exporting states. The level of reserves for some of the states, particularly Saudi Arabia, has reduced the economic opportunity costs of closure to a very low level despite their lack of development.

The relationship between international economic structure and economic growth is elusive. For small states, economic growth has generally been empirically associated with openness. Exposure to the international system makes possible a much more efficient allocation of resources. Openness also probably furthers the rate of growth of large countries with relatively advanced technologies because they do not need to protect infant industries and can take advantage of expanded world markets. In the long term, however, openness for capital and technology, as well as goods, may hamper the growth of large, developed countries by diverting resources from the domestic economy, and by providing potential competitors with the knowledge needed to develop their own industries. Only by maintaining its technological lead and continually developing new industries can even a very large state escape the undesired consequences of an entirely open economic system. For medium-size states, the relationship between international trading structure and growth is impossible to specify definitively, either theoretically or empirically. On the one hand, writers from the mercantilists through the American protectionists and the German historical school, and more recently analysts of *dependencia*, have argued that an entirely open system can undermine a state's effort to develop, and even lead to underdevelopment. On the other hand, adherents of more conventional neoclassical positions have maintained that exposure to international competition spurs economic transformation. The evidence is not yet in. All that can confidently be said is that openness furthers the economic growth of small states and of large ones so long as they maintain their technological edge.

From State Preferences to International Trading Structures

The next step in this argument is to relate particular distributions of potential economic power, defined by the size and level of development of individual states, to the structure of the international trading system, defined in terms of openness.

Let us consider a system composed of a large number of small, highly developed states. Such a system is likely to lead to an open international trading structure. The aggregate income and economic growth of each state are increased by an open system. The social instability produced by exposure to international competition is mitigated by the factor mobility made possible by higher levels of development. There is no loss of political power from openness because the costs of closure are symmetrical for all members of the system.

Now let us consider a system composed of a few very large, but unequally developed states. Such a distribution of potential economic power is likely to lead to a closed structure. Each state could increase its income through a more open system, but the gains would be modest. Openness would create more social instability in the less developed countries. The rate of growth for more backward areas might be frustrated, while that of the more advanced ones would be enhanced. A more open structure would leave the less developed states in a politically more vulnerable position, because their greater factor rigidity would mean a higher relative cost of closure. Because of these disadvantages, large but relatively less developed states are unlikely to accept an open trading structure. More advanced states cannot, unless they are militarily more powerful, force large backward countries to accept openness.

Finally, let us consider a hegemonic system—one in which there is a single state that is much larger and relatively more advanced than its trading partners. The costs and benefits of openness are not symmetrical for all members of the system. The hegemonic state will have a preference for an open structure. Such a structure increases its aggregate national income. It also increases its rate of growth during its ascendency—that is, when its relative size and technological lead are increasing. Further, an open structure increases its political power, since the opportunity costs of closure are least for a large and developed state. The social instability resulting from exposure to the international system is mitigated by the hegemonic power's relatively low level of involvement in the international economy, and the mobility of its factors.

What of the other members of a hegemonic system? Small states are likely to opt for openness because the advantages in terms of aggregate income and growth are so great, and their political power is bound to be restricted regardless of what they do. The reaction of medium-size states is hard to predict; it depends at least in part on the way in which the hegemonic power utilizes its resources. The potentially dominant state has symbolic, economic, and military capabilities that can be used to entice or compel others to accept an open trading structure.

At the symbolic level, the hegemonic state stands as an example of how economic development can be achieved. Its policies may be emulated, even if they are inappropriate for other states. Where there are very dramatic asymmetries, military power can be used to coerce weaker states into an open structure. Force is not, however, a very efficient means for changing economic policies, and it is unlikely to be employed against medium-size states.

Most importantly, the hegemonic state can use its economic resources to create an open structure. In terms of positive incentives, it can offer access to its large domestic market and to its relatively cheap exports. In terms of negative ones, it can withhold foreign grants and engage in competition, potentially ruinous for the weaker state, in third-country markets. The size and economic robustness of the hegemonic state also enable it to provide the confidence necessary for a stable international monetary system, and its currency can offer the liquidity needed for an increasingly open system.

In sum, openness is most likely to occur during periods when a hegemonic state is in its ascendency. Such a state has the interest and the resources to create a structure characterized by lower tariffs, rising trade proportions, and less regionalism. There are other distributions of potential power where openness is likely, such as a system composed of many small, highly developed states. But even here, that potential might not be realized because of the problems of creating confidence in a monetary system where adequate liquidity would have to be provided by a negotiated international reserve asset or a group of national currencies. Finally, it is unlikely that very large states, particularly at unequal levels of development, would accept open trading relations.

These arguments, and the implications of other ideal typical configurations of potential economic power for the openness of trading structures, are summarized in [Chart I].

CHART I. Probability of an Open Trading Structure with Different Distributions of Potential Economic Power

LEVEL OF DEVELOPMENT OF STATES	SIZE OF STATES		
	Relatively Equal		Very Unequal
	Small	Large	
Equal	Moderate-High	Low-Moderate	High
Unequal	Moderate	Low	Moderate-High

THE DEPENDENT VARIABLE: DESCRIBING THE STRUCTURE OF THE INTERNATIONAL TRADING SYSTEM

The structure of international trade has both behavioral and institutional attributes. The degree of openness can be described both by the *flow* of goods and by the *policies* that are followed by states with respect to trade barriers and international payments. The two are not unrelated, but they do not coincide perfectly.

In common usage, the focus of attention has been upon institutions. Openness is associated with those historical periods in which tariffs were substantially lowered: the third quarter of the nineteenth century and the period since the Second World War.

Tariffs alone, however, are not an adequate indicator of structure. They are hard to operationalize quantitatively. Tariffs do not have to be high to be effective. If cost functions are nearly identical, even low tariffs can prevent trade. Effective tariff rates may be much higher than nominal ones. Non-tariff barriers to trade, which are not easily compared across states, can substitute for duties. An undervalued exchange rate can protect domestic markets from foreign competition. Tariff levels alone cannot describe the structure of international trade.

A second indicator, and one which is behavioral rather than institutional, is trade proportions—the ratios of trade to national income for different states. Like tariff levels, these involve describing the system in terms of an agglomeration of national tendencies. A period in which these ratios are increasing across time for most states can be described as one of increasing openness.

A third indicator is the concentration of trade within regions composed of states at different levels of development. The degree of such regional encapsulation is determined not so much by comparative advantage (because relative factor endowments would allow almost any backward area to trade with almost any developed one), but by political choices or dictates. Large states, attempting to protect themselves from the vagaries of a global system, seek to maximize their interests by creating regional blocs. Openness in the global economic system has in effect meant greater trade among the leading industrial states. Periods of closure are associated with the encapsulation of certain advanced states within regional systems shared with certain less developed areas.

A description of the international trading system involves, then, an exercise that is comparative rather than absolute. A period when tariffs are falling, trade proportions are rising, and regional trading patterns are becoming less extreme will be defined as one in which the structure is becoming more open.

Tariff Levels

The period from the 1820's to 1879 was basically one of decreasing tariff levels in Europe. The trend began in Great Britain in the 1820's, with reductions of duties and other barriers to trade. In 1846 the abolition of the Corn Laws ended agricultural protectionism. France reduced duties on some intermediate goods in the 1830's, and on coal, iron, and steel in 1852. The *Zollverein* established fairly low tariffs in 1834. Belgium, Portugal, Spain, Piedmont, Norway, Switzerland, and Sweden lowered imposts in the 1850's. The golden age of free trade began in 1860, when Britain and France signed the Cobden-Chevalier Treaty, which virtually eliminated trade barriers. This was followed by a series of bilateral trade agreements between virtually all European states. It is important to note, however, that the United States took little part in the general movement toward lower trade barriers.

The movement toward greater liberality was reversed in the late 1870's. Austria-Hungary increased duties in 1876 and 1878, and Italy also in 1878; but the main breach came in Germany in 1879. France increased tariffs modestly in 1881, sharply in 1892, and raised them still further in 1910. Other countries followed a similar pattern. Only Great Britain, Belgium, the Netherlands, and Switzerland continued to follow free-trade policies through the 1880's. Although Britain did not herself impose duties, she began establishing a system of preferential markets in her overseas Empire in 1898. The United States was basically protectionist throughout the nineteenth century. The high tariffs imposed during the Civil War continued with the exception of a brief period in the 1890's. There were no major duty reductions before 1914.

During the 1920's tariff levels increased further. Western European states protected their agrarian sectors against imports from the Danube region, Australia, Canada, and the United States, where the war had stimulated increased output. Great Britain adopted some colonial preferences in 1919, imposed a small number of tariffs in 1921, and extended some wartime duties. The successor states of the Austro-Hungarian Empire imposed duties to achieve some national self-sufficiency. The British dominions and Latin America protected industries nurtured by wartime demands. In the United States the Fordney-McCumber Tariff Act of 1922 increased protectionism. The October Revolution removed Russia from the Western trading system.

Dramatic closure in terms of tariff levels began with the passage of the Smoot-Hawley Tariff Act in the United States in 1930. Britain raised tariffs in 1931 and definitively abandoned free trade at the Ottawa Conference of 1932, which introduced extensive imperial preferences. Germany and Japan established trading blocs within their own spheres of influence. All other major countries followed protectionist policies.

Significant reductions in protection began after the Second World War; the United States had foreshadowed the movement toward greater liberality with the passage of the Reciprocal Trade Agreements Act in 1934. Since 1945 there have been seven rounds of multilateral tariff reductions. The first, held in 1947 at Geneva, and the Kennedy Round, held during the 1960's, have been the most significant. They have substantially reduced the level of protection.

The present situation is ambiguous. There have recently been some new trade controls. In the United States these include a voluntary import agreement for steel, the imposition of a 10 per cent import surcharge during four months of 1971, and export controls on agricultural products in 1973 and 1974. Italy imposed a deposit requirement on imports during parts of 1974 and 1975. Britain and Japan have engaged in export subsidization. Non-tariff barriers have become more important. On balance, there has been movement toward greater protectionism since the end of the Kennedy Round, but it is not decisive. The outcome of the multilateral negotiations that began in 1975 remains to be seen.

In sum, after 1820 there was a general trend toward lower tariffs (with the notable exception of the United States), which culminated between 1860 and 1879; higher tariffs from 1879 through the interwar years, with dramatic increases in the 1930's; and less protectionism from 1945 through the conclusion of the Kennedy Round in 1967.

Trade Proportions

With the exception of one period, ratios of trade to aggregate economic activity followed the same general pattern as tariff levels. Trade proportions increased from the early part of the nineteenth century to about 1880. Between 1880 and 1900 there was a decrease, sharper if measured in current prices than constant ones, but apparent in both statistical series for most countries. Between 1900 and 1913—and here is the exception from the tariff pattern—there was a marked increase in the ratio of trade to aggregate economic activity. This trend brought trade proportions to levels that have generally not been reattained. During the

1920's and 1930's the importance of trade in national economic activity declined. After the Second World War it increased.

. . . There are considerable differences in the movement of trade proportions among states. They hold more or less constant for the United States; Japan, Denmark, and Norway . . . are unaffected by the general decrease in the ratio of trade to aggregate economic activity that takes place after 1880. The pattern described in the previous paragraph does, however, hold for Great Britain, France, Sweden, Germany, and Italy.

. . . Because of the boom in commodity prices that occurred in the early 1950's, the ratio of trade to gross domestic product was relatively high for larger states during these years, at least in current prices. It then faltered or remained constant until about 1960. From the early 1960's through 1972, trade proportions rose for all major states except Japan. Data for 1973 and 1974 show further increases. For smaller countries the trend was more erratic, with Belgium showing a more or less steady increase, Norway vacillating between 82 and 90 per cent, and Denmark and the Netherlands showing higher figures for the late 1950's than for more recent years. There is then, in current prices, a generally upward trend in trade proportions since 1960, particularly for larger states. This movement is more pronounced if constant prices are used.

Regional Trading Patterns

The final indicator of the degree of openness of the global trading system is regional bloc concentration. There is a natural affinity for some states to trade with others because of geographical propinquity or comparative advantage. In general, however, a system in which there are fewer manifestations of trading within given blocs, particularly among specific groups of more and less developed states, is a more open one. Over time there have been extensive changes in trading patterns between particular areas of the world whose relative factor endowments have remained largely the same.

Richard Chadwick and Karl Deutsch have collected extensive information on international trading patterns since 1890. Their basic datum is the relative acceptance indicator (RA), which measures deviations from a null hypothesis in which trade between a pair of states, or a state and a region, is precisely what would be predicted on the basis of their total share of international trade. When the null hypothesis holds, the RA indicator is equal to zero. Values less than zero indicate less trade than expected, greater than zero more trade than expected. For our purposes the critical issue is whether, over time, trade tends to become more concentrated as shown by movements away from zero, or less as shown by movements toward zero. . . .

There is a general pattern. In three of the four cases, the RA value closest to zero—that is the least regional encapsulation—occurred in 1890, 1913, or 1928; in the fourth case (France and French West Africa), the 1928 value was not bettered until 1964. In every case there was an increase in the RA indicator between 1928 and 1938, reflecting the breakdown of international commerce that is associated with the depression. Surprisingly, the RA indicator was higher for each of the four pairs in 1954 than in 1938, an indication that regional patterns persisted and even became more intense in the postwar period. With the exception of the Soviet Union and Eastern Europe, there was a general trend toward decreasing RA's for the period after 1954. They still, however, show fairly high values even in the late 1960's.

If we put all three indicators—tariff levels, trade proportions, and trade patterns—together, they suggest the following periodization.

Period I (1820–1879): Increasing openness—tariffs are generally lowered; trade proportions increase. Data are not available for trade patterns. However, it is important to note that this is not a universal pattern. The United States is largely unaffected: its tariff levels remain high (and are in fact increased during the early 1860's) and American trade proportions remain almost constant.

Period II (1879–1900): Modest closure—tariffs are increased; trade proportions decline modestly for most states. Data are not available for trade patterns.

Period III (1900–1913): Greater openness—tariff levels remain generally unchanged; trade proportions increase for all major trading states except the United States. Trading patterns become less regional in three out of the four cases for which data are available.

Period IV (1918–1939): Closure—tariff levels are increased in the 1920's and again in the 1930's; trade proportions decline. Trade becomes more regionally encapsulated.

Period V (1945–c. 1970): Great openness—tariffs are lowered; trade proportions increase, particularly after 1960. Regional concentration decreases after 1960. However, these developments are limited to non-Communist areas of the world.

THE INDEPENDENT VARIABLE: DESCRIBING THE DISTRIBUTION OF POTENTIAL ECONOMIC POWER AMONG STATES

Analysts of international relations have an almost pro forma set of variables designed to show the distribution of potential power in the international *political* system. It includes such factors as gross national product, per capita income, geographical position, and size of armed forces. A similar set of indicators can be presented for the international *economic* system.

Statistics are available over a long time period for per capita income, aggregate size, share of world trade, and share of world investment. They demonstrate that, since the beginning of the nineteenth century, there have been two first-rank economic powers in the world economy— Britain and the United States. The United States passed Britain in aggregate size sometime in the middle of the nineteenth century and, in the 1880's, became the largest producer of manufactures. America's lead was particularly marked in technologically advanced industries turning out sewing machines, harvesters, cash registers, locomotives, steam pumps, telephones, and petroleum. Until the First World War, however, Great Britain had a higher per capita income, a greater share of world trade, and a greater share of world investment than any other state. The peak of British ascendance occurred around 1880, when Britain's relative per capita income, share of world trade, and share of investment flows reached their highest levels. Britain's potential dominance in 1880 and 1900 was particularly striking in the international economic system, where her share of trade and foreign investment was about twice as large as that of any other state.

It was only after the First World War that the United States became relatively larger and more developed in terms of all four indicators. This potential dominance reached new and dramatic heights between 1945 and 1960. Since then, the relative position of the United States has declined, bringing it quite close to West Germany, its nearest rival, in terms of per capita income and share of world trade. The devaluations of the dollar that have taken place since 1972 are reflected in a continuation of this downward trend for income and aggregate size.

The relative potential economic power of Britain and the United States is shown in [Tables I and II].

In sum, Britain was the world's most important trading state from the period after the Napoleonic Wars until 1913. Her relative position rose until about 1880 and fell thereafter. The United States became the largest and most advanced state in economic terms after the First World War, but did not equal the relative share of world trade and investment achieved by Britain in the 1880's until after the Second World War.

TESTING THE ARGUMENT

The contention that hegemony leads to a more open trading structure is fairly well, but not perfectly, confirmed by the empirical evidence presented in the preceding sections. The argument explains the periods 1820 to 1879, 1880 to 1900, and 1945 to 1960. It does not fully explain those from 1900 to 1913, 1919 to 1939, or 1960 to the present.

TABLE I. Indicators of British Potential Power (Ratio of British value to next highest)

	PER CAPITA INCOME	AGGREGATE SIZE	SHARE OF WORLD TRADE	SHARE OF WORLD INVESTMENT*
1860	.91(US)	.74(US)	2.01(FR)	n.a.
1880	1.30(US)	.79(1874–83 US)	2.22(FR)	1.93(FR)
1900	1.05(1899 US)	.58(1899 US)	2.17(1890 GERM)	2.08(FR)
1913	.92(US)	.43(US)	1.20(US)	2.18(1914 FR)
1928	.66(US)	.25(1929 US)	.79(US)	.64(1921–29 US)
1937	.79(US)	.29(US)	.88(US)	.18(1930–38 US)
1950	.56(US)	.19(US)	.69(US)	.13(1951–55 US)
1960	.49(US)	.14(US)	.46(1958 US)	.15(1956–61 US)
1972	.46(US)	.13(US)	.47(1973 US)	n.a.

* Stock 1870–1913; Flow 1928–1950
Years are in parentheses when different from those in first column.
Countries in parentheses are those with the largest values for the particular indicator other than Great Britain.

1820–1879. The period from 1820 to 1879 was one of increasing openness in the structure of international trade. It was also one of rising hegemony. Great Britain was the instigator and supporter of the new structure. She began lowering her trade barriers in the 1820's, before any other state. The signing of the Cobden-Chevalier Tariff Treaty with France in 1860 initiated a series of bilateral tariff reductions. It is, however, important to note that the United States was hardly involved in these developments, and that America's ratio of trade to aggregate economic activity did not increase during the nineteenth century.

TABLE II. Indicators of U.S. Potential Power (Ratio of U.S. value to next highest)

	PER CAPITA INCOME	AGGREGATE SIZE	SHARE OF WORLD TRADE	SHARE OF WORLD INVESTMENT FLOWS
1860	1.10(GB)	1.41(GB)	.36(GB)	Net debtor
1880	.77(GB)	1.23(1883 GB)	.37(GB)	Net debtor
1900	.95(1899 GB)	1.73(1899 GB)	.43(1890 GB)	n.a.
1913	1.09(GB)	2.15(RUS)	.83(GB)	Net debtor
1928	1.51(GB)	3.22(USSR)	1.26(GB)	1.55(1921–29 UK)
1937	1.26(GB)	2.67(USSR)	1.13(GB)	5.53(1930–38 UK)
1950	1.78(GB)	3.15(USSR)	1.44(GB)	7.42(1951–55 UK)
1960	2.05(GB)	2.81(USSR)	2.15(1958 GB)	6.60(1956–61 UK)
1972	1.31(GERM)	n.a.	1.18(1973 GERM)	n.a.

Years are in parentheses when different from those in first column.
Countries in parentheses are those with the largest values for the particular indicator other than the United States.

Britain put to use her internal flexibility and external power in securing a more open structure. At the domestic level, openness was favored by the rising industrialists. The opposition of the agrarian sector was mitigated by its capacity for adjustment: the rate of capital investment and technological innovation was high enough to prevent British agricultural incomes from falling until some thirty years after the abolition of the Corn Laws. Symbolically, the Manchester School led by Cobden and Bright provided the ideological justification for free trade. Its influence was felt throughout Europe where Britain stood as an example to at least some members of the elite.

Britain used her military strength to open many backward areas: British interventions were frequent in Latin America during the nineteenth century, and formal and informal colonial expansion opened the interior of Africa. Most importantly, Britain forced India into the international economic system. British military power was also a factor in concluding the Cobden-Chevalier Treaty, for Louis Napoleon was more concerned with cementing his relations with Britain than he was in the economic consequences of greater openness. Once this pact was signed, however, it became a catalyst for the many other treaties that followed.

Britain also put economic instruments to good use in creating an open system. The abolition of the Corn Laws offered continental grain producers the incentive of continued access to the growing British market. Britain was at the heart of the nineteenth-century international monetary system which functioned exceptionally well, at least for the core of the more developed states and the areas closely associated with them. Exchange rates were stable, and countries did not have to impose trade barriers to rectify cyclical payments difficulties. Both confidence and liquidity were, to a critical degree, provided by Britain. The use of sterling balances as opposed to specie became increasingly widespread, alleviating the liquidity problems presented by the erratic production of gold and silver. Foreign private and central banks increasingly placed their cash reserves in London, and accounts were cleared through changing bank balances rather than gold flows. Great Britain's extremely sophisticated financial institutions, centered in the City of London, provided the short-term financing necessary to facilitate the international flow of goods. Her early and somewhat fortuitous adherence to the gold—as opposed to the silver or bimetallic—standard proved to be an important source of confidence as all countries adopted at least a *de facto* gold standard after 1870 because of the declining relative value of silver. In times of monetary emergency, the confidence placed in the pound because of the strength of the British economy allowed the Bank of England to be a lender of last resort.

Hence, for the first three-quarters of the nineteenth century, British policy favored an open international trading structure, and British power helped to create it. But this was not a global regime. British resources were not sufficient to entice or compel the United States (a country whose economy was larger than Britain's by 1860 and whose technology was developing very rapidly) to abandon its protectionist commercial policy. As a state-power argument suggests, openness was only established within the geographical area where the rising economic hegemony was able to exercise its influence.

1880–1900. The last two decades of the nineteenth century were a period of modest closure which corresponds to a relative decline in British per capita income, size, and share of world trade. The event that precipitated higher tariff levels was the availability of inexpensive grain from the American Midwest, made possible by the construction of continental railways. National responses varied. Britain let her agricultural sector decline, a not unexpected development given her still dominant economic position. Denmark, a small and relatively well-developed state, also refrained from imposing tariffs and transformed its farming sector from agriculture to animal husbandry. Several other small states also followed open policies. Germany, France, Russia, and Italy imposed higher tariffs, however. Britain did not have the military or economic power to forestall these policies. Still, the institutional structure of the international monetary system, with the City of London at its center, did not crumble. The decline in trade proportions was modest despite higher tariffs.

1945–1960. The third period that is neatly explained by the argument that hegemony leads to an open trading structure is the decade and a half after the Second World War, characterized by the ascendancy of the United States. During these years the structure of the international trading system became increasingly open. Tariffs were lowered; trade proportions were restored well above interwar levels. Asymmetrical regional trading patterns did begin to decline, although not until the late 1950's. America's bilateral rival, the Soviet Union, remained—as the theory would predict—encapsulated within its own regional sphere of influence.

Unlike Britain in the nineteenth century, the United States after World War II operated in a bipolar political structure. Free trade was preferred, but departures such as the Common Market and Japanese import restrictions were accepted to make sure that these areas remained within the general American sphere of influence. Domestically the Reciprocal Trade Agreements Act, first passed in 1934, was extended several times after the war. Internationally the United States supported the framework for tariff reductions provided by the General Agreement on Tariffs and Trade. American policy makers used their economic leverage over Great Britain to force an end to the imperial preference system. The monetary system established at Bretton Woods was basically an American creation. In practice, liquidity was provided by the American deficit; confidence by the size of the American economy. Behind the economic veil stood American military protection for other industrialized market economies—an overwhelming incentive for them to accept an open system, particularly one which was in fact relatively beneficial.

The argument about the relationship between hegemony and openness is not as satisfactory for the years 1900 to 1913, 1919 to 1939, and 1960 to the present.

1900–1913. During the years immediately preceding the First World War, the structure of international trade became more open in terms of trade proportions and regional patterns. Britain remained the largest international economic entity, but her relative position continued a decline that had begun two decades earlier. Still, Britain maintained her commitment to free trade and to the financial institutions of the City of London. A state-power argument would suggest some reconsideration of these policies.

Perhaps the simplest explanation for the increase in trade proportions was the burst of loans that flowed out of Europe in the years before the First World War, loans that financed the increasing sale of goods. Germany and France as well as Britain participated in this development. Despite the higher tariff levels imposed after 1879, institutional structures—particularly the monetary system—allowed these capital flows to generate increasing trade flows. Had Britain reconsidered her policies, this might not have been the case.

1919–1939. The United States emerged from the First World War as the world's most powerful economic state. Whether America was large enough to have put an open system in place is a moot question. As Table II indicates, America's share of world trade and investment was only 26 and 55 per cent greater than that of any other state, while comparable figures for Great Britain during the last part of the nineteenth century are 100 per cent. What is apparent, though, is that American policy makers made little effort to open the structure of international trade. The call for an open door was a shibboleth, not a policy. It was really the British who attempted to continue a hegemonic role.

In the area of trade, the U.S. Fordney-McCumber Tariff of 1922 increased protection. That tendency was greatly reinforced by the Smoot-Hawley Tariff of 1930 which touched off a wave of protective legislation. Instead of leading the way to openness, the United States led the way to closure.

In the monetary area, the American government made little effort to alter a situation that was confused and often chaotic. During the first half of the 1920's, exchange rates fluctuated widely among major currencies as countries were forced, by the inflationary pressures of the war, to abandon the gold standard. Convertibility was restored in the mid-twenties at values incompatible with long-term equilibrium. The British pound was overvalued, and the French franc undervalued. Britain was forced off the gold standard in September 1931, accelerating a trend that had begun with Uruguay in April 1929. The United States went off gold in 1933. France's decision to end convertibility in 1936 completed the pattern. During the 1930's the monetary system collapsed.

Constructing a stable monetary order would have been no easy task in the political environment of the 1920's and 1930's. The United States made no effort. It refused to recognize a connection between war debts and reparations, although much of the postwar flow of funds took the form of American loans to Germany, German reparations payments to France and Britain, and French and British war-debt payments to the United States. The great depression was in no small measure touched off by the contraction of American credit in the late 1920's. In the deflationary collapse that followed, the British were too weak to act as a lender of last resort, and the Americans actually undercut efforts to reconstruct the Western economy when, before the London Monetary Conference of 1933, President Roosevelt changed the basic assumptions of the meeting by taking the United States off gold. American concern was wholly with restoring the domestic economy.

That is not to say that American behavior was entirely obstreperous; but cooperation was erratic and often private. The Federal Reserve Bank of New York did try, during the late 1920's, to maintain New York interest rates below those in London to protect the value of the pound. Two Americans, Dawes and Young, lent their names to the renegotiations of German reparations payments, but most of the actual work was carried out by British experts. At the official level, the first manifestation of American leadership was President Hoover's call for a moratorium on war debts and reparations in June 1931; but in 1932 the United States refused to participate in the Lausanne Conference that in effect ended reparations.

It was not until the mid-thirties that the United States asserted any real leadership. The Reciprocal Trade Agreements Act of 1934 led to bilateral treaties with twenty-seven countries before 1945. American concessions covered 64 per cent of dutiable items, and reduced rates by an average of 44 per cent. However, tariffs were so high to begin with that the actual impact of these agreements was limited. There were also some modest steps toward tariff liberalization in Britain and France. In the monetary field, the United States, Britain, and France pledged to maintain exchange-rate stability in the Tripartite Declaration of September 1936. These actions were not adequate to create an open international economic structure. American policy during the interwar period, and particularly before the mid-thirties, fails to accord with the predictions made by a state-power explanation of the behavior of a rising hegemonic power.

1960–present. The final period not adequately dealt with by a state-power explanation is the last decade or so. In recent years, the relative size and level of development of the U.S. economy has fallen. This decline has not, however, been accompanied by a clear turn toward protectionism. The Trade Expansion Act of 1962 was extremely liberal and led to the very successful Kennedy Round of multilateral tariff cuts during the mid-sixties. The protectionist Burke-Hartke Bill did not pass. The 1974 Trade Act does include new protectionist aspects, particularly in its requirements for review of the removal of nontariff barriers by Congress and for stiffer requirements for the imposition of countervailing duties, but it still maintains the mechanism of presidential discretion on tariff cuts that has been the keystone of postwar reductions. While the Voluntary Steel Agreement, the August 1971 economic policy, and restrictions on agricultural exports all show a tendency toward protectionism, there is as yet no evidence of a basic turn away from a commitment to openness.

In terms of behavior in the international trading system, the decade of the 1960's was clearly one of greater openness. Trade proportions increased, and traditional regional trade patterns became weaker. A state-power argument would predict a downturn or at least a faltering in these indicators as American power declined.

In sum, although the general pattern of the structure of international trade conforms with the predictions of a state-power argument—two periods of openness separated by one of closure—corresponding to periods of rising British and American hegemony and an interregnum, the whole pattern is out of phase. British commitment to openness continued long after Britain's position had declined. American commitment to openness did not begin until well after the United States had become the world's leading economic power and has continued during a period of relative American decline. The state-power argument needs to be amended to take these delayed reactions into account.

AMENDING THE ARGUMENT

The structure of the international trading system does not move in lockstep with changes in the distribution of potential power among states. Systems are initiated and ended, not as a state-power theory would predict, by close assessments of the interests of the state at every given moment, but by external events—usually cataclysmic ones. The closure that began in 1879 coincided with the Great Depression of the last part of the nineteenth century. The final dismantling of the nineteenth-century international economic system was not precipitated by a change in British trade or monetary policy, but by the First World War and the Depression. The potato famine of the 1840's prompted abolition of the Corn Laws; and the United States did not assume the mantle of world leadership until the world had been laid bare by six years of total war. Some catalytic external event seems necessary to move states to dramatic policy initiatives in line with state interests.

Once policies have been adopted, they are pursued until a new crisis demonstrates that they are no longer feasible. States become locked in by the impact of prior choices on their domestic political structures. The British decision to opt for openness in 1846 corresponded with state interests. It also strengthened the position of industrial and financial groups over time, because they had the opportunity to operate in an international system that furthered their objectives. That system eventually undermined the position of British farmers, a group that would have supported protectionism if it had survived. Once entrenched, Britain's export industries, and more importantly the City of London, resisted policies of closure. In the interwar years, the British rentier class insisted on restoring the prewar parity of the pound—a decision that placed enormous deflationary pressures on the domestic economy—because they wanted to protect the value of their investments.

Institutions created during periods of rising ascendancy remained in operation when they were no longer appropriate. For instance, the organization of British banking in the nineteenth century separated domestic and foreign operations. The Court of Directors of the Bank of England was dominated by international banking houses. Their decisions about British monetary policy were geared toward the international economy. Under a different institutional arrangement more attention might have been given after 1900 to the need to revitalize the domestic economy. The British state was unable to free itself from the domestic structures that its earlier policy decisions had created, and continued to follow policies appropriate for a rising hegemony long after Britain's star had begun to fall.

Similarly, earlier policies in the United States begat social structures and institutional arrangements that trammeled state policy. After protecting import-competing industries for a century, the United States was unable in the 1920's to opt for more open policies, even though state interests would have been furthered thereby. Institutionally, decisions about tariff reductions were taken primarily in congressional committees, giving virtually any group seeking protection easy access to the decision-making process. When there were conflicts among groups, they were resolved by raising the levels of protection for everyone. It was only after the cataclysm of the depression that the decision-making processes for trade policy were changed. The Presidency, far more insulated from the entreaties of particular societal groups than congressional committees, was then given more power. Furthermore, the American commercial banking system was unable to assume the burden of regulating the international economy during the 1920's. American institutions were geared toward the domestic economy. Only after the Second World War, and in fact not until the late 1950's, did American banks fully develop the complex institutional structures commensurate with the dollar's role in the international monetary system.

Having taken the critical decisions that created an open system after 1945, the American Government is unlikely to change its policy until it confronts some external event that it cannot control, such as a worldwide deflation, drought in the great plains, or the malicious use of petrodollars. In America perhaps more than in any other country "new policies," as E. E. Schattschneider wrote in his brilliant study of the Smoot-Hawley Tariff in 1935, "create new politics,"[1] for in America the state is weak and the society strong. State decisions taken because of state interests reinforce private societal groups that the state is unable to resist in later periods. Multinational corporations have grown and prospered since 1950. International economic policy making has passed from the Congress to the Executive. Groups favoring closure, such as organized labor, are unlikely to carry the day until some external event demonstrates that existing policies can no longer be implemented.

The structure of international trade changes in fits and starts; it does not flow smoothly with the redistribution of potential state power. Nevertheless, it is the power and the policies of states that create order where there would otherwise be chaos or at best a Lockian state of nature. The existence of various transnational, multinational, transgovernmental, and other nonstate actors that have riveted scholarly attention in recent years can only be understood within the context of a broader structure that ultimately rests upon the power and interests of states, shackled though they may be by the societal consequences of their own past decisions.

NOTE

1. E. E. Schattschneider, *Politics, Pressures and the Tariff: A Study of Free Enterprise in Pressure Politics as Shown in the 1929–1930 Revision of the Tariff* (New York: Prentice-Hall, 1935), p. 288.

II. HISTORICAL PERSPECTIVES

A truly international economy first emerged during the "long sixteenth century," the period from approximately 1480 to 1650. In its earliest form, the modern international economy was highly mercantilistic. As Jacob Viner explains in his article, mercantilist doctrine asserted that power and wealth were closely interrelated and legitimate goals of national policy. Thus, wealth was necessary for power, and power could be used to obtain wealth. Because power is a relative concept, as one country can gain it only at the expense of another, mercantilist nations perceived themselves to be locked into a zero-sum conflict in the international economy.

Countries pursued a variety of policies during this period intended to expand production and wealth at home while denying similar capabilities to others. Six policies were of nearly universal importance. First, countries sought to prevent gold and silver, a common mercantilist measure of wealth, from being exported. Spain declared the export of gold or silver punishable by death at the beginning of the sixteenth century. Demonstrating the difficulties of enforcing such regulations, France declared the export of coined gold and silver illegal in 1506, 1540, 1548, and 1574. Second, regulations (typically, high tariffs) were adopted to limit imports to necessary raw materials. Importing raw materials was desirable because it lowered prices at home and thereby reduced costs for manufacturers. By limiting imports of manufactured and luxury items, on the other hand, countries sought to stimulate production at home while reducing it abroad. Third, exports of manufactured goods were encouraged for similar reasons. Fourth, just as they sought to encourage imports of raw materials, countries sought to limit the export of these goods—so as to both lower prices at home and limit the ability of others to develop a manufacturing capability of their own. Fifth, exports of technology—including both machinery and skilled artisans—were restricted to inhibit potential foreign competitors. Finally, many countries adopted navigation laws mandating that a certain percentage of their foreign trade had to be carried in native ships. This last trade regulation was intended to stimulate the domestic shipping and shipbuilding industries—both necessary resources for successful war making.

By the early nineteenth century, mercantilist trade restrictions were coming under widespread attack, particularly in Great Britain. Drawing upon the Liberal writings of Adam Smith and David Ricardo, Richard Cobden and other Manchester industrialists led the fight for free trade, which culminated in 1846 in the abolition of the "Corn Laws" (restrictions on grain imports)—the last remaining mercantilist impediment to trade in Britain. Other countries soon followed the United Kingdom's example. Under Britain's hegemonic leadership, a period of European free trade was ushered in which lasted from 1860 to 1879 (see Kindleberger, Reading 5). This trend toward freer trade was reversed in the last quarter of the nineteenth century. The purported causes of this reversal are many, including the decline of British hegemony, the onset of the first "Great Depression" of 1873–1896, and the new wave of industrialization on the continent, which required some measure of protection for domestic manufacturers from British competition. For whatever reason—and the debate continues even today—by 1890, nearly all countries except Great Britain had once again imposed severe restrictions on imports.

Coupled with this trend toward increased protection was a new wave of formal colonialism. For reasons discussed by V. I. Lenin (Reading 6) and John Gallagher and Ronald Robinson (Reading 7), Britain had already begun to expand its holdings of foreign territory during the period of free trade. After 1880, it was joined by Germany and France. In 1860, Great Britain possessed 2.5 million square miles of colonial territory, France held only 0.2 million square miles, and Germany had not yet entered the colonial race. By 1899, Britain's holdings had expanded to 9.3 million square miles, France's to 3.7 million, and Germany's to 1.0 million. This expansion occurred primarily in Africa and the Pacific. In 1876, slightly less than 11 percent of Africa and nearly 57 percent of Polynesia were colonized. By 1900, over 90 percent of Africa and almost 99 percent of Polynesia were controlled by European colonial powers and the United States.

The First World War, which many Realists and Marxists believe to have been stimulated by the race for colonies and particularly Germany's aggressive attempt to catch up with Great Britain, destroyed the remaining elements of the *Pax Britannica*. The mantle of leadership, which had previously been borne by Britain, was now divided between the United States and the United Kingdom. Yet, neither country could—or desired to—play the leadership role previously performed by Britain.

World War I was indeed a watershed in American international involvement. The terrible devastation caused by the war in Europe served to weaken the traditional world powers, while the war brought the United States a period of unexpected prosperity. The Allies, short of food and weapons, bought furiously from American suppliers; to finance their purchases, they borrowed heavily from American banks and, eventually, once the United States entered the war, from the

American government. As a result, American factories and farms hummed as the war dragged on; industrial production nearly doubled during the war years. And because the war forced the European powers to neglect many of their overseas economic activities, American exporters and investors were also able to move into areas they had never before influenced. When the war began, the United States was a net debtor of the major European nations; by the time it ended, the United States was the world's principal lender, and all of the allies were deeply in debt to American banks and the American government.

Despite the position of political and economic leadership the United States shared with Great Britain after World War I, the country rapidly retreated into its traditional inward orientation. To be sure, many American banks and corporations continued to expand abroad very rapidly in the 1920s, and the United States remained an important world power, but the United States refused to join the League of Nations or any of the other international organizations created in the period. American tariff levels, reduced on the eve of World War I, were once again raised. The reasons for the country's post–World War I "isolationism," as it is often called, are many and controversial. Chief among them were the continued insularity of major segments of the American public, traditionally inward-looking in political and economic matters; the resistance to American power of such European nations as Great Britain and France; and widespread revulsion at the apparently futile deaths that had resulted from involvement in the internecine strife of the Old World.

Whatever the reasons for the isolationism of the 1920s, these tendencies were heightened as the world spiraled downward into Depression after 1929. In the Smoot-Hawley Act of 1930, the United States dramatically increased its tariffs, and by 1933 the world was engulfed in a bitter trade and currency conflict. In 1933, desperate to encourage domestic economic recovery, Franklin Roosevelt significantly devalued the dollar, sounding the death knell of what remained of the nineteenth-century international economic order.

During the nearly four centuries summarized here, the international economy underwent several dramatic transformations. From a closed and highly regulated mercantilist system, the international economy evolved toward free trade in the middle of the nineteenth century. After a relatively brief period of openness, the international economy reversed direction and, starting with resurgence of formal imperialism and accelerating after the First World War, once again drifted toward closure. This historical survey highlights the uniqueness of the post–World War II *Pax Americana*, which is the focus of the rest of this reader. It also raises a host of analytic questions, many of which appear elsewhere in the book as well. Particularly important here is the question of what drives change in the international economy. In the readings that follow, Charles Kindleberger focuses on ideology, Lenin and—to a lesser extent—Gallagher and Robinson find the locus of change in the stages of capitalism, and Viner and Lake emphasize changes in the international distribution of power.

4. Power Versus Plenty as Objectives of Foreign Policy in the Seventeenth and Eighteenth Centuries

JACOB VINER

Jacob Viner analyzes the mercantilist era of the seventeenth and eighteenth centuries, an important period in the development of the modern international political economy. During this era, governments tightly regulated all international economic transactions: both imports and exports of commodities were restricted, the export of gold and silver was often punishable by death, and labor mobility was curtailed. Scholars have long debated whether mercantilist governments used their control of foreign transactions purely to enhance their national power or to enrich the nation-state (or some groups within it). Viner argues here that mercantilists used state intervention to pursue plenty as well as power while believing these goals to be legitimate, necessary, and mutually reinforcing. Viner provides a cogent summary of the mercantilist thought against which Liberal political economists and the United Kingdom would later rebel.

In the seventeenth and eighteenth centuries economic thought and practice were predominantly carried on within the framework of that body of ideas which was later to be called "mercantilism." Although there has been almost no systematic investigation of the relationship in mercantilist thought between economic and political objectives or ends in the field of foreign policy, certain stereotypes have become so prevalent that few scholars have seriously questioned or examined their validity. One of these stereotypes is that mercantilism was a "system of power," that is, that "power" was for mercantilists the sole or overwhelmingly preponderant end of foreign policy, and that wealth, or "plenty," was valued solely or mainly as a necessary means to attaining or retaining or exercising power. It is the purpose of this paper to examine in the light of the available evidence the validity of this interpretation of mercantilist thought and practice. . . .

What then is the correct interpretation of mercantilist doctrine and practice with respect to the roles of power and plenty as ends of national policy? I believe that practically all mercantilists, whatever the period, country, or status of the particular individual, would have subscribed to all of the following propositions: (1) wealth is an absolutely essential means to power, whether for security or for aggression; (2) power is essential or valuable as a means to the acquisition or retention of wealth; (3) wealth and power are each proper ultimate ends of national policy; (4) there is long-run harmony between these ends, although in particular circumstances it may be necessary for a time to make economic sacrifices in the interest of military security and therefore also of long-run prosperity.

The omission of any one of these four propositions results in an incorrect interpretation of mercantilist thought, while additions of other propositions would probably involve internal dispute among mercantilists. It is to be noted that no proposition is included as to the relative weight which the mercantilists attached to power and to plenty, respectively. Given the general acceptance of the existence of harmony and mutual support between the pursuit of power and the pursuit of plenty, there appears to have been little interest in what must have appeared to them to be an unreal issue. When apparent conflict between these ends did arise, however, differences in attitudes, as between persons and countries, did arise and something will be said on this matter later.

That plenty and power were universally regarded as each valuable for its own sake there is overwhelming evidence, in the contemporary writings of all kinds, and what follows is more or less a random sampling of the available evidence. In the text accompanying and interpreting the Frontispiece of Michael Drayton's poem, *Polyolbion*, 1622, there is the following passage:

"Through a Triumphant Arch see Albion plac'd,
In Happy site, in Neptune's arms embrac'd,
In Power and Plenty, on her Cleevy Throne"

. . . John Graunt, in 1662, states that "the art of governing, and the true politiques, is how to preserve the subject in peace, and plenty."[1] An anonymous English writer, in 1677, declares that: "The four main interests of a nation are, religion, reputation, peace, and trade . . . "[2] William III, in his declaration of war against France in 1689, gives as one of the reasons that Louis XIV's "forbidding the importation of a great part of the product and manufactures of our Kingdom, and imposing exorbitant customs upon the rest, are sufficient evidence of his design to destroy the trade on which the wealth and safety of this nation so much depends."[3] In the preamble of 3 and 4 Anne, cap. 10, are the following words: "The Royal Navy, and the navigation of England, wherein, under God, the wealth, safety, and strength of this Kingdom is so much concerned, depends on the due supply of stores for the same."[4] An English pamphlet of 1716 on the relations with Russia, after describing the Czar as "a great and enterprizing spirit, and of a genius thoroughly politic" attributes to him and his people "an insatiable desire of opulency, and a boundless thirst for dominion."[5] William Wood, a noted mercantilist writer, refers to the English as "a people . . . who seek no other advantages than such only as may enlarge and secure that, whereby their strength, power, riches and reputation, equally encrease and are preserved . . . "[6] Bernard Mandeville discusses how "politicians can make a people potent, renown'd and flourishing."[7] An anonymous English writer states in 1771 that: "Nature, reason and observation all plainly point out to us our true object of national policy, which is commerce; the inexhaustible source of wealth and power to a people."[8] In an undated memoir of Maurepas to Louis XVI, on the commerce of France, occur the following passages: "Le commerce est la source de la félicité, de la force et de la richesse d'un état . . . La richesse et la puissance sont les vrais intérêts d'une nation, et il n'y a que le commerce qui puisse procurer l'une et l'autre."[9]

Such evidence as the foregoing that in the age of mercantilism wealth and power were both sought for their own sakes could easily be multiplied many fold. In English literature of the period of all kinds, from poetry to official documents, the phrases "power and plenty," "wealth and strength," "profit and power," "profit and security," "peace and plenty," or their equivalents, recur as a constant refrain. Nor is there any obvious reason, given the economic and political conditions and views of the seventeenth and eighteenth centuries, why power *and* plenty should not have been the joint objectives of the patriotic citizen of the time, even if he had freed himself from the mercantilist philosophy. Adam Smith, though not a mercantilist, was speaking for mercantilists as well as for himself when he said that "the great object of the political economy of every country, is to increase the riches and power of that country."[10]

In all the literature I have examined, I have found only one passage which is seriously embarrassing for my thesis, not because it subordinates in extreme fashion economic to political considerations, but for the reverse reason. The passage, in an anonymous and obscure pamphlet of 1754, whose authorship I have been unable to determine, is as follows:

You want not, Gentlemen, to be informed by me, that commerce is the nearest and dearest concern of your country. It is what should be the great object of public attention in all national movements, and in every negotiation we enter into with foreign powers. Our neighbours on the continent may, perhaps, wisely scheme or quarrel for an augmentation of dominions; but *Great Britain, of herself, has nothing to fight for, nothing to support, nothing to augment but her commerce.* On our foreign trade, not only our wealth but our mercantile navigation must depend; on that navigation our naval strength, the glory and security of our country.[11]

It is much easier indeed to show that power was not the sole objective of national policy in mercantilist thought than to explain how historians ever came to assert that it was. The evidence they cite in support of this proposition is not only extremely scanty but is generally ambiguous if not wholly irrelevant to their thesis. It would be extremely difficult, I am sure, for them to cite even a single passage which unmistakably rejects wealth as a national objective worth pursuing for its own sake or unconditionally subordinates it to power as an ultimate end. It is only too probable that there has been operating here that intellectual "principle of parsimony" in the identification of causes which, whatever its service-ability in the natural sciences, has in the history of social thought worked only for ill.

Cunningham and Heckscher[12] make much of a passage of Francis Bacon's made famous by modern scholars in which he speaks of King Henry VII "bowing the ancient policy of this estate from consideration of plenty to consideration of power" when in the interest of the navy he ordered that wines from Gascony should be imported only in English bottoms. As a fifteenth century measure, this falls outside the period of present interest, but Bacon, no doubt, put much of his own ideas, perhaps more than of Henry VII's, in his *History of the Reign of King Henry the Seventh*. It is relevant, therefore, that Bacon speaks of Henry VII as conducting war for profit, and attributes to him even over-developed economic objectives. In 1493, Henry VII had declared an embargo on all trade with the Flemish provinces because the pretender, Perkin Warbeck, was being harboured there. The embargo after a time "began to pinch the merchants of both nations very sore, which moved them by all means they could devise to affect and dispose their sovereigns respectively to open the intercourse again." Henry VII, no longer apprehensive about Warbeck, was receptive. "But that that moved him most was, that being a King that loved wealth and treasure, he could not endure to have trade sick, nor any obstruction to continue in the gate-vein, which disperseth that blood," and by the *intercursus magnus* of 1495–96 with the Archduke of Austria he negotiated the end of the trade war.[13]

Not so frequently stated as that power and plenty are properly joint objectives of national policy but undoubtedly a pervasive element in the thought of the period is the proposition that they are also harmonious ends, each reinforcing and promoting the other. The idea is expressed in the maxim attributed to Hobbes: "Wealth is power and power is wealth."[14] There follow some passages in which the idea is spelled out somewhat more fully: "Foreign trade produces riches, riches power, power preserves our trade and religion."[15] "It is evident that this kingdom is wonderfully fitted by the bounty of God almighty, for a great progression in wealth and power; and that the only means to arrive at both, or either of them, is to improve and advance trade . . . "[16] "For as the honesty of all governments is, so shall be their riches; and as their honour, honesty, and riches are, so will be their strength; and as their honour, honesty, riches, and strength are, so will be their trade. These are five sisters that go hand in hand, and must not be parted."[17] "Your fleet, and your trade, have so near a relation, and such mutual influence upon each other, they cannot well be separated; your trade is the mother and nurse of your seamen; your seamen are the life of your fleet, and your fleet is the security and protection of your trade, and both together are the wealth, strength, security and glory of Britain."[18]

"By trade and commerce we grow a rich and powerful nation, and by their decay we are growing poor and impotent. As trade and commerce enrich, so they fortify, our country."

"The wealth of the nation he [the 'Patriot King'] will most justly esteem to be his wealth, the power his power, the security and the honor, his security and honor; and by the very means by which he promotes the two first, he will wisely preserve the two last."[19] . . .

George L. Beer has commented, with particular reference to the statement from Lord Haversham quoted above, that "The men of the day argued in a circle of sea power, commerce and colonies. Sea power enabled England to expand and to protect her foreign trade, while this increased commerce, in turn, augmented her naval strength."[20] Circular reasoning this may have been, but it was not, logically at least, a "vicious circle," since under the circumstances of the time it was perfectly reasonable to maintain that wealth and power mutually supported each other, that they were, or could be made, each a means to the augmentation of the other.

In contending that for the mercantilists power and plenty were regarded as coexisting ends of national policy which were fundamentally harmonious, I do not mean that they were unaware that in specific instances economic sacrifices might have to be made in order to assume national security or victory in an aggressive war. But as a rule, if not invariably, when making this point they showed their belief that such economic sacrifices in the short run would bring economic as well as political gains in the long run. The selfishness from a patriotic point of view of taxpayers resisting wartime impositions for armament or for war was always a problem for statesmen in the age of mercantilism, and sometimes the parsimony of monarchs was also a problem. It was also necessary at times for statesmen to resist the pressure from merchants to pursue petty commercial ends which promised immediate economic gain but at the possible cost of long-run military security and therefore also of long-run national prosperity. The mercantilist, no doubt, would not have denied that if necessity should arise for choosing, all other things would have to give way to considerations of the national safety; but his practice might not rise to the level of his principles, and his doctrine would not lead him to recognize that such choice was likely to face him frequently. It is not without significance that it was an anti-mercantilist economist, Adam Smith, and not the mercantilists, who laid down the maxim that "defence is more important than opulence." A typical mercantilist might well have replied that ordinarily defense is necessary to opulence and opulence to effective defense, even if momentarily the two ends might appear to be in conflict.

Queen Elizabeth was notoriously parsimonious and one of her diplomatic agents, Buckhurst, in reasoning with her in 1587 when the safety of England against the menace from Spain appeared to call for rearmament, anticipated Adam Smith's maxim:

> And alwaies when kinges and kingdoms do stand in dout of daunger, their safetie is a thing so far above all price of treasure, as there shold be no sparing to bring them even into certainty of assurans.

He accordingly advised Elizabeth to

> unlock all your cofers and convert your treasure for the advauncing of worthy men and for the arming of ships and men of war, that may defend you, sith princes' treasures serve only to that end and lie they never so fast nor so full in their chests, can no waies so defend them.[21]

Statesmen frequently found it necessary to warn against endangering political ends by unwise pursuit of temporary or petty commercial gains in response to pressure from business interests. This was especially true in connection with the relations between England and France during the Seven Years' War, which to many contemporaries seemed to be conducted with too much attention to economic considerations of minor importance. Just before the outbreak of the conflict, when it was still being debated whether the issue between the two countries should be settled by economic or military means, Lord Granville was reported as "absolutely against meddling with trade—he called it, vexing your neighbours for a little muck."[22] And in the face of the struggle itself,

Mirepoix, the French Ambassador to England, is said to have commented "that it was a great pity to cut off so many heads for the sake of a few hats."[23] . . .

To some extent this point of view may have been a reflection of a certain disdain for trade in general which was beginning to affect the aristocratic class who conducted the foreign relations of the time. It would be a mistake, however, to explain it in terms of basic disregard for economic considerations, rather than as belief that the pursuit of temporary and minor economic benefits should not be permitted to dominate foreign policy. Such is the position of John Mitchell, who makes clear elsewhere that "power and prosperity" are the proper ends of policy:

> It is well known, that our colonies in America are rather more under the tuition and influence of the merchants in Britain, than the government perhaps, and that all public measures relating to them are very much influenced by the opinions of our merchants about them. But the only things that they seem to attend to are the profits of trade . . . This, it is true, is necessary to be considered likewise, but it is not the only thing to be attended to. The great thing to be considered by all states is power and dominion, as well as trade. Without that to support and protect our trade, it must soon be at an end.[24]

While mercantilist doctrine, moreover, put great stress on the importance of national economic interests, it put equally great stress on the possibility of lack of harmony between the special economic interests of the individual merchants or particular business groups or economic classes, on the one hand, and the economic interest of the commonwealth as a whole, on the other. Refusal to give weight to *particular* economic interests, therefore, must never be identified with disregard for the national economic interest as they conceived it, in interpreting the thought of the mercantilists. In human affairs, moreover, there is always room for divergence between dogma and practice, between principles and the actual behavior of those who profess them. It is doctrine, and not practice, which is the main concern here. The task of ascertaining how much or how little they corresponded in the age of mercantilism, and what were the forces which caused them to deviate, is the difficult duty of the historian, in whose hands I gladly leave it.

It was the common belief in France, however, that commercial objectives and particular commercial interests played a much greater role in the formulation and administration of British than of French foreign policy, and some Englishmen would have agreed. There was universal agreement, also, that in "Holland" (*i.e.*, the "United Provinces"), where the merchants to a large extent shared directly in government, major political considerations, including the very safety of the country or its success in wars in which it was actually participating, had repeatedly to give way to the cupidity of the merchants and their reluctance to contribute adequately to military finance. Whether in the main the influence of the commercial classes, where they had strength, worked more for peace or for war seems to be an open question, but there appears little ground for doubt that with the merchants, whether they pressed for war or for peace, the major consideration was economic gain, either their private gain, or that of their country, or both.

The material available which touches on these strands of thought is boundless, and there can here be cited only a few passages which give the flavor of contemporary discussion. We will begin with material relating to the influence of the merchant and of commercial consider-ations on British policy.

Sir Francis Bacon, in reporting a discussion in Parliament in the fifth year of James I's reign, of the petition of the merchants with regard to their grievances against Spain, makes one of the speakers say that: "although he granted that the wealth and welfare of the merchant was not without a sympathy with the general stock and state ["estate?"] of a nation, especially an island; yet, nevertheless, it was a thing too familiar with the merchant, to make the case of his particular profit, the public case of the kingdom." The troubles of the merchants were partly their own fault: they so mismanaged their affairs abroad that "except lieger ambassadors, which are the eyes of kings in foreign parts, should leave their sentinel and become merchants' factors, and solicitors, their causes can hardly prosper." Wars were not to be fought on such minor issues. Another speaker was more sympathetic to the merchants, who were "the convoy of our supplies, the vents of our abundance, Neptune's almsmen, and fortune's adventurers." Nevertheless, the question of war should be dealt with by the King and not by Parliament, presumably because the merchants wielded too much influence there. Members of Parliament were local representatives with local interests; if they took a broader view it was accidental.[25]

Allies or potential allies of England sometimes were troubled by England's supposed obsession with commercial objectives as making her an unreliable ally where other interests were involved. In September, 1704, a minister of the Duke of Savoy issued a memorial which the English representative at that Court reported as holding that England and Holland, "the maritime powers, (an injurious term, I think, which goes into fashion,) were so attentive to their interests of trade and commerce, that, perhaps, they would . . . abandon the common interests of Europe " in the defeat of France in the war then under way.[26] When Pitt declared to Catherine the Great of Russia that no Russian conquest could give offense to England, she was skeptical, and replied: "The acquisition of a foot of territory on the Black Sea will at once excite the jealousy of the English, whose whole attention is given to petty interests and who are first and always traders"[27] . . .

The history of British policy and practice with respect to enemy and trade with the enemy during war provides abundant and occasionally startling evidence that considerations of plenty did not always automatically give way to considerations of power. There is much in British history, as in the history of Holland, of France, and of Spain, to support the statement of Carl Brinkmann that: "The history of war trade and trade war is a rich mine of interest to the economic and social historian just for the peculiar ways in which the autonomy of business connexions and traditions is seen cutting across even the sternest decrees and tendencies of political *ultima ratio.*"[28]

That in Holland commercial interests predominated was taken for granted in both France and England when foreign policy was formulated. Thurloe commented, in 1656, that all proposals "of alliances of common and mutual defense, wherein provision was to be made for the good of the Protestant religion" failed "in respect the United Provinces always found it necessary for them to mingle therewith the consideration of trade . . . The Hollanders had rather His Highness [Oliver Cromwell] be alone in it than that they should lose a tun of sack or a frail of raisins."[29] A French naval officer, writing to Colbert with reference to the failure of the Dutch to provide the fleet which they had promised for the Levant, said that he was not at all surprised: "les Hollandais n'agissent en cette occasion que par leur propre intérêt; et comme ils ont peu ou point de bâtiments en Levant, et qu'en leur pays ils ne regardent qu'au compte des marchands, ils n'ont garde d'envoyer et de faire la dépense d'une escadre de ce côté-là."[30]

In the summary given in Cobbett's *Parliamentary History* of the principal arguments made in Parliament in favor of moderating the peace settlement to be made with France to end the Seven Years' War, a contrast was made as to the policy proper for England and that for a country like Holland. The economic value of the British conquests of French colonies in America was great. Nevertheless it was to be remembered:

> . . . that the value of our conquests thereby ought not to be estimated by the present produce, but by their probable increase. Neither ought the value of any country to be solely tried on its commercial advantages; that extent of territory and a number of subjects, are matters of as much consideration to a state attentive to the sources of real grandeur, as the mere advantages of traffic; that such ideas are rather suitable to a limited and petty commonwealth, like Holland, than to a great, powerful, and warlike nation. That on these principles, having

made very large demands in North America, it was necessary to relax in other parts.[31]

There was general agreement that in France economic considerations played a lesser role in foreign policy than in England and Holland. In part, this was to be explained by the lesser importance even economically of foreign trade to France and by the lesser role of French merchants in French politics. George Lyttelton, an English observer at the Soissons Congress of 1729, where the question of the maintenance of the alliance with England was at issue, reported to his father:

> Affairs are now almost at a crisis, and there is great reason to expect they will take a happy turn. Mr. Walpole has a surprizing influence over the cardinal [Cardinal Fleury, in charge of French foreign policy]; so that, whether peace or war ensue, we may depend upon our ally. In truth, it is the interest of the French court to be faithful to their engagements, though it may not entirely be the nation's. Emulation of trade might incline the people to wish the bond that ties them to us were broke; but the mercantile interest has at no time been much considered by this court. . . . The supposition, that present advantage is the basis and end of state engagements, and that they are only to be measured by that rule, is the foundation of all our suspicions against the firmness of our French ally. But the maxim is not just. Much is given to future hopes, much obtained by future fears; and security is, upon many occasions, sought preferably to gain.[32]

Frenchmen in the period occasionally professed readiness to yield to Britain predominance in maritime trade if Britain would give France a free hand on the Continent, but it would be a mistake to conclude that this reflected a readiness to concentrate on political objectives alone. Even on the Continent there were economic prizes to be won, though less glittering ones than those naval power could win overseas.

Historians, moreover, may have been too ready to find sharp differences in kind between the role of economic considerations in the making of foreign policy in England and France, respectively, in the age of mercantilism. The differences, though probably substantial, seem in the matters here relevant to have been differences in degree rather than in kind. In particular, the extent of the influence which commercial interests in France could in one way or another exercise on policy has been seriously underestimated by many historians, and both in theory and in practice absolutist government was not as absolute in power nor as non-commercial in motivation as the school textbooks have taught us. French records have been misleading in this regard because the older generation of historians were not interested in economic issues and tended to leave out of their compilations of documents matter of a markedly economic character, and French historians seem for some time to have been moving toward a reconsideration of the role of economic factors in the formulation of foreign policy under the Ancien Régime.

There may have been monarchs who recognized no moral obligation to serve their people's interests, and there were no doubt ministers of state who had no loyalties except to their careers and perhaps to their royal masters. . . . Some monarchs were, to modern taste, childish in the weight they gave to the routine symbols of prestige and protocol. The personal idiosyncrasies of rulers and, above all, dynastic ambitions, exerted their influence on the course of events. Occasionally religious differences made the course of diplomacy run a little less smoothly by injecting an ideological factor into the range of matters out of which disputes could arise or by which they could be sharpened. But it seems clear that predominantly diplomacy was centered on and governed by considerations of power and plenty throughout the period and for all of Europe, and that religious considerations were more often invoked for propaganda purposes than genuinely operative in fashioning foreign policy. Even the cardinals, who in some degree monopolized the diplomatic profession on the Continent, granted that religious considerations must not be permitted to get in the way of vital national interests, and even genuine missionary enterprises could get seriously entangled with the pursuit of commercial privileges. When Louis XIII in 1626 sent an emissary to Persia with the primary purpose of promoting the Catholic religion, he instructed him at the same time to seek special privileges for the French trade as compensation for the diplomatic difficulties with the English and the Dutch which would result from a French attempt to catholicize Persia. . . .

The role of the religious factor in Cromwell's foreign policy has been much debated. The literature of historical debate on this question is voluminous, but it is not apparent to the layman that any progress toward a definitive decision has been made, unless it is that Cromwell was a complex personality on whom economic, religious, and power considerations all had their influence, but in varying degrees and combinations at different times. George L. Beer quotes Firth as saying about Cromwell that: "Looked at from one point of view, he seemed as practical as a commercial traveller; from another, a Puritan Don Quixote," and gives as his own verdict that "It was 'the commercial traveller' who acted, and the 'Puritan Don Quixote' who dreamt and spoke."[33] Other historians have given other interpretations.[34]

I have unfortunately not been able to find an orthodox neo-Marxian study dealing with these issues for this period. If there were one such, and if it followed the standard pattern, it would argue that "in the last analysis" the end of foreign policy had been not power, and not power and plenty, but plenty alone, and plenty for the privileged classes only, and it would charge that members of these classes would always be there in every major diplomatic episode, pulling the strings of foreign policymaking for their own special benefit. Writing a few years ago in criticism of this theory as applied to more recent times, I ventured the following comment: "While I suspect that Marx himself would not have hesitated to resort to the 'scandal' theory of imperialism and war when convenient for propaganda purposes, I am sure that he would basically have despised it for its vulgar or unscientific character."[35] I was "righter" than I deserved to be.

Karl Marx studied the British diplomacy of this period, even making use of the unpublished records in the British Foreign Office, and discussed the role played by commercial objectives in British foreign policy. The ruling oligarchy needed political allies at home, and found them in some section or other of the *haute bourgeoisie*.

> As to their *foreign policy*, they wanted to give it the appearance at least of being altogether regulated by the mercantile interest, an appearance the more easily to be produced, as the exclusive interest of one or the other small fraction of that class would, of course, be always identified with this or that Ministerial measure. The interested fraction then raised the commerce and navigation cry, which the nation stupidly re-echoed.

Eighteenth century practice thus "developed on the Cabinet, at least, the *onus* of inventing *mercantile pretexts*, however futile, for their measures of foreign policy." Writing in the 1850's, Marx found that procedure had changed. Palmerston did not bother to find commercial pretexts for his foreign policy measures.

> In our own epoch, British ministers have thrown this burden on foreign nations, leaving to the French, the Germans, etc., the irksome task of discovering the *secret* and *hidden* mercantile springs of their actions. Lord Palmerston, for instance, takes a step apparently the most damaging to the material interests of Great Britain. Up starts a State philosopher, on the other side of the Atlantic, or of the Channel, or in the heart of Germany, who puts his head to the rack to dig out the mysteries of the mercantile Machiavelism of "perfide Albion," of which Palmerston is supposed the unscrupulous and unflinching executor.[36]

Marx, in rejecting the economic explanation of British friendship for Russia, fell back upon an explanation of both a sentimental pro-Russianism in high circles in Britain and an unjustified fear of Russian power. It is a paradox that the father of Marxism should have sponsored a doctrine which now sounds so non-Marxian. I cannot believe, however, that the appeals to economic considerations which played so prominent a part in eighteenth-century British discussions of Anglo-Russian relations were all pretext, and I can find little evidence which makes it credible that friendly sentiment towards foreigners played a significant role in the foreign policy of England in the eighteenth century. Leaving sentiment aside, England's foreign policy towards Russia in the eighteenth century, like English and European foreign policy in general, was governed by joint and harmonized considerations of power and economics. That the economics at least was generally misguided, and that it served to poison international relations, is another matter which, though not relevant *here*, is highly relevant now.

NOTES

1. *Natural and Political Observations made upon the Bills of Mortality* [London, 1662], Johns Hopkins University Reprint, Baltimore, 1939, p. 78.
2. *The Present State of Christendom, and the Interest of England, with a Regard to France* [1677], in *The Harleian Miscellany*, London, 1808, I, 249.
3. As cited in *Mercator, or Commerce Retrieved*, No. 1, London, May 26, 1713.
4. Cited in G. S. Graham, *Sea Power and British North America 1783–1820*, Cambridge Mass., 1941, p. 143.
5. *The Northern Crisis; or Impartial Reflections on the Policies of the Czar* [London, 1716], as reprinted in Karl Marx, *Secret Diplomatic History of the Eighteenth Century*, London, 1899, p. 32.
6. *Survey of Trade*, 2nd ed., London, 1719, Dedication, pp. iv–v.
7. *The Fable of the Bees* [6th ed., 1732], F. B. Kaye ed., Oxford, 1924, I, 185.
8. *Considerations on the Policy, Commerce and Circumstances of the Kingdom*, London 1771, as quoted in the preface to G. S. Graham, *British Policy and Canada, 1774–1791*, London, 1930.
9. *Mémoires du Comte de Maurepas*, Paris, 1792, III, 195.
10. *Wealth of Nations*, Cannan ed., I, 351.
11. *Mercator's Letters on Portugal and Its Commerce*, London, 1754, p. 5. The italics are not in the original text.
12. Heckscher refers to this as "a very characteristic passage" (*Mercantilism*, II, 16), but I find it difficult to cite a duplicate, whether from Bacon's writings or in the period generally. See also Heckscher, "Revisions in Economic History, V, Mercantilism," *Economic History Review*, VII (1936), 48: "I think Cunningham was right in stressing the famous saying of Bacon about Henry VII: 'bowing the ancient policy of this Estate from consideration of plenty to consideration of power.'"
13. See *The Works of Francis Bacon*, James Spedding, ed., London, 1858, VI, 95–96; 172–73. Cf. also *Considerations touching a War with Spain* [1624], in *The Works of Francis Bacon*, Philadelphia, 1852 II, 214, where he says that: "whereas wars are generally causes of poverty or consumption . . . this war with Spain, if it be made by sea, is like to be a lucrative and restorative war. So that, if we go roundly on at the first, the war in continuance will find itself." On the other hand, in his *Essays or Counsels* [2nd ed., 1625], *Works*, London 1858, VI, 450–51, he makes what appears to be a clear-cut statement that the prestige of power ("grandeur") is more important than plenty.
14. J. E. Barker, *Rise and Decline of the Netherlands*, London, 1906, p. 194.
15. Josiah Child, *A Treatise concerning the East India Trade*, London, 1681, p. 29
16. *Ibid.*, *A New Discourse of Trade*, 4th ed. (ca. 1690), Preface, p. xliii.
17. Andrew Yarranton, *England's Improvement by Sea and Land*, London, 1677, p. 6
18. Lord Haversham in the House of Lords, November 6, 1707, *Parliamentary History of England*, VI, 598. . . .
19. Lord Bolingbroke, "The Idea of a Patriot King," in *Letters on the Spirit of Patriotism*, London, 1752, pp. 204, 211.
20. *The Old Colonial System, 1600–1754*, New York, 1912, I, 16.

21. "Correspondentie van Robert Dudley Graaf van Leycester," Part II, *Weken uitgiven door het Historisch Genootschap*, Utrecht, 3rd Series, No. 57 (1931), pp. 239, 240.

22. *The Diary of the Late George Bubb Dodington*, new ed., London, 1784, pp. 344–45.

23. [William Knox], *Helps to a Right Decision*, London, 1787, p. 35. . . .

24. *The Contest in America between Great Britain and France*, London, 1757, Introduction, p. xvii. Cf. also *A Letter to a certain Foreign Minister, in which the grounds of the present war are truly stated*, London, 1745, p. 6: "That we receive great benefits from trade, that trade is a national concern, and that we ought to resent any attempt made to lessen or to injure it, are truths well known and out of dispute, yet sure the British people are not to be treated like a company of merchants, or rather pedlars, who if they are permitted to sell their goods, are to think themselves well off, whatever treatment they may receive in any other respect. No, surely, the British nation has other great concerns besides their trade, and as she will never sacrifice it, so she will never endure any insult in respect to them, without resenting it as becomes a people jealous of their honour, and punctual in the performance of their engagements."

The occasion for this outburst was a Prussian "rescript" insisting that Britain should not intervene in quarrels between German states, since they had nothing to do with British commerce.

25. *The Works of Sir Francis Bacon*, Philadelphia, 1852, II, 193–99.

26. *The Diplomatic Correspondence of the Right Hon. Richard Hill*, London, 1845, I, 479; see also II, 751.

27. Cited by Edward Crankshaw, *Russia and Britain*, New York, no date (ca. 1943), pp. 45–46.

28. *English Historical Review*, CLIII (1924), 287. . . .

29. Cited by F. M. Powicke, "The Economic Motive in Politics," *Economic History Review* XVI (1946), 91.

30. A. Jal, *Abraham Du Quesne et la Marine de son Temps*, Paris, 1883, I, 470.

31. *Parliamentary History of England*, XV (1813), 1271–1272 (for December 9, 1762). . . .

32. *The Works of George Lord Lyttelton*, G. E. Ayscough, ed., 3rd ed., London, 1776, III, 243–44.

33. Cromwell's Policy in its Economic Aspects," *Political Science Quarterly*, XVII (1902), 46–47.

34. Cf. John Morley, *Oliver Cromwell*, New York, 1901, p. 434. . . .

35. "International Relations between State-Controlled National Economics," *American Economic Review Supplement*, XXXIV (1944), 324.

36. Karl Marx, *Secret Diplomatic History of the Eighteenth Century*, Eleanor Marx Aveling, ed., London, 1899, pp. 55–56. The italics are in the original.

5. The Rise of Free Trade in Western Europe

CHARLES P. KINDLEBERGER

Liberal economist Charles P. Kindleberger examines the process by which mercantilist trade restrictions were dismantled and evaluates several of the best known theses concerning the ascendance of free trade in Western Europe. According to Kindleberger, free trade initially arose in Great Britain between 1820 and 1850 as individual entrepreneurs pressured their government to lift restrictions on international trade and finance so that they could pursue overseas business opportunities. Yet, Kindleberger points out that political activity by entrepreneurs cannot explain the rapid expansion of free trade in Europe after 1850. He suggests that this "second wave" of free trade may have been motivated by ideology rather than economic or political interests. This important article offers a persuasive explanation of how and why the market principle gained dominance within the international economy during the nineteenth century.

I

. . . The beginnings of free trade internationally go back to the eighteenth century. French Physiocratic theory enunciated the slogan *laisser faire, laisser passer* to reduce export prohibitions on agricultural products. Pride of place in practice, however, goes to Tuscany, which permitted free export of the corn of Sienese Maremma in 1737, after the Grand Duke Francis had read Sallustio Bandini's *Economical Discourse*. Beset by famine in 1764, Tuscany gradually opened its market to imported grain well before the Vergennes Treaty of 1786 between France and Britain put French Physiocratic doctrine into practice. Grain exports in Tuscany had been restricted under the "policy of supply," or "provisioning," or "abundance," under which the city-states of Italy limited exports from the surrounding countryside in order to assure food to the urban populace. Bandini and Pompeo Neri pointed out the ill effects this had on investment and productivity in agriculture.

The policy of supply was not limited to food. In the eighteenth and early nineteenth century exports were restricted in, among others, wool and coal (Britain), ashes, rags, sand for glass and firewood (Germany), ship timbers (Austria), rose madder (the Netherlands), and silk cocoons (Italy). The restrictions on exports of ashes and timber from Germany had conservation overtones. The industrial revolution in Britain led further to prohibitions on export of machinery and on emigration of artisans, partly to increase the supply for local use, but also to prevent the diffusion of technology on the Continent. We return to this below.

What was left in the policy of supply after the Napoleonic War quickly ran down. Prohibition of export of raw silk was withdrawn in Piedmont, Lombardy and Venetia in the 1830's, freedom to export coal from Britain enacted in the 1840's. Details of the relaxation of restrictions are recorded for Baden as part of the movement to occupational freedom. The guild system gradually collapsed under the weight of increasing complexity of regulations by firms seeking exceptions for themselves and objecting to exceptions for others. A number of prohibitions and export taxes lasted to the 1850's—as industrial consumers held out against producers, or in some cases, like rags, the collectors of waste products. Reduction of the export tax on rags in Piedmont in 1851 produced a long drawn-out struggle between Cavour and the industry which had to close up thirteen plants when the tax was reduced. To Cavour salvation of the industry lay in machinery and the substitution of other materials, not in restricting export through Leghorn and Messina to Britain and North America.

Elimination of export taxes and prohibitions in nineteenth-century Europe raises doubt about the universal validity of the theory of the tariff as a collective good, imposed by a concentrated interest at the expense of the diffuse. The interest of groups producing inputs for other industries are normally more deeply affected than those of the consuming industries, but it is hardly possible that the consuming is always less concentrated than the producing industry.

II

The question of export duties sought by domestic manufacturers on their raw materials, and of import duties on outputs demanded by producers for the domestic market was settled in the Netherlands in the eighteenth century in favor of mercantile interests. These were divided into the First Hand, merchants, shipowners and bankers; the Second Hand, which carried on the work of sorting and packing in staple markets, and wholesaling on the Continent; and the Third Hand, concerned with distribution in the hinterland. Dutch staple trade was based partly on mercantile skills and partly on the pivotal location of Amsterdam, Rotterdam, and other staple towns dedicated to trade in particular commodities, largely perishable, non-standardized and best suited to short voyages. The First Hand dominated Dutch social and political life and opposed all tariffs on export or import goods, above a minimum for revenue, in order to maximize trade and minimize formalities. From 1815 to 1830 when Holland and Belgium were united as the Low Countries, the clash between the Dutch First Hand and Belgian producers in search of import protection from British manufactures was continuous and heated.

The First Hand objected to taxes for revenue on coffee, tea, tobacco, rice, sugar, and so on, and urged their replacement by excises on flour, meat, horses and servants. Tariffs for revenue must be held down to prevent smuggling and to sustain turnover. The safe maximum was given variously as three percent, five percent, and on transit even as one-half percent. Transit in bond, and transit with duty-cum-drawback were thought too cumbersome. The Dutch made a mistake in failing to emulate London which in 1803 adopted a convenient entrepôt dock with bonding. Loss of colonies and of overseas connections in the Napoleonic Wars made it impossible from early in the period to compete with Britain in trade. Equally threatening was Hamburg which supplied British and colonial goods to Central Europe in transit for one-half percent revenue duty maximum, many products free, and all so after 1839. More serious, however, was the rise of direct selling as transport efficiency increased. Early signs of direct selling can be detected at the end of the seventeenth century when Venice and Genoa lost their role as intermediary in traffic between Italy and the West. By the first half of the nineteenth century, they were abundant. "By the improved intercourse of our time (1840), the seller is brought more immediately into contact with the producer." Twenty years earlier, the Belgian members of a Dutch Belgian fiscal commission argued that "there was no hope of restoring Holland's general trade. Owing to the spread of civilization, all European countries could now provide for themselves in direct trading."[1]

It is a mistake to think of merchants as all alike. As indicated, First, Second and Third Hands of the Netherlands had different functions, status and power. In Germany, republican merchants of Hamburg differed sharply from those of the Imperial city, Frankfurt, and held out fifty years longer against the Zollverein. Within Frankfurt there were two groups, the English-goods party associated with the bankers, and the majority, which triumphed in 1836, interested in transit, forwarding, retail and domestic trade within the Zollverein. In Britain a brilliant picture had been drawn of a pragmatic free trader, John Gladstone, father of William, opposed to timber preferences for Canada, enemy of the East India Company monopoly on trade with China and India, but supportive of imperial preference in cotton and sugar, and approving of the Corn Laws on the ground of support for the aristocracy he hoped his children could enter via politics. The doctrinaire free traders of Britain were the cotton manufacturers like Gladstone's friend, Kirman Finlay, who regarded shipowners and corn growers as the two great monopolists.

The doctrinaire free trade of the Dutch merchants led to economic sclerosis, or economic sickness. Hamburg stayed in trade and finance and did not move into industry. In Britain, merchants were ignorant of industry, but were saved by the coming of the railroad and limited liability which provided an outlet for their surplus as direct trading squeezed profits from stapling. The economic point is simple: free trade may stimulate, but again it may lead to fossilization.

III

The movement toward freer trade in Britain began gross in the eighteenth century, net only after the Napoleonic Wars. In the initial stages, there was little problem for a man like Wedgewood advocating free trade for exports of manufactures under the Treaty of Vergennes with France, but prohibitions on the export of machinery and emigrations of artisans. Even in the 1820's and 1830's, a number of the political economists—Torrens, Baring, Peel, Nassau Senior—favored repeal of the Corn Laws but opposed export of machinery. The nineteenth century is seen by Brebner not as a steady march to *laisser-faire* but as a counterpoint between Smithian *laisser-faire* in trade matters and, after the Reform Bill, Benthamic intervention of 1832 which produced the Factory, Mines, Ten Hours and similar acts from 1833 to 1847.

First came the revenue aspect, which was critical to the movement to freer trade under Huskisson in the 1820's, Peel in the 1840's, and Gladstone in the 1850's. Huskisson and Gladstone used the argument that the bulk of revenue was produced by taxes on a few items—largely colonial products such as tea, coffee, sugar, tobacco, and wine and spirits—and that others produced too little revenue to be worth the trouble. Many were redundant (for example, import duties on products which Britain exported). Others were so high as to be prohibitory or encouraged smuggling and reduced revenue. When Peel was converted to free trade, it was necessary to reintroduce the income tax before he could proceed with repeal of 605 duties between 1841 and 1846, and reductions in 1035 others. The title of Sir Henry Parnell's treatise on freer trade (1830) was *Financial Reform*.

But Huskisson was a free trader, if a cautious one. He spoke of benefits to be derived from the removal of "vexatious restraints and meddling interference in the concerns of internal industry and foreign commerce."[2] Especially he thought that imports stimulated efficiency in import-competing industry. In 1824 the prohibition on silk imports had been converted to a duty of thirty percent regarded as the upper limit of discouragement to smuggling. In a speech on March 24, 1826, said by Canning to be the finest he had heard in the House of Commons, Huskisson observed that Macclesfield and Spitalfield had reorganized the industry under the spur of enlarged imports, and expanded the scale of output. Both Michel Chevalier and Count Cavour referred to this positive and dynamic response to increased imports in England.

Restrictions on export of machinery and emigration of artisans went back, as indicated, to the industrial revolution. Prohibition of export of stocking frames was enacted as early as 1696. Beginning in 1774 there was a succession of restrictions on tools and utensils for the cotton and linen trades and on the emigration of skilled artisans. The basis was partly the policy of supply, partly naked maintenance of monopoly. Freedom had been granted to the emigration of workmen in 1824. After the depression of the late 1830's, pressure for removal of the prohibition came from all machinery manufacturers. Following further investigation by a Select Committee of Parliament, the export prohibition was withdrawn.

The main arguments against prohibition of the export of machinery and emigration of artisans were three: they were ineffective, unnecessary, and harmful. Ineffectuality was attested to by much detail in the Select Committee reports on the efficiency of smuggling. Machinery for which licenses could not be obtained could be dispatched illegally in one of a number of ways—by another port, hidden in cotton bales, in baggage or mixed with permitted machinery and in a matter of hours. Guaranteed and insured shipments could be arranged in London or Paris for premia up to thirty percent.

That prohibition was unnecessary was justified first by the inability of foreigners, even with English machinery and English workmen, to rival English manufacturers. Britain has minerals, railways, canals, rivers, better division of labor, "trained workmen habituated to all industrious employments."[3] "Even when the Belgians employed English machines and skilled workers, they failed to import the English spirit of enterprise, and secured only disappointing results."[4] In 1825, the Select Committee concluded it was safe to export machinery, since seven-year-old machinery in Manchester was already obsolete.

In the third place it was dangerous. Restriction on emigration of artisans failed to prevent their departure, but did inhibit their return. Restriction of machinery, moreover, raised the price abroad through the cost of smuggling, and stimulated production on the Continent. Improvement in the terms of trade through restriction of exports (but failure to cut them off altogether) was deleterious for its protective effect abroad.

Greater coherence of the Manchester cotton spinners over the machinery makers spread over Manchester, Birmingham and London may account for the delay from 1825 to 1841 in freeing up machinery, and support Pincus' theory on the need of concentrated interests. But the argument of consistency was telling. In 1800 the Manchester manufacturers of cloth had demanded a law forbidding export of yarn, but did not obtain it. The 1841 Second Report concluded that machinery making should be put on the same footing as other departments of British industry. It is noted that Nottingham manufacturers approved free trade but claim an exception in regard to machinery used in their own manufacture. Babbage observed that machinery makers are more intelligent than their users, to whose imagined benefits their interests are sacrificed, and referred to the "impolicy of interfering between two classes."[5] In the end, the Manchester Chamber of Commerce became troubled by the inconsistency and divided; the issue of prohibition of machinery was subsumed into the general attack on the Corn Laws. In the 1840's moreover, the sentiment spread that Britain should become the Workshop of the World, which implied the production of heavy goods as well as cotton cloth and yarn.

Rivers of ink have been spilled on the repeal of the Corn Laws, and the present paper can do little but summarize the issues and indicate a position. The questions relate to the Stolper-Samuelson distribution argument, combined with the Reform Bill of 1832 and the shift of political power from the landed aristocracy to the bourgeois; incidence of the Corn Laws and of their repeal, within both farming and manufacturing sectors; the potential for a dynamic response of farming to lower prices from competition; and the relation of repeal to economic development on the Continent, and especially whether industrialization could be halted by expanded and assured outlets for agricultural produce, a point of view characterized by Gallagher and Robinson as "free-trade imperialism." A number of lesser issues may be touched upon incidentally: interaction between the Corn Laws and the Zollverein, and its tariff changes in the 1840's; the question of whether repeal of the Corn Laws, and of the Navigation Acts would have been very long delayed had it not been for potato famine in Ireland and on the Continent; and the question of whether the term "free-trade imperialism" is better reserved for Joseph Chamberlain's Empire preference of fifty years later.

In the normal view, the Reform Bill of 1832 shifted power from the land and country to the factory and city, from the aristocratic class to the bourgeois, and inexorably led to changes in trade policies which had favored farming and hurt manufacturing. One can argue that repeal of the Corn Laws represented something less than that and that the Reform Bill was not critical. The movement to free trade had begun earlier in the Huskisson reforms; speeches in Parliament were broadly the same in 1825 when it was dominated by landed aristocrats as in the 1830's and 1840's. Numbers had changed with continued manufacturing expansion, but nothing much more. Or one can reject the class explanation, as Polanyi does, and see something much more ideological. "Not until the 1830's did economic liberalism burst forth as a crusading passion." The liberal creed involved faith in man's secular salvation through a self-regulating market, held with fanaticism and evangelical fervor. French Physiocrats were trying to correct only one inequity, to break out of the policy of supply and permit export of grain. British political economists of the 1830's and 1840's, who won over Tories like Sir Robert Peel and Lord Russell, and ended up in 1846 with many landlords agreeable to repeal of the Corn Laws, represented an ideology. "Mere class interests cannot offer a satisfactory explanation for any long-run social process."[6]

Under a two-sector model, free trade comes when the abundant factor acquires political power and moves to eliminate restrictions imposed in the interest of the scarce factor which has lost power. In reality factors of production are not monolithic. Some confusion in the debate attached to the incidence of the tax on imported corn within both farming and manufacturing. The Anti-Corn Law League of Cobden and Bright regarded it as a tax on food, taking as much as twenty percent of the earnings of a hand-loom weaver. Cobden denied the "fallacy" that wages rose and fell with price of bread. Benefits, moreover, went to the landlord and not to the farmer or farm-laborer, as rents on the short leases in practice rose with the price of corn. There are passages in Cobden which suggest that hurt of the Corn Laws fell upon the manufacturing and commercial classes rather than labor but the speeches run mainly in terms of a higher standard of living for the laborer who would spend his "surplus of earnings on meat, vegetables, butter, milk and cheese," rather than on wheaten loaves. The Chartists were interested not in repeal, but in other amenities for the workers. Peel's conversion waited on his conclusion that wages did not vary with the price of provision, and that repeal would benefit the wage earner rather than line the pockets of the manufacturer.

In any event, with Gladstone's reductions in duties on meat, eggs and dairy products, with High Farming, and an end to the movement off the farm and out of handwork into the factory real wages did rise in the

1850's, but so did profits on manufacturing. As so often in economic debates between two alternatives, history provides the answer which economists abhor, both. Nor did repeal bring a reduction in incomes to landlords—at least not for thirty years—as the farm response to repeal, and to high prices of food produced by the potato famine, was more High Farming.

Cobden may have only been scoring debating points rather than speaking from conviction when on a number of occasions he argued that the repeal would stimulate landlords "to employ their capital and their intelligence as other classes are forced to do in other pursuits" rather than "in sluggish indolence," and to double the quantity of grain, or butter, or cheese, which the land is capable of providing, with "longer leases, draining, extending the length of fields, knocking down hedgerows, clearing away trees which now shield the corn" and to provide more agricultural employment by activity to "grub up hedges, grub up thorns, drain, ditch." Sir James Caird insisted that High Farming was the answer to the repeal of the Corn Laws and many shared his view. The fact is, moreover, that the 1850's were the Golden Age of British farming, with rapid technical progress through the decade though it slowed thereafter. Repeal of the Corn Laws may not have stimulated increased efficiency in agriculture, but they did not set it back immediately, and only after the 1870's did increases in productivity run down.

The political economists in the Board of Trade—Bowring, Jacob, MacGregor—sought free trade as a means of slowing down the development of manufacturing on the Continent. They regarded the Zollverein as a reply to the imposition of the Corn Laws, and thought that with its repeal Europe, but especially the Zollverein under the leadership of Prussia, could be diverted to invest more heavily in agriculture and to retard the march to manufacturing. There were inconsistencies between this position and other facts they adduced: Bowring recognized that Germany had advantages over Great Britain for the development of manufacturing, and that Swiss spinning had made progress without protection. The 1818 Prussian tariff which formed the basis for that of the Zollverein was the lowest in Europe when it was enacted—though the levying of tariffs on cloth and yarn by weight gave high effective rates of protection despite low nominal duties to the cheaper constructions and counts. Jacob noted that the export supply elasticity of Prussian grain must be low, given poor transport. "To export machinery, we must import corn,"[7] but imports of corn were intended to prevent the development of manufacturers abroad, whereas the export of machinery assisted it. The rise and progress of German manufacturing was attributed to restrictions on the admission of German agricultural products and wood, imposed by France and England, but also to "the natural advantages of the several states for manufacturing industry, the genius and laborious character and the necessities of the German people, and . . . especially the unexampled duration of peace, and internal tranquility which all Germany enjoyed."[8]

The clearest statements are those of John Bowring. In a letter of August 28, 1839 to Lord Palmerston he asserted that the manufacturing interest in the Zollverein "is greatly strengthened and will become stronger from year to year unless counteracted by a system of concessions, conditional upon the gradual lowering of tariffs. The present state of things will not be tenable. The tariffs will be elevated under the growing demands and increasing power of the manufacturing states, or they will be lowered by calling into action, and bringing over to an alliance, the agricultural and commercial interests."[9] In his testimony before the Select Committee on Import Duties in 1840 he went further: "I believe we have created an unnecessary rivalry by our vicious legislation; that many of these countries never would have been dreamed of being manufacturers."

On this showing, the repeal of the Corn Laws was motivated by "free trade imperialism," the desire to gain a monopoly of trade with the world in manufactured goods. Zollverein in the 1830's merely indicated the need for haste. Torrens and James Deacon Hume, among others, had been pushing for importing corn to expand exports in the 1820's, before Zollverein was a threat.

Reciprocity had been a part of British commercial policy in the Treaty of Vergennes in 1786, in treaties reducing the impact of the Navigation Laws in the 1820's and 1830's. The French were suspicious, fearing that they had been out-traded in 1786. They evaded Huskisson's negotiations in 1828. But reciprocity was unnecessary, given David Hume's law. Unilateral reduction of import duties increased exports. Restored into the British diplomatic armory in 1860, reciprocity later became heresy in the eyes of political economists, and of the manufacturing interest as well.

The view that ascribes repeal of the Corn Laws to free-trade imperialism, however, fails adequately to take account of the ideology of the political economists, who believed in buying in the cheapest market and selling in the dearest, or of the short-run nature of the interests of the Manchester merchants themselves. It was evident after the 1840's that industrialization on the Continent could not be stopped, and likely that it could not be slowed down. The Navigation Acts were too complex; they had best be eliminated. The Corn Laws were doomed, even before the Irish potato famine, though that hastened the end of both Corn Laws and Navigation Acts, along with its demonstration of the limitation of market solutions under some circumstances.

"A good cause seldom triumphs unless someone's interest is bound up with it."[10] Free trade is the hypocrisy of the export interest, the clever device of the climber who kicks the ladder away when he has attained the summit of greatness. But in the English case it was more a view of the world at peace, with cosmopolitan interests served as well as national.

It is difficult in this to find clearcut support for any of the theories of tariff formation set forth earlier. Free trade as an export-interest collective good, sought in a representative democracy by concentrated interests to escape the free rider would seem to require a simple and direct connection between the removal of the tariff and the increase in rents. In the repeal of the Corn Laws, and the earlier tariff reductions of Huskisson and Peel, the connection was roundabout—through Hume's law, which meant that increased imports would lead to increased prices or quantities (or both) exported on the one hand, and/or through reduced wages, or higher real incomes from lower food prices on the other. Each chain of reasoning had several links.

Johnson's view that free trade is adopted by countries with improving competitiveness is contradictory to the free-trade-imperialism explanation, that free trade is adopted in an effort to undermine foreign gains in manufacturing when competitiveness has begun to decline. The former might better account in timing for Adam Smith's advocacy of free trade seventy years earlier—though that had large elements of French Physiocratic thought—or apply to the 1820's when British productivity was still improving, before the Continent had started to catch up. In turn, free-trade imperialism is a better explanation for the 1830's than for the end of the 1840's, since by 1846 it was already too late to slow, much less to halt, the advance of manufacturing on the Continent.

Vested interests competing for rents in a representative democracy, thrusting manufacturers seeking to expand markets, or faltering innovators, trying as a last resort to force exports on shrinking markets—rather like the stage of foreign direct investment in Vernon's product cycle when diffusion of technology has been accomplished—none of these explanations seems free of difficulties as compared with an ideological explanation based on the intellectual triumph of the political economists, their doctrines modified to incorporate consistency. The argument took many forms: static, dynamic, with implicit reliance on one incidence or another, direct or indirect in its use of Hume's law. But the Manchester School, based on the political economists, represented a rapidly rising ideology of freedom for industry to buy in the cheapest and sell in the dearest market. It overwhelmed the Tories when it did not convert them. Britain in the nineteenth century, and only to a slightly lesser extent the Continent, were characterized by a "strong, widely-shared conviction that the teachings of contemporary orthodox economists, including Free Traders, were scientifically exact, universally applicable, and demanded assent."[11] In the implicit debate between Thurman Arnold who regarded economic theorists (and lawyers) as high priests who rationalize and sprinkle holy water on contemporary practice, and Keynes who thought of practical men as responding unconsciously to the preaching of dead theorists, the British movement to free trade is a vote, aided by the potato famine, for the view of Keynes.

IV

France after 1815 was a high-tariff country which conformed to the Pincus model for a representative democracy with tariffs, for various interests, except that (a) there were tariffs for all, and (b) it was not a democracy. The Physiocratic doctrine of *laisser-faire* for agricultural exports had been discredited in its reciprocal form by the disaster wreaked by imports up to 1789 under the Treaty of Vergennes. The Continental system, moreover, provided strong protection to hothouse industries which was continued in the tariff of 1816, and elaborated in 1820 and 1822. To the principles of Turgot, that there should be freedom of grain trade inside France but no imports except in period of drought, were added two more: protection of the consumer by regulating the right of export of wheat—a step back from Physiocratic doctrine—and protecting the rights of producers by import tariffs. In introducing the tariff of 1822 for manufactures, Saint-Cricq defended prohibitions, attacked the view that an industry which could not survive with a duty of twenty percent should perish, saying that the government intended to protect all branches together: "agriculture, industry, internal commerce, colonial production, navigation, foreign commerce finally, both of land and of sea."[12]

It was not long, however, before pressures for lower duties manifested themselves. Industries complained of the burden of the tariff on their purchases of inputs, and especially of the excess protection accorded to iron. It was calculated that protection against English iron cost industrial consumers fifty million francs a year and had increased the price of wood—used for charcoal, and owned by the many noble *maîtres de forges*—by thirty percent on the average and in some places fifty percent. Commissions of inquiry in 1828 and 1834 recommended modifications in duties, especially to enlarge supplies which local industry was not in a position to provide, and to convert prohibitions into tariffs. A tumult of conflict broke out in the Chamber among the export interests of the ports, the textile interests of Alsace and Normandy, the *maîtres de forges* and the consumers of iron, with no regard, says the protectionist Gouraud, for the national interest. The Chambers were then dissolved by the cabinet, and tariffs adjusted downward, in coal, iron, copper, nitrates, machinery, horses. Reductions of the 1830's were followed in the peaks of business by similar pressure for reductions in prosperous phases of the cycle of the 1840's and 1850's.

A troubling question that involved conflicting interests in this period was presented by sugar, for which it was impossible to find a solution agreeable at the same time to colonial planters, shipowners, port refiners, consumers and the treasury. Colonial supply was high cost and a 55 francs per 100 kilograms duty on foreign supplies was needed to keep the sugar ports content. This, however, made it economical to expand beet-sugar production, begun during the Continental blockade, and the sugar ports turned to taxing this domestic production, less heavily at first, but with full equality in 1843. By this time it was too late, and with the freeing of the slaves in 1848, French colonial sugar production no longer counted.

The free-trade movement in France had its support in Bordeaux, the wine-exporting region; Lyon, interested in silk; and Paris, producer of so-called Paris article for sale abroad (cabinet ware, perfumes, imitation jewelry, toys, and so on). Later Norman agricultural interests in the export of butter and eggs to London teamed up with Bordeaux in wine to resist the attempts by textile interests to enlist agriculture in favor of higher tariffs.

Intellectual support to free trade led by Bastiat from Bordeaux, and with Michel Chevalier as its most prestigious member, is dismissed by Lévy-Leboyer as unimportant. Nonetheless, Chevalier had an important part in the negotiation of the treaty, and in persuading Napoleon III to impose it on France in the face of the united opposition of the Chamber of Deputies. Some attention to his thought is required.

The prime interest of the *Société d'Economie Politique* and of Chevalier was growth. His two-year visit to the United States in 1833–1835 impressed him with the contribution of transport to economic growth and contributed to his 1838 major work on *The Material Interests of France in Roads, Canals and Railroads*. American protectionist doctrine of Henry Carey seems not to have affected him. Polytechnician, graduate of the *Ecole des Mines*, Chevalier's first interest in freer trade came from a project to establish woolen production in the Midi, and to obtain cheaper wool. Much of his later reasoning was in terms of the penalty to industry from expensive materials: Charging 35 francs for a quintal of iron worth 20 imposes on industry "the labor of Sisyphus and the work of Penelope."[13] His major argument, at the *Collège de France*, and in his *Examen du Système Commercial*, cited the success of Spitalfield and Macclesfield when Huskisson permitted competition of imports; and the experience of the manufacturers of cotton and woolen textiles in Saxony who were worried by the enactment of Zollverein but sufficiently stimulated by import competition so that in two or three years their industry was flourishing. The letter of Napoleon III to Fould talks in specifics of the need to abolish all duties on raw materials essential to industry to encourage production, and to reduce by stages the duties on goods which are consumed on a large scale. In the more general introduction it states that "lack of competition causes industry to stagnate," echoing the Chevalier view. Chevalier himself was one of the judges of the Universal Exposition of 1855 in Paris and noted that France received so many prizes that no one dared confess to being a protectionist.

There were economic purposes behind the Anglo-French treaty, as evidenced by the proposal in France in 1851 for tariffs of twenty percent, ten percent and a duty-free on wholly manufactured goods, semi-finished manufactures and raw materials; by actual reductions in duties on coal, iron and steel in 1852 as the railroad boom picked up; and by the legislative proposal designed by Napoleon III in 1855, but not put forward until after the Crimean War, to admit 241 items duty free, reduce tariffs on 19 others, remove all prohibitions and set a top limit of thirty percent. This last was turned down by the Chamber and Napoleon promised not to submit a new tariff proposal before 1861.

Economic interests were involved, and the theories of great men like Cobden and Chevalier. However, there was more: Napoleon III was starting to engage on foreign adventure. He wanted to rid Italy of Austrian rule by use of arms. The British opposed his military measures, despite their recent use of force in Crimea. The treaty was used to hold British neutrality, as much as or more than to stimulate growth in France. Moreover, it did not need to be submitted to the Chamber. Under the Constitution of 1851, the Emperor had the sole power to make treaties, and such treaties encompassed those dealing with trade.

The move was successful both politically and economically. With the help of the French armies, Italy was unified under the leadership of Piedmont, and French growth never faltered under the impetus of increased imports. French industries met competition successfully and checked the growth of imports after two years. While its effects are intermingled with those of the spread of the French railroad network, it "helped to bring about the full development of the industrial revolution in France."

Further, it added impetus to the free-trade movement in Europe. This was under way in the early 1850's, following repeal of the Corn Laws. The Swiss constitution of 1848 had called for a tariff for revenue only and protective duties were reduced progressively from 1851 to 1885. The Netherlands removed a tariff on ship imports and a prohibition against nationalization of foreign ships. Belgium plugged gap after gap in its protective system in the early 1850's, only to turn around at the end of the decade and adopt free trade down the line. Piedmont, as we shall see, and Spain, Portugal, Norway and Sweden (after 1857) undertook to dismantle their protective and prohibitive restrictions. With the Anglo-French treaty the trickle became a flood. France, Germany, Italy and Britain engaged in negotiating reciprocal trade treaties with the most-favored nation clause.

Following French defeat at Sedan in 1870 and the abdication of Louis Napoleon, the Third Republic brought in the protectionist Thiers. The Cobden treaty was denounced in 1872. Reversal of policy waited upon the repeal of the Le Chapelier law of 1791, taken in the heat of the French revolution against associations, which forbade economic interests from organizing. Dunham claims that a country with leadership would have accepted a moderate tariff in 1875, but that the free traders had neither organization nor conviction, that is, too many free riders.

The French movement to free trade was taken against the weight of the separate interests, in the absence of strong export interests, with an admixture of economic theory of a dynamic kind, and imposed from above. The motivation of that imposition was partly economic, partly, perhaps even mainly, political. Moreover, it had a bandwagon effect in spreading freer trade.

In the French case, the leadership overwhelmed the concentrated economic interests. That leadership earned its surplus to use Frohlich, Oppenheimer and Young's expression, in a coin different than economic, that is, in freedom to maneuver in foreign policy. It may be possible to subsume increases in leadership surplus in this form into an "economic theory of national decision-making" with costs to vested interests accepted in exchange for political benefits to a national leader, ruling by an imposed constitution, the legitimacy of which is not questioned. The effort seems tortured.

V

As mentioned earlier, the Prussian tariff of 1818 was regarded when it was enacted as the lowest in Europe. But the duties on coarse yarns and textiles were effectively high, since the tariff was levied by weight. Jacob in 1819 noted that the "system of the Prussian government has always been of manufacturing at home everything consumed within the Kingdom; of buying from others, nothing that can be dispensed with," adding "As scarcely any competition exists, but with their own countrymen, there is little inducement to adopt the inventions of other countries, or to exercise their facilities in perfecting their fabrics; none of these have kept pace. . . . "[14] Baden, on joining the Zollverein which adopted the Prussian tariff for the totality, believed itself to be raising its tariff level when it joined. What Baden did, however, was to acquire enforcement: its long border had previously been effectively open.

The Prussian tariff dominated that of the Zollverein, organized in the years from 1828 to 1833, primarily because Prussia took a very liberal view of tariff revenues. Most goods by sea entered the German states via Prussia, directly or by way of the Netherlands, but the text of the Zollverein treaty of 1833 provided that the revenues from the duties after deduction of expenses would be divided among the contracting states according to population. Prussia thus received 55 percent, Bavaria 17 percent, Saxony 6.36 percent, Wurtemberg 5.5 percent, and so on, and was said in 1848 to have sacrificed about two million thalers a year, exclusive of the fiscal loss sustained by smuggling along the Rhine and Lake Constance. This can be regarded as a side-payment made by the beneficiary of income-distribution under Pareto-optimal conditions to gain its policy, or as the disproportionate share of overhead costs of the collective good saddled on the party that most wanted it.

Despite adjustments made in Prussian customs duties between 1819 and 1833, the tariff remained low by British standards. Junker grain growers were hopeful of importing British manufactures in order to sell Britain more grain. Junker bureaucrats, brought up on Adam Smith and free trade by instinct, were fearful that highly protective rates would reduce the revenue yield.

Outside of Prussia plus Hamburg and Frankfort and the other grain-growing states of Mecklenburg, Pomerania, and so on, there was interest in higher tariffs, but apart from the Rhineland, little in the way of organized interests. Von Delbrück comments that Prussia and Pomerania had free trade interests and shipping interests, but that outside the Rhineland, which had organized Chambers of Commerce under the French occupation, there were few bureaucrats, or organs with views on questions of trade and industry. Nor did the Prussian government see a need to develop them.

Saxony was sufficiently protected by its interior location so as not to feel threatened by low tariffs, which, as mentioned, were not really low on coarse cloths. On joining the Zollverein, Baden was concerned over raising its tariff, and worried lest it be cut off from its traditional trading areas of Switzerland and Alsace. It fought with the Zollverein authorities over exemptions for imported capital equipment, but gradually evolved into a source of pressure, with Bavaria and Wurtemberg, for higher tariffs on cotton yarns and iron. Fischer points out the request for lifting the duty on cotton yarns from two talers per centner to five was resisted by the weavers of Prussia (the Rhineland) and Silesia.

Cotton yarns and iron were the critical items. Shortly after the formation of Zollverein, a trend toward protection was seen to be under way. The Leipsig consul reported a new duty on iron to the Board of Trade in February 1837 and observed that the switch from imports of cotton cloth to imports of yarn pointed in the direction of ultimate exclusion of both. Bowring's letter of August 1839 noted that the manufacturing interest was growing stronger, that the existing position was untenable, and that tariffs would be raised under the growing demands and increasing power of the manufacturing states, or would be lowered by an alliance between the agricultural and commercial interests.

Open agitation for protection began two and one-half years after the formation of the Zollverein when the South pushed for duties on cotton yarns. Linen yarns and cloth went on the agenda in 1839 and iron, protection for which was sought by Silesian and west German ironwork owners, beginning in 1842. But these groups lacked decisive power. The Prussian landed nobility covered their position by citing the interests of the consumers, and Prince Smith, the expatriate leader of the doctrinaire free traders, in turn tried to identify free trade and low tariffs with the international free-trade movement rather than with the export-interests of the Junkers. The tariff on iron was raised in 1844, those on cotton yarns and linen yarns in 1846. Von Delbrück presents in detail the background of the latter increases, starting with the bureaucratic investigations into linen, cotton, wool, and soda, with their negative recommendation, continuing through the negotiations, in which Prussia was ranged against any increase and all the others in favor, and concluding that the Prussian plenipotentiary to the Zollverein conference was right in not vetoing the increases, as he could have done, operating on the theory that a compromise was more important than the rationally correct measure of this or that tariff. The head of the Prussian Handelsamt was not satisfied with the outcome of the conference but had to accept it.

From 1846 on, the direction of Zollverein tariffs was downward, aided first by the repeal of the Corn Laws and secondly by the Cobden-Chevalier treaty. With the increases of the 1840's and English reductions, the Zollverein tariff from one of the lowest in Europe had become relatively high. Von Delbrück was one of the doctrinaire free traders in the Prussian civil service and notes that in 1863 he had been trying for a reduction on the tariff in pig iron for seven years, since the tariff reform of 1856, which reordered but did not lower duty schedules. He also wanted a reduction in the tariff on cotton cloth; duties on woolens were no longer needed. The opportunity came with the announcement of the Anglo-French treaty. He noted that Austria had gone from prohibitions to tariffs, that the Netherlands had reformed its tariffs with a five percent maximum on industrial production, and that the levels of Italian duties were lower than those in Germany. "Could we stay away from this movement? We could not."[15]

Bismarck was no barrier to the Junker bureaucracy. His view about tariff negotiations was expressed in 1879 in the question: "Who got the better of the bargain?" Trade treaties, he believed, were nothing in themselves but an expression of friendship. His economic conscience at this time, he said later, was in the hands of others. Moreover, he had two political ends which a trade treaty with France might serve: to gain her friendship in the Danish question, and to isolate Austria which was bidding for a role in the German Confederation. Austrian tariffs were high. The lower the levels of the Zollverein the more difficulty she would have in joining it and bidding against Prussia for influence. The Zollverein followed the 1863 treaty with France with a series of others.

Exports of grain from Prussia, Pomerania, and Mecklenberg to London as a percentage of total English imports hit a peak in 1862 at the time of the Civil War and proceeded down thereafter as American supplies took over. The free-trade movement nonetheless continued. Only hesitation prevented a move to complete free trade at the peak of the boom in 1873. There is debate whether the crash later in the year triggered off the return to protection in 1879 or not. Victory in 1871 had enlarged competition in iron and cotton textiles by including Alsace and Lorraine in the new German Empire. Radical free traders and large farmers achieved the reduction in duties on raw iron in 1873 and passed legislative provision for their complete removal in 1877. But Lambi notes that *Gewerbefreiheit* (freedom of occupation) had caused dissatisfaction and in some versions subsumed free trade. By 1875 the iron interests are organizing to resist the scheduled elimination of iron duties in 1877.

The difference between the 1873 depression which led to tariffs, and the 1857 crisis which did not, lay in (a) the fact that the interests were not cohesive in the earlier period and (b) that Britain did not keep on lowering duties in the later period as it had in the first. On the first score the Verein Deutscher Eisen- und Stahl Industrielle was formed in 1873 after vertical integration of steel back to iron mining had removed the opposition between the producers and consumers of iron. This much supports the view of the effectiveness of concentrated interests achieving their tariff goals when scattered interests will not—though again it has nothing to do with representative democracy. On the other hand, the free traders also organized; in 1868 the Kongress Nord-Deutscher Landwirte was organized, and in 1871 it was broadened to cover all Germany. In 1872, a Deutsche Landwirtschaftsrat was formed. Many of these organizations and the once free-trade Congress of German Economists were subverted and converted to protection after 1875, but a new Union for the Promotion of Free Trade was formed in September 1876. German economic interests as a whole became organized, and the struggle was among interests concentrated on both sides.

Abandonment of the opposition of the landed interests is perhaps critical. Consumers of iron in machinery, they opposed tariffs on iron up to 1875, but with the decline in the price of grain and the threat of imports, their opposition collapsed. It might have been possible to support tariffs for grain and free trade for iron, but inconsistency is open to attack. After von Delbrück's resignation or discharge in April 1876, Bismarck forged the alliance of bread and iron. As widely recounted, he had strong domestic political motives for higher tariffs on this occasion, as contrasted with his international political gains from lower tariffs up to 1875.

In general, however, the German case conforms to the Stolper-Samuelson explanation: the abundant factor wants free trade; when it becomes relatively scarce, through a gain in manufacturing at home and an expansion of agriculture abroad, it shifts to wanting tariffs. Doctrine was largely on the side of free trade. List's advocacy of national economy had little or no political force. His ultimate goal was always free trade, and his early proposal of ten percent duties on colonial goods, fifteen percent on Continental and fifty percent on British was more anti-British than national. In the 1840's he was regarded in Germany, or at least by the Prussians, as a polemicist whose views were offered for sale. Bismarck is often regarded as the arch-villain of the 1879 reversal of Zollverein low tariffs, but it is hard to see that his role was a major one. . . .

VI

My first conclusion reached from this survey was that free trade in Europe in the period from 1820 to 1875 had many different causes. Whereas after 1879, various countries reacted quite differently to the single stimulus of the fall in the price of wheat—England liquidating its agriculture, France and Germany imposing tariffs, though for different political and sociological reasons, Italy emigrating (in violation of the assumptions of classical economics), and Denmark transforming from producing grain for export to importing it as an input in the production of dairy products, bacon and eggs—before that the countries of Europe all responded to different stimuli in the same way. Free trade was part of a general response to the breakdown of the manor and guild system. This was especially true of the removal of restrictions on exports and export taxes, which limited freedom of producers. As more and conflicting interests came into contention, the task of sorting them out became too complex for government (as shown in *Gewerbeförderung* in Baden, and the refinement of the Navigation Laws in England), and it became desirable to sweep them all away.

Part of the stimulus came from the direct self-interest of particular dominant groups, illustrated particularly by the First Hand in the Netherlands. In Britain, free trade emerged as a doctrine from the political economists, with a variety of rationalizations to sustain it in particular applications: anti-monopoly, increases to real wages, higher profits, increased allocative efficiency, increased productivity through innovation required by import competition. In France, the lead in the direction of free trade came less from the export interests than from industrial interests using imported materials and equipment as inputs, though the drive to free trade after 1846 required the overcoming of the weight of the vested interests by strong governmental leadership, motivated by political gain in international politics. The German case was more straightforward: free trade was in the interest of the exporting grain and timber-producing classes, who were politically dominant in Prussia and who partly bought off and partly overwhelmed the rest of the country. The Italian case seems to be one in which doctrines developed abroad which were dominant in England and in a minority position in France, were imported by strong political leadership and imposed on a relatively disorganized political body.

Second thoughts raise questions. The movement to free trade in the 1850's in the Netherlands, Belgium, Spain, Portugal, Denmark, Norway and Sweden, along with the countries discussed in detail, suggests the possibility that Europe as a whole was motivated by ideological considerations rather than economic interests. That Louis Napoleon and Bismarck would use trade treaties to gain ends in foreign policy suggests that free trade was valued for itself, and that moves toward it would earn approval. Viewed in one perspective, the countries of Europe in this period should not be considered as independent economies whose reactions to various phenomena can properly be compared, but rather as a single entity which moved to free trade for ideological or perhaps better doctrinal reasons. Manchester and the English political economists persuaded Britain which persuaded Europe, by precept and example. Economic theories of representative democracy, or constitutional monarchy, or even absolute monarchy may explain some cases of tariff changes. They are little help in Western Europe between the Napoleonic Wars and the Great Depression.

NOTES

1. H. R. C. Wright, *Free Trade and Protection*, p. 124.
2. *William Huskisson, (The Speeches of the Right Honorable)* (London: John Murray, 1832), II, p. 328.
3. Report of the Select Committee on the Laws Relating to the Export of Tools and Machinery, 30 June 1825, in *Parliamentary Papers, Reports of Committee*, (1825), Vol. V, p. 12.

4. H. R. C. Wright, *Free Trade and Protection in the Netherlands, 1816–30: A Study of the First Benelux* (Cambridge: Cambridge University Press, 1955), p. 130.

5. Charles Babbage, *The Economy of Machinery and Manufactures* (London: Charles Knight, 4th ed., 1835), p. 364.

6. Karl Polanyi, *The Great Transformation* (New York: Farrar & Rinehart, 1944), p. 152–53.

7. Testimony of Thomas Ashton, in *First Report of the Select Committee*, para. 235.

8. John MacGregor, *Germany, Her Resources, Government, Union of Customs and Power under Frederick William IV* (London: Whittaker and Co., 1948), p. 68.

9. John Bowring, "Report on the Prussian Commercial Union 1840," *Parliamentary Papers*, 1840, Volume XXI, p. 287.

10. Mill, cited by Bernard Semmel, *The Rise of Free Trade Imperialism: Classical Political Economy, The Empire of Free Trade and Imperialism, 1750–1850* (Cambridge: Cambridge University Press, 1970), p. 207.

11. Kenneth Fielden, "The Rise and Fall of Free Trade," in C. J. Bartlett, ed., *Britain Pre-eminent: Studies in British World Influence in the Nineteenth Century* (London: Macmillan, 1969), p. 78.

12. Charles Gouraud, *Histoire de la politique commerciale de la France et son influence sur le progrès de la richesse publique depuis le moyen age jusqu'à nos jours*, I, II (Paris: Auguste Durand, 1854), p. 208.

13. Michel Chevalier, *Cours d'economie politique, Fait au Collège de France*, I, II, III (2nd ed., Paris: No publisher stated, 1855), p. 538.

14. William Jacob, *A View of the Agriculture, Manufactures, Statistics and Society in the State of Germany and Parts of Holland and France* (London: John Murray, 1820), pp. 201–02.

15. Rudolph von Delbrück, *Lebenserinnerungen, I* (Leipsig: Duncker u. Humblot, 1905), p. 200.

6. Selections from *Imperialism: The Highest Stage of Capitalism*

V. I. LENIN

In his 1916 pamphlet, V. I. Lenin offers both an analysis of the world's predicament at the time and a call for future action. He outlines the development of "monopoly capitalism" and the domination of the world's leading countries by finance capital. In order to escape declining rates of profit at home, according to Lenin, capitalists invest abroad with the support of their governments. As more and more land is seized by imperial powers, economic and military competition between the capitalist nation-states escalates. Lenin compares his view of this new phase of capitalism to rival Marxist

interpretations. He goes on to describe the characteristics of monopoly capitalism and the process of imperialism inherent within it. In doing so, Lenin provides an important and persuasive account of imperialism in the late nineteenth century.

THE EXPORT OF CAPITAL

Under the old type of capitalism, when free competition prevailed, the export of *goods* was the most typical feature. Under modern capitalism, when monopolies prevail, the export of *capital* has become the typical feature.

Capitalism is commodity production at the highest stage of development, when labour power itself becomes a commodity. The growth of internal exchange, and particularly of international exchange, is a special feature of capitalism. The uneven and spasmodic character of the development of individual enterprises, of individual branches of industry and individual countries, is inevitable under the capitalist system. England became a capitalist country before any other, and in the middle of the nineteenth century, having adopted free trade, claimed to be the "workshop of the world," the great purveyor of manufactured goods to all other countries, which in exchange were to keep her supplied with raw materials. In the last quarter of the nineteenth century, *this* monopoly was already undermined. Other countries, protecting themselves by tariff walls, had developed into independent capitalist countries. On the threshold of the twentieth century, we see a new type of monopoly coming into existence. First, there are monopolist capitalist combines in all advanced capitalist countries; secondly, a few rich countries, in which the accumulation of capital reaches gigantic proportions, occupy a monopolist position. An enormous "superfluity of capital" has accumulated in the advanced countries.

It goes without saying that if capitalism could develop agriculture, which today lags far behind industry everywhere, if it could raise the standard of living of the masses, who are everywhere still poverty-stricken and underfed, in spite of the amazing advance in technical knowledge, there could be no talk of a superfluity of capital. This "argument" the petty-bourgeois critics of capitalism advance on every occasion. But if capitalism did these things it would not be capitalism; for uneven development and wretched conditions of the masses are the fundamental and inevitable conditions and premises of this mode of production. As long as capitalism remains what it is, surplus capital will never be utilised for the purpose of raising the standard of living of the masses in a given country, for this would mean a decline in profits for the capitalists; it will be used for the purpose of increasing those profits by exporting capital abroad to the backward countries. In these backward countries, profits usually are high, for capital is scarce, the price of land is relatively low, wages are low, raw materials are cheap. The possibility of exporting capital is created by the entry of numerous backward countries into international capitalist intercourse; main railways have either been built or are being built there; the elementary conditions for industrial development have been created, etc. The necessity of exporting capital arises from the fact that in a few countries capitalism has become "over-ripe" and (owing to the backward state of agriculture and the impoverished state of the masses) capital cannot find "profitable" investment.

Here are approximate figures showing the amount of capital invested abroad by the three principal countries:

Capital Invested Abroad (In billions of francs)

YEAR	GREAT BRITAIN	FRANCE	GERMANY
1862	3.6	–	–
1872	15.0	10 (1869)	–
1882	22.0	15 (1880)	?
1893	42.0	20 (1890)	?
1902	62.0	27-37	12.5
1914	75-100	60	44.0

This table shows that the export of capital reached formidable dimensions only in the beginning of the twentieth century. Before the war the capital invested abroad by the three principal countries amounted to between 175 and 200 billion francs. At the modest rate of 5 per cent, this sum brought in from 8 to 10 billions a year. This provided a solid basis for imperialist oppression and the exploitation of most of the countries and nations of the world; a solid basis for the capitalist parasitism of a handful of wealthy states!

How is this capital invested abroad distributed among the various countries? *Where* does it go? Only an approximate answer can be given to this question, but sufficient to throw light on certain general relations and ties of modern imperialism.

Approximate Distribution of Foreign Capital (about 1910)
(In billions of marks)

CONTINENT	GREAT BRITAIN	FRANCE	GERMANY	TOTAL
Europe	4	23	18	45
America	37	4	10	51
Asia, Africa, Australia	29	8	7	44
Total	70	35	35	140

The principal spheres of investment of British capital are the British colonies, which are very large also in America (for example, Canada), as well as in Asia, etc. In this case, enormous exports of capital are bound up with the possession of enormous colonies, of the importance of which for imperialism we shall speak later. In regard to France, the situation is quite different. French capital exports are invested mainly in Europe, particularly in Russia (at least ten billion francs). This is mainly *loan* capital, in the form of government loans and not investments in industrial undertakings. Unlike British colonial imperialism, French imperialism might be termed usury imperialism. In regard to Germany, we have a third type; the German colonies are inconsiderable, and German capital invested abroad is divided fairly evenly between Europe and America.

The export of capital greatly affects and accelerates the development of capitalism in those countries to which it is exported. While, therefore, the export of capital may tend to a certain extent to arrest development in the countries exporting capital, it can only do so by expanding and deepening the further development of capitalism throughout the world.

The countries which export capital are nearly always able to obtain "advantages," the character of which throws light on the peculiarities of the epoch of finance capital and monopoly. The following passage, for instance, occurred in the Berlin review, *Die Bank*, for October 1913:

> "A comedy worthy of the pen of Aristophanes is being played just now on the international money market. Numerous foreign countries, from Spain to the Balkan states, from Russia to the Argentine, Brazil and China, are openly or secretly approaching the big money markets demanding loans, some of which are very urgent. The money market is not at the moment very bright and the political outlook is not yet promising. But not a single money market dares to refuse a loan for fear that its neighbour might grant it and so secure some small reciprocal service. In these international transactions the creditor nearly always manages to get some special advantages: an advantage of a commercial-political nature, a coaling station, a contract to construct a harbour, a fat concession, or an order for guns."

Finance capital has created the epoch of monopolies, and monopolies introduce everywhere monopolist methods: the utilisation of "connections" for profitable transactions takes the place of competition on the open market. The most usual thing is to stipulate that part of the loan that is granted shall be spent on purchases in the country of issue, particularly on orders for war materials, or for ships, etc. In the course of the last two decades (1890–1910), France often resorted to this method. The export of capital abroad thus becomes a means for encouraging the export of commodities. In these circumstances transactions between particularly big firms assume a form "bordering on corruption," as Schilder "delicately" puts it. Krupp in Germany, Schneider in France, Armstrong in England, are instances of firms having close connections with powerful banks and governments whose "share" must not be forgotten when arranging a loan.

France granted loans to Russia in 1905 and by the commercial treaty of September 16, 1905, she "squeezed" concessions out of her to run till 1917. She did the same thing when the Franco-Japanese commercial treaty was concluded on August 19, 1911. The tariff war between Austria and Serbia, which lasted with a seven months' interval, from 1906 to 1911, was partly caused by competition between Austria and France for supplying Serbia with war material. In January 1912, Paul Deschanel stated in the Chamber of Deputies that from 1908 to 1911 French firms had supplied war material to Serbia to the value of 45,000,000 francs.

A report from the Austro-Hungarian Consul at Sao-Paulo (Brazil) states:

> "The construction of the Brazilian railways is being carried out chiefly by French, Belgian, British and German capital. In the financial operations connected with the construction of these railways the countries involved also stipulate for orders for the necessary railway material."

Thus, finance capital, almost literally, one might say, spreads its net over all countries of the world. Banks founded in the colonies, or their branches, play an important part in these operations. German imperialists look with envy on the "old" colonising nations which in this respect are "well established." In 1904, Great Britain had 50 colonial banks with 2,279 branches (in 1910 there were 72 banks with 5,449 branches); France had 20 with 136 branches; Holland, 16 with 68 branches, and Germany had a "mere" 13 with 70 branches.

The American capitalists, in their turn, are jealous of the English and German: "In South America," they complained in 1915, "five German banks had forty branches and five English banks had seventy. . . . During the last twenty-five years, Great Britain and Germany have invested in the Argentine, Brazil and Uruguay about four billion dollars, which places under their control 46 per cent of the total trade of these three countries."

The capital exporting countries have divided the world among themselves in the figurative sense of the term. But finance capital has also led to the *actual* division of the world.

IMPERIALISM AS A SPECIAL STAGE OF CAPITALISM

We must now try to sum up and put together what has been said above on the subject of imperialism. Imperialism emerged as the development and direct continuation of the fundamental attributes of capitalism in general. But capitalism only became capitalist imperialism at a definite and very high stage of its development, when certain of its fundamental attributes began to be transformed into their opposites, when the features of the period of transition from capitalism to a higher social and economic system began to take shape and reveal themselves all along the line. The fundamental economic factor in this process is the substitution of capitalist monopolies for capitalist free competition. Free competition is the fundamental attribute of capitalism and of commodity production generally. Monopoly is exactly the opposite of free competition; but we have seen the latter being transformed into monopoly before our very eyes, creating large-scale industry and eliminating small industry, replacing large-scale industry by still larger-scale industry, finally leading to such a concentration of production and capital that monopoly has been and is the result: cartels, syndicates and trusts, and merging with them, the capital of a dozen or so banks manipulating thousands of millions. At the same time monopoly, which has grown out of free competition, does not abolish the latter, but exists alongside it and hovers over it, as it were, and, as a result, gives rise to a number of very acute antagonisms, friction and conflicts. Monopoly is the transition from capitalism to a higher system.

If it were necessary to give the briefest possible definition of imperialism we should have to say that imperialism is the monopoly stage of capitalism. Such a definition would include what is most important, for, on the one hand, finance capital is the bank capital of the few big monopolist banks, merged with the capital of the monopolist combines of manufacturers; and, on the other hand, the division of the world is the transition from a colonial policy which has extended without hindrance to territories unoccupied by any capitalist power, to a colonial policy of the monopolistic possession of the territories of the world which have been completely divided up.

But very brief definitions, although convenient, for they sum up the main points, are nevertheless inadequate, because very important features of the phenomenon that has to be defined have to be especially deduced. And so, without forgetting the conditional and relative value of all definitions, which can never include all the concatenations of a phenomenon in its complete development, we must give a definition of imperialism that will embrace the following five essential features:

1. The concentration of production and capital developed to such a stage that it creates monopolies which play a decisive role in economic life.
2. The merging of bank capital with industrial capital, and the creation, on the basis of "finance capital," of a financial oligarchy.

What are some problems w/these?

3. The export of capital, which has become extremely important, as distinguished from the export of commodities.
4. The formation of international capitalist monopolies which share the world among themselves.
5. The territorial division of the whole world among the greatest capitalist powers is completed.

Imperialism is capitalism in that stage of development in which the domination of monopolies and finance capital has established itself; in which the export of capital has acquired pronounced importance; in which the division of the world among the international trusts has begun; in which the partition of all the territories of the globe among the great capitalist powers has been completed.

We shall see later that imperialism can and must be defined differently if consideration is to be given, not only to the basic, purely economic factors—to which the above definition is limited—but also to the historical place of this stage of capitalism in relation to capitalism in general, or to the relations between imperialism and the two main tendencies in the working class movement. The point to be noted just now is that imperialism, as interpreted above, undoubtedly represents a special stage in the development of capitalism. In order to enable the reader to obtain as well grounded an idea of imperialism as possible, we deliberately quoted largely from *bourgeois* economists who are obliged to admit the particularly indisputable facts regarding modern capitalist economy. With the same object in view, we have produced detailed statistics which reveal the extent to which bank capital, etc., has developed, showing how the transformation of quantity into quality, of developed capitalism into imperialism, has expressed itself. Needless to say, all the boundaries in nature and in society are conditional and changeable, and, consequently, it would be absurd to discuss the exact year or the decade in which imperialism "definitely" became established. . . .

We notice three areas of highly developed capitalism, that is, with a high development of means of transport, of trade and of industry. These are the Central European, the British and the American areas. Among these are three states which dominate the world: Germany, Great Britain, the United States. Imperialist rivalry and the struggle between these countries have become very keen because Germany has only a restricted area and few colonies (the creation of "central Europe" is still a matter for the future; it is being born in the midst of desperate struggles). For the moment the distinctive feature of Europe is political disintegration. In the British and American areas, on the other hand, political concentration is very highly developed, but there is a tremendous disparity between the immense colonies of the one and the insignificant colonies of the other. In the colonies, capitalism is only beginning to develop. The struggle for South America is becoming more and more acute.

There are two areas where capitalism is not strongly developed: Russia and Eastern Asia. In the former the density of population is very small, in the latter it is very high; in the former political concentration is very high; in the latter it does not exist. The partition of China is only beginning, and the struggle between Japan, U.S.A., etc., in connection therewith is steadily gaining in intensity. . . .

Finance capital and the trusts are aggravating instead of diminishing the differences in the rate of development of the various parts of world economy. When the relation of forces is changed, how else, *under capitalism*, can the solution for contradictions be found, except by resorting to *violence*?

Railway statistics provide remarkably exact data on the different rates of development of capitalism and finance capital in world economy. . . .

. . . The development of railways has been more rapid in the colonies and in the independent or semi-independent states of Asia and America. Here, as we know, the finance capital of the four or five biggest capitalist states reigns undisputed. Two hundred thousand kilometres of new railways in the colonies and in the other countries of Asia and America represent more than 40,000,000,000 marks in capital, newly invested under particularly advantageous conditions, with special guarantees of a good return and with profitable orders for steel works, etc., etc.

Capitalism is growing with the greatest rapidity in the colonies and in trans-oceanic countries. Among the latter, *new* imperialist powers are emerging (*e.g.*, Japan). The struggle of world imperialism is becoming aggravated. The tribute levied by finance capital on the most profitable colonial and trans-oceanic enterprises is increasing. In sharing out this booty, an exceptionally large part goes to countries which, as far as the development of productive forces is concerned, do not always stand at the top of the list. . . .

About 80 percent of the total existing railways are concentrated in the hands of the five great powers. But the concentration of the *ownership* of these railways, that of finance capital, is much greater still: French and English millionaires, for example, own an enormous amount of stocks and bonds in American, Russian and other railways.

Thanks to her colonies, Great Britain has increased "her" length of railways by 100,000 kilometres, four times as much as Germany. And yet it is well known that the development of productive forces in Germany, and especially the development of the coal and iron industries, has been much more rapid during this period than in England—not to mention France and Russia. In 1892, Germany produced 4,900,000 tons of pig iron, and Great Britain produced 6,800,000 tons; in 1912, Germany produced 17,600,000 tons and Great Britain, 9,000,000 tons. Germany, therefore, had an overwhelming superiority over England in this respect!

We ask, is there *under capitalism* any means of remedying the disparity between the development of productive forces and the accumulation of capital on the one side, and the division of colonies and "spheres of influence" by finance capital on the other side—other than by resorting to war?

THE PLACE OF IMPERIALISM IN HISTORY

We have seen that the economic quintessence of imperialism is monopoly capitalism. This very fact determines its place in history, for monopoly that grew up on the basis of free competition, and out of free competition, is the transition from the capitalist system to a higher social economic order. We must take special note of the four principal forms of monopoly, or the four principal manifestations of monopoly capitalism, which are characteristic of the period under review.

1. Monopoly arose out of the concentration of production at a very advanced stage of development. This refers to the monopolist capitalist combines: cartels, syndicates and trusts. We have seen the important role these play in modern economic life. At the beginning of the twentieth century, monopolies acquired complete supremacy in the advanced countries. And although the first steps towards the formation of the combines were first taken by countries enjoying the protection of high tariffs (Germany, America), England, with her system of free trade, was not far behind in revealing the same phenomenon, namely, the birth of monopoly out of the concentration of production.

2. Monopolies have accelerated the capture of the most important sources of raw materials, especially for the coal and iron industry, which is the basic and most highly trustified industry in capitalist society. The monopoly of the most important sources of raw materials has enormously increased the power of big capital, and has sharpened the antagonism between trustified and non-trustified industry.

3. Monopoly has sprung from the banks. The banks have developed from modest intermediary enterprises into the monopolists of finance capital. Some three or five of the biggest banks in each of the foremost capitalist countries have achieved the "personal union" of industrial and bank capital, and have concentrated in their hands the power to dispose of thousands upon thousands of millions which form the greater part of the capital and revenue of entire countries. A financial oligarchy, which throws a close net of relations of dependence over all the economic and political insti-

tutions of contemporary bourgeois society without exception—such is the most striking manifestation of this monopoly.

4. Monopoly has grown out of colonial policy. To the numerous "old" motives of colonial policy, finance capital has added the struggle for the sources of raw materials, for the export of capital, for "spheres of influence," *i.e.*, for spheres of good business, concessions, monopolist profits, and so on; in fine, for economic territory in general. When the colonies of the European powers in Africa comprised only one-tenth of that territory (as was the case in 1876), colonial policy was able to develop by methods other than those of monopoly—by the "free grabbing" of territories, so to speak. But when nine-tenths of Africa had been seized (approximately in 1900), when the whole world had been shared out, there was inevitably ushered in a period of colonial monopoly and, consequently, a period of intense struggle for the partition and the repartition of the world.

The extent to which monopolist capital has intensified all the contradictions of capitalism is generally known. It is sufficient to mention the high cost of living and the power of the trusts. This intensification of contradictions constitutes the most powerful driving force of the transitional period of history, which began at the time of the definite victory of world finance capital.

Monopolies, oligarchy, the striving for domination instead of the striving for liberty, the exploitation of an increasing number of small or weak nations by an extremely small group of the richest or most powerful nations—all these have given birth to those distinctive features of imperialism which compel us to define it as parasitic or decaying capitalism. More and more there emerges, as one of the tendencies of imperialism, the creation of the "bondholding" (*rentier*) state, the usurer state, in which the bourgeoisie lives on the proceeds of capital exports and by "clipping coupons." It would be a mistake to believe that this tendency to decay precludes the possibility of the rapid growth of capitalism. It does not. In the epoch of imperialism, certain branches of industry, certain strata of the bourgeoisie and certain countries betray, to a greater or less degree, one or other of these tendencies. On the whole capitalism is growing far more rapidly than before, but it is not only that this growth is becoming more and more uneven; this unevenness manifests itself also, in particular, in the decay of the countries which are richest in capital (such as England).

In regard to the rapidity of Germany's economic development, Riesser, the author of the book on the great German banks, states:

"The progress of the preceding period (1848–70), which had not been exactly slow, stood in about the same ratio to the rapidity with which the whole of Germany's national economy and with it German banking progressed during this period (1870–1905), as the mail coach of the Holy Roman Empire of the German nation stood to the speed of the present-day automobile . . . which in whizzing past, it must be said, often endangers not only innocent pedestrians in its path, but also the occupants of the car."

In its turn, this finance capital which has grown so rapidly is not unwilling (precisely because it has grown so quickly) to pass on to a more "tranquil" possession of colonies which have to be captured—and not only by peaceful methods—from richer nations. In the United States, economic development in the last decades has been even more rapid than in Germany, and *for this very reason* the parasitic character of modern American capitalism has stood out with particular prominence. On the other hand, a comparison of, say, the republican American bourgeoisie with the monarchist Japanese or German bourgeoisie shows that the most pronounced political differences become insignificant during the imperialist period—not because they are unimportant in general, but because throughout it is a case of a bourgeoisie with definite traits of parasitism.

The receipt of high monopoly profits by the capitalists in one of the numerous branches of industry, in one of numerous countries, etc., makes it economically possible for them to corrupt individual sections of the working class and sometimes a fairly considerable minority, and win them to the side of the capitalists of a given industry or nation against all the others. The intensification of antagonism between imperialist nations for the partition of the world increases this striving. And so there is created that bond between imperialism and opportunism, which revealed itself first and most clearly in England, owing to the fact that certain features of imperialist development were observable there much sooner than in other countries. . . .

From all that has been said in this book on the economic nature of imperialism, it follows that we must define it as capitalism in transition, or, more precisely, as moribund capitalism. It is very instructive in this respect to note that the bourgeois economists, in describing modern capitalism, frequently employ terms like "interlocking," "absence of isolation," etc.; "in accordance with their functions and course of development," banks are "not purely private business enterprises; they are more and more outgrowing the sphere of purely private business regulations." And this very Riesser, who uttered the words just quoted, declares with all seriousness that the "prophecy" of the Marxists concerning "socialisation" has not been realised!

What then does this word "interlocking" express? It merely expresses the most striking feature of the process going on before our eyes. It shows that the observer counts the separate trees without seeing the wood. It slavishly copies the superficial, the fortuitous, the chaotic. It reveals the observer as one overwhelmed by the mass of raw material and utterly incapable of appreciating its meaning and importance. Ownership of shares and relations between owners of private property "interlock in a haphazard way." But the underlying factor of this interlocking, its very base, is the changing social relations of production. When a big enterprise assumes gigantic proportions, and, on the basis of exact computation of mass data, organises according to plan the supply of primary raw materials to the extent of two-thirds, or three-fourths of all that is necessary for tens of millions of people; when these raw materials are transported to the most suitable place of production, sometimes hundreds or thousands of miles away, in a systematic and organised manner; when a single centre directs all the successive stages of work right up to the manufacture of numerous varieties of finished articles; when these products are distributed according to a single plan among tens of hundreds of millions of consumers (as in the case of the distribution of oil in America and Germany by the American "Standard Oil")—then it becomes evident that we have socialisation of production, and not mere "interlocking"; that private economic relations and private property relations constitute a shell which is no longer suitable for its contents, a shell which must of necessity begin to decay if its destruction be postponed by artificial means; a shell which may continue in a state of decay for a fairly long period (particularly if the cure of the opportunist abscess is protracted), but which must inevitably be removed. . . .

7. The Imperialism of Free Trade

JOHN GALLAGHER AND
RONALD ROBINSON

During the 1870s, European nations began a dramatic territorial expansion in Africa and Asia; by the turn of the twentieth century, most areas of these two continents were European colonies. This process, often known as classical imperialism, has given rise to divergent interpretations. Lenin (Reading 6) saw it as an inexorable result of the development of monopoly capitalism; Realists have regarded the episode as driven primarily by national-security considerations.

In this seminal 1953 article, John Gallagher and Ronald Robinson argue that Britain's overseas territorial expansion, which led to the construction of the largest colonial empire in world history, was but part of a broader pattern of British overseas economic expansion during the nineteenth century. Britain's overriding goal throughout the Pax Britannica, *Gallagher and Robinson insist, was to tie as much of the world as possible into the British economy. At times, these economic relations came to require formal political control by the mother country; at other times, "informal empire," with independent countries dependent upon British trade and investment, was sufficient.*

This influential and controversial article is especially significant to the Marxist historiography of the period. It reinforces the view of Marxists that the marketplace is not a neutral gathering-ground but an instrument of domination, as in Gallagher and Robinson's insistence that free trade, as well as colonialism, is an imperialist tool. It is, more broadly, a good example of an analysis which links economic trends to political outcomes.

I

. . . The most striking fact about British history in the nineteenth century, as Seeley pointed out, is that it is the history of an expanding society. The exports of capital and manufactures, the migration of citizens, the dissemination of the English language, ideas and constitutional forms, were all of them radiations of the social energies of the British peoples. Between 1812 and 1914 over twenty million persons emigrated from the British Isles, and nearly 70 per cent of them went outside the Empire. Between 1815 and 1880, it is estimated, £1,187,000,000 in credit had accumulated abroad, but no more than one-sixth was placed in the formal empire. Even by 1913, something less than half of the £3,975,000,000 of foreign investment lay inside the Empire. Similarly, in no year of the century did the Empire buy much more than one-third of Britain's exports. The basic fact is that British industrialization caused an ever-extending and intensifying development of overseas regions. Whether they were formally British or not, was a secondary consideration.

Imperialism, perhaps, may be defined as a sufficient political function of this process of integrating new regions into the expanding economy; its character is largely decided by the various and changing relationships between the political and economic elements of expansion in any particular region and time. Two qualifications must be made. First, imperialism may be only indirectly connected with economic integration in that it sometimes extends beyond areas of economic development, but acts for their strategic protection. Secondly, although imperialism is a function of economic expansion, it is not a necessary function. Whether imperialist phenomena show themselves or not, is determined not only by the factors of economic expansion, but equally by the political and social organization of the regions brought into the orbit of the expansive society, and also by the world situation in general.

It is only when the polities of these new regions fail to provide satisfactory conditions for commercial or strategic integration and when their relative weakness allows, that power is used imperialistically to adjust those conditions. Economic expansion, it is true, will tend to flow into the regions of maximum opportunity, but maximum opportunity depends as much upon political considerations of security as upon questions of profit. Consequently, in any particular region, if economic opportunity seems large but political security small, then full absorption into the extending economy tends to be frustrated until power is exerted upon the state in question. Conversely, in proportion as satisfactory political frameworks are brought into being in this way, the frequency of imperialist intervention lessens and imperialist control is correspondingly relaxed. It may be suggested that this willingness to limit the use of paramount power to establishing security for trade is the distinctive feature of the British imperialism of free trade in the nineteenth century, in contrast to the mercantilist use of power to obtain commercial supremacy and monopoly through political possession.

On this hypothesis the phasing of British expansion or imperialism is not likely to be chronological. Not all regions will reach the same level of economic integration at any one time; neither will all regions need the same type of political control at any one time. As the British industrial revolution grew, so new markets and sources of supply were linked to it at different times, and the degree of imperialist action accompanying that process varied accordingly. Thus mercantilist techniques of formal empire were being employed to develop India in the mid-Victorian age at the same time as informal techniques of free trade were being used in Latin America for the same purpose. It is for this reason that attempts to make phases of imperialism correspond directly to phases in the economic growth of the metropolitan economy are likely to prove in vain. The fundamental continuity of British expansion is only obscured by arguing that changes in the terms of trade or in the character of British exports necessitated a sharp change in the process.

From this vantage point the many-sided expansion of British industrial society can be viewed as a whole of which both the formal and informal empires are only parts. Both of them then appear as variable political functions of the extending pattern of overseas trade, investment, migration and culture. If this is accepted, it follows that formal and informal empire are essentially interconnected and to some extent interchangeable. Then not only is the old, legalistic, narrow idea of empire unsatisfactory, but so is the old idea of informal empire as a separate, non-political category of expansion. A concept of informal empire which fails to bring out the underlying unity between it and the formal empire is sterile. Only within the total framework of expansion is nineteenth-century empire intelligible. So we are faced with the task of re-fashioning the interpretations resulting from defective concepts of organic constitutional empire on the one hand and Hobsonian 'imperialism' on the other.

The economic importance—even the pre-eminence—of informal empire in this period has been stressed often enough. What was overlooked was the inter-relation of its economic and political arms; how political action aided the growth of commercial supremacy, and how this supremacy in turn strengthened political influence. In other words, it is the politics as well as the economics of the informal empire which we have to include in the account. Historically, the relationship between these two factors has been both subtle and complex. It has been by no means a simple case of the use of gunboats to demolish a recalcitrant state in the cause of British trade. The type of political lien between the expanding economy and its formal or informal dependencies, as might be expected, has been flexible. In practice it has tended to vary with the economic value of the territory, the strength of its political structure, the readiness of its rulers to collaborate with British commercial or strategic purposes, the ability of the native society to undergo economic change without external control, the extent to which domestic and foreign political situations permitted British intervention, and, finally, how far European rivals allowed British policy a free hand.

Accordingly, the political lien has ranged from a vague, informal paramountcy to outright political possession; and, consequently, some of these dependent territories have been formal colonies whereas others have not. The difference between formal and informal empire has not been one of fundamental nature but of degree. The ease with which a region has slipped from one status to the other helps to confirm this. Within the last two hundred years, for example, India has passed from informal to formal association with the United Kingdom and, since World War II, back to an informal connexion. Similarly, British West Africa has passed through the first two stages and seems to-day likely to follow India into the third.

II

Let us now attempt, tentatively, to use the concept of the totality of British expansion described above to restate the main themes of the history of modern British expansion. We have seen that interpretations of this process fall into contradictions when based upon formal political criteria alone. If expansion both formal and informal is examined as a single process, will these contradictions disappear?

The growth of British industry made new demands upon British policy. It necessitated linking undeveloped areas with British foreign trade and, in so doing, moved the political arm to force an entry into markets closed by the power of foreign monopolies.

British policy, as Professor Harlow has shown, was active in this way before the American colonies had been lost, but its greatest opportunities came during the Napoleonic Wars. The seizure of the French and Spanish West Indies, the filibustering expedition to Buenos Aires in 1806, the taking of Java in 1811, were all efforts to break into new regions and to tap new resources by means of political action. But the policy went further than simple house-breaking, for once the door was opened and British imports with their political implications were pouring in, they might stop the door from being shut again. Raffles, for example, temporarily broke the Dutch monopoly of the spice trade in Java and opened the island to free trade. Later, he began the informal British paramountcy over the Malacca trade routes and the Malay peninsula by founding Singapore. In South America, at the same time, British policy was aiming at indirect political hegemony over new regions for the purposes of trade. The British navy carried the Portuguese royal family to Brazil after the breach with Napoleon, and the

British representative there extorted from his grateful clients the trade treaty of 1810 which left British imports paying a lower tariff than the goods of the mother country. The thoughtful stipulation was added 'that the Present Treaty shall be unlimited in point of duration, and that the obligations and conditions expressed or implied in it shall be perpetual and immutable.'[1]

From 1810 onwards this policy had even better chances in Latin America, and they were taken. British governments sought to exploit the colonial revolutions to shatter the Spanish trade monopoly, and to gain informal supremacy and the good will which would all favour British commercial penetration. As Canning put it in 1824, when he had clinched the policy of recognition: 'Spanish America is free and if we do not mismanage our affairs sadly she is *English*.'[2] Canning's underlying object was to clear the way for a prodigious British expansion by creating a new and informal empire, not only to redress the Old World balance of power but to restore British influence in the New. He wrote triumphantly: 'The thing is done . . . the Yankees will shout in triumph: but it is they who lose most by our decision . . . the United States have gotten the start of us in vain; and we link once more America to Europe.'[3] It would be hard to imagine a more spectacular example of a policy of commercial hegemony in the interests of high politics, or of the use of informal political supremacy in the interests of commercial enterprise. Characteristically, the British recognition of Buenos Aires, Mexico and Colombia took the form of signing commercial treaties with them.

In both the formal and informal·dependencies in the mid-Victorian age there was much effort to open the continental interiors and to extend the British influence inland from the ports and to develop the hinterlands. The general strategy of this development was to convert these areas into complementary satellite economies, which would provide raw materials and food for Great Britain, and also provide widening markets for its manufactures. This was the period, the orthodox interpretation would have us believe, in which the political arm of expansion was dormant or even withered. In fact, that alleged inactivity is seen to be a delusion if we take into account the development in the informal aspect. Once entry had been forced into Latin America, China and the Balkans, the task was to encourage stable governments as good investment risks, just as in weaker or unsatisfactory states it was considered necessary to coerce them into more co-operative attitudes.

In Latin America, however, there were several false starts. The impact of British expansion in Argentina helped to wreck the constitution and throw the people into civil war, since British trade caused the sea-board to prosper while the back lands were exploited and lagged behind. The investment crash of 1827 and the successful revolt of the pampas people against Buenos Aires blocked further British expansion, and the rise to power of General Rosas ruined the institutional framework which Canning's strategy had so brilliantly set up. The new regime was uncooperative and its designs on Montevideo caused chaos around the Rio de la Plata, which led to that great commercial artery being closed to enterprise. All this provoked a series of direct British interventions during the 1840's in efforts to get trade moving again on the river, but in fact it was the attractive force of British trade itself, more than the informal imperialist action of British governments, which in this case restored the situation by removing Rosas from power.

British policy in Brazil ran into peculiar troubles through its tactless attempt to browbeat the Government of Rio de Janeiro into abolishing slavery. British political effectiveness was weakened, in spite of economic predominance, by the interference of humanitarian pressure groups in England. Yet the economic control over Brazil was strengthened after 1856 by the building of the railways; these—begun, financed and operated by British companies—were encouraged by generous concessions from the government of Brazil.

With the development of railways and steamships, the economies of the leading Latin American states were at last geared successfully to the world economy. Once their exports had begun to climb and foreign investment had been attracted, a rapid rate of economic growth was feasible. Even in the 1880's Argentina could double her exports and increase sevenfold her foreign indebtedness while the world price of meat and wheat was falling. By 1913, in Latin America as a whole, informal imperialism had become so important for the British economy that £999,000,000, over a quarter of the total investment abroad, was invested in that region.

But this investment, as was natural, was concentrated in such countries as Argentina and Brazil whose governments (even after the Argentine default of 1891) had collaborated in the general task of British expansion. For this reason there was no need for brusque or peremptory interventions on behalf of British interests. For once their economies had become sufficiently dependent on foreign trade, the classes whose prosperity was drawn from that trade normally worked themselves in local politics to preserve the local political conditions needed for it. British intervention, in any case, became more difficult once the United States could make other powers take the Monroe doctrine seriously. The slackening in active intervention in the affairs of the most reliable members of the commercial empire was matched by the abandonment of direct political control over those regions of formal empire which were successful enough to receive self-government. But in Latin America, British governments still intervened, when necessary, to protect British interests in the more backward states; there was intervention on behalf of the bond holders in Guatemala and Colombia in the 'seventies, as in Mexico and Honduras between 1910 and 1914.

The types of informal empire and the situations it attempted to exploit were as various as the success which it achieved. Although commercial and capital penetration tended to lead to political co-operation and hegemony, there are striking exceptions. In the United States, for example, British business turned the cotton South into a colonial economy, and the British investor hoped to do the same with the Mid-West. But the political strength of the country stood in his way. It was impossible to stop American industrialization, and the industrialized sections successfully campaigned for tariffs, despite the opposition of those sections which depended on the British trade connexion. In the same way, American political strength thwarted British attempts to establish Texas, Mexico and Central America as informal dependencies.

Conversely, British expansion sometimes failed, if it gained political supremacy without effecting a successful commercial penetration. There were spectacular exertions of British policy in China, but they did little to produce new customers. Britain's political hold upon China failed to break down Chinese economic self-sufficiency. The Opium War of 1840, the renewal of war in 1857, widened the inlets for British trade but they did not get Chinese exports moving. Their main effect was an unfortunate one from the British point of view, for such foreign pressures put Chinese society under great strains as the Taiping Rebellion unmistakably showed. It is important to note that this weakness was regarded in London as an embarrassment, and not as a lever for extracting further concessions. In fact, the British worked to prop up the tottering Peking regime, for as Lord Clarendon put it in 1870, 'British interests in China are strictly commercial, or at all events only so far political as they may be for the protection of commerce.'[4] The value of this self-denial became clear in the following decades when the Pekin government, threatened with a scramble for China, leaned more and more on the diplomatic support of the honest British broker.

The simple recital of these cases of economic expansion, aided and abetted by political action in one form or other, is enough to expose the inadequacy of the conventional theory that free trade could dispense with empire. We have seen that it did not do so. Economic expansion in the mid-Victorian age was matched by a corresponding political expansion which has been overlooked because it could not be seen by that study of maps which, it has been said, drives sane men mad. It is absurd to deduce from the harmony between London and the colonies of white settlement in the mid-Victorian age any British reluctance to intervene in the fields of British interests. The warships at Canton are as much a part of the period as responsible government for Canada; the battlefields of the Punjab are as real as the abolition of suttee.

Far from being an era of 'indifference', the mid-Victorian years were the decisive stage in the history of British expansion overseas, in that the combination of commercial penetration and political influence allowed the United Kingdom to command those economies which could be made to fit best into her own. A variety of techniques adapted to diverse conditions and beginning at different dates were employed to effect this domination. A paramountcy was set up in Malaya centred on Singapore; a suzerainty over much of West Africa reached out from the port of Lagos and was backed up by the African squadron. On the east coast of Africa British influence at Zanzibar, dominant thanks to the exertions of Consul Kirk, placed the heritage of Arab command on the mainland at British disposal.

But perhaps the most common political technique of British expansion was the treaty of free trade and friendship made with or imposed upon a weaker state. The treaties with Persia of 1836 and 1857, the Turkish treaties of 1838 and 1861, the Japanese treaty of 1858, the favours extracted from Zanzibar, Siam and Morocco, the hundreds of anti-slavery treaties signed with crosses by African chiefs—all these treaties enabled the British government to carry forward trade with these regions.

Even a valuable trade with one region might give place to a similar trade with another which could be more easily coerced politically. The Russian grain trade, for example, was extremely useful to Great Britain. But the Russians' refusal to hear of free trade, and the British inability to force them into it, caused efforts to develop the grain of the Ottoman empire instead, since British pressure at Constantinople had been able to hustle the Turk into a liberal trade policy. The dependence of the commercial thrust upon the political arm resulted in a general tendency for British trade to follow the invisible flag of informal empire.

Since the mid-Victorian age now appears as a time of large-scale expansion, it is necessary to revise our estimate of the so-called 'imperialist' era as well. Those who accept the concept of 'economic imperialism' would have us believe that the annexations at the end of the century represented a sharp break in policy, due to the decline of free trade, the need to protect foreign investment, and the conversion of statesmen to the need for unlimited land-grabbing. All these explanations are questionable. In the first place, the tariff policy of Great Britain did not change. Again, British foreign investment was no new thing and most of it was still flowing into regions outside the formal empire. Finally the statesmens' conversion to the policy of extensive annexation was partial, to say the most of it. Until 1887, and only occasionally after that date, party leaders showed little more enthusiasm for extending British rule than the mid-Victorians. Salisbury was infuriated by the 'superficial philanthropy' and 'roguery' of the 'fanatics' who advocated expansion.[5]

When pressed to aid the missions in Nyasaland in 1888, he retorted: 'It is not our duty to do it. We should be risking tremendous sacrifices for a very doubtful gain.'[6] After 1888, Salisbury, Rosebery and Chamberlain accepted the scramble for Africa as a painful but unavoidable necessity which arose from a threat of foreign expansion and the irrepressible tendency of trade to overflow the bounds of empire, dragging the government into new and irksome commitments. But it was not until 1898 that they were sufficiently confident to undertake the reconquest of so vital a region as the Sudan.

Faced with the prospect of foreign acquisitions of tropical territory hitherto opened to British merchants, the men in London resorted to one expedient after another to evade the need of formal expansion and still uphold British paramountcy in those regions. British policy in the late, as in the mid-Victorian period preferred informal means of extending imperial supremacy rather than direct rule. Throughout the two alleged periods the extension of British rule was a last resort—and it is this preference which has given rise to the many 'anti-expansionist' remarks made by Victorian ministers. What these much quoted expressions obscure, is that in practice mid-Victorian as well as late-Victorian policy makers did not refuse to extend the protection of formal rule over British interests when informal methods had failed to give security. The fact that informal techniques were more often sufficient for this purpose in the circumstances of the mid-century than in the later period when the foreign challenge to British supremacy intensified, should not be allowed to disguise the basic continuity of policy. Throughout, British governments worked to establish and maintain British paramountcy by whatever means best suited the circumstances of their diverse regions of interest. The aims of the mid-Victorians were no more 'anti-imperialist' than their successors', though they were more often able to achieve them informally; and the late-Victorians were no more 'imperialist' than their predecessors, even though they were driven to annex more often. British policy followed the principle of extending control informally if possible and formally if necessary. To label the one method 'anti-imperialist' and the other 'imperialist', is to ignore the fact that whatever the method British interests were steadily safeguarded and extended. The usual summing up of the policy of the free trade empire as 'trade not rule' should read 'trade with informal control if possible; trade with rule when necessary'. This statement of the continuity of policy disposes of the over-simplified explanation of involuntary expansion inherent in the orthodox interpretation based on the discontinuity between the two periods.

Thus Salisbury as well as Gladstone, Knutsford as well as Derby and Ripon, in the so-called age of 'imperialism', exhausted all informal expedients to secure regions of British trade in Africa before admitting that further annexations were unavoidable. One device was to obtain guarantees of free trade and access as a reward for recognizing foreign territorial claims, a device which had the advantage of saddling foreign governments with the liability of rule whilst allowing Britons the commercial advantage. This was done in the Anglo-Portuguese Treaty of 1884, the Congo Arrangement of 1885, and the Anglo-German Agreement over East Africa in 1886. Another device for evading the extension of rule was the exclusive sphere of influence or protectorate recognized by foreign powers. Although originally these imposed no liability for pacifying or administering such regions, with changes in international law they did so after 1885. The granting of charters to private companies between 1881 and 1889, authorizing them to administer and finance new regions under imperial licence, marked the transition from informal to formal methods of backing British commercial expansion. Despite these attempts at 'imperialism on the cheap', the foreign challenge to British paramountcy in tropical Africa and the comparative absence there of large-scale, strong, indigenous political organizations which had served informal expansion so well elsewhere, eventually dictated the switch to formal rule.

One principle then emerges plainly: it is only when and where informal political means failed to provide the framework of security for British enterprise (whether commercial, or philanthropic or simply strategic) that the question of establishing formal empire arose. In satellite regions peopled by European stock, in Latin America or Canada, for instance, strong governmental structures grew up; in totally non-European areas, on the other hand, expansion unleashed such disruptive forces upon the indigenous structures that they tended to wear out and even collapse with use. This tendency in many cases accounts for the extension of informal British responsibility and eventually for the change from indirect to direct control.

It was in Africa that this process of transition manifested itself most strikingly during the period after 1880. Foreign loans and predatory bankers by the 1870's had wrecked Egyptian finances and were tearing holes in the Egyptian political fabric. The Anglo-French dual financial control, designed to safeguard the foreign bondholders and to restore Egypt as a good risk, provoked anti-European feeling. With the revolt of Arabi Pasha in 1881, the Khedive's government could serve no longer to secure either the all-important Canal or the foreign investors' pound of flesh.

The motives for the British occupation of 1882 were confused and varied: the desire, evident long before Disraeli's purchase of shares, to dominate the Canal; the interests of the bondholders; and the over-anxiety to forestall any foreign power, especially France, from taking advantage of the prevailing anarchy in Egypt to interpose its power across the British road to India. Nearly all Gladstone's Cabinet admitted the necessity of British intervention, although for different reasons, and, in order to hold together his distracted ministry, the Prime Minister agreed.

The British expedition was intended to restore a stable Egyptian government under the ostensible rule of the Khedive and inside the orbit of informal British influence. When this was achieved, the army, it was intended, should be withdrawn. But the expedition had so crushed the structure of Egyptian rule that no power short of direct British force could make it a viable and trustworthy instrument of informal hegemony and development. Thus the Liberal Government following its plan, which had been hastily evolved out of little more than ministerial disagreements, drifted into the prolonged occupation of Egypt it was intent on avoiding. In fact, the occupying power became directly responsible for the defence, the debts and development of the country. The perverse effect of British policy was gloomily summed up by Gladstone: 'We have done our Egyptian business and we are an Egyptian government.'[7] Egypt, then, is a striking example of an informal strategy misfiring due to the undermining of the satellite state by investment and by pseudo-nationalist reaction against foreign influence.

The Egyptian question, in so far as it was closely bound with the routes to India and the defence of the Indian empire iteself, was given the highest priority by British policy in the 'eighties and 'nineties. In order to defend the spinal cord of British trade and empire, tropical African and Pacific claims were repeatedly sacrificed as pawns in the higher game. In 1884, for example, the Foreign Office decided that British vulnerability in Egypt made it unwise to compete with foreign powers in the opening scramble for West Africa; and it was therefore proposed '. . . to confine ourselves to securing the utmost possible freedom of trade on that [west] coast, yielding to others the territorial responsibilities . . . and seeking compensation on the east coast . . . where the political future of the country is of real importance to Indian and imperial interests.'[8] British policy was not one of indiscriminate land-grabbing. And, indeed, the British penetration into Uganda and their securing of the rest of the Nile Valley was a highly selective programme, in so far as it surrendered some British West African claims to France and transferred part of East Africa to Germany.

III

Thus the mid-Victorian period now appears as an era of large-scale expansion, and the late-Victorian age does not seem to introduce any significant novelty into that process of expansion. The annexations of vast undeveloped territories, which have been taken as proof that this period alone was the great age of expansion, now pale in significance, at least if our analysis is anywhere near the truth. That the area of direct imperial rule was extended is true, but is it the most important or characteristic development of expansion during this period? The simple historical fact that Africa was the last field of European penetration is not to say that it was the most important; this would be a truism were it not that the main case of the Hobson school is founded on African examples. On the other hand, it is our main contention that the process of expansion had reached its most valuable targets long before the exploitation of so peripheral and marginal a field as tropical Africa. Consequently arguments, founded on the technique adopted in scrambling for Africa, would seem to be of secondary importance.

Therefore, the historian who is seeking to find the deepest meaning of the expansion at the end of the nineteenth century should look not at the mere pegging out of claims in African jungles and bush, but at the successful exploitation of the empire, both formal and informal, which was then coming to fruition in India, in Latin America, in Canada and elsewhere. The main work of imperialism in the so-called expansionist era was in the more intensive development of areas already linked with the world economy, rather than in the extensive annexations of the remaining marginal regions of Africa. The best finds and prizes had already been made; in tropical Africa the imperialists were merely scraping the bottom of the barrel.

NOTES

1. Quoted in A. K. Manchester, *British Pre-eminence in Brazil* (Chapel Hill, 1933), p. 90.
2. Quoted in W. W. Kaufmann, *British Policy and the Independence of Latin America, 1804–1828* (New Haven, 1951), p. 178.
3. Quoted in J. F. Rippy, *Historical Evolution of Hispanic America* (Oxford, 1946), p. 374.
4. Quoted in N. A. Pelcovits, *Old China Hands and the Foreign Office* (New York, 1948), p. 85.
5. Quoted in Cromer, *Modern Egypt* (1980), I, 388.
6. Hansard, 3rd Series, cccxxviii, col. 550, 6 July 1888.
7. Quoted in S. Gwynn and G. M. Tuckwell, *Life of Sir Charles Wentworth Dilke* (1917), II, 46.
8. F.O. Confidential Print (East Africa), 5037.

8. The Returns to U.S. Imperialism, 1890–1929

STANLEY LEBERGOTT

In this article, Stanley Lebergott challenges the radical emphasis on the exploitative effects of international investment. He looks at United States investments in Latin America around the turn of the century and finds that native workers and landowners actually benefited from American economic expansion. Opposition to imperialism came primarily from local business-people unable to compete with American investors. The article demonstrates how economic analysis can help clarify political phenomena. If indeed Lebergott is correct, many conventional interpretations of imperialism must be revised. On the one hand, United States overseas intervention had few direct economic benefits and was thus presumably motivated primarily by such noneconomic goals as national security and national chauvinism. On the other hand, local opposition to American imperialism either had few economic roots or, if it did, it came primarily from local capitalists who resented United States competition.

. . . Imperialism is a moderately ingenious system in which residents of capitalist nations are forced to transfer income among themselves. The transfer mechanism creates extraterritorial impacts as well. It increases workers' incomes in colonial nations. It benefits their landowners. And it strikes down their business monopolies. (That these benefits are conferred on developing nations helps distinguish imperialism from other modes of subsidy to business such as tariff protection.) This process creates an aura of generous patronage in the imperializing power. It stimulates a sense of outrage in the colonial nation. And it speeds the advancement of military leaders in both. Such lively consequences have obscured the primary economic struggle under imperialism—which is not between capitalists from the imperium and oppressed peasants, but between different groups of capitalists.

We focus on foreign investment—Lenin's central component—for the United States from 1890 to 1929. Part I considers how decisive such investment was for prolonging the life of U.S. capitalism. Part II looks at two specific interventions—Panama and Cuba—in terms of their overall economic profitability. Part III, taking for granted the unwisdom of U.S. interventions, goes on to consider the economic impact of U.S. foreign investment on nations abroad. What did such investments do to returns to Latin American labor, landowners and entrepreneurs?

I

Between the Civil War and 1897 American foreign investment rose from a mere $75 million to $685 million; it then rose by nearly $20 billion from 1897 to 1929. "Under the old capitalism," Lenin wrote, "the export of goods was a most typical feature. Under modern capitalism, when monopolies prevail, the export of capital has become the typical feature."[1] Rosa Luxemburg declared, "Imperialism is the political expression of the accumulation of capital in its competitive struggle for what remains still open of the non-capitalist environment."[2]

The increases in U.S. foreign investment were indeed impressive. But most numbers for continental economies look big, whether for the United States or China. How do they look when dimensioned against the entire flow of U.S. investment? Of all U.S. investment from 1869 to 1897, the foreign share accounted for 1 percent; and from 1900 to 1929, the heyday of marine intervention, it accounted for only 6 percent. Put another way: From 1900 to 1929 the entire increase of U.S. foreign investment all over the globe did not equal the increased investment in California alone.

Did so small a foreign commitment really offer a vent for surplus capital? Was it indeed the *unum porro necessarium* that enabled U.S. capitalism to create its twentieth-century hegemony?

Any approach as comprehensive as Marxism-Leninism deals comprehensively with capitalism. It does not offer a theory of Macy's profitability, or Gimbel's, or even United Fruit's. It deals with the complex, contradictory vastness of capitalism. That theory implies that U.S. investment abroad during 1890–1929 was critical in propping up the overall profit rate on U.S. capital. If so, it should have affected that rate significantly. But U.S. overseas investments from 1890 to 1929 pushed the rate of return on U.S. capital from a bit over 4.8 percent to a bit under 4.9 percent. Did so tiny an increase stave off the inevitable collapse of capitalism? Or change its character?

Most U.S. industries didn't bother to invest abroad. The aggregate impact on the profitability of the U.S. investment was small. What did occur was the seizure of lush investment opportunities in a handful of sectors. Which industries were involved? Cleona Lewis's data on U.S.

investments abroad offer us a guide. Her rich detail indicates that U.S. firms made substantial investments abroad in several industry categories. For only three of these—agriculture, manufacturing, and metals—was the ratio of foreign-to-U.S. investment more than a tenth of 1 percent. (Nor did ratios of foreign-to-domestic investment even reach 2 percent for these categories.)

For five industry/product groups, an important (significant?) ratio of foreign-to-U.S. investment appears.

1. Bananas: There were no domestic sources. Latin America provided the entire supply.
2. Sugar: All foreign sources provided about one fourth in 1897 and three fourths by 1929.
3. Copper: The share of foreign to total U.S. copper mine investment rose to perhaps 20 percent around 1900 and continued to be very substantial.
4. Oil: The foreign share rose from 3 percent in 1897 to 7 percent in 1929.
5. Precious metals: Foreign sources accounted for under 5 percent of U.S. investment.

Is there a common denominator to these concentrations of increase in U.S. foreign investment? Precious metal investment, indulged in by states from ancient Greece and the Inca empire to Soviet Russia, hardly requires any view on the theory of imperialism. The major categories—bananas, sugar, copper and oil—however, may be linked to market opportunities involving the trusts that developed in the period 1889–1900.

For bananas and sugar, U.S. trusts integrated vertically. They thereby protected themselves against combinations at the production level that might skim off their monopoly profits. By investing in banana plantations United Fruit assured its supply, and prevented any combination against it at either the farm or transport level. The American Sugar Refining Company actually had been confronted by a developing alliance of American sugar producers. U.S. beet sugar producers had expanded their output under the happy influence of the McKinley tariff. They then joined with the Louisiana cane sugar producers to block the Cuban Reciprocity Treaty. If successful they could then have raised tariffs against both Hawaiian and foreign sugar, thereby forcing the trust to divide its monopoly profits with a patriotic domestic cartel. By helping to keep the reciprocity door open, then, the trust guaranteed its supply of sugar and at the cost of only a minimum investment in Cuba by the trust itself.

Amalgamated's 30 percent stock price increase from 1898 to 1899–1901 had notified many investors of the potentially vast profits in copper. That point was italicized by the jump in its market yield (from about 2 percent in 1899 to 8 percent in the next two years). Moreover, dividends of the Michigan companies in 1899–1901 ran almost 50 percent above their 1898 level. Such prospects led both Morgan and the Guggenheims to invest heavily south of the border. They also induced other ardent investors—among them, Hearst, Frick, Haggin, and Ryan—to develop overseas copper mines. (Perhaps a more prudent trust might not have ignored the Secretan fiasco.)

It would require a more comprehensive review to determine how largely the actions of the new trusts were responsible for foreign investment in the turn-of-the-century years. For present purposes it may suffice to indicate that overseas investments by Americans in the period 1900 to 1929 do not seem particularly explicable by any general surplus of funds seeking overseas outlets. What characterized U.S. foreign investment over these decades was, instead, the seizing of the local opportunities here and there as avid entrepreneurs saw profit potential. These were pursued with no less zest than opportunities that appeared in North Dakota or New Mexico. In addition, attention concentrated on a few sectors (bananas, sugar and copper) where U.S. monopolies tried to protect future profit flows, or other entrepreneurs attempted to menace them.

II

Cuba

In April 1901 the occupying forces of the United States established a $1,000 prize to be known as "The Department of Agriculture stakes for Cuban bred horses and mares." General Wood, the American proconsul, was "acceding to the request of the 'Cuba Jockey club' . . . [for] prizes at the horse races to be held at Buenavista, Havana course." And he expressed his fond hope "that the stakes will always be considered as the 'blue ribbon' of the Cuban turf."

This improbable but thoughtful gesture symbolized how varied were opportunities seized by special interests as they utilized the power and finance of the military government for their benefit. But what major U.S. economic interests benefited?

We take as our point of departure the example given in Lenin's succinct summary:

Finance capital, concentrated in a few hands and exercising a virtual monopoly, exacts enormous and ever-increasing profits from the floating of companies, issues of stock, state loans, etc., tightens the grip of financial oligarchies and levies tribute upon the whole of society for the benefit of monopolists. Here is one example, taken from a multitude of others, of the methods of 'business' of the American trusts . . . the Sugar Trust set up monopoly prices on the market, which secured it such profits that it could pay 10 percent dividend on capital "watered" sevenfold.[3]

Imperialism centrally involved foreign investment. Mere market possibilities were perhaps primary in earlier stages of capitalism, but, Lenin states, had taken a secondary position under imperialism. Indeed a later review, by the major anti-imperialist historian of "our Cuban colony," noted that American exports to Cuba actually had fallen after the Spanish American War "as compared with those of Great Britain, France and Germany. . . . Our occupation had not promoted Cuba as a market for goods. . . . It is a common notion that people with specific economic interests beset legislators and governments with pressure to do things that will make them money. No doubt many of them do. Others need to be aroused to the work by those governments. American manufacturers in many states in 1902 and 1903 were far from anxious about export markets, or about a privileged position."[4] But pressure by Roosevelt and unspecified "industry" finally brought the Congress to pass the Reciprocity Treaty. Of all the economic interest groups to be advantaged by this legislation, confirming the returns from the Cuban invasion, presumably the trust singled out by Lenin stood foremost.

Now what did the war and the Reciprocity Treaty do to the Sugar Trust and its profits? Did they increase the demand for sugar, thereby benefiting the trust? In 1899 U.S. consumers poured $190 million worth of sugar into their coffee, tea, and lemonade and bought a further $27 million to sweeten confectionery and soft drinks. The war, therefore, had not created the consumer's sweet tooth. Could it have shifted the demand curve for sugar in any significant fashion? There is no reason to think that it intensified the demand for Moxie. Nor did it increase the demand for other sugar products.

Did the war strengthen trust control of the U.S. market? As a tough enterprise the trust was already screwing as much out of the consumer as it could, war or no war. Its powers as a trust did not depend on either the Cubans or the war.

Gains to the Sugar Trust, therefore, must have been not on the demand but on the supply side. Jenks has written:

On the face of the matter, the Reciprocity Treaty made a gift of .337 cents a pound on Cuban sugar to somebody from the United States Treasury. . . . (By 1910 . . . this benefit amounted to a total of twenty million dollars.) No one seems then to have known exactly . . . where the .337 cents went. Most of it has gone . . . either to the ultimate consumers in the United States, or to the Atlantic refiners.[5]

But Jenks's list includes those who did *not* benefit from the Reciprocity Treaty more surely than those who did.

Neither the war nor the treaty changed the supply of sugar. The Dutch were still producing in the East Indies. French, German, and American beet sugar producers were still producing. And the Hawaiians and Cubans were still producing. What the treaty did was award the Cubans a preferred market position. It cut the tariff margin between the price at which the Cubans sold and the price the American buyer had to pay.

If the American Sugar Refining Company had been the sole American purchaser of Cuban sugars it could have seized most, or all, of the reciprocity reduction. In fact, eight independent refining firms (some located on the west coast) bought over one third of U.S. raw sugar. Moreover, transport and refining costs were not changed by any of this. Hence, the benefit should have accrued almost wholly to Cuban producers. American taxpayers had simply begun to make an annual gift to Cuban sugar producers.

This is precisely and explicitly what was intended. In the authoritative words of Elihu Root, that gift permitted Cubans "to live," for the war's destruction had largely cut Cuban sugar production, and thereby Cuban incomes. Root declared:

> The peace of Cuba is necessary to the peace of the United States; the independence of Cuba is necessary to the safety of the United States. ... The same considerations which led to the war with Spain now require that a commercial agreement be made under which Cuba can live.[6]

The impact was immediate. Between 1900 and 1903 Cuban exports to the United States tripled, rising by 1.7 billion pounds. Concurrently, U.S. imports of Dutch East Indies sugar fell by 0.3 billion pounds, and imports of European (beet) sugar fell by 0.6 billion.

The Treaty, finest flower of American intervention in Cuba, had benefited neither the American consumer nor the Sugar Trust. It raised the gross receipts of Cuban sugar producers. These in turn had to pay increased rents to owners of Cuban land. For the price of the land had immediately risen, capitalizing the value of the delightful new tariff advantage. Hence the true beneficiaries were the owners of Cuban resources. As one Cuban planter told Congress, since the average developed field yielded 2½ tons of sugar, "if you took off the duty" (of about $34 a ton) you would give a bounty of about $75 to "every acre of available sugar land in Cuba." The continuing gift from the American taxpayer, therefore, increased the value of Cuban land. That capital gain was unquestionably skimmed off by landowners in subsequent years whenever they sold or rented their land.

Who owned the land in 1899, just before the war, and thereby became prime beneficiaries of the treaty? Not the Trust. Indeed all Americans taken together controlled only 16 percent of the Cuban sugar crop as late as 1902.

The benefits of that advance could, of course, have been skimmed off if buyers had foreseen the passage of the treaty and had snapped up the land in advance. However, the Cuban mortgage law was changed in 1899 to prevent forced transfers of land in those turbulent times. And it kept the land in the hands of its pre-invasion owners. The land in 1902 remained "very largely in the hands of the people who had it on the list of January, 1899." It was, therefore, primarily the landowners as of 1899 who reaped the benefit of the revolution, invasion, and Reciprocity Treaty. And it was the owners of Cuban land not already in sugar who reaped the further benefits of continuing reciprocity as the sale of Cuban sugar in American markets expanded and expanded.

The prime economic beneficiaries of the Spanish-American War, in sum, were the Spaniards and Cubans who owned Cuban sugar land at the start of the war. The generous donor of benefits to these gentlemen turned out to be—the American taxpayer. For the latter's taxes had to make up for U.S. tariff revenue foregone by the Reciprocity Treaty.

The Panama Canal

"I took the Canal," declared Theodore Roosevelt at Berkeley. Discussion of American imperialism has been entangled ever since in this much (and appropriately) quoted declaration. But Roosevelt had a very high view of his prowess. One remembers the sardonic title Mr. Dooley gave to the President's egotistic memoir of the Spanish-American War: "Alone in Cuba." Roosevelt's intervention in Panama may well have been outrageous yet not as essential in detaching Panama from Colombia as he implied.

Two climactic events marked the outbreak of American intervention. First was the resumption in 1902 by Panamanians of the revolution that had been going on since 1899. Second was a sequence of volcanic explosions in Nicaragua, Martinique, and St. Vincent in 1902. That sequence had effectively removed the Nicaraguan route as an alternative for the canal across the Isthmus. Colombia immediately recognized, and decided to monetize, its monopoly of available routes. With considerable moderation it demanded only $5 million above the $10 million provided for in the Treaty to which it had already tentatively agreed. Hay responded with asperity, informing the Colombians (in July 1903) that "no additional payment . . . can hope for approval by the United States Senate" and that any amendment whatever "would imperil the treaty."[7] Roosevelt (in his message of January 1904) restated the U.S. position: "we would give the terms that we had offered and no other; . . . if such terms were not agreed to, we would enter into an agreement with Panama direct."[8] This threatening attitude assisted those Panamanians who wished to resume their revolution.

The subsequent, 1902, revolution guaranteed the United States a harvest of ill will. Moreover, it failed to save the United States the additional Colombian money claim, which irritated the impatient president. For in 1921 the United States paid the $25 million anyway. Such brilliance in achieving the worst of both worlds is more explicable by military than by commercial motivation. As a British engineer then working for Colombia wrote: "The Canal cannot be a paying concern for any other country except the United States, and for the United States it is a paying concern not from a commercial standpoint—it will therein be a loser—but on account of its Navy."[9] After the Panamanian Revolution, the Navy's (unofficial) chief strategist, the President, could be confident that in the next war the USS Oregon need not be sent around Cape Horn before it could bring its weight to bear on the enemy.

Granting the military interests, what of the economic ones? U.S. taxpayers had made handsome expenditures for the Canal by the end of 1929 (see Table 1).

What private economic interests benefited from this sequence of gifts by the American taxpayer? The U.S. payment of $10 million (by the Act of 1902) to the New Panama Canal Company benefited few Americans. Most stockholders were French. (Of course, the Colombian government, as a major stockholder in the Canal Company, accepted its share of the $10 million—together with the $25 million the U.S. apologetically offered in 1921). Hence the revolution in Panama redistributed wealth among Americans (from taxpayers to W. N. Cromwell and associates)—and gave some gifts to Frenchmen and Colombians.

TABLE I. Panama Canal: Costs and Revenues to U.S. Taxpayers, 1909–1929

ITEM	(MILLION DOLLARS)
Costs	
1. Construction outlays, 1902–1923	388
2. Construction interest, 1902–1920	155
3. Construction interest, 1921–1929	135
4. Payment to Colombia, 1921	25
5. "National defense" construction to 1924	113
Operating Revenues	
6. Revenues from Canal operation (net)	110
Costs minus Revenue to 1929	706

Sources: (1) *Annual Report of the Governor of the Panama Canal*, 1924, Table 3; (2) Interest compounded at 3 percent on the appropriations listed in the 1924 *Report*, Table 3. (This sum necessarily exceeds the "interest on construction funds" shown in the 1942 *Report*, p. 138.) (3) *Report*, 1942, p. 144; (4) Norman J. Padelford, *The Panama Canal in Peace and War* (New York, 1942), p. 302; (5) *Annual Report*, 1924, p. 68. (6) *Report*, 1929, p. 125.

What about American shippers? Building the Canal tended to cut the real cost of ocean transport. Who then benefited? Was it the U.S. shipper? The Hay-Pauncefote Treaty of 1901 had stipulated that the Canal "shall be open to all vessels . . . on terms of entire equality . . . [with] no discrimination . . . [on] charges of traffic."[10] British ocean shippers, therefore, plus German, Dutch, and others, gained quite as much as American shippers—without their governments contributing one cent. American ocean shipping firms did benefit when some U.S. coast-to-coast traffic shifted its route, but only in the same proportion as American railroads were injured.

Shortly before the revolution in Panama a prominent Colombian lawyer estimated that the United States would profit by precisely $1,186,537,377 from the proposed Canal concession. Who could deny (or demonstrate) that American military interests, as divined by Admiral Mahan, did indeed benefit in that amount, give or take a few dollars? That American economic interests benefited is far less likely. Americans had provided some three quarters of a billion dollars to build and run the Canal to 1929 (plus a great deal more thereafter). They therefore contributed an international public work that benefited shippers throughout the world, that gave equal advantage to any nation that chose to use the Canal. Had their money been well spent? As far as economic advantage is concerned, the gains are hardly obvious. They certainly were secondary to the moral drive described so sympathetically by Roosevelt's great Democratic opponent (after the United States had taken the Canal Zone): "We are a sort of pure air blowing in world politics. . . ."[11]

III

What impact did American imperialism have on factor returns in Latin American nations in these years—the wages paid to labor, rents paid to landowners, interest rates paid to lenders, and entrepreneurial incomes? Since it is these returns that do much to determine the well being of those who work and/or invest for a living, it is somewhat surprising that so little attention has been given explicitly to such a question. Perhaps the most extended discussion appears in the statement that

> . . . foreign investment often had limited benefits for the native population. In some cases it had almost no effect, positive or negative, as where it took place in an enclave. In Peru, the guano industry used European capital, Chinese labor, and foreign markets, hardly involving the local economy at all. In mines and plantations large amounts of local labor were used. Where foreign investors build railroads, they tended to serve the needs of foreign traders. . . .[12]

We can say more than this. The economic consequences of American foreign investment and intervention can be inferred from various sources. We have chosen here to rely chiefly on the *Studies in American Imperialism* that appeared in the late 1920s. Sponsored by the American Fund for Public Service, they represent extended, careful, and tenaciously anti-imperialist studies of American intervention in various Latin American nations. The case that U.S. investment injured labor, peasants, and landowners in Latin America could hardly have been put more persuasively than by these scholarly, and strongly anti-imperialist, writers. What do their studies actually have to say on these points?

Labor

We first turn to labor. The Marxist view is well known. As a recent Chinese textbook on economics states: "Colonies are the most profitable outlets for the capital exports of imperialism. In colonies, the monopoly organizations of the suzerain can exploit and enslave the laboring people more ruthlessly."[13] Kwame Nkrumah found "imperialism is the most degrading exploitation and the most inhuman oppression of the millions of peoples in the colonies." Its purpose: "to squeeze out superprofits."[14] One of many American writers finds that "the workers and peasants in the colonies . . . countries . . . were the most oppressed owing to the fact that their labor was the source of capitalist superprofit." He refers to "the superexploitation of labor through the export of capital."[15]

What of labor in Cuba? How did the American occupation and the Reciprocity Treaty affect Cuban labor? From 1900 to 1903 Cuban cane exports responded to the Treaty by tripling. Now tripling employment with little change in the population could only tend to drive up wages.

The obvious way for new American interests to nullify such pressures would have been to import low-cost contract labor from China. The Americans had done so in Hawaii. The Spaniards had once done so in Cuba. As Machado noted, however, Chinese labor "had been absolutely prohibited" for many years. Moreover, "public sentiment in Cuba would protest against introducing an inferior race, if any attempts were made to abolish the existing law."[16] Did the U.S. military nonetheless impose such action at the behest of new American investors? On the contrary. Both Congress and the Executive sought to make Cuba the home of "the independent farmer and citizen," not of "the coolie": contract labor (largely Chinese) was therefore to be forbidden. In May 1902 the military government dutifully forbade the importation of contract labor. Moreover, when the Reciprocity Treaty was finally passed it required Cuba to enact "immigration laws as rigorous as those of the United States."[17]

Given an expanding U.S. market for Cuban sugar, together with a law forbidding the import of cheap labor, an excess demand for Cuban labor was inevitable. Hence Cuban wage rates tended to rise. Apparently they did rise. In 1900–1901, the average daily farm wage in the major sugar province of Mantanzas was 76¢. By January 1902, according to Colonel Bliss, the island average for common labor was 85½¢ a day, a rise of over 10 percent. The "most inhuman oppression" should have led wage rates, and real income, to decline. The sequence of regulations, treaties, and investment by the American conquerors did not, however, yield such a decline.

What impact did "imperialist" investment have on labor conditions in other Latin American countries? The *Studies in American Imperialism* agree on one central point: American companies paid wages at least equal to those paid by native employers, and the Americans typically offered higher real wages and better working conditions. The studies agree on quite another point, with which the first is often confused: American companies did not pay wages anywhere near as high as the writers would have liked, nor as generous as workers would have preferred. (Nor did they scatter their bounties with a charitable and loving hand.)

Rippy's discussion of Colombia deals primarily with United Fruit. He notes that United Fruit bought most of its bananas from foreman-contractors, who in turn paid piece rates for bunches of bananas. Presumably they paid the same wage rates as those contractors who sold to native entrepreneurs. In his most comprehensive comment Rippy states:

> Indeed, it appears safe to make the general statement that Colombian labor, whenever it is paid a stipulated wage, is better remunerated and granted more sanitary living quarters by foreigners than by natives, but the foreigners probably exact more systematic and strenuous effort. . . . Most of the mining is done by foreign companies who pay their laborers a better wage than they receive from the native capitalists. . . . American construction companies usually . . . [pay] the standard wage paid by the government on construction enterprises under its direct supervision and approximately the standard minimum given by native employers throughout the country. That the minimum wage allowed by the Tropical Oil Company [Standard Oil] and the United Fruit Company is considerably above this amount has already been noted, and it is believed that this is true of most other Yankee employers.[18]

Since United Fruit paid part of the wages in scrip until 1929, it is necessary to check whether the higher real wages they paid were in fact nullified by above-market store prices. Rippy states, however, that just the opposite was true:

> Much of the clothing, food and other supplies consumed by the

laborers is regularly brought into the region by the company. . . . The company store can usually sell supplies more cheaply than they can be bought from the local native merchants, who . . . often, lack(ing) a better source of supply, purchase their ware from the United Fruit Company itself.[19]

Kepner's discussion of the United Fruit Company—primarily in Costa Rica, Guatemala, Honduras, and Colombia—states flatly: "The wages paid by the United Fruit Company before the world economic crisis . . . were high in comparison to money wages paid to agricultural workers elsewhere in Central America.[20]

Knight's discussion of Santo Domingo declares that "Most of the Americans do not mistreat their labor. The complaints on this score in Santo Domingo have been directed mainly against the Italian estates."[21] His comments on wages do not indicate that American enterprises paid below-average wages. His primary focus is on how Haitian immigration depressed Dominican wages.

The Haitian profits by his seasonal move [to Santo Domingo] but his presence has a bad effect on wage levels in Santo Domingo. . . . Official sanitary reports show 70 percent or more of the population of Haiti to be suffering from venereal disease. Malaria is rife, and there are both amoebic and bacillic dysenteries . . . the Dominicans would be glad to dispense with their 100,000 or so of annual Haitian visitors. . . . Cheap imported seasonal labor digs a pit of subsistence wages at the feet of the Dominican worker in the interest of the sugar business.[22]

That both native and American employers allowed (or supported) the government in an open and loosely enforced immigration policy clearly is the center of Knight's concern. Unless foreign firms should be in the business of changing national immigration policy, however, Knight's discussion on labor policy is irrelevant to our focus of interest. Margaret Marsh's study of Bolivia provides a summary comment on wages paid in the metal mines, dominated by the Bolivian Patino interests and somewhat smaller American companies. She notes that the wages paid were "in keeping with" the "scale on which the free Indian throughout the plateau lives, and have been adjusted to a society in which it is possible to hire a fletero to trek seventy-five miles over a period of two and a half days, with a hundred pounds of coca on his back, for from six to eight bolivianos."[23] The bulk of her discussion of labor conditions focuses on conditions of labor in Bolivia that were surely appalling by American standards, conditions that were—if anything—improved by the extension of mining as a result of American investment.

It turns out that these systematic and closely studied attacks on U.S. investment abroad agree on the impact of such investment on wages and working conditions in Central and Latin America. They find wages increased (insofar as they deal with the topic). Nowhere did that impact result from any plan to do good. We assume that, in fact, the companies paid market wages, or slightly better, only to attract the quality of labor they sought. The most explicit comment on the consequences of labor was made by Jenks, in his study of Cuba.

> The coming of American companies has made for regular wage payments, cash wages, improved housing, living conditions and facilities for recreation. . . . American capital . . . has brought standards of living which can be satisfied only with American goods. . . . One hears plenty of stories of sharp practice on the part of these American concerns. That this passes the limits of business methods daily resorted to in the States or by Cubans and Spaniards in their dealings with each other and with Americans—these are statements for which there is no evidence.[24]

Land

Did North Americans succeed in gouging Latin Americans by paying below-market values for their land? The query is not whether North Americans paid what the land might be worth fifty years later. Or what its inherent fertility or beauty warranted. Or whether the price was "very few dollars per acre." Imperialistic investment is assessed against the standards of national investment: Did the foreign investor pay less than the native investor?

We are fortunate to have the testimony of Charles Kepner, a knowledgeable anti-imperialist (who wrote two books against the United Fruit Company, with its "domain of more than three million acres of tropical lowlands").[25] He focuses on the fact that United Fruit acquired these "vast areas of land . . . for trifling amounts of money or for nothing." How did United Fruit bring off such a coup? Kepner's answer is:

> Political unity, economic progress and social intercourse depend to a great extent upon efficient means of transportation. Hence for nearly a century national leaders have been anxious to connect their capital cities with the outside world. Unable, however, to finance such railway construction out of ordinary revenues these countries have sought to fulfill their aspirations by floating loans and encouraging private companies to build railroads. In exchange for promises of railroad construction, politicians have given away vast expanses of lands, which were of little immediate value to the nation.[26]

Much of the land was also of little value to the companies: they relinquished much of the land given them in Costa Rica and Guatemala. Had the companies' power enabled them to pay below-market prices for the land they did buy? Kepner's detailed discussion suggests that it did not.

First the company had to compete with native land speculators. Second, United Fruit bought through intermediaries: "Many a land-owner realizing that a fruit company wants his property will take advantage of the situation to ask a good figure for it. To avoid paying this the company frequently makes its purchase through intermediaries, who may be connected with the fruit company."[27] But if the company bought "through intermediaries," it discarded the imposing bargaining advantage of declaring its connection with two governments, the local one and the one controlling the U.S. Navy.

Kepner's discussion, in fact, indicates the weakness of the foreign firm in the local land market. The effective monopolist was the native landowner whose land the company needed to fill out a run of land for a new railroad line or plantation. In this situation the local owner recognized his monopoly power, demanding more from the large company than the market price he could charge a small buyer. Thus, the powerful foreign company either paid local landowners more than the market price for their land, or—by covertly buying through intermediaries—paid only the market price.

In sum, investments by United Fruit increased prices paid to owners of Costa Rican, Honduran and Guatemalan land, first, because a demand shift resulting from increased fruit production tended to push up land prices; and, second, because the company (as a foreign target) had to pay market or above-market prices.

Native Entrepreneurs

The classic attacks on American expansion cast a fitful light on how imperialism expanded the incomes of native workers and landowners. They reveal even less of the fate of those who supplied other factors of production. We can nonetheless infer that American expansion injured native capitalists.

Imperializing companies set up company stores. These, in Rippy's words, "usually sell supplies more cheaply than they can be bought from the local native merchants."[28] Such price cutting may have served native workers and peasants admirably. But these stores destroyed monopolies once held by native entrepreneurs. What more hateful attack on native businessmen could occur?

Expanding foreign investment in this period often involved railway construction. Such construction inevitably menaced the local entrepreneurs who carted goods, drove cattle to market, ran stage coaches, or supplied tavern accommodations to travelers. Local shoemakers, black-smiths, millers, suddenly found themselves forced to compete with goods introduced by the railway. To these entrepreneurs "the calamity of the railways" was created by foreigners.[29] In China the porters, carters, and wheelbarrow men dispossessed by the Shanghai-Woosung Railroad actually got it torn up and shipped out of the country. In Latin America, however, the imperialists had their way, and the railroads wreaked their havoc on older transport and related entrepreneurs.

Incomes created by expanded production—whether of bananas, sugar or copper—induced doctors, lawyers, money lenders, carpenters, builders, and millwrights to enter the areas affected. Such new entry ended monopolies once held by such entrepreneurs and skilled workmen. Yankee imperialism cut monopoly profits in many lines of local enterprise. The peasants benefited. The native entrepreneurial group eventually increased. But such results offered cold comfort to the monopolistic entrepreneurs thus injured.

A fourth threat was as infuriating as any. Opportunities seen by native entrepreneurs were seized by foreign ones. The clamor that resulted resembles the xenophobia voiced by American populists when they saw Scots and Englishmen investing in American lands. True, the greatest populist of them all, Bryan, fought to acquire the Philippines. But that foreigners should frustrate American entrepreneurs was quite another matter. In North and South America alike the simple motto was: Profits for the natives. Andre Gunder Frank quotes a 1911 Chilean writer:

> The foreign merchant strangled our commercial initiative abroad, and at home he eliminated us from the international trade. . . . The foreigner owns two thirds of our nitrate production and continues to acquire our most valuable copper deposits. The merchant marine . . . continues to cede ground to foreign shipping even in the coastwide trade. The majority of the insurance companies that operate among us have their head office abroad. The national banks . . . keep ceding ground to the branches of the foreign banks. . . .

Frank adds, "foreign capital acquired an importance that was almost equal to that of foreign trade in transforming . . . Latin America in a way that would consolidate the structure of its underdevelopment."[30]

Native businessmen, and their supporters, inevitably mourned their lost profit opportunities.

One could merely dismiss such regrets. After all, with local interest rates at 10 and 30 percent it was hardly to be expected that they could engage in long-range development of mines and plantations. Profit seekers from lands where government bonds were paying 2 percent (as the United States) were a more likely source for long-term investment, in which profits were often deferred for years. For example, the Cerro de Pasco mine yielded net returns only after 15 years.

On the other hand, one might conclude such investment opportunities should have lain fallow until native businessmen were able to take advantage of them. Perhaps some inevitable historic sequence even requires the growth of a native bourgeoisie before its downfall and (with it) the advance to socialism. Or one might believe, with Felipe Pazos, that foreign investment only "brings with it ready-made development. . . . There is no wait for training of technicians and managers, nor for try-outs and for gaining of experience . . . it may inhibit the emergence . . . of local personnel . . . and institutions needed for self-sustaining development."[31]

In any event, foreign investors seized opportunities that native entrepreneurs had been unable to seize. The unsuccessful investor, or lover, never wholly ceases to regret.

In summary, American imperialism after the Spanish American War worked systematic effects on economic interest groups in Latin America. (a) It increased the income of workers and peasants because it expanded the demand for labor. Moreover, anti-imperialist writers assure us that American companies in that expanding market paid wages that were average, and sometimes above average. (b) Workers' real wages often increased more than their money wages. The introduction of company stores ended monopolies once exercised by local general stores and taverns, thereby reducing the monopoly profits once provided by workers and peasants. (c) Imperialist investment increased the value of land held by local landholders, whether they held small plots of land or vast acreage. Such increases proved most substantial when the United States offered new and especially advantageous terms for native products entering the U.S. market (for example, as in Cuba). They also occurred whenever American companies bought land for plantations and railroads. The assertions by anti-imperialist writers that the United Fruit Company sometimes bought land through intermediaries suggest that American companies generally paid at least the price for land that native buyers did (and whenever the identity of the company became known, the company presumably paid somewhat above market prices). (d) American imperialism injured the vested interests of the existing native business group by destroying monopoly profits. The provision of general stores by American companies brought new competition to isolated farm and village areas. Such expansion inevitably menaced the monopoly profits of existing native entrepreneurs, even as it induced the creation of a new entrepreneurial group. Moreover, American investments would have snatched away opportunities that would-be native entrepreneurs saw, coveted, and sometimes might even have been able to finance. The heart of the anti-imperialist struggle, then, may prove to be a squabble between two capitalist groups, one native and the other foreign, fighting over the spoils of progress.

NOTES

1. Eugen Varga and L. Mendelsohn, *New Data for V. I. Lenin's Imperialism*, (New York, 1940), p. 138.

2. Rosa Luxemburg, *The Accumulation of Capital* (New Haven, 1951), p. 446. In response to criticism I am obligated to warn any unwary reader that agreement between Lenin and Luxemburg on this point does not imply their further agreement on imperialism, on the multiplication table, or on anything else.

3. See Varga, *New Data*, p. 120.

4. Leland Jenks, *Our Cuban Colony* (New York, 1928), p. 136.

5. Jenks, *Our Cuban Colony*, p. 138–39.

6. Quoted by Jenks, *Our Cuban Colony*, p. 133. The underlying strategic considerations seem no different from, nor better thought through than, those apparently operative in planning the second Cuban invasion, the Bay of Pigs.

7. 58th Congress, 2nd Sess., S.D. 51, *Correspondence Concerning . . . Interoceanic Canal Across Isthmus of Panama* (Washington, D.C., 1903), p. 40.

8. Quoted by Harmodio Arias, *The Panama Canal* (London, 1911), p. 63.

9. The engineer, J. T. Ford, was consulting engineer to the Colombian government and manager of the Cartegena Harbor, Railway and River Companies. 58th Cong., *Correspondence Concerning . . . Interoceanic Canal*, pp. 41, 43.

10. John B. Moore, *A Digest of International Law*, vol. 3. (Washington, D.C., 1912), pp. 220. Various Congressmen proposed legislation to give American shippers preference, but their bills failed.

11. Woodrow Wilson, speech on "Patriotism," January 28, 1904, in Arthur S. Link, ed., *The Papers of Woodrow Wilson*, vol. 15 (Princeton, 1972), p. 143. See vol. 14, pp. 419, 454, 491 for versions of the speech back to April 1903.

12. Charles Kindleberger, *Power and Money, the Economics of International Politics and the Politics of International Economics* (New York, 1970), pp. 76–77.

13. Fundamentals of Political Economy Writing Group, Shanghai, in George C. Wang, ed., *Fundamentals of Political Economy* (White Plains, N.Y., 1977), p. 173.

14. Kwame Nkrumah, *Towards Colonial Freedom* (London, 1962), p. 38.

15. Stanley Aranowitz, *False Promises* (New York, 1973), pp. 184, 139.

16. 57th Cong., 1st Sess., H.R. 535, *Reciprocity with Cuba* (1902), p. 445.

17. Jenks, *Our Cuban Colony*, p. 133.

18. J. Fred Rippy, *The Capitalists and Colombia* (New York, 1931), pp. 190–91.

19. Ibid., p. 182.

20. Charles Kepner, Jr., *Social Aspects of the Banana Industry* (New York, 1936), p. 129.

21. Melvin Knight, *Americans in Santo Domingo* (New York, 1928), p. 143.

22. Ibid., p. 158 . . . .

23. Margaret Marsh, *The Bankers in Bolivia* (New York, 1928), p. 42.

24. Jenks, *Our Cuban Colony*, p. 301.

25. Kepner, *Social Aspects of the Banana Industry*, p. 70.

26. Ibid., pp. 70–71.

27. Ibid., p. 84 . . . .

28. Rippy, *The Capitalists*, p. 182.

29. The phrase is Sir James McAdam's and is quoted by H. M. Hallsworth, "The Future of Rail Transport," *The Economic Journal*, 44 (Dec. 1934), p. 537 . . . .

30. Quoted by Andre Gunder Frank, *Lumpenbourgeoisie: Lumpendevelopment* (New York, 1972), p. 70, from a 1912 study of Chile . . . .

31. Felipe Pazos, "The Role of International Movements of Private Capital in Promoting Development," in John H. Adler, ed. *Capital Movements and Economic Development* (New York, 1967), p. 196 . . . .

9. International Economic Structures and American Foreign Economic Policy, 1887–1934

DAVID A. LAKE

David Lake looks at American foreign economic policy before the United States' rise to world leadership. Lake relates changes in the American position in the international economy to particular changes in the nation's tariff. He begins with a discussion of hegemonic stability theory (see also Krasner, Reading 3) and of the international economic structure. He applies a differentiated analysis of changes in the United States international economic position to four periods of American foreign economic policy from 1887 to 1934. Lake argues that when Great Britain was the dominant economic power, the United States could adopt protectionist policies at home while pursuing export expansion abroad. As Britain declined, the United States was forced to reduce its tariffs. With the collapse of the international economy during the Great Depression, American policy swung first toward greater protection and then, after 1934, toward freer trade and world leadership. Lake's analysis in this article builds on the Realist approach to foreign economic policy. For Lake, as for most Realists, national policies are dictated first and foremost by the nation's international environment and only secondarily by the domestic setting.

In the 1890 tariff debate, Representative William McKinley stated, "This is a domestic bill; it is not a foreign bill."[1] Many scholars have echoed this view of the tariff and American foreign economic policy. Tom E. Terrill argues that tariff policies in the United States during the late 19th century resulted from the struggle between the Democratic and Republican parties to break the political equipoise of the era. Theodore J. Lowi, drawing upon E. E. Schattschneider, contends that tariff policy before 1934 was primarily shaped by the distributive nature of the issue area. And nearly every account of the passage of the Reciprocal Trade Agreements Act of 1934, which overturned America's century-old commitment to protectionism, attributes an important role to the personal beliefs of Secretary of State Cordell Hull.

Recently, the "theory of hegemonic stability" has been put forth as a systemic-level explanation of international economic regime change. Despite this emergence of a "third image" in international political economy, comparatively little attention has been devoted to the international sources of foreign economic policy in individual countries. This is unfortunate. Not only do state policies provide additional cases to refine and test the theory of hegemonic stability—and this is important because of the limited number of international economic regimes available for study—but the central propositions of the theory of hegemonic stability form the basis for a powerful and parsimonious explanation of foreign economic policy and policy change in individual countries over time.

In this article, I examine the international sources of American foreign economic policy between 1887 and 1934, an era of rapid and dramatic changes. Immediately after the Civil War, the United States had sought to insulate itself from the international economy; it adopted protectionism at home and a *laissez faire* policy toward exports. After 1887, the United States began actively to promote exports through bilateral reciprocity treaties and duty-free raw materials while maintaining the essential structure of protection. Between 1897 and World War I, America's recognition that its policies could and did affect the international economy was primarily reflected in the pursuit of the Open Door abroad. After 1913, the United States undertook a greater leadership role within the international economy. It lowered its tariff wall at home and, at the end of the war, attempted to create and maintain a new and fundamentally liberal international economy based on the Open Door principle. In the late 1920s, the United States briefly abdicated its position of international economic leadership and returned to protectionism via the Smoot-Hawley Tariff Act of 1930, but reversed direction again in the Reciprocal Trade Agreements Act of 1934.

Between 1887 and 1934, the United States evolved from a highly protectionist into an internationally liberal country. In this article, I offer an alternative explanation of this evolution in American foreign economic policy from that contained in the several domestic approaches summarized in the opening paragraph. My central proposition is that American foreign economic policy, and policy change during the period 1887–1934, was shaped in important ways by the international economic structure and the position of the United States within it. The source of American foreign economic policy, in other words, was within the international political economy.

The discussion is divided into two principal sections. First, I review and refine the theory of hegemonic stability, proposing a new category of international actor which better describes the position of the United States within the international economic structure. Second, I examine the theory of hegemonic stability through an analysis of American foreign economic policy between 1887 and 1934. In the conclusion, I discuss the strengths and weaknesses of an explanation of foreign economic policy derived from international economic structures, and summarize the implications of this analysis for the theory of hegemonic stability.

THE THEORY OF HEGEMONIC STABILITY

There are two variants of the theory of hegemonic stability. The first, associated with Charles P. Kindleberger's *The World in Depression 1929–1939*,[2] focuses on the provision of the collective good of international stability, where instability is defined as a condition in which small disruptions (e.g., the stock market crash of 1929) have large consequences (the Great Depression). Assuming that markets are inherently unstable—or nonhomeostatic systems—and tend toward stagnation and fragmentation, Kindleberger argues that the international economy will be stable only if a single leader is willing to assume responsibility for "(a) maintaining a relatively open market for distress goods; (b) providing countercyclical long-term lending; and (c) discounting in a crisis."[3] He has subsequently added two additional responsibilities: (d) "managing, in some degree, the structure of exchange rates," and (e) "providing a degree of coordination of domestic monetary policies."[4]

Leadership, for Kindleberger, is altruistic. A stable international economy is produced only at a net physical cost to the country in exchange for the amorphous "privilege" of leading. The ability of a country to assume responsibility for stabilizing the international economy is primarily determined by its position within the international economic structure, which Kindleberger defines along the single dimension of size: "Small countries have no economic power. At the same time they have no responsibility for the economic system, nor any necessity to exert leadership."[5] Small states, in other words, are "free riders." Middle-sized countries are "big enough to do damage to the system, but not substantial enough to stabilize it. . . ."[6] Since they tend to act as if they were small free riders, middle-sized countries are extremely destabilizing and are the "spoilers" of the system. Only large states have both the capability and responsibility for leading the international economy. "The main lesson of the inter-war years," Kindleberger states, is that, "for the world economy to be stabilized, there has to be a stabilizer, one stabilizer."[7]

The second variant, drawn from the works of Robert Gilpin,[8] differs from the first in three substantive ways: the phenomenon to be explained, the nature of leadership, and the definition of the international economic structure. Gilpin does not address the question of stability directly; rather, he seeks to explain why regimes—or the rules and norms that govern international economic relations—emerge and change. In addressing this question, Gilpin subsumes much of Kindleberger's argument and draws heavily upon the collective goods approach. Despite this intellectual debt, Gilpin moves beyond Kindleberger's conception of altruism and develops an interest-based explanation of leadership. While noting that all countries gain from a liberal regime, Gilpin asserts that the strongest and most advanced countries reap a disproportionate share of the benefits. Britain and the United States, in other words, constructed and maintained liberal international economic regimes at their hegemonic zeniths because the benefits outweighed the costs. When this favorable payoff disappeared, the hegemonic powers stopped leading.

Gilpin defines the position of a country within the international economy along two dimensions: political-military power and efficiency. In Gilpin's conceptualization, political-military power primarily indicates the quantity of influence a state possesses over the international economic regime. Efficiency, on the other hand, largely determines the degree to which a state's interests are associated with a liberal international economic regime. The more efficient the nation, the larger the relative gains from trade, and the greater the country's support for a liberal regime. Within this definition of the international economic structure, Gilpin identifies three categories of international actors: peripheral states, which because of their small size are of little consequence for the regime; "growth nodes," which emerge as challengers to the liberal regime and, presumably, are of relatively low efficiency; and hegemonic leaders, which are extremely large and highly efficient countries. Although "growth nodes" are a more active threat to a liberal international economy than are Kindleberger's "middle-sized" countries, the two sets of categories are essentially similar; I refer to them as free riders, spoilers, and hegemonic leaders.

These three categories of international actors do not exhaust the logical possibilities presented within a two-dimensional conception of the international economic structure. Nor do they adequately describe the position of the United States within the international economy between 1887 and 1934. The theory of hegemonic stability, perhaps due to its focus on the absence or presence of hegemony, has failed to develop the analytic tools necessary to comprehend adequately the interests and policies of all countries within the international economy. To accomplish this task, Gilpin's two dimensions of political-military power and efficiency must be redefined. Political-military power may be a necessary condition for economic hegemony, but the relationship between political-military power and influence over the international economic regime diminishes once the analysis is extended beyond the category of hegemonic leadership. West Germany and Japan, for instance, possess much greater influence over the international economic regime today than their political-military strength would indicate. Relative size, operationalized by issue area, is a more appropriate indicator of international economic influence. Because the following discussion focuses primarily on trade policy, relative size is measured here by a country's proportion of world trade.

Gilpin's second dimension suffers less from a problem of theory than from one of semantics. Strictly defined, efficiency refers to the least wasteful means of production and is specific to time, place, and the available mix of the factors of production. Efficiency has little impact upon the absolute or relative gains from trade. Rather, the concept to which Gilpin appears to be referring is relative productivity—defined as relative output per unit of labor input. . . .

The three categories of nations identified by Gilpin and Kindleberger are defined graphically in Figure 1 within the two dimensions of relative size and relative productivity. . . . An important fourth category of international actor—supporters—has not been examined by either of these authors. Supporters are middle-sized countries of high relative productivity; they are not simply smaller or less effective hegemonic leaders. Supporters cannot unilaterally lead the international economy, nor—unlike a hegemonic leader—are they willing to accept high short-term costs for long-term gains. Rather, supporters seek to balance their short-term costs and benefits, and prefer to bargain for collective movement toward specified goals. Similarly, while hegemonic leaders forsake protectionism at home in order to lead the international economy as a whole toward greater openness, supporters are in most cases unwilling to do so. Even the most productive countries possess internationally uncompetitive industries. If a hegemonic leader were to protect such industries, it would undercut its ability to lead the international economy. Indeed, some measure of self-sacrifice in the short run may be necessary for a hegemonic leader to achieve its goal of constructing a liberal international economy. Supporters, on the other hand, are not subject to the same constraints of leadership; they will protect their least competitive industries whenever possible.

When a hegemonic leader exists within the international economy, supporters will free-ride, protecting industry at home and expanding exports abroad. They assume, in short, that the hegemonic leader will

FIGURE 1.   Four Categories of International Economic Actors

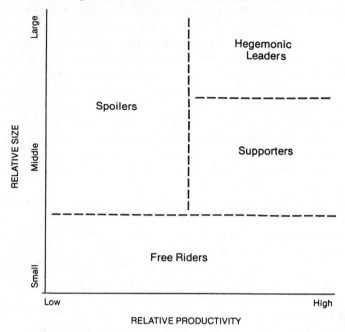

carry the burden of preserving their export markets while they remain free to pursue self-seeking policies at home.

When no hegemonic leader exists and two or more supporters are present in the international economy, their mutual desire to export will constrain protectionism in each other. Supporters, because of their high relative productivity, value export markets more than protection at home, but will sacrifice the latter only if necessary to obtain the former. An international economic structure of bilateral (or multilateral) supportership is likely, as a result, to contain higher levels of protectionism than a hegemonic structure, but will not experience extremely high levels of protection because the interaction between supporters places limits on protectionism in any single supporter. Bilateral supportership can be a stable system in which protectionism or beggar-thy-neighbor policies are moderated by mutual constraints between supporters, and in which a measure of cooperation and collective international leadership exists. Considerable potential for instability does exist, however. Either supporter may try to "cheat" on the other, or either may be unwilling to carry an equitable share of the leadership burden.

International economic structures with only one supporter, by contrast, are highly unstable. When no hegemonic leader exists and only a single supporter is present, there are no constraints on protectionism within the supporter. Although it will continue to value export markets and may attempt to lead the international economy, a single supporter will lack the resources to stabilize the international economy successfully, or to create and maintain a liberal international economic regime. If the supporter believes that it cannot preserve its export markets, the protectionist fires at home will be fueled. The growing flames may precipitate the abdication of whatever leadership role had been held by the supporter.

The foreign economic policy of any individual country is affected both by the international economic structure (defined as the number and category of states within the international economy), and by the state's position within it. The international economic structure from 1870 to 1938 is detailed in Table 1 and illustrated in Figure 2. Throughout the period, the United States was a supporter. Its share of world trade rose steadily from 8.8 percent in 1870 to a high of 13.9 percent in 1929, only to decline to 11.3 percent in 1938. Its relative productivity was high and rising steadily until 1929; it surpassed the level of productivity of the United Kingdom in the late 1890s. Germany and France were spoilers throughout the period. Germany's proportion of world trade and its relative productivity gradually increased until World War I. After the war, its share of world trade and relative productivity declined to approximately the levels that had obtained in 1870. France's share of

TABLE 1. The International Economic Structure, 1870-1938

	UNITED STATES		UNITED KINGDOM		GERMANY		FRANCE	
	Proportion of World Trade	Relative Productivity [i]	Proportion of World Trade	Relative Productivity [i]	Proportion of World Trade	Relative Productivity [i]	Proportion of World Trade	Relative Productivity [i]
1870	8.8[a]	1.22	24.0[a]	1.63	9.7[a]	.66	10.8[a]	.65
1880	8.8[c]	1.29	19.6[c]	1.50	10.3[b]	.64	11.4[c]	.69
1890	9.7[d]	1.37	18.5[d]	1.45	10.9[d]	.69	10.0[d]	.63
1900	10.2[e]	1.42	17.5[e]	1.30	11.9[e]	.74	8.5[e]	.65
1913	11.1[f]	1.56	14.1[f]	1.15	12.2[f]	.73	7.5[f]	.68
1929	13.9[g]	1.72	13.3[g]	1.04	9.3[g]	.66	6.4[g]	.74
1938	11.3[h]	1.71	14.0[h]	.92	9.0[h]	.69	5.2[h]	.82

[a] Mulhall data, 1870, 1880; see Simon Kuznets, *Modern Economic Growth* (Yale University Press, 1966), 306.
[b] Mulhall data, 1880, 1889, *ibid.*, 306.
[c] League of Nations data, 1876–1880. League of Nations, *Industrialization and Foreign Trade* (Geneva, 1945), 157-67.
[d] League of Nations data, 1886–1890, in Kuznets, 307.
[e] League of Nations data, 1896–1900, *ibid.*, 307.
[f] League of Nations data, 1911–1913, *ibid.*, 307.
[g] League of Nations, *Review of World Trade*, 1927–1929.
[h] *Ibid.*, 1936–1938.
[i] Relative Productivity data derived from Angus Maddison, "Long Run Dynamics of Productivity Growth," *Banca Nazionale del Lavoro Quarterly Review*, No. 128 (March 1979), 43.

FIGURE 2.   The International Economic Structure, 1870–1938

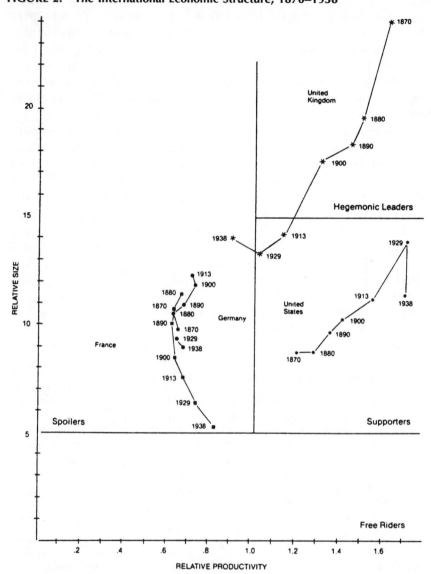

world trade eroded throughout the period after having reached a high of 11.4 percent in 1880. Its relative productivity was low and fluctuated before World War I; it was somewhat higher after the war than before, although it was still below the levels attained by the United Kingdom and the United States. The United Kingdom changed from a hegemonic leader into a supporter immediately before World War I, and into a spoiler in the late 1920s. Its share of world trade fell from a high of 24.0

percent in 1870 to a low of 13.3 percent in 1929, while its relative productivity dropped from 1.67 in 1870 to .92 in 1938.

The position of the United Kingdom changed most dramatically between 1870 and 1938, creating three distinct international economic structures. A hegemonic structure under British leadership existed from before 1870 until approximately World War I. Next, a structure of bilateral supportership, in which the United States and the United Kingdom were the key actors, was present from approximately 1913 to the late 1920s. Finally, a structure of unilateral supportership, centering on the United States, existed from 1929 through World War II.

If my basic proposition is correct, these changes in the international economic structure and the position of the United States as a supporter should be reflected in American foreign economic policy and changes in that policy. Specifically, the United States should have attempted to free-ride within the structure of British hegemony. As the British position began to decline, however—and particularly after the United States had surpassed the United Kingdom in productivity—America should have gradually moved toward a more active and liberal policy in the international economy. Once the structure was transformed from hegemony to bilateral supportership, the United States should have adopted more liberal policies and sought to negotiate the rules and norms of a new, more protectionist yet still liberal international economic regime. Finally, both United States policy and the international economy should have entered into a period of instability after the United Kingdom evolved from supporter to spoiler. Within this structure of unilateral supportership, the United States should have remained liberal in its policies only so long as it believed it could maintain or expand its export markets.

AMERICAN FOREIGN ECONOMIC POLICY

There were four phases in American foreign economic policy during the period 1887–1934. The goals of this policy remained the same they had been for over a century: national development and domestic prosperity. What changed were the policies and strategies best suited to the attainment of these goals. We will now examine how the international economic structure, and the position of the United States within it, affected American foreign economic policy.

1887–1897

Prior to 1887, exports were not regarded as a proper sphere of government intervention; the tariff was perceived as a strictly domestic issue. The "American system" of moderately high tariff protection was explicitly enacted to stimulate and encourage the industrialization of the country. The agrarian community—still the largest sector of the economy—was encouraged to accept the American system through promises that an adequate and sufficiently stable home market would be created for its surplus.

While exports gradually became more important to agricultural interests, most manufacturers continued to regard exports as secondary to their main markets and primarily as a means of dumping (in the economic sense) their occasional surpluses. Those Americans who did seek to expand exports systematically did not link foreign expansion and the tariff. Rather, their emphasis was on infrastructural improvements, such as port and canal construction, and railroad development and regulation.

After 1887, under the efforts of David Ames Wells, James G. Blaine, and President Grover Cleveland, the tariff was reconceptualized as an instrument of foreign economic policy whose manipulation could serve to expand American exports. The opening of this new debate was marked by Cleveland's Annual Message to Congress in 1887, which he devoted entirely to the tariff question. While focusing primarily on the high consumer prices and favoritism that resulted from protectionism, Cleveland also sounded the theme of export expansion through cheaper raw materials and lower duties. This latter theme was developed more fully in the debate over the legislatively unsuccessful Mills bill, based on Cleveland's tariff principles, and in the "Great Tariff Debate" in the presidential election of 1888.

Cleveland and other leading Democrats were heavily influenced by the ideas of Wells. A former Republican Commissioner of Revenue, Wells had maintained as early as 1868 that American farmers and manufacturers faced a condition of chronic overproduction. Unless the United States increased its exports, he contended, periodic depressions would result. Wells consistently linked his diagnosis and prescription to tariff policy. In an analysis reminiscent of the British Anti-Corn Law League, Wells argued that high tariffs restricted the market place. Low tariffs, on the other hand, would broaden the market and stimulate exports by easing the exchange of goods and services, and reducing the costs of manufacturing through cheaper raw materials.

Even though Cleveland lost the Great Debate of 1888 at the polls and failed to enact his tariff reform principles in the Wilson-Gorman Tariff of 1894 in the face of protectionist opposition in the Senate (see Table 2 for a comparison of rates of duty) during his second administration, the export expansionists were ultimately victorious. In response to Democratic demands for tariff reduction, the majority of Republicans limited themselves to reciting the litany of protectionist arguments and emphasizing the adequacy of the home market. A minority of Republicans, however, under the leadership of Blaine, began to formulate a new perspective which shared Wells's assumption of overproduction, but maintained the essential structure of protection. Rather than seeking to lower the entire tariff wall, as the Democrats advocated, Blaine sought to expand exports by negotiating tariff reciprocity treaties with other countries. Despite initial opposition from the majority of Republicans, Blaine's conception of reciprocity prevailed in the McKinley Tariff of 1890 and, to a lesser extent, in the Dingley Act of 1897 (see Table 2).

Blaine's success illustrates how far the reconceptualization of the tariff had progressed. By the early 1890s, the leaders of both political parties agreed on the need for export expansion and on the proposition that the tariff could serve as a useful instrument for accomplishing this aim. They disagreed only on the means of expansion: the Democrats favored duty-free raw materials, with the market mechanism determining the level of imports; the Republicans preferred reciprocity, with the government determining which raw materials from which countries would be admitted to the United States.

Despite this desire for export expansion, there was little recognition of the effects United States policy had upon the international economy. To Americans of this period, it appeared that exports could be expanded indefinitely through adjusting the tariff without damaging the principle of protection. For the Cleveland Democrats, duty-free raw materials were a means of increasing the competitiveness of American manufactured exports. For the Republicans, reciprocity based primarily on the admittance of raw materials at a preferential rate of duty was a wedge to pry open additional markets for American exports. The proposition that, in order to sell to the world, a country must buy from the world was not readily accepted outside a small circle of academic economists and "free trade" Democrats. Nor was there any widespread recognition that American exports depended on the continued willingness of other countries—particularly the United Kingdom, America's single largest trading partner—to accept American goods. Rather, existing markets tended to be taken for granted and new markets were perceived to be ripe for picking.

As predicted above, so long as the United Kingdom remained a hegemonic leader, the United States would free-ride even though it was a supporter. America remained protectionist and sought to expand its exports. It contributed little or nothing to the stability of the international economy and actually helped to undermine the existing liberal international economic regime. During this first phase, in short, the United States free-rode on free trade.

1897–1912

By the late 1890s, the country's growing productivity and events in Europe and China forced the United States to recognize the effects of its policies on other nations. Confronted with an American commercial "invasion" spurred by rising relative productivity in the United States, several European statesmen began to advocate protecting their markets against American imports. "The destructive competition with transoceanic countries," Count Agenor Goluchowski, Foreign Minister of Austria-Hungary, stated on November 20, 1897, "requires prompt and thorough counteracting measures if vital interests of the peoples of Europe are not to be gravely compromised. . . . The European nations must close their ranks in order successfully to defend their existence."[9] Three weeks later, Baron von Thielmann, Secretary of the German Treasury and a former Ambassador to the United States, argued before the Reichstag that the recently passed Dingley Tariff put America in the position of a pike in a carp pool. The carp, he warned, must combine. Though these statements were noted with some alarm in the American press, more ominous, perhaps, was the growing movement in the United Kingdom for an imperial preference system led by Joseph Chamberlain, who had been appointed Colonial Secretary in 1895. It was unlikely that the highly divided Europeans of the late 19th century would combine into the customs union proposed by Goluchowski and Thielmann, but for Britain to adopt imperial preferences would have been a matter of concern for the United States and was recognized as such.

Events in China, which threatened to disrupt American trade with that country—important more for its promise than for its actual levels—drew a more concrete response from the United States. In March 1898, after several years of increasing Russian, German, and French encroachments on China's territory and sovereignty, Britain approached the United States and inquired "whether they could count on the cooperation of the United States in opposing any such action by Foreign Powers and whether the United States would be prepared to join with Great Britain in opposing such measures should the contingency arise."[10] The United States refused. Britain, in a significant departure from its past policy of free trade and nondiscrimination, then began to move away from the principle of the Open Door, leasing the port of Kowloon and expelling the Chinese Imperial Maritime Customs Service. In September 1899, Secretary of State John Hay issued the now famous Open Door notes.

The Open Door principle had existed long before the United States issued these notes. Lord Balfour, in the parliamentary debates of 1898, referred to it as "that famous phrase that has been quoted and requoted almost *ad nauseam*."[11] In the September notes, the United States invited

Russia, Germany, Great Britain, France, and Japan to adhere to three principles: noninterference with the vested interests within the existing spheres of influence in China, the uniform application of Chinese treaty tariffs at all ports, and nondiscrimination regarding railroad and harbor charges. All the powers responded, though some quite vaguely, that they would respect the Open Door to the extent that all other nations did. Hay, in what is generally regarded as a brilliant tactical move, announced that all the powers had agreed to uphold the Open Door in China and that he considered their replies to be "final and definitive."[12]

The Open Door notes in themselves had little practical effect. It was clear that the United States would not use more than moral suasion to enforce the principle. Moreover, the notes were almost swallowed up in the march of events in China. The military intervention of the foreign powers (including the United States) to put down the Boxer Rebellion in 1900 soon led to an increase in the authority exerted by foreign governments in China. Yet, the Open Door notes were significant for three reasons. First, as Thomas McCormick writes:

> the promulgation of the [Open Door notes] did pass the scepter of open door champion from Great Britain to the United States. For a half-century the British had successfully used an open door policy to create and maintain their economic supremacy in the Chinese Empire. . . . Now, as Britain's power waned—and with it her commitment to the open door, the United States made a concerted effort to adapt the nineteenth-century policy to the expansive needs of a twentieth-century industrial America."[13]

Second, the Open Door notes demonstrated the important effect that Britain's move away from free trade had in shaping American foreign economic policy after 1898. Third, while they were not recognized as doing so at that time, the Open Door notes repudiated the concept of reciprocity and signaled a new era in which the principle of nondiscrimination, or the Open Door, was to be the cornerstone of American foreign economic policy.

This new commitment to nondiscrimination was reflected in the next Republican tariff bill—the Payne-Aldrich Act of 1909. In this bill, Congress established a system of minimum and maximum tariff rates. The President was given the authority to impose duties 25 percent higher than the minimum rates on goods from any country that discriminated against American exports. During the House debate, Representative Edgar D. Crumpacker of Indiana (R), a member of the House Ways and Means Committee, argued:

> It is a wise provision, and its main virtue is in the retaliatory power it contains to compel foreign countries to accord our exports the same treatment they give to those of other countries. *Our foreign commercial*

and industrial policy ought to be that of the open door. We ask only equal consideration at the hands of foreign countries, and that we should insist upon. I have little respect for reciprocity in its narrow sense—in the sense that it is a system of international dickers under which one line of products may secure special advantages in foreign markets in consideration of a grant of special advantages to a particular line of products in return. . . . The broad reciprocity of treating all competitors and all producers exactly alike is the principle that this country ought to encourage as the permanent commercial policy of the civilized world.[14]

Despite this commitment to the liberal principle of the Open Door, the United States remained unwilling to abolish its tariff wall. Pressure on the government for tariff reduction rose throughout the first decade of the 20th century. Active on the issue were, on the one hand, the Progressives, who perceived the tariff as aiding the process of consolidation in American industry, and, on the other, the large and internationally competitive businesses, which defined their interests in broad internationalist terms. President Theodore Roosevelt, who feared that revising the tariff would split his then-dominant Republican party, successfully avoided the issue and bequeathed the problem to this successor. Although William Taft had run on an election platform that advocated tariff reform, he was unable to contain protectionist pressures within his party once he was in office. The Payne-Aldrich Act, which contained the minimum-maximum schedule with the aim of expanding the Open Door, only slightly lowered the average rates of duty from those of the Dingley Act of 1897 (see Table 2). Taft's inability to fulfill his promise of tariff reform engendered a considerable groundswell of resentment. This negative reaction effectively thwarted Taft's ability to utilize the higher maximum schedule so as to secure a further expansion

TABLE 2. Levels of Duty by Tariff Act, 1887–1934*

TARIFF ACT, DATE	LEVEL OF DUTY ON ALL IMPORTS	LEVEL OF DUTY ON DUTIABLE IMPORTS	PERCENTAGE OF ALL IMPORTS ON FREE LIST
McKinley, 1890	23.7	48.4	50.8
Wilson-Gorman, 1894	20.5	41.2	50.0
Dingley, 1897	26.2	47.6	45.1
Payne-Aldrich, 1909	20.0	41.0	51.3
Underwood, 1913	8.8	26.8	67.5
Fordney-McCumber, 1922	13.9	38.2	63.5
Smoot-Hawley, 1930	19.0	55.3	65.5

Source: *Statistical Abstract of the United States,* selected years.

* Average rates of duty and average percentage of imports on free list for all full years during which the tariff was in effect (e.g., McKinley Tariff Act passed in October 1890; duties calculated on 1891–1893).

of the Open Door abroad because he feared popular condemnation of a further increase in the tariff.

As Britain's hegemony waned and the United States' productivity rose, the latter—as predicted by the refined theory of hegemonic stability—adopted more liberal policies within the international economy, but continued to free-ride. The Open Door policy was a significant recognition that the United States depended on export markets and that it could no longer rely entirely upon the United Kingdom to maintain openness abroad. Still, Washington was unwilling to accept the costs of enforcing the Open Door principle in China, or of restricting protection for American industry.

1913–1929

Woodrow Wilson, in accepting the Democratic presidential nomination, stated: "The tariff was once a bulwark; now it is a dam. Foreign trade is reciprocal; we cannot sell unless we also buy."[15] Pledged to tariff reform, Wilson called Congress into special session in order to enact the Underwood Tariff Act of 1913. In a speech before Congress, he declared:

> It is clear to the whole country that the tariff duties must be altered. They must be changed to meet the radical alteration in the conditions of our economic life which the country has witnessed within the last generation. While the whole face and method of our industrial and commercial life were being changed beyond recognition the tariff schedules have remained what were before the change began or have moved in the direction they were given when no large circumstance of our industrial development was what it is to-day. Our task is to square them with actual facts.[16]

The Underwood Act, when passed, lowered the average rate of duty on all imports into the United States to 8.8 percent and on dutiable imports alone to 26.8 percent (see Table 2). While it abolished the minimum and maximum schedules of the Payne-Aldrich Act, the new tariff constituted a major step by the United States toward supporting a liberal international economy.

During and after World War I, the liberal international economy, to which the United States had just made an important contribution, was threatened by rising economic nationalism in Europe. At the Paris Economic Conference in 1916, France and Britain agreed on a plan to organize trade on a state capitalist basis around exclusive regional trading blocs. This plan was never fully implemented, however, because of American pressure and inter-Ally disagreements. After the war, Britain adopted a moderate form of imperial preference; France enacted a two-tiered tariff in which the highest duties did not apply to countries that discriminated against French goods (as this type of tariff had traditionally been used), but to those that imposed "high" duties on French exports. Both policies contravened America's conception of the Open Door.

The principal instrument in the effort to extend the Open Door abroad was the "bargaining tariff," or the Fordney-McCumber Act of 1922. The concept of a flexible tariff, which was similar to the minimum and maximum provisions of the Payne-Aldrich Act, had gained wider acceptance in the United States after the Paris Economic Conference. In 1916, the National Foreign Trade Council called for the development of an effective bargaining tariff and expressed its willingness to work with the newly created Tariff Commission in writing such a bill. Immediately after the war, however, there was renewed interest in the concept of reciprocity as an instrument for acquiring special trading advantages. The Harding Administration, under the leadership of William S. Culbertson, argued for the Open Door. Culbertson, with the aid of Senator Smoot, was successful: the final version of the bill provided the President with the authority to impose penalty duties against countries that discriminated against American goods. The Fordney-McCumber Act, though it had been passed as a protectionist measure, did not raise tariff levels dramatically. The average tariff on all imports was raised to 13.9 percent while the tariff on dutiable imports was raised to 38.2 percent; both measures were below the average tariffs found in the first two phases discussed earlier.

In 1922, the Harding Administration also decided to abandon the conditional form of the most-favored-nation (MFN) principle and adopt a more liberal unconditional variant. Previously, trade concessions granted by the United States to second-party states had been extended to third-party states only upon the receipt of equivalent concessions. After it adopted the unconditional form of the MFN principle, the United States automatically extended concessions to all nations with which it had an MFN treaty. In conjunction with the flexible tariff provision of the Fordney-McCumber Tariff, this shift in policy illustrates the desire of the United States to play a greater and more liberal role within the international economy.

Constrained by domestic partisanship and a commitment to moderate protectionism, however, the Republicans were unable to wield the tariff as an effective offensive weapon to break down the barriers to discrimination abroad. The Europeans remained recalcitrant. In response to American criticism, they argued that the greatest obstacles to world trade were not their discriminatory tariff schedules, but the relatively high rates all nations faced in the United States. Americans, and especially Secretary of Commerce Herbert Hoover, replied that aggregate imports by the United States continued to rise despite the higher Fordney-McCumber duties and, indeed, that imports were rising faster than exports. Neither side would yield, and little progress was made.

Thus, the United States quest for a worldwide Open Door was not achieved in the 1920s. Even though the Europeans finally agreed at the Geneva International Economic Conference in 1927 that the unconditional MFN principle was the most desirable basis upon which to organize international trade, they continued to evade the Open Door principle in practice.

The United States recognized that its export trade was dependent not only on a liberal international economic regime, but also on a revitalized Europe; it therefore sought to assist in the rebuilding of the war-torn European economy. American decision makers perceived the isolation and embitterment of Germany as the central threat to European stability; once the United States had failed to join the League of Nations, however, few instruments remained by which it could attempt to induce or coerce the Europeans, and particularly France, into reintegrating Germany into the European economic and political orders. As a result, Washington was forced to expand its conception of foreign economic policy beyond the trade policy arena, and to include, for the first time, the issue areas of international finance and investment.

The outstanding war debts provided one of two instruments to influence European policies toward Germany. France, minimizing its responsibility for debts incurred during the war, wanted to extract the largest possible indemnity from Germany. The United States, focusing on Europe's long-term stability, sought a much lighter reparations burden. By denying any linkage between war debts and reparations—in contravention of the European view—the United States sought to limit the size of the final reparations settlement; it refused to yield until its allies agreed to make significant concessions to Germany.

The second major instrument available to American decision makers was the loan control program. The voluntary program adopted by the government in March 1922 stated that no loans by American bankers would be approved for "governments or citizens in countries who have failed to maintain their obligations to the United States."[17] In this way, the loan-control program was intended to apply pressure on the Europeans through the war-debt issue. Subjected to both official and unofficial American pressure and facing increasing financial difficulties, all the relevant European nations became increasingly willing to compromise. Between 1924 and 1926, the London Conference and the Dawes Loan temporarily settled the reparations issue; the Locarno Treaties helped stabilize the European political order by resolving several outstanding points of disagreement between France and Germany; and the Mellon-Berenger Agreement settled the war-debt program (again temporarily). In each of these cases, the final agreement was close to the position advocated by the United States.

In this third phase, the United States emerged as a significant but nonhegemonic leader within the international economy. Washington closely conformed to the policies expected of a supporter in an international economic structure of bilateral supportership as outlined above. Before the war, it made a significant move toward greater liberalism in its foreign economic policies through the Underwood Tariff Act. It also attempted to rebuild a liberal international economy during the 1920s. The United States could not unilaterally lead the international economy; as a result, it sought to bargain with the Europeans in order to meet its objectives. There were significant elements of cooperation with the United Kingdom, particularly in the area of international finance and currency stabilization. On the other hand, considerable criticism and threats of retaliation from the Europeans, and from the United Kingdom in particular, helped to restrain protectionism within the United States. Relatively high U.S. tariffs and the instruments used by the United States—primarily the outstanding war-debt issue and the loan-control program—to influence European policies did engender considerable controversy and conflict within the international community. Considering the magnitude of the war's destruction, the international economy was relatively stable during the 1920s even though no clear hegemonic leader was present. But it was not without tension.

1930–1934

The modicum of international stability that existed during the 1920s disappeared by 1929. In the presidential campaign of 1928, the Republicans pledged to relieve farm distress, which had been a problem throughout the 1920s, by raising tariffs on agricultural goods imported into the United States. Congress was called into special session by President Herbert Hoover for this purpose, but the legislative mandate was soon redefined as a general upward revision of the tariff. The domestic advocates of protectionism, who had been restrained during the 1920s, took this opportunity to press for special favors. The Smoot-Hawley Act of 1930, which raised tariffs on all imports to 19.0 percent and on dutiable imports to 55.3 percent (see Table 2), sparked a global increase in protectionism. In the two years that followed, Canada, Switzerland, Austria, France, Germany, Italy, and many other countries also adopted increased protection. The United Kingdom passed the protectionist Abnormal Importations and Horticultural Products Acts in 1931. In 1932, it adopted the Import Duties Act, which imposed a 10 percent *ad valorem* tariff on all imports into the country. And, in the Ottawa Agreements of 1932, the United Kingdom accepted a full-scale imperial preference system as first advocated by Chamberlain in 1895.

The London Economic Conference was organized in 1933 to discuss measures to halt the proliferation of protectionist and beggar-thy-neighbor policies throughout the international economy. While the Conference was in session, President Franklin D. Roosevelt dashed any hopes of success by his "bombshell" message of July 2, in which he deplored the emphasis on currency stabilization and stated that the creation of sound domestic economies should be the Conference's principal concern.

One year later, the wheels of international trade having ground to a halt, President Roosevelt reversed American policy with the passage of the Reciprocal Trade Agreements Act (RTAA). This act gave the President three years to negotiate foreign trade agreements that could reduce American tariffs by as much as 50 percent from the Smoot-Hawley levels. The emphasis on tariff reduction distinguishes the RTAA from all past American trade policies. For the first time, the United States sought to bargain not only for equality of access or for the Open Door, but for lower tariffs in foreign countries. Between 1934 and 1938, America negotiated 18 treaties that lowered duties at home and abroad. Each contained the unconditional MFN clause. These treaties were among the major stimuli of the resurgence of world trade in the late 1930s.

American foreign economic policy after 1930 was in accord with the prediction for a single supporter within the international economy. When the mutual constraints of bilateral supportership were lifted from the United States, protectionism was unleashed. Once retaliation had occurred and world trade was diminished, the United States stood to gain only if it expanded its export markets. This expansion could be accomplished only by lowering tariffs abroad; hence, the RTAA. The United States was not a hegemonic leader in the 1930s, however. It did not act altruistically or accept short-term costs for long-term gains. It continued to behave as predicted for a supporter: it bargained over tangible goods (tariffs) to achieve a specific goal (reductions) with immediate rewards.

CONCLUSIONS

American foreign economic policy between 1887 and 1934 generally conformed with the behavior predicted for a supporter. While the United Kingdom remained a hegemonic leader, the United States attempted to free-ride. Once the British position began to weaken and American productivity had surpassed that of the United Kingdom, the

United States began to play a more active and liberal role in the international economy. Within the structure of bilateral supportership, the United States emerged as a leader, restraining protectionism at home, attempting to reestablish the rule of nondiscrimination or the Open Door in the international economy, and seeking to stabilize Europe. Once Britain evolved from a supporter into a spoiler, leaving the United States as the sole supporter within the IES, both American policy and the international economy became unstable. In sum, the international economic structure and the position of the United States within it appear to provide a parsimonious and reasonably powerful explanation of American foreign economic policy and policy change. . . .

The structural theory outlined earlier lacks a conception of process, or an explanation of how the constraints or interests derived from the international economic structure are transformed into decisions or political strategies within particular countries. As a result, the causal link between the systemic-level international economic structure and national-level policy is open to question. Ultimately, structure and process must be integrated in a theory of political economy. In this article, however, I have only attempted to clarify the constraints facing the United States in the period 1887–1934 and to demonstrate the strength and usefulness of a purely structural argument as a first and necessary step toward an integrated theory. . . .

NOTES

1. *Congressional Record*, 51st Cong., 1st sess. (1890), 4250.
2. Kindleberger, *The World in Depression 1929–1939* (Berkeley: University of California Press, 1973).
3. *Ibid.*, 292.
4. Kindleberger, "Dominance and Leadership in the International Economy: Exploitation, Public Goods, and Free Rides," *International Studies Quarterly* 25 (June 1981), 247.
5. *Ibid.*, 249.
6. *Ibid.*, 250.
7. Kindleberger, *The World in Depression*, 305.
8. See Robert Gilpin, *U.S. Power and the Multinational Corporation: The Political Economy of Foreign Direct Investment* (New York: Basic Books, 1975), and "Economic Interdependence and National Security in Historical Perspective," in Klaus Knorr nd Frank N. Trager, eds., *Economic Issues and National Security* (Lawrence, Kansas: Regents Press of Kansas, 1977), 19–66.
9. Quoted in Charles S. Campbell, Jr., *Special Business Interests and the Open Door Policy* (Hamden, Conn.: Archon Books, 1968), 6.
10. George F. Kennan, *American Diplomacy 1900–1950* (Chicago: University of Chicago Press, 1951), 25–26.
11. *Ibid.*, 25.
12. *Ibid.*, 32.
13. Thomas J. McCormick, *China Market: America's Quest for Informal Empire 1893–1901* (Chicago: Quadrangle Books, 1967), 127.

14. *Congressional Record*, 61st Cong., 1st sess., 1909, 285; emphasis added.

15. Quoted in William Diamond, "The Economic Thought of Woodrow Wilson," *Johns Hopkins University Studies in Historical and Political Science* 61 (No. 4, 1943), 134.

16. H. R. Richardson, *Messages and Papers of the Presidents*, XVIII (New York: Bureau of National Literature), 8251–52.

17. Herbert Feis, *The Diplomacy of the Dollar: First Era 1919–1932* (Baltimore: The Johns Hopkins University Press, 1950), 11.

III. THE *PAX AMERICANA*

A. Overview

The United States has been the dominant force in international politics and economics since World War II. For over forty years, the general pattern of relations among non-Communist nations has been set by American leadership. In the political arena, formal and informal alliances have tied virtually every major non-Communist nation into an American-led network of mutual support and defense. In the economic arena, a wide-ranging set of international economic organizations—including the International Monetary Fund, the General Agreement on Tariffs and Trade, and the European Common Market—grew up under a protective American umbrella, and often as direct American initiatives. The world economy itself has been heavily influenced by the rise of modern multinational corporations and banks, whose contemporary form is largely of United States origin. It is virtually impossible to understand the postwar international political economy without also understanding the role the United States plays within it.

American plans for a reordered world economy go back to the mid-1930s. After World War I, the United States retreated into relative economic insularity, for reasons explored above (see "Historical Perspectives," page 69). When the Great Depression hit, American political leaders virtually ignored the possibility of international economic cooperation in their attempts to stabilize the domestic economy. Yet, even as the Roosevelt administration looked inward for recovery, by 1934 new American initiatives were signaling a shift in America's traditional isolation. Roosevelt's Secretary of State, Cordell Hull, was a militant free trader, and in 1934 he convinced Congress to pass the Reciprocal Trade Agreements Act, which allowed the Executive to negotiate tariff reductions with foreign nations. This important step toward trade liberalization and international economic cooperation was deepened as war threatened in Europe and the United States drew closer to Great Britain and France.

The seeds of the new international order, planted in the 1930s, began to grow even as World War II came to an end. The Bretton Woods Agreement reached among the Allied powers in 1944 established a new series of international economic organizations that became the foundation for the postwar American-led system. As the wartime American-Soviet alliance began to shatter, a new economic order emerged in the non-Communist world. At its center were the three pillars of the Bretton Woods system: international monetary cooperation under the auspices of the International Monetary Fund, international trade liberalization negotiated within the General Agreement on Tariffs and Trade, and investment in the developing countries stimulated by the International Bank for Reconstruction and Development (World Bank). All three pillars were essentially designed by the United States and dependent on American support.

As it developed, the postwar capitalist world reflected American foreign policy in many of its details. One principal concern of the United States was to build a bulwark of anti-Soviet allies; this was done with a massive inflow of American aid under the Marshall Plan, and the encouragement of Western European cooperation within a new Common Market. At the same time, the United States dramatically lowered its barriers to foreign goods, and American corporations began to invest heavily in foreign nations. Of course, the United States was not acting altruistically; European recovery, trade liberalization, and booming international investment helped bring and ensure great prosperity within the United States as well.

American policies, whatever their motivation, had an undeniable impact on the international political economy. Trade liberalization opened the huge American market to foreign producers. American overseas investment provided capital, technology, and expertise for both Europe and the developing world. American government economic aid—whether direct or channeled through such institutions as the World Bank—helped finance economic growth abroad. In addition, the American military "umbrella" allowed anti-Soviet governments in Europe, Japan, and the developing world to rely on the United States for security and to turn their attentions to encouraging economic growth.

All in all, the non-Communist world's unprecedented access to American markets and American capital provided a major stimulus to world economic growth—not to mention to the profits of American businesses and to general prosperity within the United States. For over twenty-five years after World War II, the capitalist world experienced impressive levels of economic growth and development, all within a general context of international cooperation under American political, economic, and military tutelage.

This period is often referred to as the *Pax Americana* because of its broad similarity to the British-led international economic system that reigned from about 1820 until World War I known as the *Pax Britannica*. In both instances, general political and economic peace prevailed under the leadership of an overwhelming world power—the United Kingdom in one case, the United States in the other.

Just as the *Pax Britannica* eventually ended, the *Pax Americana* will not last forever. Already in the early 1970s, strains were developing in the postwar system. Between 1971 and 1975, the postwar international monetary system, which had been based on a gold-backed United States dollar, fell apart and was replaced by a new, improvised pattern of floating exchange rates in which the dollar's role was still strong but no longer quite so central. All through the 1970s and 1980s, pressures for trade protection mounted from uncompetitive industries in North America and Western Europe, and, although tariff levels remained low, a variety of such nontariff barriers to world trade such as import quotas proliferated. In the political arena during the 1970s, détente between the United States and the Soviet Union seemed to make the American security umbrella less relevant for the Japanese and Western Europeans; in the less developed countries, North-South conflict appeared more important than East-West strife. Even as Soviet-American relations fell back into Cold-War patterns during the 1980s, the political solidarity of the West was never totally restored. Western Europeans and Japanese, unlike the United States, valued their improved economic and political ties with the Communist world and hesitated to break them; the Third World remained far more concerned about problems of development than about American-Soviet conflict. In both the economic and the political realms, by the mid-1980s the future of the *Pax Americana* seemed in question.

As might be expected, the post–World War II rise of American world hegemony has led to great scholarly controversy. Some analysts of the period view American political goals as determinant, especially as concerns the battle against Soviet influence. Others see United States economic interests as primary, and point to the massive expansion of American overseas economic interests since 1945. The future of the current American-led order is also a theme for debate, with some scholars projecting the end of United States hegemony and others expecting American international predominance to continue for the foreseeable future.

Most of the remainder of this book is devoted to the *Pax Americana*. In the sections that follow, a variety of thematic issues are addressed; in each cluster of issues, alternative theoretical and analytical perspectives compete. The selections in the remainder of this book thus serve both to illuminate important substantive issues in the modern international political economy and to illustrate divergent theoretical approaches to the analysis of these issues.

B. Production

Productive activity is at the center of any economy. Agriculture, mining, and manufacturing are the bases upon which domestic and international commerce, finance, and other services rest. No society can survive without producing, and production is thus crucial to both domestic and international political economies.

In the international arena, production abroad by large corporations has gained enormously in importance since World War I. However, the establishment of productive facilities in foreign lands is nothing new; the planters who settled the southern portion of the Thirteen Colonies under contract to, and financed by, British merchant companies were engaging in foreign direct investment in plantation agriculture. Before the twentieth century, indeed, foreign investment in primary production—mining and agriculture—was quite common. European and North American investors financed copper mines in Chile and Mexico, tea and rubber plantations in India and Indochina, and gold mines in South Africa and Australia.

Around the turn of the century, and especially after World War I, a relatively novel form of foreign direct investment arose: the establishment of overseas branch factories of manufacturing corporations. In its origin, the phenomenon was largely North American, and remained so until the 1960s, when European and then Japanese manufacturers also began investing in productive facilities abroad. The name given to this internationalized industrial firm was the *multinational* or *transnational corporation* (*MNC* or *TNC*), usually defined as a firm with productive facilities in three or more countries. Such corporations have been extraordinarily controversial for both scholars and politicians.

By 1980, there were about sixteen thousand MNCs in the world. Most are relatively small, but the top several hundred are so huge, and so globe-straddling, as to dominate major portions of the world economy. It has in fact been estimated that the 350 largest MNCs in the world in 1980, with over twenty-five thousand affiliates, accounted for 28 percent of the non-Communist world's output. The largest MNCs have annual sales larger than the Gross National Product of all but a few of the world's nations.[1]

Most Americans take MNCs for granted—few even realize that such firms as Shell, Bayer, American Motors, and Nestlé are foreign-owned. Yet, neither scholars nor politicians in much of the world are so

170

lackadaisical; for the former, the rise of the MNC presents major analytical problems, while for the latter, political problems are much more immediate.

The principal analytical task is to explain the very existence of multinational manufacturing corporations. It is, of course, simple to understand why English investors would finance tea plantations in Ceylon—they could hardly have grown tea in Manchester. Yet, in the abstract, there is little logic in Bayer producing aspirin in the United States. If the German aspirin industry is more efficient than the American, Bayer could simply export the pills from its factories at home and sell them in the United States. Why, then, does Ford make cars in England, Volkswagen make cars in the United States, and both companies make cars in Mexico, instead of simply shipping them, respectively, across the Atlantic or the Rio Grande?

For the answer, students of the MNC have examined both economic and political factors. The political spurs to overseas direct investment are straightforward: Many countries maintain trade barriers in order to encourage local industrialization; this makes exporting to these nations difficult, and MNCs thus choose to "jump trade barriers" and produce inside protected markets. Similar considerations apply where the local government uses such policies as "Buy American" regulations, which specify, for example, that government purchases must be domestically produced or where, as in the case of Japanese auto investment in the United States, overseas producers fear the onset of protectionist measures.

Economic factors in the spread of MNCs are many and complex. Unquestionably, the most influential and widely accepted explanation of them is the "product-cycle theory" developed by Raymond Vernon of the Harvard Business School and presented in Reading 10. The picture that emerges from Vernon's analysis, successfully applied to a number of industries and historical periods, is one in which leading firms introduce new products, export to foreign markets, eventually engage in foreign investment, and then see their goods come to be more and more standardized, at which point presumably the leaders move on to other new products. This jibes with the frequent observation that MNCs tend to operate in oligopolistic markets with products that have a great deal of embodied new technology, and that MNCs tend to have important previous exporting experience.

Other economic stimuli to foreign direct investment can also be advanced. Because MNCs are very large in comparison to local firms in most countries, they can mobilize large amounts of capital more easily than local enterprises. Foreign corporations may then, simply by virtue of their vast wealth, buy up local firms in order to eliminate real or potential competitors. In some lines of business, such as large-scale appliances or automobiles, the initial investment necessary to begin production may be prohibitive for local firms, giving MNCs a decisive advantage. And the widespread popularity of consumption patterns formed in North America and Western Europe and then transplanted to other nations—a process which often leads to charges of "cultural imperialism"—may lead local consumers to prefer foreign brand names to local ones: much of the Third World brushes with Colgate and drinks Coke, brands popularized by American literature, cinema, television, and advertising.

If the origins of MNCs are analytically controversial, their effects are debated with far more ferocity. Because most developed countries have technically developed regulatory agencies, and relatively large and sophisticated economies, MNCs have aroused far less opposition in the advanced industrial nations than in the Third World. Most less developed countries (LDCs) have economies smaller than the largest MNCs, and the regulatory bureaucracies of many LDC governments are no match for MNC executives. In many LDCs, then, the very presence of MNCs is viewed with suspicion. MNCs have been known to interfere in local politics, and the competition huge foreign enterprises present to local businesspeople is often resented. Since 1970, most LDCs have imposed stringent regulations on foreign direct investors, although most of them simultaneously believe that on balance the MNCs have a beneficial impact on national economic and political development. In the section that follows, the articles by Edith Penrose and by Richard Sklar deal specifically with the economic and political implications of the spread of MNCs to the less developed countries.

The rise of enormous business corporations whose activities span many nations is also a fact of great interest to analysts of world politics. Yet, scholars disagree over the independent importance of MNCs. For many, especially those associated with Realist or structural Marxist schools of thought, MNCs are not so much a new, independent political and economic force as they are adjuncts to their home countries' more general national goals. Thus, the spread of American MNCs, argue many, was an essential component of United States global strategy, a strategy that saw the burgeoning presence of American firms abroad as a major vehicle for American political influence. Robert Rowthorn (Reading 12) argues from a Marxist perspective that MNCs have not eliminated competition among capitalist nations, and indeed have become a major form in which such competition takes place.

For other scholars, especially those from a Liberal perspective and many other Marxists, MNCs have begun to surpass the power of individual nation-states. The concentrated economic power of the MNCs, and their ability to move rapidly from nation to nation, leaves states nearly powerless to control them. For some Marxists, this implies the creation of a new supranational bourgeoisie *above* nationality; this is essentially Stephen Hymer's position (Reading 2). Others far from the Marxist tradition, such as leading businessman and statesman George Ball, a quintessential Liberal, also believe that MNCs are making divisions between national markets more and more irrelevant (see Reading 11). For Liberals, the increased integration of national markets is a major spur to global economic efficiency and governments should refrain from interfering in this process.

Multinational corporations will in the view of some lead to a new era in world politics, making national distinctions unimportant. For others, MNCs are simply one more tool in the hands of still-powerful nation-states. Whether the truth lies with one or another view, or somewhere in between, there is little doubt that MNCs will remain an important topic in the study of the international political economy, as well as a live issue in domestic and world politics.

NOTE

1. United Nations Centre on Transnational Corporations, *Transnational Corporations in World Development: Third Survey* (New York: UN, 1983), p. 46.

10. International Investment and International Trade in the Product Cycle

RAYMOND VERNON

In this influential 1966 essay, Raymond Vernon theorizes that foreign direct investment is a natural stage in the life cycle of products. When a product is first introduced, the firm that developed it has an innate technological and cost advantage; it therefore produces the goods at home and exports to foreign markets. In the second stage of the cycle, the successful marketing of the goods stimulates foreign competitors who, because they are more familiar with the local market and possess labor and transportation cost advantages, begin to displace the innovator's exports. To maintain its market, the originator invests in and begins to produce in its former export markets. In the third stage, production technology is so standardized that labor costs become crucial and manufacture shifts to the less developed countries. From here, the product is now exported to the innovators' home market. The "product cycle" thus combines ideas on innovation, production location, and national market characteristics to predict where and when trade and foreign direct investments will occur. This article presents a powerful theory that draws upon both market and institutional factors to explain the rise and growth of multinational corporations.

Anyone who has sought to understand the shifts in international trade and international investment over the past twenty years has chafed from time to time under an acute sense of the inadequacy of the available analytical tools.[1] While the comparative cost concept and other basic concepts have rarely failed to provide some help, they have usually carried the analyst only a very little way toward adequate understanding. For the most part, it has been necessary to formulate new concepts in order to explore issues such as the strengths and limitations of import substitution in the development process, the implications of common market arrangements for trade and investment, the underlying reasons for the Leontief paradox, and other critical issues of the day.

As theorists have groped for some more efficient tools, there has been a flowering in international trade and capital theory. But the very proliferation of theory has increased the urgency of the search for unifying concepts. It is doubtful that we shall find many propositions that can match the simplicity, power, and universality of application of the theory of comparative advantage and the international equilibrating mechanism; but unless the search for better tools goes on, the usefulness of economic theory for the solution of problems in international trade and capital movements will probably decline.

The present paper deals with one promising line of generalization and synthesis which seems to me to have been somewhat neglected by the main stream of trade theory. It puts less emphasis upon comparative cost doctrine and more upon the timing of innovation, the effects of scale economies, and the roles of ignorance and uncertainty in influencing trade patterns. It is an approach with respectable sponsorship, deriving bits and pieces of its inspiration from the writings of such persons as Williams, Kindleberger, MacDougall, Hoffmeyer, and Burenstam-Linder.

Emphases of this sort seem first to have appeared when economists were searching for an explanation of what looked like a persistent, structural shortage of dollars in the world. When the shortage proved ephemeral in the late 1950's, many of the ideas which the shortage had stimulated were tossed overboard as prima facie wrong. Nevertheless, one cannot be exposed to the main currents of international trade for very long without feeling that any theory which neglected the roles of innovation, scale, ignorance and uncertainty would be incomplete.

LOCATION OF NEW PRODUCTS

We begin with the assumption that the enterprises in any one of the advanced countries of the world are not distinguishably different from those in any other advanced country, in terms of their access to scientific knowledge and their capacity to comprehend scientific principles. All of them, we may safely assume, can secure access to the knowledge that exists in the physical, chemical and biological sciences. These sciences at times may be difficult, but they are rarely occult.

It is a mistake to assume, however, that equal access to scientific principles in all the advanced countries means equal probability of the application of these principles in the generation of new products. There is ordinarily a large gap between the knowledge of a scientific principle and the embodiment of the principle in a marketable product. An entrepreneur usually has to intervene to accept the risks involved in testing whether the gap can be bridged.

If all entrepreneurs, wherever located, could be presumed to be equally conscious of and equally responsive to all entrepreneurial opportunities, wherever they arose, the classical view of the dominant role of price in resource allocation might be highly relevant. There is good reason to believe, however, that the entrepreneur's consciousness of and responsiveness to opportunity are a function of ease of communication; and further, that ease of communication is a function of geographical proximity. Accordingly, we abandon the powerful simplifying notion that knowledge is a universal free good, and introduce it as an independent variable in the decision to trade or to invest.

The fact that the search for knowledge is an inseparable part of the decision-making process and that relative ease of access to knowledge can profoundly affect the outcome are now reasonably well established through empirical research. One implication of that fact is that producers in any market are more likely to be aware of the possibility of introducing new products in that market than producers located elsewhere would be.

The United States market offers certain unique kinds of opportunities to those who are in a position to be aware of them.

First, the United States market consists of consumers with an average income which is higher (except for a few anomalies like Kuwait) than that in any other national market—twice as high as that of Western Europe, for instance. Wherever there was a chance to offer a new product responsive to wants at high levels of income, this chance would presumably first be apparent to someone in a position to observe the United States market.

Second, the United States market is characterized by high unit labor costs and relatively unrationed capital compared with practically all other markets. This is a fact which conditions the demand for both consumer goods and industrial products. In the case of consumer goods, for instance, the high cost of laundresses contributes to the origins of the drip-dry shirt and the home washing machine. In the case of industrial goods, high labor cost leads to the early development and use of the conveyor belt, the fork-lift truck and the automatic control system. It seems to follow that wherever there was a chance successfully to sell a new product responsive to the need to conserve labor, this chance would be apparent first to those in a position to observe the United States market.

Assume, then, that entrepreneurs in the United States are first aware of opportunities to satisfy new wants associated with high income levels or high unit labor costs. Assume further that the evidence of an unfilled need and the hope of some kind of monopoly windfall for the early starter both are sufficiently strong to justify the initial investment that is usually involved in converting an abstract idea into a marketable product. Here we have a reason for expecting a consistently higher rate of expenditure on product development to be undertaken by United States producers than by producers in other countries, at least in lines which promise to substitute capital for labor or which promise to satisfy high-income wants. Therefore, if United States firms spend more than their foreign counterparts on new product development (often misleadingly labeled "research"), this may be due not to some obscure sociological drive for innovation but to more effective communication between the potential market and the potential supplier of the market. This sort of explanation is consistent with the pioneer appearance in the United States (conflicting claims of the Soviet Union notwithstanding) of the sewing machine, the typewriter, the tractor, etc.

At this point in the exposition, it is important once more to emphasize that the discussion so far relates only to innovation in certain kinds of products, namely to those associated with high income and those which substitute capital for labor. Our hypothesis says nothing about industrial innovation in general; this is a larger subject than we have tackled here. There are very few countries that have failed to introduce at least a few products; and there are some, such as Germany and Japan, which have been responsible for a considerable number of such introductions. Germany's outstanding successes in the development and use of plastics may have been due, for instance, to a traditional concern with her lack of a raw materials base, and a recognition that a market might exist in Germany for synthetic substitutes.

Our hypothesis asserts that United States producers are likely to be the first to spy an opportunity for high-income or labor-saving new products. But it goes on to assert that the first producing facilities for such products will be located in the United States. This is not a self-evident proposition. Under the calculus of least cost, production need not automatically take place at a location close to the market, unless the product can be produced and delivered from that location at lowest cost. Besides, now that most major United States companies control facilities situated in one or more locations outside of the United States, the possibility of considering a non-United States location is even more plausible than it might once have been.

Of course, if prospective producers were to make their locational choices on the basis of least-cost considerations, the United States would not always be ruled out. The costs of international transport and United States import duties, for instance, might be so high as to argue for such a location. My guess is, however, that the early producers of a new product intended for the United States market are attracted to a United

States location by forces which are far stronger than relative factor-cost and transport considerations. For the reasoning on this point, one has to take a long detour away from comparative cost analysis into areas which fall under the rubrics of communication and external economies.

By now, a considerable amount of empirical work has been done on the factors affecting the location of industry. Many of these studies try to explain observed locational patterns in conventional cost-minimizing terms, by implicit or explicit reference to labor cost and transportation cost. But some explicitly introduce problems of communication and external economies as powerful locational forces. These factors were given special emphasis in the analyses which were a part of the New York Metropolitan Region Study of the 1950's. At the risk of oversimplifying, I shall try to summarize what these studies suggested.

In the early stages of introduction of a new product, producers were usually confronted with a number of critical, albeit transitory, conditions. For one thing, the product itself may be quite unstandardized for a time; its inputs, its processing, and its final specifications may cover a wide range. Contrast the great variety of automobiles produced and marketed before 1910 with the thoroughly standardized product of the 1930's, or the variegated radio designs of the 1920's with the uniform models of the 1930's. The unstandardized nature of the design at this early stage carries with it a number of locational implications.

First, producers at this stage are particularly concerned with the degree of freedom they have in changing their inputs. Of course, the cost of the inputs is also relevant. But as long as the nature of these inputs cannot be fixed in advance with assurance, the calculation of cost must take into account the general need for flexibility in any locational choice.

Second, the price elasticity of demand for the output of individual firms is comparatively low. This follows from the high degree of production differentiation, or the existence of monopoly in the early stages. One result is, of course, that small cost differences count less in the calculations of the entrepreneur than they are likely to count later on.

Third, the need for swift and effective communication on the part of the producer with customers, suppliers, and even competitors is especially high at this stage. This is a corollary of the fact that a considerable amount of uncertainty remains regarding the ultimate dimensions of the market, the efforts of rivals to preempt that market, the specifications of the inputs needed for production, and the specifications of the products likely to be most successful in the effort.

All of these considerations tend to argue for a location in which communication between the market and the executives directly concerned with the new product is swift and easy, and in which a wide variety of potential types of input that might be needed by the production unit are easily come by. In brief, the producer who sees a market for some new product in the United States may be led to select a United States location for production on the basis of national locational considerations which extend well beyond simple factor cost analysis plus transport considerations.

THE MATURING PRODUCT

As the demand for a product expands, a certain degree of standardization usually takes place. This is not to say that efforts at product differentiation come to an end. On the contrary; such efforts may even intensify, as competitors try to avoid the full brunt of price competition. Moreover, variety may appear as a result of specialization. Radios, for instance, ultimately acquired such specialized forms as clock radios, automobile radios, portable radios, and so on. Nevertheless, though the subcategories may multiply and the efforts at product differentiation increase, a growing acceptance of certain general standards seems to be typical.

Once again, the change has locational implications. First of all, the need for flexibility declines. A commitment to some set of product standards opens up technical possibilities for achieving economies of scale through mass output, and encourages long-term commitments to some given process and some fixed set of facilities. Second, concern about production cost begins to take the place of concern about product characteristics. Even if increased price competition is not yet present, the reduction of the uncertainties surrounding the operation enhances the usefulness of cost projections and increases the attention devoted to cost.

The empirical studies to which I referred earlier suggest that, at this stage in an industry's development, there is likely to be considerable shift in the location of production facilities at least as far as internal United States locations are concerned. The empirical materials on international locational shifts simply have not yet been analyzed sufficiently to tell us very much. A little speculation, however, indicates some hypotheses worth testing.

Picture an industry engaged in the manufacture of the high-income or labor-saving products that are the focus of our discussion. Assume that the industry has begun to settle down in the United States to some degree of large-scale production. Although the first mass market may be located in the United States, some demand for the product begins almost at once to appear elsewhere. For instance, although heavy fork-lift trucks in general may have a comparatively small market in Spain because of the relative cheapness of unskilled labor in that country, some limited demand for the product will appear there almost as soon as the existence of the product is known.

If the product has a high income elasticity of demand or if it is a satisfactory substitute for high-cost labor, the demand in time will begin to grow quite rapidly in relatively advanced countries such as those of Western Europe. Once the market expands in such an advanced country, entrepreneurs will begin to ask themselves whether the time has come to take the risk of setting up a local producing facility.

How long does it take to reach this stage? An adequate answer must surely be a complex one. Producers located in the United States, weighing the wisdom of setting up a new production facility in the importing country, will feel obliged to balance a number of complex considerations. As long as the marginal production cost plus the transport cost of the goods exported from the United States is lower than the average cost of prospective production in the market of import, United States producers will presumably prefer to avoid an investment. But that calculation depends on the producer's ability to project the cost of production in a market in which factor costs and the appropriate technology differ from those at home.

Now and again, the locational force which determined some particular overseas investment is so simple and so powerful that one has little difficulty in identifying it. Otis Elevator's early proliferation of production facilities abroad was quite patently a function of the high cost of shipping assembled elevator cabins to distant locations and the limited scale advantages involved in manufacturing elevator cabins at a single location. Singer's decision to invest in Scotland as early as 1867 was also based on considerations of a sort sympathetic with our hypothesis. It is not unlikely that the overseas demand for its highly standardized product was already sufficiently large at that time to exhaust the obvious scale advantages of manufacturing in a single location, especially if that location was one of high labor cost.

In an area as complex and "imperfect" as international trade and investment, however, one ought not anticipate that any hypothesis will have more than a limited explanatory power. United States airplane manufacturers surely respond to many "noneconomic" locational forces, such as the desire to play safe in problems of military security. Producers in the United States who have a protected patent position overseas presumably take that fact into account in deciding whether or when to produce abroad. And other producers often are motivated by considerations too complex to reconstruct readily, such as the fortuitous timing of a threat of new competition in the country of import, the level of tariff protection anticipated for the future, the political situation in the country of prospective investment and so on.

We arrive, then, at the stage at which United States producers have come around to the establishment of production units in the advanced countries. Now a new group of forces are set in train. . . .

As far as individual United States producers are concerned, the local markets thenceforth will be filled from local production units set up abroad. Once these facilities are in operation, however, more ambitious possibilities for their use may be suggested. When comparing a United States producing facility and a facility in another advanced country, the obvious production-cost differences between the rival producing areas are usually differences due to scale and differences due to labor costs. If the producer is an international firm with producing locations in several countries, its costs of financing capital at the different locations may not be sufficiently different to matter very much. If economies of scale are being fully exploited, the principal differences between any two locations are likely to be labor costs. Accordingly, it may prove wise for the international firm to begin servicing third-country markets from the new location. And if labor cost differences are large enough to offset transport costs, then exports back to the United States may become a possibility as well.

Any hypotheses based on the assumption that the United States entrepreneur will react rationally when offered the possibility of a lower-cost location abroad is, of course, somewhat suspect. The decision-making sequence that is used in connection with international investments, according to various empirical studies, is not a model of the rational process. But there is one theme that emerges again and again in such studies. Any threat to the established position of an enterprise is a powerful galvanizing force to action; in fact, if I interpret the empirical work correctly, threat in general is a more reliable stimulus to action than opportunity is likely to be.

In the international investment field, threats appear in various forms once a large-scale export business in manufactured products has developed. Local entrepreneurs located in the countries which are the targets of these exports grow restive at the opportunities they are missing. Local governments concerned with generating employment or promoting growth or balancing their trade accounts begin thinking of ways and means to replace the imports. An international investment by the exporter, therefore, becomes a prudent means of forestalling the loss of a market. In this case, the yield on the investment is seen largely as the avoidance of a loss of income to the system.

The notion that a threat to the status quo is a powerful galvanizing force for international investment also seems to explain what happens after the initial investment. Once such an investment is made by a United States producer, other major producers in the United States sometimes see it as a threat to the status quo. They see themselves as losing position relative to the investing company, with vague intimations of further losses to come. Their "share of the market" is imperiled, viewing "share of the market" in global terms. At the same time, their ability to estimate the production-cost structure of their competitors, operating far away in an unfamiliar foreign area, is impaired; this is a particularly unsettling state because it conjures up the possibility of a return flow of products to the United States and a new source of price competition, based on cost differences of unknown magnitude. The uncertainty can be reduced by emulating the pathfinding investor and by investing in the same area; this may not be an optimizing investment pattern and it may be costly, but it is least disturbing to the status quo.

Pieces of this hypothetical pattern are subject to empirical tests of a sort. So far, at any rate, the empirical tests have been reassuring. The office machinery industry, for instance, has seen repeatedly the phenomenon of the introduction of a new product in the United States, followed by United States exports, followed still later by United States imports. (We have still to test whether the timing of the commencement of overseas production by United States subsidiaries fits into the expected pattern.) In the electrical and electronic products industry, those elements in the pattern which can be measured show up nicely. A broader effort is now under way to test the United States trade patterns of a group of products with high income elasticities; and, here too, the preliminary results are encouraging. On a much more general basis, it is reassuring for our hypotheses to observe that the foreign manufacturing subsidiaries of United States firms have been increasing their exports to third countries. . . .

THE STANDARDIZED PRODUCT

. . . At an advanced stage in the standardization of some products, the less-developed countries may offer competitive advantages as a production location.

This is a bold projection, which seems on first blush to be wholly at variance with the Heckscher-Ohlin theorem. According to that theorem, one presumably ought to anticipate that the exports of the less-developed countries would tend to be relatively labor-intensive products.

One of the difficulties with the theorem, however, is that it leaves marketing considerations out of account. One reason for the omission is evident. As long as knowledge is regarded as a free good, instantaneously available, and as long as individual producers are regarded as atomistic contributors to the total supply, marketing problems cannot be expected to find much of a place in economic theory. In projecting the patterns of export from less-developed areas, however, we cannot afford to disregard the fact that information comes at a cost; and that entrepreneurs are not readily disposed to pay the price of investigating overseas markets of unknown dimensions and unknown promise. Neither are they eager to venture into situations which they know will demand a constant flow of reliable marketing information from remote sources.

If we can assume that highly standardized products tend to have a well-articulated, easily accessible international market and to sell largely on the basis of price (an assumption inherent in the definition), then it follows that such products will not pose the problem of market information quite so acutely for the less-developed countries. This establishes a necessary if not a sufficient condition for investment in such industries.

Of course, foreign investors seeking an optimum location for a captive facility may not have to concern themselves too much with questions of market information; presumably, they are thoroughly familiar with the marketing end of the business and are looking for a low-cost captive source of supply. In that case, the low cost of labor may be the initial attraction drawing the investor to less-developed areas. But other limitations in such areas, according to our hypothesis, will bias such captive operations toward the production of standardized items. The reasons in this case turn on the part played in the production process by external economies. Manufacturing processes which receive significant inputs from the local economy, such as skilled labor, repairmen, reliable power, spare parts, industrial materials processed according to exacting specification, and so on, are less appropriate to the less-developed areas than those that do not have such requirements. Unhappily, most industrial processes require one or another ingredient of this difficult sort. My guess is, however, that the industries which produce a standardized product are in the best position to avoid the problem, by producing on a vertically-integrated self-sustaining basis.

In speculating about future industrial exports from the less-developed areas, therefore, we are led to think of products with a fairly clear-cut set of economic characteristics. Their production function is such as to require significant inputs of labor; otherwise there is no reason to expect a lower production cost in less-developed countries. At the same time, they are products with a high price elasticity of demand for the output of individual firms; otherwise, there is no strong incentive to take the risks of pioneering with production in a new area. In addition, products whose production process did not rely heavily upon external economies would be more obvious candidates than those which required a more elaborate industrial environment. The implications of remoteness also would be critical; products which could be precisely described by standardized specifications and which could be produced for inventory without fear of obsolescence would be more relevant than those which had less precise specifications and which could not easily be ordered from remote locations. Moreover, high-value items capable of absorbing significant freight costs would be more likely to appear than bulky items low in value by weight. Standardized textile products are, of course, the illustration par excellence of the sort of product that meets the criteria. But other products come to mind such as crude steel, simple fertilizers, newsprint, and so on.

Speculation of this sort draws some support from various inter-regional experiences in industrial location. In the United States, for example, the "export" industries which moved to the low-wage south in search of lower costs tended to be industries which had no great need for a sophisticated industrial environment and which produced fairly standardized products. In the textile industry, it was the grey goods, cotton sheetings and men's shirt plants that went south; producers of high-style dresses or other unstandardized items were far more reluctant to move. In the electronics industry, it was the mass producers of tubes, resistors and other standardized high-volume components that showed the greatest disposition to move south; custom-built and research-oriented production remained closer to markets and to the main industrial complexes. A similar pattern could be discerned in printing and in chemicals production.

In other countries, a like pattern is suggested by the impressionistic evidence. The underdeveloped south of Italy and the laggard north of Britain and Ireland both seem to be attracting industry with standardized output and self-sufficient process.

Once we begin to look for relevant evidence of such investment patterns in the less-developed countries proper, however, only the barest shreds of corroboratory information can be found. One would have difficulty in thinking of many cases in which manufacturers of standardized products in the more advanced countries had made significant investments in the less-developed countries with a view of exporting such products from those countries. To be sure, other types of foreign investment are not uncommon in the less-developed countries, such as investments in import-replacing industries which were made in the face of a threat of import restriction. But there are only a few export-oriented cases similar to that of Taiwan's foreign-owned electronics plants and Argentina's new producing facility, set up to manufacture and export standard sorting equipment for computers.

If we look to foreign trade patterns, rather than foreign investment patterns, to learn something about the competitive advantage of the less-developed countries, the possibility that they are an attractive locus for the output of standardized products gains slightly more support. The Taiwanese and Japanese trade performances are perhaps the most telling ones in support of the projected pattern; both countries have managed to develop significant overseas markets for standardized manufactured products. According to one major study of the subject (a study stimulated by the Leontief paradox), Japanese exports are more capital-intensive than is the Japanese production which is displaced by imports. . . . Apart from these cases, however, all that one sees are a few provocative successes such as some sporadic sales of newsprint from Pakistan, the successful export of sewing machines from India, and so on. Even in these cases, one cannot be sure that they are consistent with the hypothesis unless he has done a good deal more empirical investigation.

The reason why so few relevant cases come to mind may be that the process has not yet advanced far enough. Or it may be that such factors as extensive export constraints and overvalued exchange rates are combining to prevent the investment and exports that otherwise would occur.

If there is one respect in which this discussion may deviate from classical expectations, it is in the view that the overall scarcity of capital in the less-developed countries will not prevent investment in facilities for the production of standardized products.

There are two reasons why capital costs may not prove a barrier to such investment.

First, according to our hypotheses, the investment will occur in industries which require some significant labor inputs in the production process; but they will be concentrated in that subsector of the industry which produces highly standardized products capable of self-contained production establishments. The net of these specifications is indeterminate so far as capital-intensiveness is concerned. A standardized textile item may be more or less capital-intensive than a plant for unstandardized petro-chemicals.

Besides, even if the capital requirements for a particular plant are heavy, the cost of the capital need not prove a bar. The assumption that capital costs come high in the less-developed countries requires a number of fundamental qualifications. The reality, to the extent that it is known, is more complex.

One reason for this complexity is the role played by the international investor. Producers of chemical fertilizers, when considering whether to invest in a given country, may be less concerned with the going rate for capital in that country than with their opportunity costs as they see such costs. For such investors the alternatives to be weighed are not the full range of possibilities calling for capital but only a very restricted range of alternatives, such as the possibilities offered by chemical fertilizer investment elsewhere. The relevant capital cost for a chemical fertilizer plant, therefore, may be fairly low if the investor is an international entrepreneur.

Moreover, the assumption that finance capital is scarce and that interest rates are high in a less-developed country may prove inapplicable to the class of investors who concern us here. The capital markets of the less-developed countries typically consist of a series of water-tight, insulated, submarkets in which wholly different rates prevail and between which arbitrage opportunities are limited. In some countries, the going figures may vary from 5 to 40 per cent, on grounds which seem to have little relation to issuer risk or term of loan. (In some economies, where inflation is endemic, interest rates which in effect represent a negative real cost are not uncommon.)

These internal differences in interest rates may be due to a number of factors: the fact that funds generated inside the firm usually are exposed to a different yield test than external borrowings; the fact that government loans are often floated by mandatory levies on banks and other intermediaries; and the fact that funds borrowed by governments from international sources are often reloaned in domestic markets at rates which are linked closely to the international borrowing rate, however irrelevant that may be. Moreover, one has to reckon with the fact that public international lenders tend to lend at near-uniform rates, irrespective of the identity of the borrower and the going interest rate in his country. Access to capital on the part of underdeveloped countries, therefore, becomes a direct function of the country's capacity to propose plausible projects to public international lenders. If a project can plausibly be shown to "pay its own way" in balance-of-payment and output terms at "reasonable" interest rates, the largest single obstacle to obtaining capital at such rates has usually been overcome.

Accordingly, one may say that from the entrepreneur's viewpoint certain systematic and predictable "imperfections" of the capital markets may reduce or eliminate the capital-shortage handicap which is characteristic of the less-developed countries; and, further, that as a result of the reduction or elimination such countries may find themselves in a position to compete effectively in the export of certain standardized capital-intensive goods. This is not the statement of another paradox; it is not the same as to say that the capital-poor countries will develop capital-intensive economies. All we are concerned with here is a modest fraction of the industry of such countries, which in turn is a minor fraction of their total economic activity. It may be that the anomalies such industries represent are systematic enough to be included in our normal expectations regarding conditions in the less developed countries. . . .

NOTE

1. The preparation of this article was financed in part by a grant from the Ford Foundation to the Harvard Business School.

11. Cosmocorp: The Importance of Being Stateless

GEORGE W. BALL

In this 1967 essay, originally a speech to the International Chamber of Commerce, prominent investment banker and former Undersecretary of State George Ball presents an eloquent defense of economic liberalism and the principle of minimal political interference in business. Ball points out that, with the rise of the multinational corporation, economic interests have come to surpass the ability of nation-states to control them. He then describes the tension between national governments and multinational corporations, and suggests ways of defusing this tension in order to maintain an open international economy.

During the several millennia of our history there have been long periods when time seemed to stand still. Now in this last third of the twentieth century it has not only caught up, but seems at times to be moving ahead of us. Caught in a whirlwind of pervasive and accelerating change, we have barely enough time to inquire as to its larger implications, and where they may lead us a decade hence.

We recognize that we live in a world whose resources are finite and whose demands are exploding. To avoid a Darwinian debacle on a global scale we will have to use our resources with maximum efficiency and a minimum of waste.

In these twenty postwar years, we have come to recognize in action, though not always in words, that the political boundaries of nation-states are too narrow and constricted to define the scope and activities of modern business. This recognition has found some reflection, though not enough, in political action. . . .

International trade, as everyone knows, is as old as time. Internationalized production is less familiar. Businessmen in the United Kingdom are old hands at making their living in world markets and exporting capital to produce goods abroad. This has not always been true of the

United States. Except in extractive industries, most U.S. enterprises until recent times have concentrated their activities on producing for the national market, exporting only their surplus. Many still do. However this is no longer adequate for the requirements of the world we live in. In order to survive, man must use the world's resources in the most efficient manner. This can be achieved only when all the factors necessary for the production and use of goods—capital, labor, raw materials, plant facilities and distribution—are freely mobilized and deployed according to the most efficient pattern. And this in turn will be possible only when national boundaries no longer play a critical role in defining economic horizons.

It is a fact of great import, therefore, that, at a time when politicians have been moving to create regional markets to supersede national markets, businessmen have been making quiet progress on an even larger scale: The great industrial enterprises of the world are moving to recast their plans and design their activities according to the vision of a total world economy.

In this development, as is so often the case in history, commerce has been in advance of politics. In a thoroughly pragmatic spirit it has improvised the fictions needed to shake free from strangling political impediments. To make possible the global activities of modern business, it has extended the fiction of the corporation—that artificial person invented by lawyers to free entrepreneurs of personal liability in doing business and thus enable them to mobilize capital from diverse financial sources. The corporate form was originally conceived as a special privilege granted by states to some businessmen for attainment of the states' political purposes. But, over the years, the corporate form of business has become common everywhere and enabled business to roam the world with substantial freedom from political interference, producing and selling in a multiplicity of national markets and creating corporate offspring of various nationalities.

AN EMANCIPATED PERSONALITY

Today we recognize the immense potentials of this emancipated corporate person. For at least a half century a handful of great companies have bought, produced and sold goods around the world. Since the Second World War the original handful has multiplied many fold. Today a large and rapidly expanding roster of companies is engaged in taking the raw materials produced in one group of countries, transforming these into manufactured goods with the labor and plant facilities of another group, and selling the products in still a third group. And, with the benefit of instant communications, quick transport, computers and modern managerial techniques, they are redeploying resources and altering patterns of production and distribution month to month in response to changes in price and availability of labor and materials.

This is an achievement of impressive magnitude and we are only beginning to know its implications. By no means all industries in the United States or elsewhere have comprehended the full meaning and opportunity of the world economy. But they will soon. Meanwhile we can detect the extent to which the concept shapes corporate thinking by the attitudes of management toward liberal trade.

By and large, those companies that have achieved a global vision of their operations tend to opt for a world in which not only goods but all of the factors of production can shift with maximum freedom. Other industries—some of great size and importance in the United States, such as steel and textiles—which have confined their production largely or entirely to domestic markets, anxiously demand protection whenever a substantial volume of imports begins to invade national markets.

HOLD THE HAILSTONES

At the moment, in the United States the free-trade movement is again threatened by protectionist storm clouds. I am confident that these clouds will blow by with more wind than hailstones. American businessmen have become involved in world trade to an extent where they can no longer turn their backs on it. But trouble will always arise in some places as business continues to expand its horizons. Conflict will increase between the world corporation, which is a modern concept evolved to meet the requirements of the modern age, and the nation-state, which is still rooted in archaic concepts unsympathetic to the needs of our complex world.

The lack of phasing between the development of our archaic political and modern business structures is sometimes abrasive. The abrasion has already surfaced in several places. The phenomenon is complex. It reflects not only honest business anxiety but a kind of neo-mercantilism. Even in economically advanced Western Europe the concern of local enterprises over the superior size and resources of the global company is being loudly voiced. European businessmen are worried because the measures taken to liberate the movement of goods have preceded adequate modernization of the structure of their own enterprises. They have not had time to build up their strength. They have not yet effected the across-boundary industrial concentration that is essential for European industry to stand on its feet and meet the competition of direct investment by the great global corporations.

The problem is perhaps even graver in Canada, where business and political leaders are deeply worried about how they can maintain their national integrity while living next to an economy fourteen times the size of their own, and yet not jeopardize the inflow of investment capital on which their prosperity depends.

We see comparable phenomena in the developing countries. Hypersensitive to anything that suggests colonialism, they are afraid their economies will fall under foreign domination and, to prevent this, they impose obstacles to the entry of foreign firms, thereby blocking the inflow of the capital they desperately need.

Yet though the anxieties of local business cannot be ignored, I doubt that this is the most serious danger to worldwide corporate enterprise. A greater menace may come from the actions of governments addicted to a regime of planning, who see in the global corporation a foreign instrumentality that may frustrate their economic designs. The basis for their concern is easy to understand, especially in countries where a world company, if allowed in, would become the largest employer of national labor and consumer of national materials. The problem is something like this: how can a national government make an economic plan with any confidence if a board of directors meeting 5,000 miles away can by altering its patterns of purchasing and production affect in a major way the country's economic life? . . .

Thus there is an inherent conflict of interest between corporate managements that operate in the world economy and governments whose points of view are confined to the narrow national scene. We are going to have to ponder the problem far more in order to find the means to resolve the conflict.

One obvious solution is to modernize our political structures—to evolve units larger than nation-states and better suited to the present day. But that is going to take a long time. Meanwhile, many company managements, sensitive to the problem if not always to the full range of considerations that produce it, have developed corporate diplomacy to a high level of sophistication. Not only do they take great pains to ease pressures on national governments but many seek to attach a kind of national coloration to their local subsidiaries.

These commendable efforts take a variety of forms. For example, some world corporations associate themselves with local partners; others take only minority holdings in their local affiliates. In some cases they leave effective control of local subsidiaries to local managers while inserting only a minimum of direction.

While leaving control to the local managers sometimes works well, often it gives rise to additional problems. It is clear to me that national ownership in local subsidiaries impedes the fulfillment of the world corporation's full potential as the best means yet devised for utilizing world resources according to the criterion of profit: an objective standard of efficiency.

The obvious drawback of local ownership interests is that they necessarily think in national and not in world terms. Thus they are likely to impress their narrowly focused views on vital policies having to do with prices, dividends, employment, the use of plant facilities in one country rather than another, even to the source of component materials. In other words, once the central management of a global company is restricted to the divergent interests of national partners, it loses its ability to pursue the true logic of the global economy.

"DENATIONALIZATION"

This leads me to suggest that we might do well to approach the problem at a different level, not by nationalizing local subsidiaries but by internationalizing or perhaps more accurately denationalizing the parent. Only in this way can we preserve the full economic promise of the world corporation as an institutional instrument of the world economy.

A solution in these terms represents a step well in advance of solutions that have been generally considered. Perhaps it may seem utopian and idealistic, but I would be prepared to wager that over the next decade or two we shall have to find a solution along this line if world companies are to avoid being increasingly hamstrung and emasculated by national restrictions.

BY SPECIAL STATUTE

The essence of this suggestion is that those artificial persons whom I have referred to as world corporations should become quite literally citizens of the world. What this implies is the establishment by treaty of an international companies law, administered by a supranational body, including representatives drawn from various countries, who would not only exercise normal domiciliary supervision but would also enforce antimonopoly laws and administer guarantees with regard to uncompensated expropriation. An international companies law could place limitations, for example, on the restrictions nation-states might be permitted to impose on companies established under its sanction. The operative standard defining those limitations might be the quantity of freedom needed to preserve the central principle of assuring the most economical and efficient use of world resources.

Obviously such an international company would have a central base of operations. It would not be like Mohammed's coffin, suspended in air. It is clearly unnecessary that there be a single profit center. The international company's operations in its home country would be subject to local laws, to the extent that they do not infringe the overriding regulations of the organic treaty.

I recognize, of course, that a company will not become effectively a citizen of the world merely by a legal laying on of hands. It requires something more than an international companies law to validate a company's passport; the company must in fact become international. This means among other things that share ownership in the parent must be spread through the world so that the company cannot be regarded as the exclusive instrument of a particular nation. Of course, in view of the underdeveloped state of most national capital markets, even in economically advanced countries, this is not likely to occur very soon. But eventually, as savings are effectively mobilized for investment in more and more countries, companies will assume an increasingly international character. At the same time, we can expect a gradual internationalizing of boards of directors and parent company managements.

These suggestions are offered in tentative and speculative terms. They are not the only solution. One can envisage an international treaty, for example, directed at resolving jurisdictional conflicts and limiting national restrictions on trade and investment. Yet an international companies act, as I see it, has intrinsic merits. It offers the best means I can think of to preserve the great potential of the world corporation for all society.

Nor is this suggestion far beyond present contemplation. It is merely an adaptation in a larger arena of what is likely to be created within the next few years in Europe: a common companies law for the European Economic Community together with a body of regulations to be administered by the EEC.

But let me be quite clear on one point. This proposal does not rest on the notion of world government or anything resembling it. I have lived far too long on the exposed steppes of diplomacy and practical policies to believe in such an apocalyptic development within foreseeable time. Nonetheless what I am suggesting necessarily has its political implications. Freeing commerce from national interference through the creation of new world instrumentalities would inevitably, over time, stimulate mankind to close the gap between the archaic political structure of the world and visions of commerce vaulting beyond confining national boundaries to exploit the full promise of the world economy.

12. Imperialism in the Seventies—Unity or Rivalry?

BOB ROWTHORN

In this 1971 article, Marxist Bob Rowthorn explores three possible futures for the international political economy: (1) United States super-imperialism, in which American capitalists dominate all others; (2) ultra-imperialism, in which capitalists forge greater bonds among themselves to the detriment of the nation-state; and (3) imperial rivalry, where capitalists retain their nationalistic ties. Unlike some other Marxists (see Hymer, Reading 2), Rowthorn argues that competition among the capitalist states will heighten. He examines the international trade and investment of various national capitalist classes to support his position, and asserts that European and Japanese capital will soon challenge the hegemonic position of American capitalists. Rowthorn rather accurately predicts the very rapid growth of European and Japanese foreign investment in the 1970s and 1980s, as well as the enlargement of the European Economic Community (EEC) in order to strengthen Europe's ability to compete internationally. On the other hand, open conflict between the American, European, and Japanese states over investment and trade issues is far less evident than Rowthorn projected in 1971. Nonetheless, the article is a representative attempt to apply Marxist analysis to a problem in the contemporary international political economy.

This essay will discuss the effects of recent economic trends on the unity of the imperialist bloc and on the autonomy of its constituent elements—the individual nations. Three broad possibilities may be distinguished:

U.S. super-imperialism in which all other capitalist states are dominated by the United States and have comparatively little freedom to choose their policies and control their economies in ways opposed by the American state. America acts as the organizer of world capitalism, preserving its unity in the face of socialism. This domi-

193

nation may not, of course, operate smoothly—for antagonisms will not be eliminated but merely contained.

Ultra-imperialism in which a dominant coalition of relatively autonomous imperialist states performs the organizing role necessary to preserve the unity of the system. For this to work the antagonisms between the members of the coalition must not be so severe that they overcome the interest they have in maintaining the coalition.

Imperial Rivalry in which the relatively autonomous states no longer perform the necessary organizing role, or perform it so badly that serious conflicts break out between them and the unity of the system is threatened. For this to happen the antagonisms between states must be severe.

Recent Marxist writers have been divided in their views on which of these three variants of imperialism is most likely. The majority, amongst whom are to be found Sweezy, Magdoff, Jalée and Nicolaus, believe that the United States is not only the dominant imperial power today, but that it will become increasingly dominant in the future. Their argument runs, with variations, roughly as follows. American firms are much bigger, more advanced and faster growing than their foreign rivals. They are using this strength to take over key sectors of European industry, and are using American state power to force their way into Japan. Eventually American firms will dominate the economies of Europe and Japan, and, as a result, large sections of the national bourgeoisies of these countries will be denationalized, becoming objectively—if not subjectively—representatives of American capital. Moreover, European and Japanese capital surviving this process will be weak and completely subordinate to American capital. Even today, they argue, a coalition of dominant American and subordinate foreign capital is creating a unified imperialism under the hegemony of the United States and the contradictions between national capitalisms are becoming of increasingly little significance. The significant contradiction is more and more between a unified imperialism and the 'third world.' These writers have been criticized, in my opinion fairly, as 'third-worldists' by Ernest Mandel. For convenience I shall also use this term.

On the opposite side stand Mandel and perhaps Kidron, who believe that the hegemony of the United States is being challenged by the Europeans and the Japanese. Mandel argues as follows. A combination of mergers, accumulation and rationalization is destroying the size advantage of American firms, and as a result non-American productivity levels are catching up with those of the Americans. The formation of a supranational state in Europe would speed up this process considerably, but even in the absence of such a state the Europeans are closing the gap. Since non-American wages are much lower than American wages, increases in productivity could make goods produced in Europe and

Japan so cheap that exports from these countries could flood American markets, creating severe contradictions within that country as American capitalists try to hold down wages in an attempt to stem this flood. Moreover, American penetration of Europe or Japan has by no means reached the point where the bourgeoisies of these countries have been denationalized. National states still defend the interests of national capital. Neither Europe nor Japan are anywhere near to being neo-colonies. As the struggle for world markets intensifies there will be increasing conflict between nation states as they attempt to defend their respective firms. In particular, the non-Americans will come into conflict with the Americans. Indeed the European states may even form an alliance or perhaps a supranational state to enable them to stand up to the Americans on equal or near equal terms. Internally, within the non-American nations, contradictions will become increasingly severe as states try to hold down wages to enable their firms to compete more effectively. Thus Mandel's view is of an imperialism increasingly wracked by internal contradictions, although he does not believe these will be severe enough to break out into wars. The need to defend the system as a whole will be too great to allow this to happen. . . .

POINTS OF DIFFERENCE

It is clear that there are three central issues on which the various schools of thought differ: 1. the relative strength of U.S. capital and the related question of the degree to which it can dominate Europe and Japan by capturing most key industrial sectors; 2. the severity and nature of the antagonisms between different national capitals; 3. the extent to which the common fear of socialism can overcome those antagonisms which do exist.

It is impossible in the space of this article to discuss in depth all of these points of difference. On the third, I shall content myself with the following observations. The degree to which the common fear of socialism can overcome antagonisms depends on the nature and severity of these antagonisms, and the extent to which states perceive that in pursuing the interests of their national capitals they are putting the entire system in jeopardy. China and Eastern Europe would never have been invaded if the Japanese and German imperialists had realized that the outcome would not be the colonization of these areas but their detachment from the imperialist system as a whole. To ascribe this myopia to madness, as does Varga when he says that capitalism will no longer be dominated by madmen like Hitler, is to ignore the objective conditions which determine whether or not 'madmen' are in control. Amongst these objective conditions must be counted the nature and extent of the antagonisms between national capitals. A high degree of antagonism may induce a high degree of myopia. Indeed this may even be 'structural' myopia in the sense that those concerned may individually understand what is happening but be powerless to prevent it. We do not, of course, need to take such an extreme example as that of imperialism and war. The system may be put in jeopardy by contradictions between capital and labour within the imperial countries, contradictions brought to explosion-point by antagonisms between national capitals. A crisis caused by the collapse of the international monetary system might, for example, lead to a socialist revolution in Italy or France. So might competitive attempts by the imperialist states to contain inflation, attempts which had their roots not in a contradiction between imperialism and the third world but in antagonisms between national capitals. Rather than pursue such an obvious, if neglected, line of argument, let us pass on to the remaining two questions at issue.

THE STRENGTH OF U.S. CAPITAL

The relative strength of U.S. capital and its advantages in the struggle for world markets have been greatly exaggerated by the 'third-worldists'.

First, although American firms are still, on average, larger than their foreign rivals, mergers, takeovers and high rates of accumulation in Europe and Japan have done much to close this gap. In many industries such as chemicals, machinery, oil or steel the differences in size have ceased or are rapidly ceasing to be significant. In others, such as computers or automobiles, the differences are still significant, although in most cases they are being lessened by the continued concentration and centralization of capital in Europe and Japan. Indeed, if the Common Market, with or without Britain, can develop a common company law facilitating mergers between European firms of different nationalities, all but a few of the existing inequalities in size will be eliminated or reduced to the point where they no longer matter.

Secondly, although it is true that American firms are the leading innovators and have monopolies or near-monopolies in the production of many advanced or 'modern' products, the 'third-worldists' almost exclusive focus on these products and the research and development expenditures associated with them is seriously misleading. It ignores both the temporary nature of technological monopolies and the faster growth of European and Japanese capital in products other than the most advanced. As leaders, American firms must spend enormous amounts making mistakes which others can avoid and discovering things which others can imitate or adapt cheaply. Within a few years of their introduction, 'modern' products in which the Americans initially had monopolies become 'traditional' and are produced efficiently and in bulk by European and Japanese firms. To maintain their lead, therefore, or to prevent it being eroded too rapidly, American firms are forced to spend far more on research and development than their rivals overseas. This is the price they pay for being leaders.

As the gap between the Americans and the non-Americans closes, the scope for catching-up will, of course, diminish and the non-Americans will be increasingly forced to become innovators themselves and competition will become increasingly centred on advanced products. Indeed the growing chorus of demands in Europe and Japan for technological cooperation and for more state expenditure on research and development suggests that this is already happening, and that non-American capital is preparing to challenge the Americans in areas where they have, until now, reigned supreme. It is quite wrong, therefore, to see these demands as evidence of a desperate last-ditch attempt on the part of weakening European and Japanese capitals to resist 'technological colonization' by the Americans. Their growing need to become innovators themselves and not merely imitators is a direct consequence of their past dynamism and the increasing sophistication of both their markets and products. If the European and Japanese challenges fail these firms will, of course, be compelled to tail along behind the Americans. However, their failure is by no means a foregone conclusion, as the third-worldists seem to believe. On the contrary, the growing strength of European and Japanese capital, caused by mergers and accumulation, together with the growing size and sophistication of their markets, suggests that they will be able to mount an effective challenge in most, if not all, advanced products.

Finally, the third-worldists have over-emphasized the offensive aspects of American direct investment overseas and under-emphasized its defensive aspects. With the exception of a brief period in the late sixties, when the United States experienced a boom at the same time as Germany experienced a recession, continental Europe has grown substantially faster than the United States during the last two decades. Japan has grown even faster than continental Europe, its GNP rising from one twentieth of the American GNP in 1953 to nearly one sixth in 1968. This growth has affected American firms in two ways. On the one hand, growing markets overseas have offered them the chance to expand overseas, often in products for which American demand has begun to level out as domestic markets become saturated. On the other hand, the growth of overseas economies has enabled many foreign firms to strengthen themselves to the point where they have begun to threaten the world position of American giants. American investment in Europe and other areas can only be appreciated if both these aspects of non-American growth are taken into account. In addition to increasing the sales of American firms, overseas investment has served to frustrate foreign competition and preserve American monopolies. If American firms had not taken over actual or potential foreign rivals and established subsidiaries overseas, they would have been forced to rely upon exports—not a very effective means of penetrating foreign markets— and today would be faced with an even greater foreign challenge.

Despite their phenomenal expansion overseas, however, big American firms are having and will have increasing difficulty in keeping ahead of their foreign rivals. The fast growth of American firms in the late sixties was based largely on an accelerated growth of the U.S. economy and a rapid increase in the level of concentration in that economy, neither of which is likely to last. The U.S. economy is once again stagnating and American giants will experience increasing difficulty in raising their share of the domestic economy. Thus, viewed in a longer perspective, the cause of the American invasion of Europe must be seen as the erosion of a previously impregnable position. So long as they were absolutely superior American firms could rely mainly on exports, and could regard European and Japanese recovery with certain indulgence. With European and Japanese recovery, however, the firms of these countries have become dangerous challengers and American firms are forced to invest overseas for their own defence. Hence their massive investment in Europe and their increasing pressure on Japan to allow the entry of foreign capital. So much for the supposedly overwhelming and increasing superiority of American capital. Let us now turn to the question of antagonisms.

ANTAGONISMS

Relations between capitals are always to some extent antagonistic, the degree of antagonism depending both on the area of actual or potential competition and on its intensity. Thus, in the present case, where we are concerned with relations between capitals of different nationalities, it is important to know: 1. over what areas the firms of North America, Europe and Japan are or will be in competition with each other; 2. what form this competition will take—will, for example, Continental and Japanese capitals create or at least attempt to create international firms of their own or will they rely mainly on exports as a means of penetrating foreign markets? To answer these questions, let us begin by discussing international trade and investment.

1. International Trade and Investment

The post-war economic growth of advanced capitalist countries has been accompanied by an increasing dependence on international trade as both imports and exports have risen considerably faster than output. Much of this increase has consisted of manufactured goods either sold to or imported from other advanced capitalist countries. As a result, trade within the advanced capitalist bloc is now three times as large as between this bloc and the rest of the world, and exports account for a significant proportion of the output of many manufacturing firms.

Exports have not, however, been the only way in which firms, particularly big firms, have penetrated foreign markets. Direct investment, whereby firms establish and operate production and distribution facilities overseas, has played an important role in the penetration of foreign markets by the firms of at least five countries—Britain, the United States, the Netherlands, Canada and Switzerland. Indeed, it has been more important than exports in the case of Britain and the United States. Between 1957 and 1965 direct investment accounted for five-sixths and three-fifths respectively of the overseas expansion of the average American and British manufacturing firm. . . .

Overseas investment has enabled the firms of certain countries to establish powerful and sometimes dominant positions in foreign markets, even where their export performance has been poor. Indeed, it is only by looking at overseas production as well as exports that one gets an idea of the penetration of American or British firms into such areas as Europe, South Africa, Australia or Canada. . . .

The significance of overseas investment in international competition goes far beyond the example we have just been discussing. An examination would reveal:

(i) Trade in manufactures between industrialized capitalist countries is usually in rough balance. Collectively, the manufacturing firms of one of these countries lose about as much of their domestic markets to foreign imports as they gain by exporting to other industrialized capitalist countries. Only in trade with underdeveloped and other resource-producing countries do industrialized countries have substantial surpluses in manufactures.

(ii) Overseas investment is becoming the most effective means of penetrating the world's major markets. It is becoming increasingly important both as a means of defending existing markets and of capturing new ones.

(iii) Direct investment, unlike trade, is often highly unbalanced. Britain, the United States, the Netherlands and Switzerland have invested far more overseas than foreign firms have invested in these countries. As a result, their big firms have made considerable net gains, capturing markets overseas without sacrificing an equivalent amount of home markets in return.

If Lenin's words were something of an exaggeration when he wrote them in 1916, they have become true today: 'Under the old capitalism when free competition prevailed, the export of *goods* was the most typical feature. Under modern capitalism, when monopolies prevail, the export of *capital* has become the typical feature.'[1]

2. European and Japanese Capital

A well-established, if not so well understood, feature of capitalism is the tendency for capital to expand outwards and seek new markets overseas. Since European and Japanese firms are manifestly not exceptions to this rule, it follows from the above conclusion regarding the role of direct investment in overseas expansion that these firms will be forced to rely increasingly on overseas investment if their objectives are to be attained.

As well as what might be called the universal reasons for overseas expansion, however, European firms have an added reason in the form of an already massive American investment in Europe. . . . This investment has enabled American manufacturing and petroleum firms to penetrate European markets to such an extent that their sales in Europe exceeded European sales in the United States by $30,000 millions a year in 1966. Clearly, American firms derive a considerable advantage from this net penetration of European markets and to eliminate or greatly reduce the deficit will be one of the future objectives of European big capital.

The deficit can, in principle, be tackled in one of two ways: *defensively* by reducing the size and growth of American sales in Europe, or *offensively* by increasing European sales abroad, both in the United States and elsewhere. Since American capital is already well-established in Europe, a defensive approach would have to be based on drastic state intervention if it were to have any real effect. The result would be a confrontation with America on a scale which, for obvious reasons, European capital wants to avoid; although, as we suggest below such a confrontation may eventually come about if America protects its domestic capital against the incursion of European and other foreign capital. We can assume, however, that European capital will not initiate such a confrontation and that, until the American state initiates it, American firms will be allowed to operate fairly freely in Europe. In so far as European capital attempts to reduce the American advantage it will adopt, therefore, an offensive approach and counter-attack overseas either by exporting more or by establishing more overseas subsidiaries.

Exports cannot, however, provide anything like the necessary increase in overseas sales. Quite apart from what might be called the micro-

reason of rising European wage costs, . . . there is a crucial macro-reason relating to the equilibrium of the world monetary system. Annual European *exports* would have to increase by a gigantic amount, $20,000 millions to $30,000 millions over and above any offsetting increase in *imports*.

Europe as a whole would have, therefore, to run massive current account surpluses with the rest of the world. Moreover, since the bulk of non-European purchasing power is located in America, a large proportion of the extra exports would have to be bought by that country, and America would have to run massive current account deficits. Thus, if the Europeans were successful in their export drive, the result would be European surpluses and American deficits of unprecedented magnitude, qualitatively larger than the surpluses and deficits which have plagued the capitalist world during the last few years. Within a short time either the world monetary system would collapse and with it trade, or else a major realignment of currencies, in which some were revalued and others devalued, would take place, thereby destroying the cost advantage of European firms and restoring the equilibrium of the world monetary system. In other words, the very success of the export drive, by creating huge surpluses and deficits, would undermine the conditions which made it successful. This argument, it should be noted, applies quite generally to the question of overseas expansion by means of exports. Any country which exports so successfully that it obtains massive surpluses tends to undermine the conditions of its own success.

It seems then that a defensive approach, although technically possible, would do more harm than good to European firms and that an offensive approach based on exports could not provide surpluses large enough to compensate for more than a small proportion of the enormous American sales in Europe. Only by investing heavily overseas, establishing production facilities in other countries, could European firms hope to compensate for losses to American firms in Europe.

Thus for both general reasons relating to the outward expansion of capital and particular reasons relating to the already massive American stake in Europe, European firms must invest heavily overseas. For the same general reasons Japanese firms will have to follow suit. As yet, however, the incentive for the latter to do so is not quite so great, for they have managed to pursue a successful defensive strategy in which the operation of American capital in Japan has been severely circumscribed. American pressure is, however, causing Japan to relax some of its restrictions and, should the stage be reached where American capital has more or less free entry into Japan, Japanese firms will be forced to adopt an offensive strategy which seeks to compensate for domestic losses by investing overseas. . . .

. . . Initially the growing ability of Continental and Japanese firms to finance overseas investment will manifest itself, indeed is already manifesting itself, in an expansion into areas other than the United States. As the process of merger, rationalization and accumulation continues, however, it is inevitable that these firms will turn increasingly to the United States itself. To help them they may have state aid, disguised wherever possible to prevent American retaliation. If international mergers such as that between Dunlop and Pirelli become the fashion, European investment in America will take place on an enormous scale. Similarly, if Japanese industry consolidates still further and the Japanese economy continues growing at its present rate, Japanese firms will invest heavily both in the United States and elsewhere.

We may sum up this argument by saying that rising costs at home, greater strength, and established overseas markets for European and Japanese products are all combining to make the big firms of these countries move towards investment as the most effective way of penetrating foreign markets, both in America and elsewhere. European-wide mergers would accelerate this process but it will occur even without them. This does not, of course apply to all products or all firms. It is likely that we shall see both a more intensive export drive by some firms, particularly those too small to invest, and a massive investment drive by others.

This discussion has been concerned with manufacturing firms. For obvious strategic and economic reasons, however, a similar growth of non-American investment overseas will occur in the field of natural resources. Indeed, it is already beginning.

3. Conclusions

The above discussion, although by no means definitive, points to the following conclusions:

   (i) European and Japanese capital is strong enough not only to fight back against American capital but also to counter-attack by expanding overseas.
  (ii) The overseas expansion of big European and Japanese firms will increasingly take the form of direct investment in other countries, including the United States itself. Exports will, however, continue to be important both for small firms and certain products.
 (iii) Continent-wide mergers in Europe and further consolidation in Japan would accelerate the process considerably and the firms of these countries would invest overseas on an enormous scale. . . .

PERSPECTIVES

. . . As European and Japanese firms expand overseas, they will increasingly threaten the position of American firms, both in the United

States and elsewhere. Initially the American state is likely to respond to this threat, indeed is already responding, by restricting certain kinds of imports, aiding domestically controlled firms and attempting to obtain or maintain American privileges in overseas markets. If these measures prove inadequate, as they probably will in the face of heavy European and Japanese investment, the American state will be tempted to restrict the operations of foreign capital in the United States, and where possible persuade its more dependent allies to do the same.

Thus, as non-American capital counter-attacks, the American state will intervene more vigorously on behalf of American capital. To penetrate the United States and other areas under its hegemony non-American capital will, therefore, be forced to rely increasingly on the use of its own state power: financial and technological support to lower costs of production and to provide the funds for expansion; economic or even military inducements to weaken America's grip on its satellites; and, finally, counter-threats against American capital in Europe. If these measures fail, European and Japanese expansion in the United States and its satellites will be severely hampered, and European and Japanese capital will be forced to operate mainly outside the U.S. sphere of influence. Thus, the medium-term prospect is one of increasing intervention by the American state in the face of a growing non-American challenge, threatened or actual retaliation by non-American states, and perhaps a partial reversal of existing tendencies towards interpenetration as the capitalist world fragments into more self-contained regions.

The extent to which the American state can be deterred from intervening on behalf of American capital depends on the extent to which non-American states are able to act in a concerted fashion and to form effective alliances. A European bloc, for example, embracing virtually the whole of Western Europe would have tremendous bargaining power with the United States. With sales in Europe of over $60,000 million a year, American subsidiaries would be extremely vulnerable to retaliatory action by the combined European powers in the event of a conflict with the United States, and at the present time the loss of a substantial proportion of these sales would far outweigh the benefits to American firms of vigorous state intervention on their behalf. Thus, although not enough to guarantee that America would continue to follow liberal policies, the threat of retaliation by the combined European powers would, in the short run, be enough to guarantee the existence of a powerful liberal lobby in the United States. In the medium run, however, the formation of a European bloc would have the opposite effect, for by facilitating European-wide mergers and mobilizing massive state resources on behalf of European firms, this bloc would so strengthen European capital that it could expand overseas on an enormous scale, both into the United States and elsewhere. Before long the Europeans would pose such a serious threat to the operations of American firms in Latin America, Canada, Australia, the Middle East and even the United States itself that many firms of formerly liberal views would be forced to call upon the American state to defend their interests in these areas, even if the price of such defence was a restriction of their activities in Europe. Thus, although in the short run the formation of a European bloc might deter the American state from acting too vigorously on behalf of American capital, in the medium run it would have the opposite effect and would only serve to intensify the pressures for state action.

It is clear from the above discussion that the ability of firms to compete internationally, both in capturing new markets and sources of supply and in defending existing ones, will come to depend increasingly on the use of state power. If, for one reason or another, the state power available to capital is nowhere near commensurate with its needs, then not only will this capital be at a serious disadvantage in world competition, but even the state power it does command will not be exploited to the full for fear of provoking retaliatory action by other states.

To overcome this disability there are several obvious courses of action. The state concerned can ally itself or even merge with other states, thereby placing greater state power at the disposal of its capital. Britain's application to join the Common Market, for example, is intended to serve both of these objectives. British capital, being highly international in its operation and perspectives, needs a greater state power than Britain alone can provide, and at the same time is frightened that, if Britain remains outside the Common Market, the state power of continental countries will be used against it. Alternatively, failing an alliance or merger of states, capital can change its nationality. For example, provided the British state agreed, certain British firms operating mainly within the U.S. sphere of influence might change their nationality and become American. Under certain circumstances even the agreement of the British state would be unnecessary.

These two courses of action are not, of course, mutually exclusive. Indeed alliances may actually facilitate changes of nationality. Within the Common Market, for example, it may become relatively easy for say a French firm to merge with a German firm and gradually shift the balance of its activities and eventually its headquarters into Germany, becoming thereby effectively and one day legally German. Given a merger between states, on the other hand, the situation is less simple, for then all capitals adopt the 'nationality' of the new unit. This change will not, however, affect the original nations and national capitals equally and the degree to which it can be considered a true change of nationality will vary from country to country.

Although changes of nationality may eventually turn out to be important, alliances or mergers of states are likely to be of more immediate significance in view of the growing unity of the Common Market and Britain's application for membership. At its widest, an extended Common Market might cover virtually the whole of Western Europe, and, at its most complete, so many basic economic and military decisions would be irreversibly centralized that the resulting 'United Europe' would be a single nation. As well as increasing considerably the state power at the disposal of European capital, this unification would have the effect of 'renationalizing' the operations of many European firms and of giving them a much greater interest in the health of the newly created 'home' economy. All West European markets would be brought under the control of what amounted to a single state power, and, from the point of view of European firms, many formerly overseas markets, i.e. those located in other European countries, would become home markets. Many firms which were previously international under the old system of separate European states would become 'national' under the new system—most of their production and sales would be located within the 'national' boundaries of a United Europe. As a result, these firms would have a strong interest in a fast-growing 'national' economy, even where the price of this growth was conflict with America or some other capitalist state. This does not imply, of course, that all of these firms would have a corresponding interest in their growth of their original national economies. On the contrary, capital based on the more backward areas of Europe or those where the working class was particularly militant would migrate to more prosperous or more congenial parts of Europe, with possibly disastrous consequences for the areas left behind.

Since European big capital would depend closely on the health of the West European economy and would derive considerable benefits from the use of European state power, it would act as a 'nationalist' force, supporting an autonomous economic development for Western Europe and relying on the use of state power overseas. The relationship of European capital to the European 'state' would be much the same as that of American capital to the American state and this European state would, therefore, be autonomous *vis-à-vis* other states and would act vigorously on behalf of its own capital when necessary. Thus, a United Europe would constitute what, for want of a better name, we may call an 'imperialist metropolis', i.e. it would be autonomous and imperialist.

It is not necessary to assume such an all-embracing West European unity in order to deduce the existence of imperialist metropolises other than the United States. If the existing Common Market unified to the point where crucial economic and military decisions were irreversibly centralized, then capital would have much the same relationship to the 'state' as we observed in the case of a United Europe, and the Common Market would constitute a single imperialist metropolis.

At the present time of writing, of course, a number of existing nations constitute imperialist metropolises in their own right. Most firms, big or small, based on such countries as France, Germany or Japan are and will remain closely dependent on their home economies for some years to come. In times of economic crisis these firms will have an overriding interest in domestic growth and will, therefore, support an autonomous economic policy. Moreover, these states are able to extend substantial, if not entirely adequate, protection and support for the relatively limited overseas operations of their firms, either in the form of direct economic and even military aid, such as Japan is likely to offer its firms in South East Asia, or else in the form of retaliatory measures against foreign interest in the home economy, such as continental Europe may take if America restricts imports from Europe. Thus, even in the absence of European unification, an ideal solution from the point of view of most big European firms, there will be autonomous non-American states which will use their power vigorously on behalf of their own capital.

CONCLUSIONS

We shall make no attempt to summarize what is contained above, other than to say that the prospect is one of imperial rivalry, in which a number of relatively autonomous states, which we have called 'imperialist metropolises', are in conflict with each other as they try to support their respective capitals. Whether these metropolises will consist of certain of today's nation states or of wider units will depend on a number of political and other factors, most of which have not been discussed. There are strong forces pushing European states into closer and closer alliance with each other, but whether this alliance will become sufficiently close to constitute a single true metropolis is not yet clear. Unless they can find allies, certain nation states, of which Britain is the leading example, will become, or perhaps already are, relatively subordinate. In contrast to the imperialist metropolises they might be called 'imperialist satellites'.

The reason these countries are or will be satellites is not necessarily to be found in the weakness of their capital, but in some cases may be in a lack of correspondence between the needs of this capital and the state power available to it. Where big capital operates internationally on a large scale and the state is relatively powerless, one of its prime needs is to keep on good terms with powerful foreign states. Thus, in economic affairs it will oppose the policies necessary for an indigenous solution to economic crises, for such policies may lead to foreign retaliation, and in foreign affairs it will not want the state to antagonize those states upon whose good will it depends.

Although these conclusions have important implications for the future of the imperialist system, we shall not discuss them here. One point is, however, worth making. The problems and prospects facing the working class and revolutionary movements in advanced capitalist countries will depend partly on the extent to which big capital is prepared to support an indigenous path of economic development in times of crisis, i.e., on the extent to which it acts as a nationalist force, where the term 'nationalist' must be interpreted widely to include such phenomena as Common Market or European 'nationalism'. In a metropolis where this is the case, the danger exists of a new kind of 'social imperialism', whereby—in return for the benefits of an indigenous development—the working class accepts the capitalist system and supports or at least acquiesces in imperialist policies. 'Benefits' need not, of course, mean an actual increase in the standard of living of the working class. On the contrary, in a severe world crisis, the main benefit of an indigenous development would be to cushion the shock rather than actually to improve the workers' position. In a satellite, by contrast, where big capital is not prepared to support an indigenous development and acts, therefore, as a cosmopolitan force, the state's room for manoeuvre is greatly reduced and at times of crisis it is correspondingly more difficult to provide any benefits for the working class. Indeed, within the constraints imposed by the international needs of big capital, the state may be compelled to tackle the crisis by making a frontal attack on working-class living standards.

NOTES

1. *Imperialism, The Highest Stage of Capitalism*, in *Selected Works*, Moscow 1967, Vol. 1, p. 723.

13. Postimperialism: A Class Analysis of Multinational Corporate Expansion

RICHARD L. SKLAR

Richard Sklar examines the role of the multinational corporation and challenges the view that capital will retain its national links. Sklar identifies the modern corporation as a major political institution both domestically and internationally. As firms become international, they develop transnational ties, most notably between multinational corporate managers and executives from Third World state-operated enterprises. Sklar thus predicts that multinational corporations and national—even nationalist—politicians will co-exist peacefully in the developing countries.

This reading is an example of the application of class analysis to the politics of Third World economic development. Like some Marxists, Sklar believes that transnational class formation has emerged as a major force in the international political economy; unlike other Marxists, Sklar is confident of the ability of nation-states to resist assaults on their nationalist integrity by transnational corporations.

I

. . . The multinational corporation (or enterprise or firm) may be suitably defined according to these criteria: it consists of a parent company and subsidiary companies, the latter of which are located in a few or more countries and are engaged in the performance of basic economic, typically productive, activities in addition to trade. The various national components of the enterprise are mutually supportive and subject to central direction. The management of each component is designed to promote the overall interests of the group as a whole. If, for example, it should appear to be in the interest of the enterprise as a whole to move certain productive operations from one country to another in quest of cheaper labor or lower taxes, the inclination to do so is likely to prevail. Inevitably, it will be suggested that the interests of the whole normally coincide with the interests of the controlling part. Since the parent company does have a national identity and since it is normally controlled by directors of a specific nationality, or a small set of nationalities, the spread of multinational enterprise appears to result in the perpetuation and intensification of hegemonic domination by the industrial capitalist powers. In short, the national and organizational loyalties of transnational businessmen may be expected to fuse with imperialistic force. This argument has been made from a Marxist-Leninist standpoint as a matter of doctrine:

> Capital without a state is . . . unthinkable. But in the world as it is constituted today only nations have states: there is no such thing as a supranational state. If, for example, the state of the nation to which it belonged were to collapse, capital would lose its indispensable protector. It would then either be incorporated into the capital of another nation, or cease to be capital, by coming under the jurisdiction of a revolutionary regime dedicated to the abolition of the entire set of relations of production of which capital is one part. . . . [T]he historic course of the global capitalist system is leading to one of two outcomes: world empire or world revolution.[1]

An empirically based demonstration of the thesis that multinational corporations promote imperialism by economic means has been presented by Stephen Hymer. The basis of his argument is his insistence upon the differing effects of the technological and organizational determinants of economic development. In his view, technological diffusion alone does not produce or serve to perpetuate imperialist domination. This condition is plainly the result of corporate organization, which typically distributes the functions of planning, coordination, and routine operation according to the principle of hierarchy. The result is a proliferation of subsidiary firms, whose actions are coordinated at regional levels by higher subsidiaries of parent corporations, themselves located in the major geographical centers of corporate power and planning.

Marxists in general assume that domination (of the underindustrialized countries by the industrial capitalist countries) and exploitation go hand in hand—that in the course of multinational corporate expansion, relatively poor and weak countries are compelled by various means to pay for the benefits that accrue to the advanced capitalist countries. Few people today would bother to challenge this assumption by resuscitating the late Victorian doctrine of beneficent, paternalistic imperialism. However, another somewhat paradoxical thesis to the effect that imperialism is not only injurious to subjugated peoples but also harmful to the imperialist nations themselves—John A. Hobson's distinctive viewpoint—has been reiterated by anti-imperialists of diverse ideological orientations. Thus, Barnet and Müller hold that by means of "transfer pricing" and other exploitative/manipulative devices, multinational corporations systematically cheat, and thereby retard the economic development of, poor countries. At the same time, they contend, in the spirit of Hobson, that such corporations are directly responsible for retrogressive tendencies in their industrial "home" countries, especially the United States, as shown by symptoms of economic, political, and social decay that are reminiscent of conditions in underdeveloped countries. American workers, they state, are especially liable to suffer from the transfer of productive and distributive operations from the United States to low wage "host" countries.

These observations suggest that the domination of one people or nation by another, which, strictly speaking, defines the concept of imperialism, should not be confused with the calculation of benefits and costs that result from such domination. Benefit/cost calculations involve an assessment of outcome rather than power. Until the mid-twentieth century, it was widely assumed that exploitative economic relations between countries at different levels of economic development were established and maintained by means of imperial domination. With the advent of colonial freedom in Asia and Africa, and the emergence of communist powers comparable in strength to their capitalist adversaries, it became reasonable to expect that the causes of economic exploitation would be clearly identified and progressively eliminated. Proponents of multinational enterprise do hold that this, in fact, is the direction of movement within the noncommunist sphere. Responding to the charge of exploitation, they say that multinational corporations diffuse modern skills, technologies, and urgently needed capital resources to the nonindustrial countries, that they contribute handsomely to governmental revenues in such countries, and that they provide secure access to world markets for their exports. Since there are both benefits and costs on either side of all international economic relationships, the calculation of *relative* benefit and cost is crucial to this argument. If it can be shown, contrary to the case for transnational enterprise, that the economic position of given industrial nations is enhanced relative to (or at the expense of) particular non- or less-industrialized nations, the relationships in question may be deemed to promote or perpetuate imperialist domination. In fact, the debate about relative benefit and cost in relationships mediated by multinational corporations has been intense; it is also likely to be interminable and inconclusive, as powerful arguments are marshalled on both sides.

Advocates of the exploitation-imperialism thesis have had to assume an added theoretical burden in addition to the weight of their evidence on costs. They need to explain the persistence of exploitation despite the passing of colonialism and other overtly imperialistic forms of political control. Obviously, it will not suffice merely to infer domination from a (usually rebuttable) demonstration of exploitation. To this author's mind, the elements of controversy about imperialist domination (whether and why it persists) have not been identified with anything like the clarity that recent studies have shed upon the question of relative benefit and cost. For want of satisfactory formulations of specific matters of controversy relating to the question of domination, the debate about imperialism in the age of multinational enterprise has not been properly joined.

II

Whereas the benefit/cost calculation, upon which a finding of "economic" imperialism depends, does not directly bear upon the bases and exercise of power, the issue of managerial authority is directly and indubitably pertinent to the study of corporate power. Managers exercise authority. But the heralds of managerial autonomy misperceived the evolving relationship between management and ownership-interest as a case of divorcement. Recent evidence relating to the major American "global" corporations has been summarized by Barnet and Müller thus: ". . . in the upper reaches of America's corporations there is no 'technostructure' made up of managers with interests distinct from those of the owners. Increasingly, the managers are the owners, deriving an increasing proportion of their income not from their managerial skills but from the stock they own in their own corporations."[2] Paradoxically, the thesis of managerial autonomy may be revived in connection with multinational corporate expansion mainly as a result of conditions in the nonindustrial and newly developing countries, where corporate enterprise has been established upon foundations of foreign capital.

To be sure, the detection of managerial rule in nonindustrial societies would not mark the first removal of this idea from its original setting. Heretofore, expositors of the "managerial revolution" have cited developments in socialist countries, especially the Soviet Union, to corroborate their thesis. Trotsky's harsh judgement, in *The Revolution Betrayed*, has been repeated and refined by Marxist critics of "bureaucratic" autocracy in the Soviet Union, some of whom identify a "new class," comprising a party-bureaucratic formation, while others, who are equally critical, do not. Charles Bettelheim uses the term "state bourgeoisie" to describe and condemn the ruling stratum in the Soviet

Union, holding, in a Maoist vein, that its existence actually portends nothing less than the restoration of capitalism.

As in the socialist countries, bureaucratic cadres in the nonsocialist, newly developing countries have increasingly come to the forefront of public affairs. Typically, the bureaucratic elites of such countries enjoy incomes and social privileges far beyond the dreams or expectations of all but a few of their relatively impoverished compatriots. In his moving critique of social inequality and poor economic performance in newly independent African states, the French agronomist, René Dumont, observes that "a new type of bourgeoisie is forming in Africa . . . a bourgeoisie of the civil service."[3] The concept of a "bureaucratic bourgeoisie" as the new ruling class has been applied effectively in African studies. But it does not appear to match the social realities of countries such as Nigeria, where an entrepreneurial bourgeoisie is well established; nor has this term been widely adopted by students of those Asian and Latin American societies where private enterprise is the principal economic form.

As in the study of industrial societies, so also in the study of nonindustrial societies the relationship between bureaucratic and entre-preneurial class power becomes a matter of serious controversy. The theoretical problems are compounded by widespread uncertainty as to the approximate degree to which the private enterprise sectors of most newly developing countries are dependent upon state patronage and support. Invariably, a degree of dependence that is deemed to be either too great or too small will automatically activate theoretical defense mechanisms against the specter of an indistinct analytical boundary between the bureaucratic and entrepreneurial spheres of life. In this circumstance, a complex idea is needed to comprehend businessmen, members of the learned professions, leading politicians, and upper level bureaucrats as members of a single class. Perhaps the term "managerial bourgeoisie" will suggest an idea of merit. Inasmuch as this term clearly refers to the private business elite as well as to the managers of public enterprises and to high government officials, it may be preferred to either "bureaucratic" or "state" bourgeoisie. Moreover, this term, in contrast with the term "entrepreneurial bourgeoisie," reflects the appar-ent disposition of bourgeois elements in the nonindustrial and newly developing countries to manage the production and distribution of wealth rather than to create new wealth-producing enterprises.

In many postcolonial and nonindustrial countries, as C. B. Macpherson has observed, the state is conceived and appraised mainly in terms of its contribution to development.[4] Development itself is a value-laden idea, connoting progress toward the achievement of desired goals. The political aspect of development, as distinct from those value premises that involve political goals, may be understood to signify the improvement of a society's ability to control the rate and direction of change. The concept of control is crucial to this definition, since it implies the ability to formulate and implement strategies for solving problems and achieving goals. In newly developing countries, drastic changes in the organization of authority—organizational revolutions— are frequently required to facilitate the effective exercise of social control. These political transformations are themselves contingent upon the recruitment of unprecedented numbers of trained people to staff the new and rejuvenated state agencies. To this end, certain democratic and egalitarian devices, such as equal educational opportunity, are useful if not indispensable. However, the new organizational men and women, taken together with their immediate families and social peers, constitute a minor fraction of the population, about 5 to 10 percent. The organizational revolution, spurred by material incentives, is a forcing house for class formation and privilege.

In all societies, "revolutions from above" are prone to develop deeply conservative tendencies. In newly developing countries, modern conservatism, as distinct from traditionalism, normally connotes a disposition to arrest the transformation of organizational revolutions into social revolutions or shifts in the class content of power. Typically, the managerial bourgeoisie, virtually born (as a class) to authority, takes care to contain radicalism and maintain its position as the predominant class. Insecure as it is and not strongly committed to liberal principles, this class has shown a marked disposition to take refuge in various forms of political monopoly, such as the one-party state and the "caesarist" military regime. Populist and socialist rhetoric may be "poured on" to obscure and excuse the imposition of political monopoly. Normally, however, this kind of arrangement serves to protect and consolidate the rule of the bourgeoisie.

To what extent does empirical evidence sustain the hypothesis of widespread class domination of the nonindustrial countries by the managerial bourgeoisie, as herein defined? The evidence is not inconsiderable, although Maurice Zeitlin has correctly noted the present need for studies of "dominant classes" in underdeveloped countries. Regional studies would be especially valuable. In African studies, the hypothesis in question is supported by a formidable body of literature; in Asian studies, a few works on India and Iran have corroborative value; and in Latin American studies, evidence relating to Brazil is particularly relevant.

It would not be correct to hold that the presence of a managerial bourgeoisie as the dominant class necessarily means that a given country will be receptive to capitalist principles of development. Anticapitalist— including Marxist—strategies of development may be chosen, as in the case of Tanzania. Thus far, however, the vast majority of such governments have chosen to adopt mixed economy strategies in conjunction with various forms of foreign investment. Increasingly, "partnerships" between state investment agencies and multinational corporations serve to promote the organizational revolution and, by extension, the class interests of the managerial bourgeoisie. Leading members of the bourgeoisie are constantly tempted to imbibe the capitalistic and managerial attitudes of their foreign business associates. Some of them may aspire to careers in the wider business world. Given the obviously bourgeois life-styles of individuals in this elite social stratum, they may be expected to embrace an elitist ideology. The influence of international capitalism functions to reinforce immanent tendencies toward embourgeoisment of the state bureaucratic elite.

No one should assume that a policy of partnership with the agencies of international capitalism portends the abandonment of nationalist principles on the part of governments in the nonindustrial countries. It is the singular failing of many "radical," including Marxist, analyses of such countries to underestimate the strength and historic importance of bourgeois class formation as well as the nationalist integrity of that class. Too often, the generic term "bourgeoisie" is casually qualified with the contemptuous adjective "comprador," a synonym for "puppet"—entirely dependent and subservient. It is thereby suggested that the emergent bourgeoisie is a "clientele" class that betrays the national interest of its own country to foreign capitalist powers. This notion is fundamental to the closely related doctrines of "dependency" and "neocolonialism." Indeed, these doctrines purport to supply a theory of postcolonial domination that cannot be derived from the traditional economic theories of imperialism. Beholden as they are to Marxism, these doctrines are disabled, as is standard Marxism itself, by the inadequate conception of class upon which they are founded. As Stanislaw Ossowski has observed, in his Marxist criticism of the Marxist conception of class, the relevant determinants of class include relationships to the means of production, consumption, *and* compulsion. Given its control over the means of consumption and compulsion, the managerial bourgeoisie, as herein identified, must be comprehended, contrary to the doctrines of dependency and neocolonialism, as an autonomous social force—the veritable ruling class in most of those countries that comprise the so-called "Third World." The identity of this class becomes more firmly established with each passing year. Its ardent desire for autonomy is unmistakable. And it yields to no other class in the intensity of its nationalism.

Intense nationalism on the part of the managerial bourgeoisie poses an historic challenge to the leaders of international capitalism. Will they be able to harmonize their practices with the nationalistic values of bourgeois governments in the newly developing countries? Only, we may answer, if it is in their perceived interest to do so. Adam Smith taught successive generations that businessmen who pursue their own interests serve the general interest as well. The business creed comprehends this even more plausible corollary: He who serves another benefits himself.

Is it not logical to expect the subsidiaries of a multinational business group to harmonize their policies with the interests of various host governments insofar as they seek to survive and prosper in the host countries concerned? Corporate policies of precisely this nature are described in my study of multinational mining companies that operate in the several states of central and southern Africa. In particular, I have observed that South African and American controlled mining corporations domiciled in the Republic of Zambia complied faithfully with Zambian national policies of economic disengagement from the white-ruled states of southern Africa even before the Zambian Government acquired majority ownership of those companies in 1970. They did so at considerable cost to themselves and despite the fact that the Zambian policies in question were largely inconsistent with economic values and policies espoused by the directors of the parent companies in South Africa and the United States. On the other hand, these companies made no apparent concession to the Zambian point of view in implementing their policies of equally good corporate citizenship on the part of subsidiaries domiciled in other states, including the white-dominated states of southern Africa.

These observations suggest a corporate doctrine of domicile, meaning that individual subsidiaries of an international business group may operate in accordance with the requirements of divergent and conflicting policies pursued by the governments of their respective host states. Ultimately, the aim of local adaptation is to promote the interests of the enterprise as a whole. Meanwhile, the policy of good corporate citizenship will appeal to the leaders of newly developing host countries who would like to establish stable relationships with international business organizations. Positing a mutuality of interest, the doctrine of domicile justifies transnational corporate expansion while it also legitimizes large-scale foreign investments in the eyes of the host country. Furthermore, it commands subservience to the local authority of the managerial bourgeoisie.

My formulation of the doctrine of domicile as a tenet of corporate ideology is based upon political and logistical evidence from a turbulent and, in many ways, atypical region. It will be tested again within that region by relations between the giant corporations and the newly independent, avowedly anticapitalist governments of Angola and Mozambique. In southern Africa, as elsewhere, it would be far more difficult to make out a prima facie case for compliance with host country interests at the expense of corporate group interests with evidence derived from routine business practices. Having surveyed the "transfer pricing" practices, "cross subsidization" strategies, and sundry exploitative devices to which multinational enterprises normally resort, Barnet and Müller conclude that comprehensive regulatory policies by the governments of the capitalist states themselves will be required to discipline and humanize the global corporations. Other commentators, more sympathetic to multinational enterprise, have discerned a greater capacity for the exercise of corporate statesmanship in the quest for policies that will satisfy transnational corporate managers and the nationalist governments of newly developing countries at one and the same time. Joint ventures, involving the transfer of substantial, even majority, ownership to agencies of host states have become increasingly familiar. Rarely do such schemes silence the cry of exploitation; nor do they settle the question of control, since minority owners may yet retain effective control of a given venture, while the reality of self-management by the host state is contingent upon many circumstances, including the attainment of technical competence in diverse fields. Nonetheless, joint ventures do facilitate the "revolution from above," and thereby help to produce the institutional conditions and climate of opinion that enhance the authority of the bourgeoisie and promote its growth as a class.

III

Within its sphere of control—specifically, a newly developing, nonindustrial, and nonsocialist country—the managerial bourgeoisie rises above a larger, normally far larger, national bourgeoisie, the diversity and extent of which depends mainly upon the size of the country and its level of economic development. In effect, the managerial bourgeoisie is the ruling stratum of the national bourgeoisie. Its distinctive identity as a subclass is manifest behaviorally in the collective actions and attitudes of its members. The action which, more than any other, sets this subclass apart from the bourgeoisie as a whole is its tendency to coalesce with bourgeois elements at comparable levels of control in foreign countries. To the extent that the doctrine of domicile becomes a maxim of corporate action, it helps to reconcile the staunch nationalism of the managerial bourgeoisie with the cosmopolitan values of bourgeois leaders abroad who have global interests and perspectives. Thus, it functions to promote transnational class cohesion.

It may be enlightening to think of the worldwide corporate and managerial bourgeoisie as a class in formation that now comprises three overlapping entities. . . . The corporate bourgeoisie, based mainly in the industrial capitalist countries, includes a corporate international segment. The managerial bourgeoisie of the newly developing, nonsocialist countries also overlaps with the corporate international bourgeoisie. These transnational extensions of, and linkages between, comparable segments of the bourgeoisie depend upon the creation and perfection of transnational institutions. The multinational corporation is probably the most effective institution for this purpose. It should, therefore, be analyzed and understood in terms of transnational class development. In this process, the bourgeoisie, true to its epoch-making tradition, has taken the lead.

Corporate internationalism is a social movement and a rising class interest. With its advent as a major social force, the working classes of the world confront a corporate bourgeoisie in industrial capitalist countries, and a managerial bourgeoisie in newly developing countries. Where the transition of a given developing country to the stage of industrial capitalism is sustained, indigenous elements of the corporate bourgeoisie will emerge. In the long run, if capitalism in that country is preserved, the corporate bourgeoisie may be expected to supersede the managerial bourgeoisie as the ruling class. This essay presents a short-term analysis. It draws attention to the coalescent relationship between two dominant classes—the managerial bourgeoisie and the corporate international bourgeoisie. In so doing, it seeks to make the hypothesis of transnational class formation credible.

Wars of redistribution between rival capitalist powers, specified by Lenin as the distinctive product of imperialism, may yet disrupt and abort the transnational evolution of the bourgeoisie. But that danger is counteracted by the emergence of the managerial bourgeoisie as a cohesive ruling class in newly developing countries in conjunction with the growth and spread of multinational enterprise. Increasingly, power in world affairs comes to be organized in accordance with class rather than national interests and values. Imperialism, as a stage of capitalism, gives way to corporate international capitalism. We may anticipate severe ideological strain between the doctrinaire liberalism of the corporate bourgeoisie and the paternalistic authoritarianism of the managerial bourgeoisie. However, the fate of the bourgeoisie—corporate and managerial—will probably be determined by domestic struggles, not by anti-imperialist struggles that pit insurgent nations against foreign powers.

NOTES

1. Harry Magdoff and Paul M. Sweezy, "Notes on the Multinational Corporation," in K. T. Fann and Donald C. Hodges, eds., *Readings in U.S. Imperialism* (Boston, 1971), pp. 100, 133.

2. Richard J. Barnet and Ronald E. Müller, Global Reach: The Power of the Multinational Corporations (New York, 1974), pp. 294, 246, 458.

3. René Dumont, *False Start in Africa*, 2nd Ed., rev. trans. Phyllis Nauts Ott (New York, 1969), p. 81.

4. C. B. Macpherson, *The Real World of Democracy* (London, 1966).

14. The State and Multinational Enterprises in Less-Developed Countries

EDITH PENROSE

In this reading, Edith Penrose questions the Liberal notion that international economic integration is rendering national political institutions obsolete. Penrose looks at the role of foreign firms in the Third World and points out that the expansion of multinational corporations in the developing countries has not served to erode these countries' sense of political identity. Penrose concludes that foreign direct investment is more likely to bolster the position of the nation-state than to reduce it, and argues that less developed countries' governments will continue to attempt to control multinational corporations. The implication of her analysis, originally published in 1971, is that nation-states are unlikely to be superseded by international economic integration in the foreseeable future.

INTRODUCTION

In a recent series of lectures an eminent American economist predicted, rather hopefully, that the 'nation state is just about through as an economic unit'.[1] This prediction comes just at the moment when large numbers of countries in the Afro-Asian world have become politically independent for the first time—members in their own right of the society of nations, and under the impression that the era of the independent 'nation state' has, for them, just begun. Professor Kindleberger's prediction implies that the peoples of these countries are under a grave illusion if they think that their newly-won independence will include any real influence over their economic affairs. Nevertheless, within Asia and Africa, which after all includes China, reside the majority of the world's population, and it is of some interest to enquire whether this 'cosmopolitan' point of view, so vigorously put forward in different contexts by a number of North American economists, seems likely to prevail in the near future. True, Kindleberger does not specify the time horizon of his prediction, but one has the impression that he is not peering into far-distant historical vistas but into the foreseeable future. Already, he says, 'Tariff policy is virtually useless. . . . Monetary policy is in the process of being internationalized. The world is too small. It is too easy to get about. Two-hundred-thousand-ton tank and ore carriers and containerization . . . airbuses, and the like will not permit sovereign independence of the nation state in economic affairs.'[2]

True also, there is no hint that the 'nation state' is 'through' as a political unit, which may be of some comfort for those countries under the illusion that their time had just begun. But historically political independence—like political dependence—has had very important implications for economic policy. No one, of course, assumes that any state can, by virtue of its political independence, be completely independent of the rest of the world in its economic affairs. Sharp limits to the power of governments to shape the economic life of their countries as they would wish if no other country existed, are imposed by many types of circumstance, including the possibility of war, and are very different for countries of different sizes, with different endowments and in different locations. Such limits have always existed, but have not called into question the importance of the modern state as a significant economic unit. Hence, the issue must turn on the extent to which contemporary developments are imposing such extensive new limits on the power of the state to adopt and implement independent economic policies that one will soon be unable to consider it as an important 'unit' from an economic point of view.

In this chapter I shall deal with the question only so far as it relates to the countries of the third world. First, I shall briefly recapitulate the contemporary developments that have led to the so-called 'nation state controversy' and to conclusions which, from almost any standpoint outside North America, seem bordering on the absurd. Secondly, I shall examine the way in which the countries of the world are to become so closely 'integrated' into the international economy that they lose their economic identity; I shall then look at the relation of this process to conditions widely prevalent in the less-developed countries. Finally, I shall suggest what seems to me a more likely course of events.

THE LARGE ENTERPRISE AND ECONOMIC INTEGRATION

The new developments in the modern world that are to bring about the economic obsolescence of the state relate to technology and (or including) techniques of organization. These have reached the highest stages in their evolution so far in the United States and have enabled the large business corporations of that country not only to dominate or, if you like, 'integrate' the US economy, but also to reach abroad on a hitherto unimagined scale and directly to organize economic activity in other countries. It is not surprising, therefore, that American economists should take the lead in drawing attention to the prospect that these corporations (aided perhaps by some from other countries) will now proceed to accomplish in the international economy what they have accomplished at home. The emergence and spread of the large national corporation in the United States is held to provide a pattern, or prototype, not only for the evolution of the international corporation, but of the international economy as well.

The future economic organization of the world under the aegis of the large corporation is seen, therefore, as the culmination on a global scale of an evolutionary process that has been long in the making. Kuznets has looked at economic history in terms of 'economic epochs', the distinctive features of an epoch being determined by 'epochal innovations'.[3] He finds that the innovation distinguishing the modern economic epoch is 'the extended application of science to problems of economic production'.[4] It is within this framework that the modern corporation has developed. From small beginnings in the introduction of simple technology, the basic economic units in the organization of production,—the factory and the firm—have grown steadily in size and in complexity.

This growth has been characterized by increasing division of labour, increasing use of capital, and continuous innovation in the techniques of both production and organization and in the nature of output. The potentialities of the corporate form of organization have been progressively developed as a means of raising capital, spreading risk and expanding the scope of the enterprise through merger and acquisition. It became possible for one firm to integrate vertically entire industries within its scope and to spread horizontally over wide geographical areas. Because the potentialities for the growth of the firm tend to exceed the growth of demand for a given product after a point, the aggressive enterprise will forever be seeking new fields of activity, devising new products, and developing new markets. This process has been especially prominent in the United States where 'product development and marketing replaced production as a dominant problem of business enterprise.'[5]

This is how Capitalism works!

Such diversification brought with it an appropriate internal structure of organization, for it was found desirable to create separate central divisions to deal with the several activities of the firm, although the activities themselves were often carried on in separately incorporated subsidiaries. The 'multidivisional' form of organization is extremely flexible, for new activities can be taken on and old ones thrown off with relative ease, while the central activities of planning and directing overall corporate development and strategy can be concentrated in head offices with a very long view and a very wide horizon, which even curves round the earth. In these circumstances, and given the scope for profitable expansion abroad, the international spread of US corporations, as well as of corporations in similar positions in other countries, is easily explicable. The chief older incentives to direct foreign investment—the development of new sources of supply of raw materials or control over old ones—were increasingly supplemented by the need to secure and control markets. New methods of organization supported and induced by new technology in office machinery and data processing seem to have greatly extended the limits to size which had previously been imposed by the requirements of administrative co-ordination. Extensive decentralization of responsibility and authority are characteristic of the new forms of organization, but do not seem to have prevented the central planning of strategy and control. . . .

As I understand the argument of those who predict that the economic future of the world lies in the hands of the large corporation, it is by an extension abroad of the same type of managerial control now exercised by the 'technostructure' in the United States, that the big corporations are supposed to integrate the world and reduce to insignificance the economic importance of 'nation states'. We now turn to a discussion of the way in which this state of affairs might be achieved.

A NEW STRUCTURE FOR THE WORLD ECONOMY

I have seen very little concrete discussion of the process by which the world economy is to be integrated under the impact of the international corporations. The analysis seems to consist mostly of drawing analogies with the United States and sometimes with US/Canadian relations. In the United States the large corporations have not had to contend with independent states and national boundaries, for the local states have never had the type of power which could seriously interfere with interstate investment, trade, money flows, or migration. On the other hand, in spite of national boundaries, there has been considerable integration of the Canadian and US economies through the agency of the international corporations. I shall return to this later.

It is true, as Kindleberger has emphasized, that the national corporation raised capital in those parts of the United States where funds could be obtained most cheaply and invested where labour was relatively cheap, thus helping to equalize wages and the cost of capital throughout the country, and that through national advertising it created the same wants and brand attachments from coast to coast, thus creating a national market. In addition, its managerial and technical personnel (the 'technostructure') are highly mobile, further reducing regional attachments within the corporation. On all this type of thing is hung the generic label 'integration' which, as the opposite of disintegration, is supposed to be a very good thing indeed. It is easy to see in broad terms that a similar process may take place internationally—in fact, that it already is taking place in some degree. But how is it to reduce the economic significance of the state? . . .

. . . If the type of development outlined is to 'integrate' the world economy so successfully that national frontiers become relatively insignificant, the international corporations will have to be able to carry on their activities—and especially those relating to their investment, trade, financial affairs and labour and recruitment policies—with minimal interference from individual governments. It is envisaged, at least by Kindleberger, that the national interests of the countries involved would be protected by independent international bodies or through international agreements. The international arrangements would presumably be established partly as a result of free negotiations, such as those of the European Common Market, and partly also because the force of circumstances left little alternative to the governments concerned. The truly international corporation, without national attachments, with no 'citizenship' and therefore indifferent to all national considerations, would attempt to equalize return on assets at the margin subject only to 'the discount for risk which applies realistically at home as well as abroad',[6] and would be free to do so within the internationally agreed constraints.

According to this 'cosmopolitan', or 'international' thesis, such corporations would do for the world economy what national corporations have allegedly already done for the United States economy: their capital would flow to raw materials and the cheaper sources of labour, with the result that the benefits of modern technology would reach the poorer and backward areas of the world, opportunities for all peoples, both at home and abroad, especially as internationally mobile employees of the large corporations would be widened, and consumption standards would rise everywhere. In short, the classical advantages of the international division of labour and free international trade would bring about greater world output and greater efficiency in the allocation of world resources.

It is not my purpose here to discuss the merits of this argument. Rather I now want to turn to an examination of the relationship that is envisaged between the international corporation and the state in the light of conditions and attitudes now widely prevalent among the less-developed countries.

ATTITUDES TOWARD INWARD INVESTMENT

In discussing the problem from the point of view of the less-developed countries I shall deal with three broad interrelated considerations: first, the emphasis that the new states place on 'nation-building', an integral part of which is the economic development of their own countries with a view to increasing the opportunities and standard of living of their own peoples in their own lands; second, the emphasis commonly placed on national economic 'planning' and the role of the so-called public sector, sometimes referred to loosely as 'socialism'; and finally, the ambivalent attitude toward foreign enterprise and the widely-expressed fear of foreign 'exploitation', again loosely referred to as 'imperialism'.

There is no doubt whatsoever that the less-developed countries in general take a 'narrowly-nationalistic' view of their situation. Economists from the industrialized countries, the riches of which are spilling over the frontiers may, with impeccable theoretical credentials and considerable practical force, point out to the poorer countries the folly of their ways, but one must deal with the world as it is. And the fact is that these countries are obsessed with their own economic problems and care not a bean for 'world allocative efficiency'. It follows, therefore, that their leaders must be convinced that the economic development of their own countries will be hastened if they give reasonably free rein to foreign corporations, or else they must be forced to do so by a variety of economic or political pressures to 'liberalize' their policies.

There are very great differences in the attitudes of the countries of the third world in this respect, but even in countries where foreign firms are reasonably welcome, restrictions are usually placed on their freedom of action, and these restrictions are often of a kind that force the foreign corporations to pay as much attention to national development needs as to international efficiency, if not more. There must be few underdeveloped countries in which foreign companies feel really secure and at ease, for suspicion of them is very widespread indeed. Are such attitudes likely to change in the foreseeable future? I think not, for three reasons.

My first reason (not necessarily the most important) relates to the inconclusiveness of the relevant economic analysis. That I should suggest such a consideration as an important influence on the attitudes of the leaders in less-developed countries may cause many to doubt my sanity, let alone my experience of these countries. Nevertheless, I submit that if all Western economists were agreed that direct private foreign investment always brought important net benefits to developing countries, benefits that were maximized when foreign companies were allowed to operate as freely as they chose, and if all the students from the developing countries studying economics in the Western world were firmly taught these propositions, it would be very much easier to persuade their economic ministers of the truth of this point of view. In practice, all relevant economic theory places much emphasis on the possible conflict between social and private benefit and on the dangers of monopoly, and some of it emphasizes the wastes of competition. In certain fields of international economics, special stress is laid on the specific problems raised for national economies by the operations of foreign firms. Considerable attention is paid in modern theory to the role of 'learning by doing' (which, of course, suggests that one does not gain by allowing foreigners to do too much). The list could be lengthened. My point is that serious and competent economists can make a strong case against a permissive attitude toward private foreign investment and thus bring respectability even to attitudes originally based upon an unthinking, emotional reaction.

My second reason for thinking that the role of the international corporation will be limited by the state in the third world for a long time to come is in a sense a continuation of the first. Economic planning, one of the most outstanding characteristics of the large corporation itself, is now widely accepted as an important function of the state in the interest of the development and stability of its national economy. The term 'planning' is only a generic one, covering many qualitatively different species of activity, but it carries with it the notion of establishing priorities among objectives, of setting targets and then of attempting systematically to achieve these targets.

Development planning is almost universal in the less-developed countries, aided and supported by international organizations and by developed countries of all political shades. In my view, development planning is not necessarily inconsistent with a large and growing private sector, nor with a high degree of autonomy for both private and public enterprises. But this is by the way the fact is that many developing countries have conceived of planning as the antithesis of private-enterprise capitalism responding to the profit motive. Attributing much of their present lack of development to colonialist exploitation or capitalist imperialism, and with an eye on the alternative modes of economic organization seen in the communist world, many of them enthusiastically adopted—at least formally—a centralized type of planning, nationalizing their major industries and creating in the process a large 'public sector'. For the most part their reach exceeded their grasp, and their first enthusiasm has given way to much disillusion. A public commitment to 'socialism' usually remains, but in many countries reappraisal and retrenchment is the order of the day.

It would be a very grave mistake, however, to interpret retrenchment as a return to the older system, as a complete reversal of policy. More freedom and autonomy for enterprises there may be, and more sympathy and encouragement for the private sector, but governments will continue to be concerned with priorities, and will continue to intervene in attempts to ensure that the private sector, including foreign enterprises, will operate in ways consistent with overall government objectives. The priorities and objectives will differ for countries in different economic positions, but there is no reason to think that they will be consistent with the objectives of international corporations, were the latter free from state interference. They will continue to find that the state will remain a powerful and difficult economic unit. This is not to say that international corporations will become less important than they are now; on the contrary, their contribution should increase as countries develop, but this contribution will have to fit in with national priorities.

Finally, I come to my third reason why governments in the third world can be expected to continue to assert their economic independence *vis-à-vis* foreign corporations—a widespread dislike of foreign domination, ranging from obsessive fears of 'imperialist exploitation' to simple political pride in the ability to maintain a high degree of independence. These attitudes will tend to persist as long as there are really glaring disparities in the economic position of the peoples of different countries.

As noted above, some countries trace many of their present problems to imperialist exploitation in the past, and their governments make great political play with anti-imperialist slogans in attempts to rally their people to support their policies. This is particularly common among governments which consider themselves 'revolutionary'. But even when governments are relatively conservative, there are always vocal groups which use such slogans in appealing to the people for support, and which governments can rarely afford to ignore. The roots of these attitudes, and the justifications for them, are far too complicated to explore here. They lie deep in grievances, real or imagined, inherited from the past, and in bitter feelings of inferiority directly traceable to the wide disparities in standards of living, technology and education that exist between the rich and the poor areas of the world. These feelings are exacerbated by sheer frustration and a sense of helplessness in the face of the overwhelmingly difficult problems inherent in attempts to force economic development and political progress at anywhere near the pace considered essential. They therefore become a potent political force in internal political struggles, and can be used to arouse class antagonism when conservative or 'reasonable' governments come too close to foreign business interests.

Because xenophobia is often used as a scapegoat for domestic troubles, there is a tendency among Western observers to put this entire complex of attitudes and behaviour into the box labelled 'irrationality' with no further attempt at analysis, or else to assume that the source of the trouble lies with 'communists' and the cold war. No one can deny that there is often much stupidity, illogicallity and unthinking emotionalism to contend with, as well as genuine ideological controversy, but I think that there is a real problem underneath the froth worthy of serious attention—and this apart from the seriousness with which one must examine the ideological basis of conflicting views.

It is, of course, irrational of economists to label other people's preferences 'irrational', provided that these preferences are consistent and that their implications are appreciated by those who express them. It has always been understood that welfare encompasses much more than objectively measurable economic goods and services—workers (and businessmen) may prefer leisure to income after a point without being thought irrational, 'psychic utility' lies at the basis of the theory of consumers' choice. Even the notion of 'community preferences' is respectable in much welfare theory, in spite of the obvious difficulties, and surely it is not unreasonable to postulate that some peoples may prefer to run their own affairs as far as possible rather than have them run by foreigners. In other words, extensive and dominant foreign control of economic activities may in itself be a positive disutility to a community, and the community may be willing to incur a cost to avoid it.

If 'disutility' of this kind exists, it may take the form of complaints that the country is being 'exploited' by foreign companies, who may then be accused of 'neo-imperialism'. It is very difficult to give a concrete meaning to such terms as 'exploitation', but there can be no doubt that a feeling of being exploited is one of the compelling forces behind much of the hostility directed toward large foreign firms. Their size, international scope, political, managerial and technological expertise, and in general the apparently wider 'options' open to them in determining their policies, all give rise to a feeling in their less well-endowed host countries that bargaining power is grossly unequal, with the result that the foreigner obtains a disproportionate gain from his activities in the country. The notion of *disproportionality* rather than the notion that the country necessarily loses *absolutely* is, in my view, the important consideration on which to focus in explaining the prevalence of the belief that foreign investment tends to be exploitative. The larger and more internationally powerful as foreign firm becomes, the greater may be its need to demonstrate its value to the host countries by contributing even more extensively to their development in terms of their own objectives.

Resentment, and difficulties, are sometimes intensified by attempts of dominant industrial countries to put pressure on less-developed countries in order to force them to admit private investment more freely. There is a certain analogy here with what has been called the "imperialism of free trade" in the nineteenth century. Britain was committed to free trade and she sometimes forced it on other areas under her political domination. It may be that she did so in the firm belief that, for all of the classical economic reasons, it was economically advantageous to the colonies as well as to the mother country. Nevertheless, one consequence was the destruction of some local industries with nothing to take their place. Today, infant industry (or infant country) arguments are almost universally accepted as grounds for making exceptions to free trade. But as Robinson and Gallagher have pointed out, the function of imperialism was to integrate new regions into an expanding economy, and it did so for a variety of agricultural and mining activities in an earlier period, but probably at an unnecessary cost to local development.

Today we have what might be called the 'imperialism of free investment', with precisely the same function, supported by arguments similar to those advanced for free trade, and enforced where possible by the dominant industrial power. From the point of view of the regions peripheral to the industrially advanced economies, however, 'free private investment' may have disadvantages similar to those attaching to free trade. Indeed, it is for this reason that even the most enthusiastic supporters of it admit the necessity for some sort of international controls. . . .

To summarize this section, I suggest that the state will remain an overwhelmingly important economic unit in the less-developed world, at least so long as that world is poor and technologically backward: (1) because the arguments designed to persuade it that its welfare would be increased by rapid and comprehensive 'integration' with the advanced countries via the international firm are inconclusive and unconvincing; (2) because their peoples seem to want to demonstrate their competence and independence and to establish their own economic priorities—and insist on doing so; and (3) because inequality breeds fear of the more powerful. Where foreign domination has been extensive, as it has apparently been, and still is in Latin America, it seems to raise political problems consistent with these considerations. It has even been suggested that some Latin American regimes are maintained in power only with the help of the great capital-exporting country whose firms have achieved dominant positions. In other instances there are signs that

This is what I used to get

national governments are attempting to assert their economic autonomy against international firms. *And to do.*

`'IPRA'`

THE FUTURE ROLE OF THE MULTINATIONAL ENTERPRISE

What, then, is the role of the multinational enterprise *vis-à-vis* the state? In spite of all the difficulties and attitudes outlined above, the less-developed countries, by and large, are prepared to accept—even to welcome—foreign enterprise and foreign help on their own terms where they believe it is clearly advantageous. 'Socialistically' inclined governments tend to insist on partnership arrangements; countries more sympathetic to private enterprise may also do so in less restrictive ways. For their part, the great international enterprises are likely to invest wherever they consider it profitable to do so, without worrying overmuch about ideological considerations if only they feel reasonably secure—which means if expected profit will compensate for any additional risk. These enterprises have a great contribution to make to the less-developed countries, but it is very different from what it is in the developed countries.

It has been persuasively argued that continual innovation in technology, and in methods of stimulating and sustaining consumers' demand with new products, new designs, new methods of marketing are necessary to maintain the momentum of the great industrial economies. Even if this is true, however, innovation and change of the kind that is characteristic of the United States economy, for example, is not the need, nor the popular demand, of the poor world. Many of their governments are aware of this, as are many international firms, some of whom devote special efforts to research into the ways of meeting their real needs—agricultural development, the provision of water supplies, special health or nutritional problems, etc. Moreover, much of the nascent industry of many countries has been established with the help of the great international corporations, which have provided technical advice, granted licences and help under their own patents, given managerial assistance and even made training facilities of various kinds available for local technical people. If attention were focused on this kind of thing instead of on the more sweeping and spectacular generalizations about the 'integration of the world' through the multinational enterprise and the economic absorption of the 'nation state', I wonder which type of activity would really turn out to be generally the most important in the developing countries?

A firm is a pool of managerial and technological expertise. It is also an efficient operating machine for both production and distribution. It can enter areas of inefficiency and set up and operate efficient units. It can also train others to do so, making much of its own expertise available in the process. Both of these are important activities, but I have not yet understood why the former will take precedence, or why world-wide planning on an industry level is the most efficient way to raise the standards of living of all peoples.

The notion that firms will integrate the industries, and thus the economies, of the world within their own administrative framework, and that this will maximize world welfare, rests basically on the notion that planning on a world-wide scale is not only the inevitable outcome of present trends and United States economic power, but is also the most effective way of bringing the peoples of the world closer to the United States levels of living. It seems to me equally likely that they will continue to function as important international organizations, complementing and aiding the economic efforts of independent countries to develop their economies, and that such enterprises will have an important independent role in all sorts of international economic relations, but will also have to conduct continuous negotiations with states whose economic sovereignty they must respect as they try to 'harmonize' their own interests with those of the countries in which they operate.

I have not tried to discuss 'welfare' considerations here or the extent to which integration by firms would advance the development of any particular country, both economically and politically. My primary thesis has been that so long as the inequalities among the nations of the world are so great that a large proportion of the peoples of some are in real poverty, the governments of these peoples will be unwilling to give the rich and favoured foreign economic interests a dominating position in their economies. I also think it probable that, for as long as we can conveniently foresee, governments must insist on a high degree of sovereignty over their economic affairs in order to provide a national economic framework for the activities of their people on the one hand, and on the other to ensure that their economic needs are represented as identifiable claimants for international consideration. If the basic economic unit for planning is the independent country—or a group of countries where some of the national units are very small—it may be less likely that pockets of backwardness in the world will be forgotten and left to rot. It is argued that the existence of the economic sovereignty of the state leads to economic cleavages along national lines, but if national differences were eliminated through integration, would not cleavages of an even more intractable nature along class (or even colour) lines tend to be accentuated?

The concern of a government for the economic welfare of its country must inevitably encompass a variety of considerations which would not be important to a great international enterprise. Indeed, I suspect that multinational enterprises as we know them today would find their life intolerable if the 'state as an economic unit' really did disappear!

NOTES

1. C. P. Kindleberger, *American Business Abroad: Six Lectures on Direct Investment*, New Haven and London, Yale University Press, 1969, p. 207.
2. Kindleberger, *op. cit.*, pp. 207–8.
3. S. Kuznets, *Modern Economic Growth: Rate, Structure and Spread*. New Haven and London, Yale University Press, 1966, pp. 2 ff.
4. *Ibid.*, p. 9.
5. See S. Hymer, 'The Multinational Corporation and the Law of Uneven Development', in J. N. Bhagwati (ed.), *Economics and World Order*, New York, World Law Fund, 1970.
6. Kindleberger, *op. cit.*, p. 183.

15. The Several Faces of the Multinational Corporation: Political Reaction and Policy Response

ROBERT T. KUDRLE

In this reading, Robert Kudrle examines national policies toward multinational corporations in both developed and developing countries. He notes the wide variety of ways in which foreign corporations are viewed, from unwanted extensions of foreign powers to valuable resources for national development. Kudrle explains in this survey how different nations have reacted toward foreign direct investment, and points out that developing countries are far more sensitive to issues of national control than are developed nations.

. . . The multinational corporation (MNC) exemplifies the era of transnationalism and the increasingly complex problems nearly all national governments face in devising effective, coherent international economic policies. The relative importance of the MNC has grown steadily over most of the postwar period. From 1960 until the late 1970s, annual foreign production of MNCs grew at over 10 percent, while world trade grew at 9.5 percent and world production at about 8 percent. Moreover, the enormous growth in world trade has taken place in large part under the aegis of the MNC. Over half of all U.S. exports are now accounted for by MNC activity.

The growing interdependence of the world economy presents a threat to national sovereignty, and direct foreign investment (DFI) appears as perhaps the most palpable specific threat. The word "direct" implies control by a foreign-owned economic presence within a sovereign state, so that suspicion and conflict come almost automatically. The threat seems particularly formidable when the sizes of many of the firms are considered. Dozens of MNCs have sales greater than the GNPs of most members of the United Nations.

The focus of this chapter is government policy toward the MNC. I look at how the MNC penetrates a country's national consciousness and generates political reaction and ultimately policy response. More specifically, I endeavor to explain why developed countries (DCs) and less developed countries (LDCs) have systematically different policy responses to MNC activities within their borders. . . .

INCOMING DIRECT FOREIGN INVESTMENT

I assume that the MNC presents several faces to politically conscious persons around the world. The reactions of these persons are mediated by political institutions that determine policies that governments actually pursue toward the MNC. A model of this policy process is presented later. Most writing on the MNC over the past quarter-century suggests that nearly all stimuli can be considered under three broad headings: the MNC as "extension of the home country," the MNC as "rival," and the MNC as "resource." Broadly speaking, the first face stresses the general foreign influences brought by the firm, the second its claim on resources that might otherwise go to some domestic element, and the third its augmentation of the productive capacity of the host country's economy.

The MNC as Extension of the Home Country

Incoming Direct Foreign Investment (IDFI) can be seen as an extension of the home country (1) because the firm appears protected by its home government (protégé), (2) because it seems to act at the behest of the home government (agent), or (3) because it serves as a means whereby broad foreign influences are injected into the host country (conduit for alien influence).

Protégé. The MNC generates politically relevant stimuli in the host country when the home country is seen to safeguard the MNC's interests. In the developed countries this face has not typically been prominent. The pre-World War II experience of more developed countries with IDFI generally was not dramatic. After the war, the U.S. government exercised influence to gain comparable treatment for its MNCs in European nations under the Treaty of Rome, but little in the way of further specific action on behalf of individual firms or the business community in a particular DC has been seen until recently. In 1982, the U.S. Congress considered legislation designed to counter pending measures before the EEC commission requiring MNCs to share their future plans with host governments and employees. Such exceptional behavior was widely regarded with dismay in Europe.

The less developed countries provide a sharp contrast. The large trading and producing companies of the colonial empires became despised symbols of hierarchy and privilege. In many popular versions of imperialism the principal purpose of political control was to help these enterprises develop and prosper. In many of the republics of Latin America the relation was experienced just as vividly. They saw their claims as sovereign states thwarted by the superior power of Europeans and North Americans who intervened militarily over many decades to assert the property rights and to protect the safety of home country citizens. Thus did the prerogatives of foreign capital become virtually defined as an offense to nationalism. The United States formally abandoned intervention claims for such purposes in 1933, but military action in Guatemala in 1954 and in the Dominican Republic in 1965, as well as CIA activity in Chile in 1971, were widely regarded as intended mainly to protect U.S. business there. . . . France appears willing to intervene for similar purposes in Black Africa.

LDCs also feel that the Hickenlooper and Gonzales amendments—which oblige the United States to withhold international assistance from states that have not paid adequate compensation in cases of nationalization of U.S.-owned industries—are a continuing affront to the general Third World doctrine that such disputes should not extend beyond the borders of the host country.

Agent. The MNC may also be perceived as an agent of the home country. In contrast to the image (and often the reality) in many LDCs, the United States has most often used MNCs in the industrialized countries to achieve broad goals of foreign and domestic policy rather than to assist in covert activities.

The U.S. government in the 1960s forbade overseas subsidiaries from selling to China and Cuba and obliged them to find non-U.S. finance in the face of U.S. balance-of-payments problems. U.S. authorities also blocked mergers that were thought likely to affect adversely the U.S. domestic market. Changes in the international monetary system in the 1970s ended most conflicts arising from the balance of payments, however. The other two sources of conflict, also based on the extraterritorial claims of U.S. law, continue. By claiming that its laws extend to its MNCs operating abroad, the United States has aroused almost universal condemnation abroad from all parts of the political spectrum. Legislatures of many countries have attempted to assist their bureaucrats and courts in resisting the U.S. reach by passing specific legislation directing noncompliance.

In the LDCs the provocation stems less frequently from explicit claims of extraterritoriality and more often from evidence or rumor of spying and covert manipulation of the political system. The activities of the CIA in Latin America, sometimes working with U.S. business, and the claims of close ties between intelligence services of other countries and their MNCs have generated widespread suspicion and revulsion across a broad range of domestic politics.

The potential threat to national security perceived from the connections of MNCs with their host governments has led both DCs and LDCs to block foreign firms from defense-related industries. France, largely because of her determination to maintain an independent foreign policy, has been particularly cautious in this area. Several Latin American governments in recent years have increased attention to such concerns. Dominguez suggests that limiting foreign participation in industries related to national defense is particularly likely where the military exercises strong political influence.

Conduit for Alien Influence. The apparent Americanization of the developed world, largely, or so it seemed, under the auspices of the MNC, stirred passion from the mid-1950s until perhaps the early 1970s. Servan-Schreiber stated the issues forcefully in *Le Défi Americain* of 1967. Except for Japan, most industrialized countries responded to the U.S. challenge by adapting more than resisting, as Servan-Schreiber recommended. His book was much less an attack on the United States or its MNCs than it was an indictment of the slowness of European public policy to respond to the challenges posed by the complex relations among technology, wealth, and especially power in the postwar world. His observations about Europe's educational system and social structure prompted policy responses, as did some of his suggestions for industrial policy. Governments became heavily involved in subsidized research, encouraged mergers, and increased their preferential purchasing from national firms—not merely European Community-based firms. The major states encouraged "national champions" in key industries.

Despite the pivotal role they seem to have played in provoking broad policy responses by other Western governments, the U.S.-based MNCs did not typically generate a large amount of political tension toward specific firms or even the home government. The policy changes, even when they directly affected MNCs, did so in a way that left them a broad range of attractive, permissible activity.

An apparent threat to autonomy—and in some cases to security as well—was countered by disallowing or limiting foreign participation in certain basic sectors of the economy in addition to defense-related industries. Some countries that have no restriction on the right of establishment of foreign firms have used foreign exchange laws to monitor and perhaps occasionally modify foreigners's plans (Britain and Italy). But some have not (Germany, Switzerland, and the United States). Other countries have employed direct screening. Norway and Sweden examine all incoming investment but with little apparent deterrent effect, while France does so with great thoroughness. In France, the rejection rate on proposed IDFI ventures in the late 1970s was estimated to be much higher than elsewhere in Europe—at perhaps 5 percent. And where takeovers have been proposed (even from elsewhere in the European Economic Community) the French government has frequently tried to find a French buyer instead. France presents yet another contrast to most of the rest of Europe. Because the intimate role of the French government in business decision making is well known, the government is likely to take much of the blame or credit for specific incursions by foreign capital.

A third pattern of entry control is followed by Canada, Australia, and Japan. Entry, expansion, and takeovers are monitored by a distinct entity. In Canada, about half of all manufacturing output and 70 percent of oil production were in foreign hands in 1970. Canada's Foreign Investment Review Agency (FIRA), established in 1974, now requires "significant benefit" for the country from the proposed foreign-based activity. Its rejection rate of 8 percent on new activity and 16 percent on takeovers in 1977 was far higher than in Europe. FIRA has been attacked both by international business and from within the country because its rationale for decisions is not public and is ultimately decided at the cabinet level. The issue is kept constantly in the public eye by the greater enthusiasm for IDFI in poorer provinces. Regional differences in attempting to attract IDFI may be less politically important in more centralized states.

In Australia, where IDFI penetration is in many respects similar to that in Canada, there is an additional emphasis on local participation, with the required percentage varying by sector. Among the Western developed countries, Canada and Australia are unique, not simply because of their stringency but because IDFI has long been a major issue in their mass electoral politics, with a significant part of the political leadership actively cultivating nationalist sentiment.

Japan presents the most restrictive case; foreign investment in more than negligible amounts has been permitted only in recent years. Japan's sense of uniqueness and vulnerability after an extremely unhappy series of early contacts with Europeans on Japanese soil set an enduring pattern of minimizing any permanent foreign presence, let alone one of substantial influence or control. In 1970 there were fewer than 25,100 residents from Western countries in Japan. Instead of allowing substantial DFI, Japan increasingly broadened the scope of licensed technology. Pressure from major home countries, particularly the United States, has led in recent years to a nominal lessening of restrictions but only minor changes in actual penetration.

Again, the conduit face of MNCs appears more dramatic and threatening in the less developed countries than elsewhere. In many LDCs, the MNC has virtually become the symbolic embodiment of the modern world in broad ranges of national life. Foreign business thus becomes a source of annoyance and frustration to those who must modify their behavior to work successfully as employees, customers, or suppliers. Those most wedded to the traditional society regard the MNC as a principal symbol of evil. There are many who welcome the modernization that the MNC symbolizes, but even most of these would prefer such change to take place under national auspices and control. One looks in vain for a strong defense of direct foreign influence from any part of the political spectrum in any country, rich or poor.

Foreign penetration leading ultimately to social decay features prominently in the *dependéncia* literature from Latin America. The comprehensiveness of the approach is captured by Sunkel:

> Foreign factors are seen not as external but as intrinsic to the system, with manifold and sometimes hidden or subtle political, financial, economic, technical, and cultural effects inside the underdeveloped country. These contribute significantly to shaping the nature and operation of the economy, society, and polity, a kind of "fifth column" as it were.[1] . . .

The threat to autonomy presented by the three dimensions of the MNC as extension of the home country take on different significance for most LDCs relative to DCs. In the developed world most people regard the challenges posed by MNCs as discrete and visible, but among the newly modernizing countries the fear of pervasive and largely invisible domination by MNCs has become widespread.

The MNC as Rival of Government

Although the MNC as conduit encompasses political phenomena generated by the MNC largely unintentionally, as a result of its pursuit of profit, the MNC as government rival encompasses certain intentional activities. The latter may be as minor as tax minimization within the apparent discretion of the law, or as major as deception and corruption, manipulation, and even system disruption.

In the developed countries direct rivalry between foreign firms and host-country governments has been far less of an issue than in the developing world. Although there are exceptions, foreign enterprises have generally operated within the realm of accepted law. Tax avoidance has seldom provided an important source of conflict. Whenever such rivalry has become overt, however, the MNC has received condemnation in the media and in other public discourse. The opposition of the U.S. Chamber of Commerce in West Germany to certain elements of the co-determination legislation of the 1970s caused a furor in a country whose general hospitality toward DFI is very high. The lobbying action taken by the Chamber was, in essence, declared illegitimate by the West German chancellor.

The DCs have also experienced a vague uneasiness that the economic outlook of the MNC is somehow incongruent with that of the host state, or more specifically that a foreign firm can never be sufficiently subordinate to state power to be entirely satisfactory. The French adduce as evidence the ability of U.S. firms in the 1960s to obtain funds not controlled by the French government and hence to escape *le plan*. Special competitive assets virtually define the MNC; nonetheless, most evidence suggests that foreign and domestic firms now usually see and react to most economic situations quite similarly. However, some apprehension remains.

The history of rivalry between the MNC and host-country governments in the Third World is typically of a wholly different order from the situation elsewhere. Prior to World War II the overwhelming share of all direct investment in Third World countries was in natural resource extraction or public utilities. Even in the industrialized countries these two sectors have given rise to great policy difficulties because ownership often confers excess profits or rent. Excess profits of one kind or another thus frequently became a central focus of LDC government concern from the very earliest period. And yet, for extended periods, policymaking groups were frequently so inept, corrupt, or easily coopted that the host government gained little from the MNC relative to the host's potential. Foreign firms frequently manipulated not just specific decisions, but the broader political process. . . .

The recent history of the rivalry between the MNC and developing country governments is recounted quite similarly in both the conventional and the radical literature. In the early postwar years, the broad security interests of the host countries, their lack of sophistication in dealing with the MNC, and the absence of alternative sources of foreign resources gave foreign—usually U.S.—firms the upper hand. U.S. MNCs established well over two-thirds of all new foreign-owned subsidiaries in LDCs between 1946 and 1959. Washington later reconsidered its security interests, excluding the protection of U.S. capital. MNCs could no longer count on strong support in disputes with host country governments.

Other developments also diminished MNC power. Host governments developed much stronger skills and monitoring capacities during the 1960s and 1970s, a time when the emerging alternative of non-U.S. MNCs provided additional leverage. In industries with large fixed investments and familiar technologies, including much of natural resource exploitation and public utilities, nationalization often became an irresistibly attractive option. Where nationalization was rejected as an appropriate policy, governments learned that whatever bargain was initially struck, the rules could be continually changed on the foreign investor—up to the point at which the firm could no longer meet its out-of-pocket costs. This is Vernon's "obsolescing bargain."[2]

In natural resources and elsewhere, the increasingly sophisticated policies of many Third World governments, including virtually all where large amounts of capital are invested, have focused on reducing the profitability of a broad range of foreign direct investments. By the end of the 1970s, many countries had developed specialized agencies to act as sole national representatives to bargain directly with the MNCs for the best possible terms regardless of the type of activity.

Most recent case histories of the MNC in LDCs suggest few covert attempts to manipulate the political system. Corruption and attempts to evade profit-reducing regulations certainly continue, but now the MNCs sometimes assure that necessary payments are made indirectly. Spectacular exceptions such as ITT's vendetta against the Allende government notwithstanding, contemporary practice by foreign firms appears in general to be politically cautious, a recognition both of the extent to which such activity is regarded as illegitimate and of the effectiveness of retribution.

Several factors beyond those already mentioned explain the sharp and systematic difference between DC and LDC practice on the stringency and specificity of controls on IDFI. First, there is typically little international competition in heavily protected LDC markets, and the MNC frequently fills a niche in the economy where there will also be little domestic competition. Second, the developing world has favored greater asymmetry of treatment between LDCs and DCs and sees no merit in the nondiscriminatory treatment of domestic and foreign business. This position is bolstered by laws and social attitudes toward private property that are typically extremely flexible and often present no barrier to treating each case on its own apparent merits with no necessity for consistent application of general rules.

Finally, while nineteenth-century liberalism prevails less in nearly all countries, rich and poor, than it does in the United States, the history of all political factions in most developing countries reveals a particular willingness to use the state to any extent necessary to create the conditions for economic development. Even where the prevailing elite ideology has seen private enterprise as the principal engine of material advance, the state has been regarded as a crucial, positive actor.

A very broad notion of what constitutes infrastructural activity has characterized most poor countries; and, in most, the state also engages in a large amount of activity that is clearly substitutive for what could be done by the private sector. Observers have identified at least three major rationales for the extension of state enterprise into the commercial sphere: First, there are occasions when domestic private firms appear to lack the capital or other requisites that the government deems necessary for national development; second, local private attempts to play such a role may have failed, with the state taking over; third, the state has often intervened to counteract "denationalization" of industry by MNC.

The third possible motive generates a variety of policies. Nationalization has already been mentioned. Compensation is typically paid, although it is often modest relative to the owners's valuation. Often the state becomes the operator of the enterprise. In other cases, the state moves into a promising new area to avoid entrance there by the MNC. Finally, increasing numbers of countries have laws prescribing the minimum amount of domestic ownership that foreign capital must employ in endeavors of various kinds. Mexico has a highly elaborated structure. There, the government may simply become the last resort investor when private firms do not come forward.

The MNC as Rival of Domestic Business

Rivalry for gain between domestic and foreign business has been a pervasive and significant political issue in the DCs. Particularly in the 1950s and 1960s, domestic firms in many countries felt deeply threatened both by the superior competitive potential of foreign firms (cost, design, and marketing advantages) and their relatively unrestrained exercise of that potential in what had often previously been an environment of mutual accommodation. This adverse but diffuse feeling generated little in the way of political product. Nevertheless, partly as a result of domestic business lobbying, sectors in addition to defense-related industries have been closed to foreign capital or meet resistance to foreign penetration from DC authorities. These include private utilities, transportation and communications including the media, banking and finance, and to a widely varying extent, natural resources and land.

The typical developing country entirely excludes foreign capital from at least as broad a range of activity as do most industrialized states. Moreover, several severely restrict operations in wholesale and retail trade. In the early period of modern development, there were many firms whose activities complemented those of foreign firms and rather few that could have ambitions to duplicate them. But over time acquisition of skills and experience by indigenous firms typically shifted the balance quite radically and greatly increased elements wishing to displace foreign investment. Several developments reflect this shift. Because of the absence of notions of nondiscriminatory treatment, locally-owned LDC business has lobbied for preferential government purchasing in a wide variety of industries and in some countries has successfully blocked MNCs from access to the local capital market. Such discrimination encourages the formation of joint ventures between local and foreign capital even where they are not mandated by law.

Although the relative size of the state entrepreneurial sector varies widely, the growing strength of both the entrepreneurial bureaucracy and private business has accompanied more negative attitudes by both toward foreign business and, in some countries, has produced a more exclusionary policy.

The MNC as Rival of Labor

A third major rivalry is with organized labor, and in the DCs it takes several forms. One is the traditional quest for above-market wages, a goal that seems generally to have been achieved more fully in dealings with MNCs than with domestic firms. However, U.S. MNCs have typically been assertive about workplace organization and resistant to responsibility for the stability of employment. The greater paternalism of Japanese firms operating in the United States has generated tension.

In most DCs, labor has understandably tried to gain some package of high wages and increased employment as it stands firm against foreigners's preferences that threaten other goals. Vernon has observed that most European unions oppose the MNC because they feel that their bargaining power is threatened by its mobility and they see the welfare state threatened by decreased national autonomy. As a practical matter, however, national EEC unions must be concerned for jobs; they understand that presenting difficulties for foreign firms may simply drive these firms elsewhere. Effective opposition to foreign capital awaits a Europe-wide labor organization, which shows little sign of developing. In the United States the AFL-CIO has shown little opposition to foreign investment in general but has criticized its frequent preference for location in right-to-work states. This position is consistent with U.S. labor's largely nonideological character.

Rivalry between the MNC and labor typically attains less importance in LDCs than in the DCs because industrial workers in LDCs usually have less power in both the political system and the workplace. Some successful industrializing countries, such as Singapore, Malaysia, Indonesia, and South Korea, have attracted foreign capital in part by promising and delivering a quiescent labor force. Elsewhere, however, including Mexico, the government has sometimes encouraged nationalism in general and its own political base in particular by supporting organized labor in disputes with foreign capital.

The MNC as Resource

Despite the other manifestations, often negative, of foreign penetration, the major governments of the Western industrialized countries have generally regarded IDFI mainly as a means of increasing national material welfare by adding tangible resources. The Organization for European Economic Cooperation (OEEC) Council recommended the liberalization of capital movements in Europe in 1957 as part of the general restoration of normal economic activity; much liberalization was accomplished in the following few years. The successor Organization for Economic Cooperation and Development (OECD) incorporated these provisions and expanded cooperation on matters related to DFI, with the objective of nondiscrimination between foreign and domestic capital. Elite surveys reveal that this policy has generally reflected informed opinion, and most economic analyses have confirmed the contribution of IDFI to national income through its capital, technology, management, and marketing innovations. Although administrative discretion may be used to discourage acquisition in some sectors to an extent that is not fully public, most countries continue to welcome investment in most sectors of the economy. They give special incentives—usually also available to domestic firms—for new operations in regions of high unemployment.

In Japan, management and marketing have been largely irrelevant to the country's unique social system, and Japan's high savings rate has greatly diminished the appeal of a foreign capital contribution. The only compelling MNC offering has been technology, much of which has become available through licensing. When Japan's general attitude toward foreign presence is combined with its actual economic needs, the tight restrictions on the MNC become easily understandable.

All of the negative political phenomena generated by the MNC in LDCs should not obscure the fact that most countries still actively recruit MNCs in many sectors of the economy and that this posture is consistent with informed opinion. For example, a substantial role for DFI is supported by a diverse set of groups in Latin America.

Foreign borrowing grew enormously in the 1970s, but it cannot completely replace DFI unless the other resources that equity brings are redundant or can be easily purchased separately. A richer set of international markets in management and technology coupled with increased domestic sophistication has certainly increased the second possibility. And yet a nearly universal demand for substantial MNC activity remains. In many fields the most attractive technology and expertise does not come in "unbundled" form; the advantages in foreign market access that are inherent in most manufacturing MNCs often cannot be duplicated except at a very high price. A rapid and premature jettisoning of the MNC—even in natural resource industries—has led some countries to economic disaster.

In 1975, OPEC accounted for 23 percent of all IDFI in LDCs; ten other countries hosted 41 percent. Much of the rest of the developing world, although maintaining a nominally complex set of requirements for entering investment, actively recruits DFI with various incentives but finds rather little interest.

NOTES

1. Sunkel, O., "Big Business and 'Dependéncia'", *Foreign Affairs* April 1972, p. 519.
2. Vernon, R. *Sovereignty at Bay: The Multinational Spread of U.S. Enterprises* (New York: Basic Books, 1971).

C. Money and Finance

The international economy, like domestic economies, requires a common monetary standard to function smoothly. For individuals and firms to buy and sell and to save and invest, they need some generally acceptable and predictable *unit of account* against which other goods can be measured, a *medium of exchange* with which transactions can be carried out, and a *store of value* in which wealth can be held. National currencies serve this purpose within countries: Americans buy, sell, save, and invest in dollars. In international trade and payments, a variety of possible common measures can be imagined; in practice, the two purest cases are a commodity standard and an international currency standard. Economic actors could use a widely traded commodity, such as gold or pork bellies, against which to measure other goods; or they might arrive at some fictitious unit in which goods could be priced. The former approximates the classical gold standard; the latter present-day Special Drawing Rights, which are a sort of "paper gold" issued by the International Monetary Fund and equal to a mix of national currencies. Because agreement on a fictitious international currency is difficult, such national currencies as the dollar or the pound sterling have often been used.

If the international monetary system provides the measures needed to conduct world trade and payments, the international financial system provides the means by which actual trade and payments are carried out. For many hundreds of years, financial institutions—especially banks—have financed trade among clients in different nations, sold and bought foreign currencies, transferred money from one country to another, and lent capital for overseas investment. If, as is often averred, the international monetary system is The Great Wheel that allows goods to move in international trade, the international financial system is the grease that allows the wheel itself to turn.

In the modern era, since 1820 or so, there have been essentially four well-functioning international monetary systems in the non-Communist world; each had corresponding international financial characteristics. From about 1820 until World War I, the world was on the classical gold standard, in which many major national currencies were tied to gold at a legally fixed rate. In principle, as Benjamin J. Cohen explains in a reading that follows, the gold standard was self-regulating; should any national currency (and economy) get out of balance, it would be forced back into equilibrium by the very operation of the system. In practice, the pre–World War I system was actually a gold-sterling standard; the British pound sterling, backed by a strong government and the world's leading financial center, was "as good as gold," and most international trade and payments were carried out in sterling. The world financial system in the century before World War I was indeed dominated by British banks, who financed much of world trade and channeled enormous amounts of investment capital to such rapidly developing countries as the United States, Australia, Argentina, and South Africa. As time wore on, the financial institutions of other European powers, especially France and Germany, also began to expand abroad. The result was a highly integrated system of international monetary and financial interactions under the *Pax Britannica*.

Even before World War I, strains and rivalries were beginning to test the system. Once the war started in 1914, international trade and payments collapsed: of all the world's major financial markets, only New York stayed open for the duration of the conflict. Indeed, by the time World War I ended, the center of international finance had shifted from London to New York, and Wall Street remained the world's principal lender until the Great Depression of the 1930s. As might be expected, given the reduced economic might of Great Britain, the prewar gold-sterling standard could not be rebuilt. Yet neither was the United States—beset by the isolationist-internationalist conflict at home—willing to simply replace Great Britain at the apex of the world monetary system. What emerged was the so-called "gold-exchange standard," where most countries went back to tying their currencies to gold, but no one national currency came to dominate the others. Dollars, sterling, and French francs were all widely used in world trade and payments, yet, given the lack of lasting international monetary cooperation in the period, the arrangement was quite unstable and short-lived. Normal international economic conditions were only restored by 1924, and within a few years, the Depression drove sterling and the dollar off gold. With the collapse of the gold-exchange standard and the onset of the Depression and World War II, the international monetary and financial systems remained in disarray until after 1945.

As World War II came to an end, the Allied powers led by the United States began reconstructing an international monetary system. This Bretton Woods system was based, in the monetary sphere, on an American dollar tied to gold at the rate of thirty-five dollars an ounce; other Western currencies were in turn tied to the dollar. This was a modified version of the pre-1914 gold standard, with the dollar at its center rather than sterling. As in the *Pax Britannica*, massive flows of capital from the leading nation—Great Britain in the first instance, the United States in the second—were crucial to the proper functioning of the mechanism. Whereas in the British case these capital flows were primarily private loans, from 1945 to 1965 they were essentially government or multilateral loans and foreign direct investment. Only after 1965 did private international finance become significant—but then it rapidly grew to historically unprecedented proportions and characteristics, as Jim Hawley notes.

Even as the new international financial system, generally known as the Euromarket, was gathering steam, the Bretton Woods monetary system was beginning to weaken. It was, as Benjamin J. Cohen points out, more and more difficult to maintain the dollar's price of thirty-five dollars an ounce. As pressure built on the dollar, and attempts at reform stagnated, the Nixon administration finally decided that the system was unsustainable. In August 1971, President Richard Nixon "closed the gold window," ending the dollar's free convertibility into gold. The dollar was soon devalued. By 1975, the gold-dollar standard had been replaced by a floating-rate system, in which the value of most currencies is set more or less freely in world currency markets. Thus, the values of the dollar, the deutsche mark, the franc, and so on, fluctuate on international currency markets. This has led to frequent and rapid changes in the relative prices of major currencies, as well as to frequent complaints about the unplanned nature of the new system. Some support the development of a new international money, of which Special Drawing Rights might be a precursor; others desire a return to the gold standard. Nonetheless, although there have been some moves in the direction of more concerted international monetary cooperation in the 1980s, no real replacement to the floating-rate system has emerged, and it is likely to remain in place for the foreseeable future.

In international finance, the period since 1965 has been extraordinarily eventful. The Euromarket grew to well over a trillion dollars, international banks lent hundreds of billions of dollars to developing and Communist countries; in 1982, an international financial crisis began to unfold. Jeff Frieden's article (Reading 19) describes the growth in developing-country debt; Charles Lipson's contribution explains the role of the International Monetary Fund and international banks in managing debt crises.

Postwar monetary and financial affairs have given rise to both academic and political polemics. Developing countries especially have argued that the existing system works to their detriment, and have proposed sweeping reforms. Most developed nations believe that, imperfect as current arrangements may be, they are the best available and that reform schemes are simply unrealistic.

Among scholars, international monetary and financial relations raise important analytical issues. As in other arenas, the very rapid development of globe-straddling international financial markets has led some scholars, such as Jim Hawley, to believe that the rise of supranational banks has eroded the power of national states. In this view, international monetary relations are essentially a tool of increasingly global international banks and their allies in such international institutions as the International Monetary Fund. Other analysts believe that national governments are still the primary determinants of international monetary and financial trends. The specific policies of major states toward their own banks and their own currencies are, in this view, set in line with national interests; banks and currency movements are instruments of national policy and not the other way around. The tension between a monetary and financial system that is in a sense beyond the reach of individual states, and currencies and banks that clearly have home countries, gives rise to a fundamental tension in world politics and in the study of the international political economy.

16.   A Brief History of International Monetary Relations

BENJAMIN J. COHEN

Benjamin Cohen describes the evolution of the international monetary system over the past century. He shows how the system has evolved away from a gold standard toward the use of national currencies, not backed by precious metals, for international trade and payments. As Cohen indicates, the national goals of independent states have often conflicted with the more general international goal of a stable, workable means of international payments. The two most successful experiences in overcoming the contradiction between national desires and global cooperation have been, Cohen argues, in the periods before World War I and after World War II, in which Great Britain and the United States, respectively, served as bankers to the world. In these eras, one nation managed and enforced international monetary relations in ways that conformed both to the hegemon's national goals and to the maintenance of international monetary stability—which is not to say that the resultant order was benevolent to all concerned, as Cohen points out. In any case, just as the decline of British political and economic power undermined the classical gold standard, so too has the United States' relative decline since 1970 led to a reshuffling of existing international monetary arrangements.

THE CLASSICAL GOLD STANDARD

. . . It is impossible to specify a precise date when the international monetary order began. The origins of international monetary relations, like those of money itself, are shrouded in the obscurity of prehistory. We know that there were well-defined monetary areas in many parts of the ancient world. But it is only with the rise of the Roman Empire that we begin to find documentary evidence of a very explicit international monetary order. The Roman monetary order, which was based initially on the gold coinage of Julius Caesar and later on the gold solidus (bezant, nomisma) for Byzantium, lasted some twelve centuries in all. Though confronted from the seventh century on with competition from a silver bloc centered on the newly emergent Muslim dinar, the Roman system did not break down completely until the sacking of Constantinople in 1203. The next five centuries were characterized by fluctuating exchange rates and a succession of dominant moneys—the "dollars of the Middle Ages," one source has called them[1]—including in later years the Florentine fiorino, the Venetian ducato, the Spanish reale, and the Dutch florin. After the beginning of the Industrial Revolution, it was the British pound sterling that rose to a position of preeminence in world monetary affairs.

As its name implies, the pound sterling was originally based on silver. In fact, however, England began practicing a loose sort of bimetallism— gold coins circulating alongside silver ones—even as early as the fourteenth century. (Gold coinage was first introduced into England in 1344, during the reign of Edward III.) Gresham's Law was coined during the reign of Queen Elizabeth I. Sir Isaac Newton, as Master of the Mint, tried to cope with the problem of bad money driving out good by calculating the value of the gold guinea (named after the region in West Africa where gold was mined) in terms of silver shillings. And in 1817 gold was formally declared legal tender in England alongside silver. From the time of the Napoleonic Wars, the United Kingdom moved rapidly from bimetallism to a single-money system. In 1798 the free coinage of silver was suspended and a £25 limit set on the legal-tender power of silver coins. In 1816 silver's legal-tender powers were further limited to £2. And after 1819 silver could no longer be used to redeem circulating bank notes: paper could be redeemed in gold coin only. From that date onward, the pound was effectively based on gold alone. The British were on a full gold standard.

Other countries, however, resisted the gold standard for several decades more. Most European nations, as well as the United States, remained legally bimetallic for at least another half century; most others, especially in Asia, formally retained silver standards. It was only in the 1870s that the movement toward a full-fledged international gold standard picked up momentum, and it is from this decade that the modern history of international monetary relations is customarily dated. In 1871 the new German empire adopted the gold mark as its monetary unit, discontinuing the free coinage and unlimited legal-tender powers of silver. In 1873 a parallel decision followed in the United States (the "Crime of '73"), and by 1878 silver had been demonetized in France and virtually every other European country as well. During this decade, the classical gold standard was born. During succeeding decades, it spread to encompass virtually all of the world's independent countries, as well as all of the various colonial empires of Europe.

The classical gold standard was a comparatively brief episode in world history, ending with the outbreak of World War I in 1914. It was defined by two key features. A country was considered to be "on" the gold standard if (1) its central bank pledged to buy and sell gold (and only gold) freely at a fixed price in terms of the home currency, and (2) its private residents could export or import gold freely. Together, these two features defined a pure fixed-exchange-rate mechanism of balance-of-payments adjustment. Fixed exchange rates were established by the ratios of the prices at which central banks pledged to buy and sell gold for local currency. Free export and import of gold in turn established the means for reconciling any differences between the demand and supply of a currency at its fixed exchange rate. Deficits, requiring net payments to foreigners, were expected to result in outflows of gold, as residents converted local currency at the central bank in order to meet transactions obligations abroad. Conversely, surpluses, were expected to result in gold inflows. Adjustment was supposed to work through the impact of such gold flows on domestic economic conditions in each country.

The mechanism of liquidity creation under the classical gold standard was very nearly a pure commodity standard—and that commodity, of course, was gold. Silver lost its role as an important reserve asset during the decade of demonetization in the 1870s. And national currencies did not even begin to enter into monetary reserves in significant quantities until after 1900. The most widely held national currency before World War I was the pound; its principal rivals were the French franc and the German mark. But even as late as 1914, the ratio of world foreign-exchange reserves to world gold reserves remained very low. The monetary standard even then was still essentially a pure commodity standard.

After World War I, observers tended to look back on the classical gold standard with a sense of nostalgia and regret—a sort of Proustian *Recherche du temps perdu*. As compared with the course of events after 1918, the pre-1914 monetary order appeared, in retrospect, to have been enormously successful in reconciling the tension between economic and political values. During its four decades of existence, world trade and payments grew at record rates, promoting technical efficiency and economic welfare; yet, looking back, it seemed that problems of balance-of-payments adjustment and conflicts of policy between nations had been remarkably rare. The gold standard seemed to have succeeded to a unique degree in accommodating and balancing the efficiency and consistency objectives. For many, it had literally been a "Golden Age" of monetary relations.

The image of a Golden Age, however, was a myth, based on at least two serious misconceptions of how the gold standard had actually operated in practice. One misconception concerned the process of balance-of-payments adjustment, the other involved the role of national monetary policies. The process of balance-of-payments adjustment was said to have depended primarily on changes of domestic price levels. The model was that of the so-called "price-specie-flow" mechanism: outflows of gold (specie) shrinking the money supply at home and deflating the level of domestic prices, inflows expanding the money supply and inflating domestic prices. National monetary policies, although reinforcing the adjustment process, were said to have been actually concerned exclusively with defense of the convertibility of local currencies into gold. Central banks were said to have responded to gold flows more or less mechanically and passively, with a minimum of discretionary action or judgment. They simply played the "rules of the game," allowing gold flows to have their full impact on domestic money supplies and price levels. Combined, these misconceptions produced a myth of an impersonal, fully automatic, and politically symmetrical international monetary order dependent simply on a combination of domestic price flexibility and natural constraints on the production of gold to ensure optimality of both the adjustment process and reserve supply.

More recent historical research has revealed just how misleading this myth of the Golden Age really was. Regarding the role of monetary policy, for example, Arthur Bloomfield has convincingly demonstrated that central banks before 1914 were rarely quite as mechanical or passive as observers later believed. In fact, central banks exercised a great deal of discretion in reacting to inward or outward flows of gold. The rules of the game could be interpreted in either a negative or a positive sense. In the negative sense, central banks could simply refrain from any actions designed to counteract the influence of gold flows on domestic money supplies; in the positive sense, central banks might have been expected to magnify the domestic monetary influence of gold flows according to their deposit-reserve ratios. Bloomfield has shown that under the classical gold standard, central banks hardly ever adhered to the rules in the positive sense, and sometimes even departed from them in the negative sense. Of course, this was still an era of predominantly laissez-faire attitudes in government economic policy. Yet, even then, central banks were neither entirely unaware of, nor indifferent to, the effects of gold flows on domestic prices, incomes, or public confidence. To counteract such effects when it suited them, monetary authorities developed a variety of techniques for evading the rules of the game— including manipulation of the margins around exchange rates (technically, the "gold points"), direct intervention in the foreign-exchange market, and loans between central banks. Monetary policies in this period were never really either fully passive or simply automatic.

Similarly, regarding the process of balance-of-payments adjustment, Robert Triffin has convincingly demonstrated that domestic price levels rarely played as much of a role before 1914 as observers later believed. In fact, the process of adjustment depended at least as much on changes of domestic income and employment as on price changes. But most of all, the process depended on capital movements. The role of international capital movements in adjusting to payments disequilibria was far more important than any role that the terms of trade may have played. . . .

However, capital movements were not something that all countries could avail themselves of with equal facility. Triffin drew a distinction between countries that were capital exporters and those that were capital importers. Capital-exporting countries usually could avoid the consequences of balance-of-payments deficits—domestic deflation or a possible threat to the gold convertibility of the local currency—simply by slowing down investment abroad. The customary instrument in this regard was the central-bank discount rate (in England, Bank rate); that is, the rate at which the central bank discounted collateral when lending to commercial banks. A rise of the discount rate, cutting back cash reserves of banks, could normally be relied upon to reduce the rate of capital outflow and improve the balance of payments. Borrowing countries, on the other hand, were far less able to control the rate of their capital imports, these being primarily determined by credit conditions in the capital-exporting countries. The Golden Age, therefore, was really limited only to the "core" of advanced nations of Europe and the so-called "regions of recent settlement" (including North America, Australia, South Africa, and Argentina). Elsewhere, the gold standard was far less successful in preserving payments stability or avoiding policy conflict. . . .

Thus, not only was the gold standard neither impersonal nor fully automatic; it was also not politically symmetrical. In fact, the pre-1914 monetary order was arranged in a distinctly hierarchical fashion, with the countries of the periphery at the bottom, the core countries above, and at the peak—Britain. Great Britain dominated international monetary relations in the nineteenth century as no state has since, with the exception of the United States immediately after World War II. Britain was the supreme industrial power of the day, the biggest exporter of manufactured goods, the largest overseas investor. London was by far the most important world financial center, sterling by far the most widely used of the world's currencies for both current- and capital-account transactions. It is sometimes claimed that the gold standard was in reality a sterling-exchange standard. In one sense this appellation is misleading, insofar as most monetary reserves before 1914 (as mentioned above) were still held in gold, not sterling, and insofar as governments continued to be concerned with maintaining the gold value of their currencies, not the sterling value. Yet in another sense the fact cannot be denied: the classical gold standard *was* a sterling standard—a hegemonic regime—in the sense that Britain not only dominated the international monetary order, establishing and maintaining the prevailing rules of the game, but also gave monetary relations whatever degree of inherent stability they possessed.

This stability was ensured through a trio of roles which at that time only Britain had the economic and financial resources to play: (1) maintaining a relatively open market for the exports of countries in balance-of-payments difficulties; (2) providing contracyclical foreign long-term lending; and (3) acting as lender of last resort in times of exchange crisis. These were not roles that the British deliberately sought or even particularly welcomed. As far as the Bank of England was concerned, its monetary policies were dictated solely by the need to protect its narrow reserves and the gold convertibility of the pound. It did not regard itself as responsible for global monetary stabilization or as money manager of the world. Yet this is precisely the responsibility that was thrust upon it in practice—acquired, like the British Empire itself, more or less absentmindedly. The widespread international use of sterling and the close links between the larger financial markets in London and smaller national financial markets elsewhere inevitably endowed Britain with the power to guide the world's monetary policy. Changes of policy by the Bank of England inevitably imposed a certain discipline and coordination on monetary conditions in other countries. . . .

It is important to recall, however, that the stability ensured by British monetary management was confined largely to the core of advanced nations in Europe and the regions of recent settlement—countries that were themselves capital exporters or, when necessary, were capable of availing themselves of the lending facilities of London or other financial centers. The less-developed countries of the periphery were, as emphasized, far less able to control the rate of their foreign capital imports; moreover, they suffered from Britain's related power to avoid the continuing cost of adjustment by manipulating its international terms of trade. . . . As Fred Hirsch has argued, Britain " 'managed' the system partly at the expense of its weakest members."[2] Over time, this was bound to become a source of serious policy conflict in the monetary order.

In fact, it may be argued that behind the deceptive facade of the Golden Age, the classical gold standard actually bore within itself the seeds of its own destruction. Not only did the order require the continued acquiescence of periphery countries in order to preserve a semblance of stability in the core; it also depended on the continued hegemony of Great Britain in the world's economic affairs. But as many economic historians have noted, this dominance was already beginning to fade, even as early as the turn of the century. From the decade of the 1870s onward, British industrialists were faced with a mounting wave of competition in world export markets, first from Germany and the United States, and later from France, Russia, and Japan. From the 1890s onward, London was faced with growing competition from newly emergent financial centers like Paris, Berlin, and later New York; the pound found itself rivalled *inter alia* by the franc, the mark, and eventually the dollar. As a result of these developments, the British gradually lost a good part of their power to manage the international monetary order. Thus, when it was brought down by the outbreak of World War I, the classical gold standard had already become a rather fragile thing. It is perhaps too much to argue, as does one economic historian, that "the tree felled by the crisis was already rotten."[3] But signs of decay there most certainly were.

THE INTERWAR PERIOD

When World War I broke out, all of the belligerent nations—and soon most others as well—took action to protect their gold reserves by suspending currency convertibility and embargoing gold exports. The classical gold standard was dead. Private individuals could no longer redeem paper currency in gold, nor could they sell it abroad. But they could still sell one paper currency for another (exchange control not being invented until the 1930s) at whatever price the exchange market would bear. The fixed exchange-rate mechanism of the gold standard, therefore, was succeeded by its absolute opposite: a pure floating exchange-rate regime. In the ensuing years, as currency values varied considerably under the impact of wartime uncertainties, the international monetary order could not even come near to realizing its potential for joint gain.

Accordingly, once the war was over and peace arrangements taken care of, governments quickly turned their attention to the problem of world monetary reform. Lulled by the myth of the Golden Age, they saw their task as a comparatively simple one: to restore the classical gold standard (or a close approximation thereof). The major conundrum seemed to be an evident shortage of gold, owing to the extreme price inflations that had occurred in almost all countries during and immediately after the war. These had sharply reduced the purchasing power of the world's monetary gold stock, which was still valued at its old prewar parities. One plausible solution might have been an equally sharp multilateral devaluation of currencies in terms of gold, in order to restore the commodity value of gold reserves. But that was ruled out by most countries on the grounds that a return to "normal" (and to the Golden Age) must include a return to prewar rates of exchange. Yet at the same time, governments understandably wanted to avoid a scramble for gold that would have pushed up the metal's commodity value through competitive deflations of domestic prices. Some other solution had to be found.

The "solution" finally agreed upon was to *economize* on the use of gold. An international economic conference in 1922 (the Genoa Conference) recommended worldwide adoption of a gold-exchange standard in order to "centralize and coordinate the demand for gold, and so avoid those wide fluctuations in the purchasing power of gold which might otherwise result from the simultaneous and competitive efforts of a number of countries to secure metallic reserves."[4] Central banks were urged to substitute foreign-exchange balances for gold in their reserves as a "means of economizing the use of gold."[5] Gold holdings were to be systematically concentrated in the major financial centers (e.g., London); outside the centers, countries were to maintain their exchange rates by buying and selling "gold exchange" (i.e., currencies convertible into gold, such as sterling) instead of gold itself. The monetary order was thus to combine a pure fixed exchange-rate mechanism of balance-of-payments adjustment modeled on the classical gold standard, with a new mixed commodity-currency standard to cope with the shortage of gold.

The gold-exchange standard came into formal existence early in 1925, when Britain reestablished the gold convertibility of the pound and eliminated restrictions on gold exports. Within a year nearly forty other nations had joined in the experiment, either de jure or de facto, and most other independent governments joined not much later. But the experiment did not last long. In 1931, following a wave of bank failures on the European continent, the British were forced by a run on their reserves to suspend convertibility once again, and in the chaos that ensued the international monetary order broke up into congeries of competing and hostile currency blocs. The largest of these was the sterling bloc, comprising Britain, its overseas dependencies and dominions (except Canada, which had closer financial ties with the United States), and a variety of independent states with traditionally close trading and banking connections with Britain. This bloc was a shrunken remnant of the world that the British had dominated and in effect managed prior to 1914. Members were identified by two main characteristics: they pegged their currencies to sterling, even after convertibility was suspended; and they continued to hold most of their reserves in the form of sterling balances in London. A second bloc after 1931 was informally grouped around the United States (the dollar area), and a third around France (the "gold bloc"). In addition, there was a large group of miscellaneous countries (including, especially, Germany and the states of Eastern Europe) that abandoned convertibility altogether in favor of starkly autarkic trade and financial policies.

The decade of the 1930s, the decade of the Great Depression, was a period of open economic warfare—a prelude to the military hostilities that were to follow after 1939. Never had the conflictual element in international monetary relations been laid quite so bare. It was truly a free-for-all regime. With public confidence shattered, exchange rates tended to fluctuate widely, and governments consciously engaged in competitive depreciations of their currencies in attempting to cope with their critical payments and unemployment problems. As in the years during and immediately after World War I, the monetary order failed to come even near to realizing its potential for joint gain. In 1936 a semblance of cooperation was restored by the Tripartite Agreement among Britain, France, and the United States for mutual currency stabilization. But this was only the barest minimum that might have been done to restore consistency to international monetary relations. Genuine monetary reconstruction had to wait until after World War II.

Why did the interwar experiment fail? Why did the attempt to return to the Golden Age end so disastrously? Mainly because the Golden Age *was* a myth, a myth based on misconceptions and a fundamental misunderstanding of how much the world economy had really changed. Governments failed to read the signs of decay in the prewar era; more importantly, they failed to realize how anachronistic a restored gold standard would be in the new circumstances of the postwar era. Conditions in the 1920s simply did not lend themselves to the adoption of an impersonal and fully automatic monetary order. In reality, the experiment was doomed from the start.

In the first place, governments were in the process of abandoning their inherited attitudes of laissez-faire in general economic policy. Social and political conditions had changed. A Bolshevik revolution had succeeded in Russia; elsewhere, socialism was almost universally on the rise. Governments could no longer afford to tolerate a certain amount of price or income deflation or inflation simply for the sake of maintaining convertibility of their currencies at a fixed price. Domestic stability now had to take precedence if politicians were to hold onto their jobs. If before World War I central banks rarely adhered to the gold-standard rules of the game in the positive sense, after the war they rarely adhered to them even in the negative sense. Instead, a variety of new instruments were devised to counteract and neutralize the domestic monetary influence of external payments disequilibria, just the opposite of what was needed to make a restored gold standard work. . . .

In the second place, prices and wages were becoming increasingly rigid, at least in a downward direction, under the impact of rising trade unionism and expanding social welfare legislation. Domestic price flexibility was a key requirement for a restored gold standard. Without it (and with exchange rates fixed), a disproportionate share of the adjustment process had to consist of changes of domestic incomes, output, and employment. It was precisely in order to avoid such impacts, of course, that governments were becoming increasingly interventionist in economic affairs. But the consequences of such interventionism inevitably included a complete short-circuiting of the external adjustment mechanism that the same governments were laboring so hard to rebuild.

A third problem was the distorted structure of exchange rates established under the new gold-exchange standard. In insisting upon a return to convertibility at their prewar parities, governments were taking insufficient note of the fact that price relationships between national economies had been dramatically altered since 1914. Inconvertibility and floating exchange rates had broken the links between national price movements, and domestic inflation rates had varied enormously. When convertibility was finally reestablished after 1925, many governments found themselves with currencies that were overvalued and undervalued by quite significant amounts. Yet they were prevented from doing much about it by the straitjacket of fixed exchange rates. The pound, for example, restored to convertibility at its old prewar parity of $4.86, was overvalued by at least 10 percent; but since subsequent changes of the parity were ruled out by the gold-standard rules of the game, it was not surprising that the British balance of payments stayed under almost continuous strain until 1931, and British unemployment rates remained uncomfortably high. The French, on the other hand, who were an exception to the general rule in returning to gold (de facto in 1926, de jure in 1928) at just one-fifth of their prewar parity, undervalued the franc by perhaps as much as 25 percent. The result in this case was an almost immediate drainage of funds from London to Paris, adding to Britain's woes and, in the end, contributing importantly to the final collapse of the ill-fated experiment in 1931.

A fourth problem was the war's legacy of international indebtedness, which imposed a severe strain on monetary relations throughout the 1920s. The United States was the net creditor in a complicated network of obligations arising from wartime interallied loans and postwar German reparations; the biggest debtor, of course, was defeated Germany. As it turned out, most countries simply did not have the capacity to generate the net current-account surpluses necessary to effect their obligated transfers on capital account. In large measure, therefore, they had to rely instead on private capital outflows from the United States (much of which went to Germany) in a vast circular flow of funds. The Germans paid their reparations essentially with funds borrowed from America; Germany's creditors then used the same funds or other American loans to pay off their debts in the United States. How precarious all of this was became clear in 1929, when the stock-market crash and ensuing Great Depression abruptly cut off virtually all U.S. investment overseas. It is no accident that within two years reparations and interallied debt payments were abruptly cut off as well.

Finally, there was the problem of divided responsibility in the monetary order. If what ensured the apparent stability of the classical gold standard before 1914 was a single dominant center capable of acting as money manager of the world, what ultimately brought down its successor in 1931 was the emergence of competitive financial centers effectively rendering Britain's traditional hegemonic role impossible. Rivals to London had begun emerging even before World War I. During the 1920s this process continued, as Paris reasserted itself as a financial center and New York suddenly appeared on the scene. Still losing ground industrially and now saddled with an overvalued currency as well, Britain was no longer capable of playing the trio of roles that had provided the prewar monetary order with its semblance of stability. Unfortunately, neither were the French capable of shouldering such heavy responsibilities—they lacked the requisite economic and financial resources—and the Americans, who did have the resources, were as yet unwilling to do so. As a result, the system drifted without a leader. As Charles Kindleberger has written: "The United States was uncertain of its international role. . . . The one country capable of leadership was bemused by domestic concerns and stood aside. . . . The instability [came] from the growing weakness of one driver, and the lack of sufficient interest in the other."[6]

Could the two drivers, together with France, possibly have managed the monetary order cooperatively? Perhaps so. But this would have called for greater mutual trust and forebearance than any of the three seemed capable of at the time. Britain was still trying to lead, albeit from weakness, and the United States had not yet learned how to lead from strength. The French, meanwhile, resented both Anglo-Saxon powers, and all three were competing actively for short-term money flows—and even for gold itself. (After 1928, for example, the Bank of France added to the pressures on the British by suddenly opting to convert its sizable accumulation of sterling balances into gold.) The result of this lack of coordination was a continual problem of large-scale transfers of private funds ("hot money" movements) from one financial center to another— the confidence problem. "This shifting of balances from one market to another [was] inevitable in a gold standard system without a single dominating center."[7] In the end, it was such a shifting of balances out of London in 1931 that finally brought the system down. In fact, it was not until 1936, with the Tripartite Agreement, that the three powers eventually got around to acknowledging formally their mutual responsibility for the monetary order. By that time, however, it was too late.

THE BRETTON WOODS SYSTEM

World War II brought exchange control everywhere and ended much of what remained of the element of cooperation in international monetary relations. But almost immediately, planning began for postwar monetary reconstruction. Discussions centered in the Treasuries of Britain and the United States, and culminated in the creation of the International Monetary Fund at a conference of 44 allied nations at Bretton Woods, New Hampshire, in 1944. The charter of the IMF was intended to be the written constitution of the postwar monetary order—what later became known as the Bretton Woods system. The Bretton Woods system lasted only twenty-seven years, however, and died in August 1971.

The Origins of the Bretton Woods System

The Bretton Woods system originated as a compromise between rival plans for monetary reconstruction developed on the one hand by Harry Dexter White of the U.S. Treasury, and on the other hand by Lord Keynes of Britain. In 1944 the differences between these two plans seemed enormous. Today their differences appear rather less impressive than their similarities. Indeed, what is really striking, a third of a century later, is how much common ground there really was among all the participating governments at Bretton Woods. All agreed that the interwar experience had taught them several valuable lessons; all were determined to avoid repeating what they perceived to be the errors of the past. Their consensus of judgment was reflected directly in the contents of the IMF's Articles of Agreement.

Four points in particular stand out. First it was generally agreed that the interwar period had demonstrated (to use the words of one authoritative source) "the proved disadvantages of freely fluctuating exchanges."[8] The floating rates of the 1930s were seen as having discouraged trade and investment and encouraged destabilizing speculation and competitive depreciations. Nations were loath to return to the free-for-all regime of the Depression years. But at the same time, they were also unwilling to return to the exchange-rate rigidity of the 1920s. The experience of those years was seen as having demonstrated the equal undesirability of the opposite extreme of permanently fixed rates. These, it was agreed, could "be equally harmful. The general interest may call for an occasional revision of currency values."[9] Accordingly, the negotiators at Bretton Woods were determined to find some compromise between the two extremes—one that would gain the advantages of both fixed and flexible rates without suffering from their disadvantages.

What they came up with has since been labeled the "pegged-rate" or "adjustable-peg" regime. Members were obligated to declare a par value (a "peg") for their currencies and to intervene in the exchange market to limit fluctuations within maximum margins (a "band") one percent above or below parity; but they also retained the right, whenever necessary and in accordance with agreed procedures, to alter their par values to correct a "fundamental disequilibrium" in their balance of payments. What constituted a fundamental disequilibrium? Although key to the whole operation of the Bretton Woods adjustment mechanism, this notion was never spelled out in any detail anywhere in the Articles of Agreement. The omission was to come back to haunt members of the Fund in later years.

Second, all governments generally agreed that if exchange rates were not to be freely fluctuating, countries would need to be assured of an adequate supply of official monetary reserves. An adjustable-peg regime "presupposes a large volume of such reserves for each single country as well as in the aggregate."[10] The experience of the interwar period—the gold shortage of the 1920s as well as the breakdown of fixed rates in the 1930s—was thought to have demonstrated the dangers of inadequate reserve volume. Accordingly, a second order of business at Bretton Woods was to ensure a supplementary source of reserve supply. Negotiators agreed that what they needed was some "procedure under which international liquidity would be supplied in the form of pre-arranged borrowing facilities."[11]

What they came up with, in this instance, was the IMF system of subscriptions and quotas. In essence, the Fund was to be nothing more than a pool of national currencies and gold subscribed by each country.

Members were assigned quotas, according to a rather complicated formula intended roughly to reflect each country's relative importance in the world economy, and were obligated to pay into the Fund a subscription of equal amount. The subscription was to be paid 25 percent in gold or currency convertible into gold (effectively the U.S. dollar, which was the only currency still convertible directly into gold) and 75 percent in the member's own currency. Each member was then entitled, when short of reserves, to "purchase" (i.e., borrow) amounts of foreign exchange from the Fund in return for equivalent amounts of its own currency. Maximum purchases were set equal to the member's 25-percent gold subscription (its "gold tranche"), plus four additional amounts each equal to 25 percent of its quota (its "credit tranches"), up to the point where the Fund's holdings of the member's currency equaled 200 percent of its quota. (If any of the Fund's holdings of the member's initial 75 percent subscription of its own currency was borrowed by other countries, the member's borrowing capacity was correspondingly increased: this was its "super-gold tranche.") The member's "net reserve position" in the Fund equaled its gold tranche (plus super-gold tranche, if any) less any borrowings by the country from the Fund. Net reserve positions were to provide the supplementary liquidity that was generally considered necessary to make the adjustable-peg regime work.

A third point on which all governments at Bretton Woods agreed was that it was necessary to avoid a recurrence of the kind of economic warfare that had characterized the decade of the 1930s. Some "code of action" was needed to "guide international exchange adjustments," some framework of rules to ensure that countries would remove their existing exchange controls and return to a system of multilateral payments based on currency convertibility. At Bretton Woods such a code was written into the obligations of Fund members. Governments were generally forbidden to engage in discriminatory currency practices or exchange-control regulation, although two exceptions were permitted. First, convertibility obligations were extended to current international transactions only. Governments were to refrain from regulating purchases and sales of foreign exchange for the purpose of current-account transactions. But they were not obligated to refrain from regulation of capital-account transactions; indeed, they were formally encouraged to make use of capital controls to maintain equilibrium in the face of "those disequilibrating short-term capital movements which caused so much trouble during the 'thirties.' "[12] And second, convertibility obligations could be deferred if a member so chose during a postwar "transitional period." Members deferring their convertibility obligations were known as Article XIV countries; members accepting them had so-called Article

VIII status. One of the functions assigned to the IMF was to oversee this code of action on currency convertibility.

Finally, governments agreed that there was a need for an institutional forum for international consultation and cooperation on monetary matters. The world could not be allowed to return to the divided responsibility of the interwar years. "International monetary relations especially in the years before the Tripartite Agreement of 1936 suffered greatly from the absence of an established machinery or procedure of consultation."[13] In the postwar era, the Fund itself would provide such a forum. Of all the achievements of Bretton Woods, this was potentially the most significant. Never before had international monetary cooperation been attempted on a permanent institutional basis. Judged against the anarchy of the 1930s, this could be considered a breakthrough of historic proportions. For the first time ever, governments were formally committing themselves to the principle of collective responsibility for management of the international monetary order.

These four points together defined the Bretton Woods system—a monetary order combining an essentially unchanged gold-exchange standard, supplemented only by a centralized pool of gold and national currencies, with an entirely new pegged-rate mechanism of balance-of-payments adjustment. The Fund itself was expected to perform three important functions: regulatory (administering the rules affecting exchange rates and currency convertibility), financial (supplying supplementary liquidity), and consultative (providing a forum for the cooperative management of monetary relations). The negotiators at Bretton Woods did not think it necessary to alter in any fundamental way the mixed commodity-currency standard that had been inherited from the interwar years. Indeed, it does not even seem to have occurred to them that there might be any inherent defect in the structure of a gold-exchange standard. The problem in the 1920s, they felt, had not been the gold-exchange standard itself but the division of responsibility—in short, a problem of management. "The nucleus of the gold exchange system consisted of more than one country; and this was a special source of weakness. With adequate cooperation between the centre countries, it need not have been serious."[14] In the Bretton Woods system the IMF was to provide the necessary machinery for multilateral cooperation. The management problem would thus be solved and consistency in monetary relations ensured.

Implicit in this attitude was a remarkable optimism regarding prospects for monetary stability in the postwar era. Underlying the choice of the pegged-rate adjustment mechanism, for instance, seemed to be a clear expectation that beyond the postwar transitional period (itself expected to be brief) payments imbalances would not be excessive. The adjustment mechanism was manifestly biased in principle against frequent changes of exchange rates, presumably because of the experience of the 1930s; governments had to demonstrate the existence of a fundamental disequilibrium before they could alter their par values. At the same time, no government was prepared to sacrifice domestic stability for the sake of external equilibrium. Yet nations were left with few other instruments, other than capital controls, to deal with disturbances to the balance of payments. This suggests that the negotiators at Bretton Woods felt that the major threat to stability was likely to come from private speculation rather than from more fundamental price or income developments. It also suggests that they were confident that most disequilibria would be of a stochastic rather than nonstochastic nature. Underlying the IMF's financial function seemed to be a clear expectation that its centralized pool of liquidity would be sufficient to cope with most financing problems as they emerged.

As matters turned out, this optimism proved entirely unjustified. Monetary relations immediately after the war were anything but stable, and the transitional period anything but brief. Only the United States, Canada, and a small handful of other countries (mainly in Central America) were able to pledge themselves to the obligations of Article VIII right away. Most others were simply too devastated by war—their export capacities damaged, their import needs enormous, their monetary reserves exhausted—to commit their currencies to convertibility. Payments problems, especially in Europe and Japan, could hardly be described as stochastic; the Fund's initial pool of liquidity was anything but sufficient. After a short burst of activity during its first two years, mainly to the benefit of European nations, the Fund's lending operations shrank to an extremely small scale. (In 1950 the Fund made no new loans at all, and large-scale operations did not begin again until 1956.) The burden instead was shifted to one country, the only country after the war immediately capable of shouldering the responsibility for global monetary stabilization—namely, the United States.

Fortunately, this time, for reasons of its own (see below), the United States was willing. As dominant then as Britain had been in the nineteenth century, America rapidly assumed the same trio of managerial roles—in effect, taking over as money manager of the world. A relatively open market was maintained for the exports of foreign goods. A relatively generous flow of long-term loans and grants was initiated first through the Marshall Plan and other related aid programs, then through the reopened New York capital market. And a relatively liberal lending policy was eventually established for the provision of short-term funds in times of exchange crisis as well. Since monetary reserves were everywhere in such short supply—and since the IMF's pool of liquidity was manifestly inadequate—the United States itself became the residual source of global liquidity growth through its balance-of-payments deficits. At the war's end, America owned almost three-quarters of the world's existing monetary gold; and prospects for new gold production were obviously limited by the physical constraints of nature. The rest of the world, therefore, was more than willing to economize on this scarce gold supply by accumulating dollars instead. The dollar thus was enshrined not only as principal "vehicle currency" for international trade and investment but also as principal reserve asset for central banks. In the early postwar years, America's deficits became the universal solvent to keep the machinery of Bretton Woods running. It may be misleading, as I have indicated, to call the classical gold standard a sterling-exchange (though not, I have suggested, to call it a hegemony); it is not at all misleading to call the postwar monetary standard a dollar-exchange standard. Indeed, the Bretton Woods system became synonymous with a hegemonic monetary order centered on the dollar. Though multilateral in formal design, in actual practice (like the classical gold standard before it) the Bretton Woods system was highly centralized.

In effect, what the United States did was to abjure any payments target of its own in favor of taking responsibility for operation of the monetary order itself. Other countries set independent balance-of-payments targets; America's external financial policy was essentially one of "benign neglect." Consistency in monetary relations was ensured not by multilateral cooperation but by America's willingness to play a passive role in the adjustment process, as the nth country, in effect: "other countries from time to time changed the par value of their currencies against the dollar and gold, but the value of the dollar itself remained fixed in relation to gold and therefore to other currencies collectively."[15] The growth of the world's liquidity supply was largely determined, consequently, by the magnitude of America's deficits—modified only to the extent that these deficits were settled in gold, rather than dollars, reflecting the asset preferences of surplus countries.

Like the British in the nineteenth century, the Americans did not deliberately seek the responsibility of global monetary management (In the interwar period they had evaded it.) On the other hand, unlike the British, once the Americans found themselves with it, they soon came to welcome it, for reasons that were a mixture of altruism and self-interest. Being money manager for the world fit in neatly with America's newfound leadership role in the Western Alliance. The cold war had begun, and isolationism was a thing of the past. The United States perceived a need to promote the economic recovery of potential allies in Europe and Japan, as well as to maintain a sizable and potent military establishment overseas. All of this cost money: the privilege of liability-financing deficits meant that America was effectively freed from balance-of-payments constraints to spend as freely as it thought necessary to promote objectives believed to be in the national interest. The United States could issue the world's principal vehicle and reserve currency in amounts presumed to be consistent with its own policy priorities—and not necessarily with those of foreign dollar holders. Foreign dollar holders conceded this policy autonomy to America because it also directly contributed to their own economic rehabilitation. America accepted the necessity, for example, of preferential trade and payments arrangements in Europe, despite their inherent and obvious discrimination against U.S. export sales; likewise, America accepted the necessity of granting Japanese exporters access to the U.S. internal market at a time when other markets still remained largely closed to goods labeled "Made in Japan." In effect, as I have argued elsewhere, an implicit bargain was struck.[16] America's allies acquiesced in a hegemonic system that accorded the United States special privileges to act abroad unilaterally to promote U.S. interests. The United States, in turn, condoned its allies' use of the system to promote their own economic prosperity, even if this happened to come largely at the expense of the United States. . . .

The History of the Bretton Woods System

The subsequent history of the Bretton Woods system may be read as the history of this implicit bargain. The breakdown of the system in 1971 may be read as the bargain's final collapse. . . .

The chronology of Bretton Woods can be divided into two periods: the period of the "dollar shortage," lasting roughly until 1958; and the period of the "dollar glut," covering the remaining dozen years or so. The period of the dollar shortage was the heyday of America's dominance of international monetary relations. The term "dollar shortage," universally used at the time, was simply a shorthand expression of the fact that only the United States was capable of shouldering the responsibility for global monetary stabilization; only the United States could help other governments avoid a mutually destructive scramble for gold by promoting an outflow of dollar balances instead. As David Calleo has written: "Circumstances dictated dollar hegemony."[17] Dollar deficits began in 1950, following a round of devaluations of European currencies, at American insistence, in 1949. (Dollar surpluses prior to 1950 were financed largely by grants and long-term loans from the United States.) In ensuing years, deficits in the U.S. balance of payments (as conventionally measured) averaged approximately $1.5 billion a year. But for these deficits, other governments would have been compelled by their reserve shortages to resort to competitive exchange depreciations or domestic deflations; they would certainly not have been able to make as much progress as they did toward dismantling wartime exchange controls and trade restrictions. Persistent dollar deficits thus actually served to avoid monetary instability or policy conflict before 1958. Not since the Golden Age before World War I, in fact, had the monetary order been so successful in reconciling the tension between economic and political values. The period to 1958 has rightly been called one of "beneficial disequilibrium."

After 1958, however, America's persistent deficits began to take on a different coloration. Following a brief surplus in 1957, owing to an increase of oil exports to Europe caused by the closing of the Suez Canal, the U.S. balance of payments plunged to a $3.5 billion deficit in 1958 and to even larger deficits in 1959 and 1960. This was the turning point. Instead of talking about a dollar shortage, observers began to talk about a dollar glut; consistency in monetary relations no longer appeared quite so assured. In 1958, Europe's currencies returned to convertibility. In subsequent years the former eagerness of European governments to obtain dollar reserves was transformed into what seemed an equally fervent desire to avoid excess dollar accumulations. Before 1958, less than 10 percent of America's deficits had been financed by calls on the gold stock in Fort Knox (the rest being liability-financed). During the next decade, almost two-thirds of America's cumulative deficit was transferred in the form of gold. Almost all of this went to governments on the continent of Europe.

It was clear that the structure of Bretton Woods was coming under increasing strain. Defects were becoming evident both in the mechanism of liquidity creation and in the mechanism of payments adjustment.

Credit for first drawing attention to the defects in the liquidity-creation mechanism of Bretton Woods is usually given to Robert Triffin for his influential book *Gold and the Dollar Crisis*.[18] The negotiators at Bretton Woods, Triffin argued, had been too complacent about the gold-exchange standard. The problem was not simply one of management. Rather, it was one of structure—an inherent defect in the very concept of a gold-exchange standard. A gold-exchange standard is built on the illusion of convertibility of its fiduciary element into gold at a fixed price. The Bretton Woods system, though, was relying on deficits in the U.S. balance of payments to avert a world liquidity shortage. Already, America's "overhang" of overseas liabilities to private and official foreigners was growing larger than its gold stock at home. The progressive deterioration of the U.S. net reserve position, therefore, was bound in time to undermine global confidence in the dollar's continued convertibility. In effect, governments were caught on the horns of a dilemma. To forestall speculation against the dollar, U.S. deficits would have to cease. But this would confront governments with the liquidity problem. To forestall the liquidity problem, U.S. deficits would have to continue. But this would confront governments with the confidence problem. Governments could not have their cake and eat it too.

Not that governments were unwilling to try. On the contrary, during the early 1960s a variety of ad hoc measures were initiated in an effort to contain speculative pressures that were mounting against the dollar. These included a network of reciprocal short-term credit facilities ("swaps") between the Federal Reserve and other central banks, as well as enlargement of the potential lending authority of the IMF (through the "General Arrangements to Borrow"). Both were intended to facilitate recycling of funds in the event of speculative currency shifts by private investors. They also included creation of a "gold pool" of the major financial powers to stabilize the price of gold in private markets. Later, in 1968, the gold pool was replaced by a two-tier gold-price system—one price for the private market, determined by supply and demand, and another price for central banks, to remain at the previous fixed level of $35 per ounce. These several measures were moderately successful in helping governments cope with the threat of private speculation against the dollar—the private confidence problem. The official confidence problem, however, remained as acute a danger as ever.

Meanwhile, in the mid-1960s, negotiations were begun whose aim was to establish a substitute source of liquidity growth, in order to reduce reliance on dollar deficits in the future. These negotiations were conducted among ten industrial countries—the so-called Group of Ten (G-10)—compromising Belgium, Canada, France, Germany, Italy, Japan, the Netherlands, Sweden, the United Kingdom, and the United States. What came out of the G-10 negotiations was the agreement to create Special Drawing Rights, an entirely new type of world fiduciary reserve asset. The SDR agreement was confirmed by the full membership of the International Monetary Fund in 1968 and activated in 1969. Between 1970 and 1972 some 9.5 billion SDR units were allocated to members of the Fund. Governments were confident that with SDRs "in place," any future threat of world liquidity shortage could be successfully averted. On the other hand, they were totally unprepared for the opposite threat—a reserve surfeit—which in fact is what eventually emerged.

Any number of authors could be credited for drawing attention to the defects in the payments adjustment mechanism of Bretton Woods. Virtually from the time the Charter was first negotiated, observers began pointing to the ambiguity surrounding the notion of fundamental disequilibrium. How could governments be expected to alter their par values if they could not tell when a fundamental disequilibrium existed? And if they were inhibited from altering their par values, then how would international payments equilibrium be maintained? I have already noted that the adjustment mechanism was biased in principle against frequent changes of exchange rates. In practice during the postwar period it became biased even against infrequent changes of exchange rates. At least among the advanced industrial nations, the world seemed to have returned to the rigidities of the 1920s. Governments went to enormous lengths to avoid the "defeat" of an altered par value. (A particularly sad example of this was the long struggle of the British government to avoid devaluation of the pound—a struggle that ended when sterling was devalued by 14.3 percent in 1967.) The resulting stickiness of the adjustment process not only aggravated fears of a potential world liquidity shortage. It also created irresistible incentives for speculative currency shifts by private individuals and institutions, greatly adding to the confidence problem as well.

Speculative currency shifts were facilitated at the time by the growing integration of money and capital markets in all of the advanced industrial nations. Large-scale capital movements had not originally been envisaged by the negotiators at Bretton Woods; as I have indicated, governments actually were encouraged to *control* capital movements for the purpose of maintaining payments equilibrium. In reality, however, capital movements turned out to be promoted rather than retarded by the design of the Bretton Woods system—in particular, by the integrative power of the par-value regime, and by the return to currency convertibility in Europe in 1958. (Japan did not pledge itself to Article VIII of the IMF Charter until 1964.) After 1958, capital mobility accelerated *pari passu* with the growth of the Eurocurrency market—that well-known market for currencies deposited in banks located outside of the country of issue. From its origin in the mid-1950s, the Eurocurrency market rapidly expanded into a broad, full-fledged international financial market; subject to just a minimum of governmental guidance, supervision, and regulation, it became during the 1960s the principal vehicle for private speculation against official exchange parities. Increasingly, governments found it difficult to "defend" unadjusted par values in the face of the high degree of international capital mobility that had been generated.

The most serious adjustment problem during this period was, of course, the dollar glut—more accurately, the persistent payments imbalance between the United States and the surplus countries of Europe and Japan. On each side, complaints were heard about the policies of the other. America felt that its erstwhile European and Japanese allies could do more to eliminate the international payments disequilibrium by inflating or revaluing their currencies; the Europeans and Japanese argued that it was the responsibility of the United States to take the first steps to reduce its persistent deficit. Each felt discriminated against by the other. The surplus countries felt that America's privilege of liability-financing deficits, growing out of the dollar's reserve-currency role, created an asymmetry in the monetary order favorable to the United

States. None of them, after all, had such a degree of policy autonomy. America, on the other hand, felt that the use of the dollar by other governments as their principal intervention medium to support par values—the intervention-currency role of the dollar—created an asymmetry in the monetary order more favorable to Europe and Japan. Many sources argued that the dollar was over valued. Yet how could its value in terms of foreign currencies be changed unilaterally unless all other countries agreed to intervene appropriately in the exchange market? The United States felt it had no effective control over its own exchange rate (no exchange-rate autonomy) and therefore did not feel it could easily devalue to rid itself of its deficit.

In fact, the debate over asymmetries masked a deeper political conflict. The postwar bargain was coming unstuck. In the United States, concern was growing about the competitive threat from the European Common Market and Japan to American commercial interests. The period of postwar recovery was over: Europe and Japan had become reinvigorated giants, not only willing but able to compete aggressively with America in markets at home and abroad. The cost of subordinating U.S. economic interests to the presumed political advantage of now strengthened allies was becoming ever more intolerable. Conversely, concern was growing in Europe and Japan about America's use of its privilege of liability-financing to pursue policies abroad which many considered abhorrent (one example was the U.S. involvement in Vietnam), the "exorbitant privilege," as Charles de Gaulle called it. The Europeans and Japanese had just one major weapon they could use to restrict America's policy autonomy—their right to demand conversion of accumulated dollar balances into gold. Robert Mundell has written that "the sole function of gold convertibility in the Bretton Woods arrangement was to discipline the U.S."[19] But by the mid-1960s this was a discipline that most major financial powers were growing somewhat reluctant to use. America's overhang of liabilities was by now far larger than its gold stock. A concerted conversion campaign could have threatened to topple the whole of the Bretton Woods edifice. Governments—with one major exception—did not consider it in their interest to exacerbate the official confidence problem and provoke a systemic crisis. The one major exception was France, which in 1965, in a move strikingly reminiscent of its behavior toward sterling after 1928, began a rapid conversion of its outstanding dollar balances into gold, explicitly for the purpose of exerting pressure on the United States. France alone, however, was unable to change America's policies significantly.

At bottom, the Bretton Woods system rested on one simple assumption—that economic policy in the United States would be stabilizing. Like Britain in the nineteenth century, America had the power to guide the world's monetary policy. The absence of an effective external discipline on U.S. policy autonomy could not threaten the system so long as this assumption held. And indeed, before 1965, the assumption did seem quite justified. America clearly had the best long-term record of price stability of any industrial country; even for some time after 1958 the United States could not justly be accused of "exporting" inflation, however much some governments were complaining about a dollar glut. After 1965, however, the situation reversed itself, as a direct consequence of the escalation of hostilities in Vietnam. America's economy began to overheat, and inflation began to gain momentum. The Bretton Woods system was tailor-made to promote the transmission of this inflation abroad. With exchange rates pegged, tradable-goods price increases in the largest of all trading nations were immediately radiated outward to the rest of the world economy. And with governments committed to defending their pegged rates by buying the surfeit of dollars in the exchange market, a huge reserve base was created for monetary expansion in these other countries as well. Now the United States could justifiably be accused of exporting inflation overseas.

The gathering world inflation after 1965 exposed all of the latent defects of Bretton Woods. American policy was no longer stabilizing, yet other governments were reluctant to use the one power of discipline they had. (Indeed, after the creation of the two-tier gold-price system in 1968, the U.S. government made it quite plain that if a serious depletion of its gold stock were threatened, it would be prepared to close the window and refuse further sales.) The adjustment mechanism was incapable of coping with the widening deficit in the U.S. balance of payments (which soared to $9.8 billion in 1970 and an incredible $29.8 billion in 1971), and the confidence problem was worsening as private speculators were encouraged to bet on devaluation of the dollar or revaluations of the currencies of Europe and Japan. Ultimately, it was the United States that brought the drama to its denouement. Concerned about the rapidly deteriorating U.S. trade balance, as well as about rising protectionist sentiment in the Congress, President Richard Nixon was determined to force the Europeans and Japanese to accept an adjustment of international exchange-rate relationships that would correct the overvaluation of the dollar. Feeling that he lacked effective control over the dollar exchange rate under the prevailing rules of the game, the President decided that the rules themselves would have to be changed. Thus, on August 15, 1971, the convertibility of the dollar into gold was suspended, in effect freeing the dollar to find its own level in the exchange market. With that decision, the Bretton Woods system passed into history.

NOTES

1. Carlo M. Cipolla, *Money, Prices, and Civilization in the Mediterranean World: Fifth to Seventeenth Century* (Princeton: Princeton University Press, 1956), chap. 2.

2. Fred Hirsch, *Money International* (London: Penguin, 1967), p. 28.

3. Marcello de Cecco, *Money and Empire: The International Gold Standard, 1890-1914* (Oxford: Basil Blackwell, 1974), p. 128.

4. Currency Resolution of the Genoa Conference, as quoted in League of Nations, *International Currency Experience* (1944), p. 28.

5. Ibid. As another economy measure, central banks were also urged to withdraw gold coins from circulation.

6. Charles P. Kindleberger, *The World in Depression* (Berkeley: UC Press, 1973), pp. 298–301.

7. W. A. Brown, *The International Gold Standard Reinterpreted* (New York: NBER, 1944), 2:769.

8. League of Nations, *International Currency Experience*, p. 211.

9. Ibid.

10. Ibid., p. 214.

11. Ibid., p. 218.

12. Ibid., p. 220.

13. Ibid., pp. 226–227.

14. Ibid., p. 46.

15. Marina v. N. Whitman, "The Current and Future Role of the Dollar: How Much Symmetry?" *Brookings Papers on Economic Activity*, no. 3 (1974): 542.

16. Benjamin J. Cohen, "The Revolution in Atlantic Economic Relations: A Bargain Comes Unstuck," in Wolfram Hanrieder, ed. *The United States and Western Europe: Political, Economic and Strategic Perspectives* (Cambridge, Mass.: Winthrop, 1974), pp. 113–120.

17. David P. Calleo, "American Foreign Policy and American European Studies: An Imperial Bias?", in Hanrieder, *United States and Western Europe*, p. 62.

18. Robert Triffin, *Gold and the Dollar Crisis* (New Haven: Yale University Press, 1960). The book first appeared in the form of two long journal articles in 1959.

19. Robert A. Mundell, "Optimum Currency Areas," *Economic Notes* 3 (September–December 1975): 36.

Bring Elizabeth $8.—
for dinner .

17. The Internationalization of Capital: Banks, Eurocurrency and the Instability of the World Monetary System

JIM HAWLEY

Jim Hawley relates the activities of private banks to changes in the international monetary system and argues that the internationalization of capital has fundamentally transformed contemporary international monetary relations. The rise of both the multinational corporation and, more importantly, the Euromarket has dramatically increased international holdings of the dollar and international liquidity. Yet, while capital has been "denationalized," the state steering mechanism has not. In the absence of an international "lender of last resort," a highly unstable international financial system has emerged. Hawley thus identifies an important contradiction underlying the present international capitalist system, a contradiction that threatens a new period of economic crisis.

. . . The post World War II period has seen the transformation of the international economy from one characterized by integration primarily through the market to a world system linked together by global corporations and international banks. Along with this process of internationalization of direct investment capital has come a new complex, rapidly growing system of international finance. These developments have created massive new problems for policy formulation and implementation among and within capitalist nations, for capital itself and for the traditional organizations of the working class, especially trade unions and labor, socialist and communist parties. The political implications of this increasing internationalization of capital are significant. One important result is that capital's "interests" become more diffuse and contradictory. The ability to adjust the organization and operations of national economies (including the state steering mechanisms of economic planning and/or management, social policy and so on) becomes more problematic. In short, a tendency towards a "denationalization" of capital takes place without the concomitant ability to "denationalize"— that is, internationalize—state policy and operations. Denationalization means the increased ability of capital to maintain cross-national investments (especially direct investment and international branch banking) and to play one part against another when it is economically and/or politically advantageous. Thus, the state steering mechanisms become increasingly less effective.

This essay will examine [three] major related aspects of the most recent financial and monetary developments: the qualitative rise of a world commercial banking system since the middle 1960s; the related growth of the massive Eurocurrency system; and finally, although briefly, the significance of the recent growth of privately held debt to Third-World countries. It will also look at these developments in terms of their impact on the overall instability of the capitalist world system and their relation to the generation and transmission of inflation.

The past decade and a half has witnessed the internationalization of the U.S. commercial banking system. A similar tendency, although not nearly as developed, exists among all the advanced capitalist banking systems. The primary mechanism for this development has been the massive growth of the Eurocurrency system,* the first truly international money and capital market, unregulated by any national government or transnational governmental agency. The result has been the emergence with a vengeance of "laissez-faire" banking on the international level.

Recent developments in world monetary events tend to support the argument that conflict and rivalry between the U.S. and Western European nations, and the U.S. and Japan, are on the rise. This flows from the breakdown of U.S. hegemony in the late 1960s and early 1970s, on the one hand; and on the other hand, from the relative rise of competing capitalist nations. Yet the decline of U.S. hegemony has not implied the balanced nor parallel rise of another or other imperial powers. The U.S. remains the most powerful capitalist nation economically, politically and militarily. But the relative strength of the U.S.

---

* In brief, the Eurocurrency system is composed of banks of many nationalities which hold currencies (most importantly dollars, marks, pounds and Swiss francs) outside of their countries of origin. Short and long term debt instruments are issued by the banks on the basis of these deposits. There has come into existence both long- and short-term money and capital markets, as well as a large interbank market which operates on thin interest rate differentials.

vis-à-vis Western Europe (as a whole, and its various parts) and Japan has severe limits. U.S. strength is a contradictory strength, no longer hegemonic, yet more than first among equals.

The process of internationalizing capital has brought with it a concomitant "denationalization" of the interests (economic, political, cultural, etc.) of certain of the most developed sectors of capital. Hence, if ever the nation state was the direct or indirect "instrument" of capital's rule (doubtful in itself), the internationalization process has qualitatively weakened the links between nation states and global capital. The weakening has two sides. From capital's point of view, it may be difficult to know where its "true" interests lie when, say, 30–60% of assets, sales and/or profits originate from abroad. From a state manager's position—even one who is most in tune with the accumulation imperative of the state—it is virtually impossible to formulate policy which both fosters international interests and domestic ones in a stagflationary world economy increasingly characterized by protectionism, rivalry and competition among both nation-states and "their" capitals. . . .

A "GOLDEN INTERNATIONAL"

The overseas expansion of U.S. commercial banks has created a truly international chain of branch banking. This new financial network has been and remains a major part of the more general process of the internationalization of capital. There are two important elements in the internationalization of U.S. commercial banking. The first is the expansion of the commercial bank network itself, and its implications for banking operations, especially in terms of the decreasing effectiveness of state central-bank regulation. The second element lies in the related development of the Eurocurrency market—the first "denationalized" and therefore authentically international banking system. This section will discuss the international banking network. The following section will analyze the Eurocurrency system.

The growth sector of the largest international banks after 1960 was in their overseas branches and assets. . . . Thus, while total domestic assets grew about 3½ times between 1960–1974, overseas assets grew about 42 times.

The composition of funds controlled by U.S. banks abroad is significant. In the 1960s, U.S. branches in London and the Bahamas—the main Eurocurrency centers—had between 59% and 66% of their liabilities in foreign commercial banks. This was about 52% for all overseas branches, and about two-fifths outside of the U.S. and Bahamas. By the end of September, 1974, there had been a general decline in the interbank market. That is, U.S. branch bank liabilities were concentrated less in liabilities for foreign banks. Given the world recession and inflation, there was a general decline of interest rates on the Eurocurrency markets, and a relative lack of outlets for funds. The profitability of branches declined markedly, thereby forcing the closing of many of the smaller banks' offices, especially in London where operating costs were extremely high. Brimmer and Dahl comment:

> . . . once foreign branches had been established, they were open to a continued sizable inflow of funds—although the demand for funds by their own internal systems had declined appreciably. To employ such resources, the foreign branches began to engage progressively in what was essentially a brokerage rather than a banking business. The competition to place funds in the interbank market led to a significant narrowing in lender margins, and this had a significant adverse impact on the profitability of foreign branches.[1]

The significance of these developments is that participation in the Eurocurrency market, a large proportion of which is an interbank market, works on extremely thin profit margins and interest rate differentials. In a period of high overall demand for funds and related rising interest rates, the business is both profitable and, while built as a house of cards, stable. However, given a sharp contradiction in the world economy and/or bank failures, as in 1974–1975, interest rates decline and outside (nonbank) demand for funds decrease. There was a general shakedown, as well as possible crisis of confidence. While ahead of the story in that the Eurocurrency market itself is yet to be discussed, the point is that the internationalization of U.S. commercial banking has led to the growth in the Eurocurrency market, while at the same time the Eurocurrency market encouraged bank internationalization.

The dependence on overseas operations for a disproportionate share of earnings has raised the issue of the soundness of the largest U.S. banks. One indicator of soundness is a bank's capital-to-asset ratio. The largest 20 U.S. multinational banks had a ratio of only 4.1% in 1974. This contrasts with a 6.4% for all U.S. banks. The decline from the 1960 average of 8.8% (8.7% for banks with over $5 billion assets) was greatest for banks with over $5 billion in assets. The significance of using capital rather than total assets as a measure of a bank's loans outstanding is that capital is related to a bank's function as a margin of safety. Since the liabilities of overseas branches are uninsured (averaging 33% foreign branch liabilities to domestic—insured and uninsured—for the 20 largest U.S. multinational banks) the margin of safety for these banks is, in the words of a Congressional study, "quite slim."[2] This puts the Federal Reserve Board as the lender of last resort in the position of bailing out a U.S. bank for possible overseas—uninsured—failures, as happened with the Franklin National failure in 1974. The growth of U.S. international banking is not merely a "policy" decision, capable of being changed by legislative or executive decision, but is rather a rational business response to the globalization of productive capital, to the re-emergence of intercapitalist competition after the rebuilding efforts out of World War II, and finally to the various forms of national restrictions on capital movement. The culmination of this process has been the tremendous growth of the Eurocurrency system.

EUROCURRENCY: THE FIRST INTERNATIONAL "MONEY"

This section traces the development of the Eurocurrency market from the so-called Eurodollar market into its full development as the Eurocurrency system. It defines and explains the sources and uses of Eurocurrency funds (Eurofunds), and argues that the nature of the Eurocurrency system is similar to a fractional reserve banking system in certain important respects.

If the developments of the last twenty years in international banking have created the first truly "golden international," then the key element in this development has been the growth of the Eurocurrency system. The Eurocurrency markets had their origins in the Eurodollar market in the late 1950s and early 1960s. The original Eurodollar market (so-called because the great majority of the assets and loans were denominated in dollars) was as a short-term market which borrowed and lent dollars and other currencies (e.g., yen, marks, francs, etc.) which were nonresident from their country of origin. The market dealt in foreign branches and subsidiaries of national banks which issued interest bearing deposits denominated in currencies other than that of the country in which they operated. Large amounts of liquid and near liquid "money" was thus able to be mobilized outside of the normal channels of national monetary control, regulation and issuance. After 1963, as a partial result of the U.S. government's restrictions on the export of certain types of capital from the U.S., the Eurocurrency market grew rapidly, from a gross size of $9.0 billion in 1964 to well over $400 billion by 1978 (est.)— four times as large as in 1972. In 1973, total Eurocurrencies were somewhat larger than total government international reserve assets. By mid-1978 Eurocurrencies were almost twice as large as total official reserve assets.

While the initial growth of the Eurocurrency market from 1963 to 1971 was closely related to the U.S. government's capital export controls and restrictions, it most likely would have developed without the catalyst of the controls, although not as rapidly. The spread of the global corporation as the main institution dominating economic intercourse between the leading industrial capitalist nations created the need for international money and capital markets. By the mid-1960s the U.S. money and capital markets, due in part to the capital controls, were no longer adequate to meet the needs for world liquidity expansion. The growth of the Eurocurrency markets meant that various national banking and investment institutions could expand in a new way: on a truly international basis free from almost all restrictions imposed by national central banks. In a very specific sense, the Eurocurrency markets, a result of various national restrictions on free flows of money and capital, developed much like the wildcat banks which grew up in the western United States in the 1830s and 1840s. They were unregulated, unrestrained, laissez-faire in nature, usually undercapitalized, fiercely competitive and speculative, and in times of crisis proved unstable and often insolvent. Operating without a lender of last resort, the Eurocurrency market grew serving its main clients: global corporations, various local governmental agencies and increasingly since 1971 state agencies of both Third-World countries as well as the weaker sisters of the core capitalist states, Italy and Great Britain.

The significance of operating without a lender of last resort is twofold. First, by definition the Eurocurrency system was unregulated, hence potentially unstable and unsafe in time of crisis. Specifically, the banks involved—the top 200–300 largest in the world, but especially the top 30–50—thrived on foreign exchange speculation which was fostered by the alleged "efficiency" of the Eurocurrency system itself. Comments *Business Week:* "The new [Euro] banking order tremendously increases the efficiency of moving cash around the globe, and that very ease of shifting billions at a moment's notice makes currency instability chronic and dollar weakness inevitable."[3]

The second significance of operating without a lender of last resort is that its absence means that to a degree the Eurocurrency system is able to create and/or constrict world credit much as a national fractional-reserve banking system does. The amount of credit created by the Eurobanks is uncontrolled and unplanned. Since the expansion of a money supply can be too fast or too slow given the rate of real economic expansion or contraction, the money supply itself can be an important short-term factor in the real expansion or contraction of the world economy. Such was the case, for instance, with the over-supply of credit by the Eurobanking system during 1970–1971, contributing to both the transmission of inflation as well as its generation and thereby also contributing to the recession of 1974–1975. The impact of the Eurocurrency system on the explosion of world monetary reserves since the 1971 collapse of the Bretton Woods system has been profound.

WHAT IS A EURODOLLAR?

To answer the seemingly transparent question: "What is a Eurodollar, or a Eurocurrency?" is in fact quite complex. The Eurocurrency market began as a short-term market in which assets and liabilities were usually interest-bearing time deposits, often for extremely short periods: e.g., overnight, 2 and 7 days; as well as for longer periods, 30, 60, 90, 180 and 360 days. Daily (fixed) quotations applied to the above periods, while maturities over one year were usually negotiated. Shortly after the money market aspect of the Eurocurrency system developed (around 1959–1964) a longer-term capital market developed (1963–1964), known as the Eurobond market, with maturities of usually over five years. A medium-term market of one to five years also developed. By the late 1960s and early 1970s the Eurocurrency system had developed a full range of financial instruments, which cut through the usual American division between investment and commercial banks: Eurocommercial paper, Eurocredits, Eurocertificates of deposit and so on.

The Eurodollar (or mark, franc, yen, etc.) section of the market—the highly liquid "hot" money section of the Eurocurrency system—itself consists of two parts. The first is of money lent by the original owners to a bank (say a corporation or oil-exporting nation), and in turn lent by the bank to a final user (say another corporation or a government). This constitutes the net size of the market. The second section of the market consists of interbank transactions in which banks within the Eurocurrency system lend money to each other at fractions of percentage points due to interest-rate differentials. The difference between the net and gross size of the Eurocurrency system is the size of interbank deposits. The often-drawn and reassuring parallel between interbank depositing and the borrowing of Federal Funds by U.S. banks is not correct. Federal funds are borrowed overnight and short term by U.S. commercial banks in order to make up cash reserves and/or due to interest-rate arbitrage. The funds are controlled and interest-rate ceilings set by the Federal Reserve Board. Thus they are as secure as the entire U.S. commercial banking system as backed by the resources of the U.S. Treasury and the state. The inter-bank deposits in the Eurocurrency system (amounting to over $150 billion in late 1974) are liabilities drawn on other banks in the system and are not backed by any final authority. Bank regulators and bankers themselves tended (at least prior to the credit crunch of 1974) to view inter-bank deposits as riskless transactions; not as loans but as adjustments to cash balances similar to U.S. Federal Funds. In fact, the interbank market is a form of speculation. For instance, in 1974, the North Carolina National Bank, one of the smaller Eurobanks, had $550 million placed with other Eurobanks, usually at longer maturities than the deposits coming into its own system. The NCNB would have shown a profit (called an arbitrage profit) if interest rates had decreased or remained the same; but interest rates shot up in the spring of 1974, and the bank lost more than $1 million.

The Eurobanking system has linked together hundreds of banks of various sizes around the world, many knowing little about each other. In an expansionary period, trust is characteristic; but in a contraction, mutual mistrust based on increasing competition means that one bank's problems usually spread rapidly throughout the entire system. The failure in 1974 of a variety of smaller world banks (Herstatt, Franklin National, and so on) for reasons not directly related to the Eurocurrency system, caused a massive, although temporary, contraction in the market; a weeding out of the smaller Eurobanks and enormous deposits in the twenty or so largest Eurobanks. Thus, the largest Eurobanks had a surplus of oil-exporting nations income (petrodollars), while the majority of smaller banks did not have deposits to cover liabilities. The end result of this chain was that many of the smaller banks reduced their share of the market, or got out altogether. This left borrowers holding loans which could not be rolled over at terms' end or which could not be renegotiated. One of the more sensational results of this process was collapse of the Burmah Oil Company as a result of its inability to roll over or renegotiate a $420 million Eurodollar loan from the previous year, which prior to 1974 was considered a standard operating procedure.

SOURCES AND USES OF EUROFUNDS

As of September, 1976, the oil-exporting nations were the single largest suppliers of funds to the Eurocurrency system, making a net contribution of $33 billion. With the sudden oil price increase in 1973, the surplus funds of the oil exporting nations were first invested in short-term, large-Eurobank, Eurocurrency-denominated issues. Since that time surplus oil funds have been concentrated in domestic investment and consumer-importing projects, investments in core capitalist countries (primarily in real estate and equity), and in the purchase of long-term Eurobonds (and a corresponding decline in short-term Eurocurrencies). The significance of the tendency to switch from highly liquid holdings in Eurocurrencies to the purchase of long-term Eurobonds is that it gives a certain initial stability to the Eurocurrency system, minimizing maturity transformation problems while at the same time supporting the ability of Eurobonds to issue increasing amounts of long-term loans to a variety of nonoil producing countries. Thus, the massive shift of location and ownership of world capital since 1973 has been handled in part through the mechanism of the Eurocurrency system. In 1975, 12% of Middle East money was in Eurocurrency instruments and holdings. In 1976, this increased to 19%. The actual rate of oil producers' surplus in the Eurocurrency system is higher since the Middle-East classification excludes Algeria, Nigeria, and Venezuela.

The most significant shift in the makeup of the Eurosystem since the credit crunch of 1974 has been the move of funds from the short-term capital markets into long-term bond markets. Between 1974–1976 total bond issues (including Eurobonds and all foreign bonds issued in various countries) increased from 18.9% of the international capital markets to 50.4%. Conversely, Eurocurrency bank credits (short term) decreased proportionately from 88.1% to 49.6%. Ugeux summarizes the trend in the ten years up to 1978: ". . . the supremacy of Eurocurrency loans has progressively been eroded and the bond market is now a major source of international financing."[4] Whether the shift away from Eurocurrency to Eurobond issues is a long-term trend reflective of basic structural changes in the market, or whether it is a cyclically related response to the massive liquidity in which international capital markets have found themselves awash since 1975 remains to be seen. The abundance of funds, especially in U.S. banks, has not been counter-balanced by demand for loans from advanced capitalist countries. The outcome, in part due to the resultant decline of interest rates, spreads and length of maturities and in part related to the increase of loans for nonoil exporting Third-World nations, has been that Eurobank lending to Third-World nations has increased dramatically.

The shift to Eurobond issues has been accompanied by the increased domination of the Eurobond market by European based investment and/or commercial banks to the relative exclusion of U.S. commercial and investment banks and banking houses. Among the ten largest bond underwriters in 1977 only one was U.S. Among the largest twenty, only three were U.S.

It is often argued by banks and many government officials that with the shift into Eurobonds, the Euromarkets as a whole have developed more stability than previously. This has led to the greater participation in the market by institutional investors such as insurance companies and pension funds. However, while there has been relative growth of the bond market, both the short-term and long-term sections have grown massively in absolute terms and remain closely interconnected. Thus, the potential for instability is dependent not only on the quality of the bond-type development loans—itself problematic in some important cases (e.g., Iran, Peru, Zaire, etc.)—but also on the nature of the "hot money" flows in the huge short-term market.

In sum, from the early 1970s to date, the major and significant shift which occurred in the Eurocurrency system was from providing working capital to major U.S., European and Japanese corporations to one of providing much longer-term credit to official agencies and institutions of primarily Third-World countries and other nations with balance of payments deficits. The political risks involved in such a transition are obviously of an entirely higher order of magnitude than previously. This has created a long-term problem (especially intense in 1974–1975) of a maturity imbalance between deposits and loans—"borrowing short to lend long." In part, this problem has recently been somewhat offset by the purchase of Eurobonds by oil exporting nations; but given the increasing demand for and supply of long-term loans, it is far from certain to what degree this can effectively deal with the problem.

THE EXPLOSION OF WORLD LIQUIDITY

To the extent the Eurocurrency system functions as a fractional-reserve banking system (and it has tended to function differently depending on the specifics of time and place), it has the ability to create credit (liquidity), and to transfer with increasing rapidity this liquidity around the world depending on the smallest margin of interest-rate differentials. (This is so because of the use of telex and telephone communication systems as the medium of Eurocurrency transactions, save for the longer-term instruments; e.g., Eurocredits, Euro-CDs, Eurobonds, etc.). Central to the Eurocurrency system's ability to increase world liquidity has been the role of various central banks themselves in the Eurocurrency markets. This is highly ironic since more than any other development in the last twenty years which has served to destabilize and undercut the ability of the nation state to manage and/or "plan" its economic development, the growth of the Eurocurrency system is responsible for this subversion.

The Eurocurrency system is similar to a national banking system based on fractional-reserve banking* On the basis of an original dollar deposit

*For those unfamiliar with fractional reserve-banking; a national commercial banking system is able to expand its credit base because it makes loans on the basis of its capital assets plus its deposits, keeping a "prudent," or legally determined, proportion of its assets as reserves. For instance, assume an original deposit of $X minus a reserve is lent to a borrower (X-R). For the sake of simplicity, the borrower buys a commodity. The borrower's check is cashed by the owner of the commodity in his/her bank, and the borrower's bank honors the check. While the borrower's bank loses $(X-R), the original deposit in the borrower's bank remains so that two banks together have on the basis of the original deposit (X), $X + (X-R). The two banks acting together have created additional credit. The second bank, of course, now has $(X-R) sitting idle and, we assume, will make a loan of this amount, minus a reserve fund. Depending on the amount of the reserve fund this multiplier process will continue until the original deposit is used up to its reserve limit. (The level and trend of interest rates also affect the limits, but for our purposes, this is secondary). The key assumption here is that no part of the original deposit (X) leaves the banking system. In reality, a proportion will leave for "cash" purposes, for funds outside the country and so on.

(from whatever source: the U.S., a central bank, an oil-exporting country, a global corporation, etc.), in a Eurobank that bank makes a loan, outside of the U.S. If this loan (and here we are referring to highly liquid "short-term" loans) is to a domestic U.S. bank (or in the case of Euromarks, a German bank, and so on), there can be no credit creation since the dollar (or mark, etc.) returns to the domestic money supply. If the dollar (or mark, etc.) remains in the Eurosystem, then there is no reason for the multiplier effect not to work, providing that the deposit is lent to a final nonbank, non-U.S. (or non-German, etc.) resident user, who in turn (directly or indirectly) must redeposit the money into the Eurosystem. Since there are no legally defined reserve limits in the Eurosystem (and we have no way of ascertaining the actual reserve practice of Eurobanks since the information is highly protected), the theoretical possibility for a high multiplier exists. However, in fact the Eurosystem has many "leaks" and in this regard is quite different from a national banking system.

In sum, the theoretical possibility for a high multiplier impact of the Eurobanking system exists. So far this has been considered without the influence of the central banks. Once the practice of central banks intervening in the Eurosystem is taken into consideration, the liquidity creating functions of the Eurocurrency system take on a more concrete and definitive picture. . . .

Bank intermediation is of obvious importance to all forms of capitalist economic growth. The liquidity functions of the Euromarkets, however, are not necessarily geared to economic growth as an abstraction, but rather to growth or potential growth as indicated by the profit-maximizing potentials of individual Eurobanks in a highly competitive world market. The very laissez-faire nature of the Euromarkets—while aiding their "efficiency," read profit—recapitulates on a world scale the essential elements of the history of financial booms and busts in all capitalist countries. This is particularly so prior to the development of at least minimally effective central bank institutions as credit regulators and as lenders of last resort. The best recent example of private profit leading to an overextension of credit is the case of Euroloans to many Third-World countries. The growth of liquidity must be in relation to potential real economic growth or intermediation itself becomes a fetter on growth and transforms into its opposite—disintermediation.

Whatever amount of addition to world liquidity the Eurocurrency system has produced, there is also an indirect inflationary effect due to the system's very existence. Even if the German central banks had not deposited its surplus dollars back into the market during 1970–1971, as in the previous example (either directly or via the Bank for International Settlements), it could have bought U.S. Treasury bills with the dollars. U.S. domestic banks are, in turn, able and willing to lend the money so injected into the U.S. domestic money supply back to the Germans in order to gain interest arbitrage, which by definition of the situation, is more profitable than similar U.S. domestic money-market instruments. Thus, the Eurocurrency system responds to more underlying forces at work within the fabric of the world economy as a whole and is not in any simple way only dependent on the policies of various national governments.

Similarly, in defense of the Eurocurrency system, it has been argued that the system does not add to the impact of speculation in the world money markets, but merely makes those markets more "efficient." However, the existence of the Eurocurrency system has the potential for increasing the rate and institutionalizing foreign exchange speculation, given floating exchange rates. . . .

The anarchy of the Euromarkets has led to pressures for the coordination of interest-rate policies among the advanced capitalist nations. This will work well, however, only if economic conditions and trends are similar among all the European countries, the U.S. and Japan. That is, if national business cycles are synchronized. Characteristic of the post World War II period, however, is the asynchronized nature of the cycles, with the initial exception of the oil related recession of 1974–1975. Thus the cycles have usually put the U.S. in opposition to most of the European nations and Japan in terms of interest-rate coordination. This has been so between 1976–1978. The actual coordination of interest rate and other monetary policies would mean that some nations would have to sacrifice domestic priorities (whether these are social legitimating priorities such as unemployment levels, social welfare spending, etc.; or whether they are accumulation priorities such as the level of domestic capital formation). Real and effective coordination would mean the elimination of capitalist competition. That continually proves impossible. Thus, the coordination of interest rate policy becomes merely a fair weather strategy. A good recent example of national political pressures is France's response to the state policy of "sustained noninflationary growth" announced by the leaders of the major capitalist countries at the London economic summit in May, 1977. According to the *New York Times:* "While the leaders were assembling in London . . . France's Jacques Chirac announced a campaign program to defeat the opposition Socialist-Communist coalition by putting the fight against unemployment above all other concerns and by "adjusting to temporary dislocations which may arise," in other words, creating jobs by letting inflation soar and the franc fall."[5]

In sum, the Eurocurrency system has developed in response to the underlying growth of various forms of internationalized capital and on the basis of the ability to transfer funds immediately to any corner of the world. At various points in its history the sources and uses of its funds have shifted in response to the changing needs and contradictions of global capital and the increasing instability of the international monetary system. The Eurocurrency system is extremely volatile, capable of rapid expansion to meet (and most likely exceed) world liquidity needs during a boom, and just as capable of rapid contraction, if not panic, leading to a major crisis of "confidence."

EUROCURRENCY DEBT AND THE INTERNATIONAL MONETARY SYSTEM

Since the 1973 oil price increases and the elimination of the U.S. capital controls in 1974, the majority of final users of Eurofunds has shifted to non-U.S. global corporations and increasingly, as has been noted, to the more rapidly "developing" nonoil exporting nations. Given the increasingly close connection between the extension of private sector loans and the related private sector domination of the world monetary system itself, two central issues should be touched on relative to the impact of the loans on the world monetary system. The first issue is the nature of the debt: its extent, soundness and more immediate impact on balance of payments and trade. The second and more underlying issue is the relation between the debt burden and economic growth of the indebted nations. These two issues together focus attention on a major weak point in the world economy and monetary system, and in particular in terms of the Eurocurrency markets.

A thorough discussion of the nature of international debt is beyond the scope of this article. However, brief attention to some points is critical in order to understand the relation of debt to the Eurosystem. The issue of the soundness of debt mixes economics and politics. Peru and Zaire, for instance, have recently experienced serious political turmoil related to the economic stagnation in large part necessitated by their debt-servicing problems and the austerity programs initiated by those governments. Other countries (such as South Korea, Mexico and Brazil) have recently been able to prepay and/or renegotiate their debts to their advantage resulting from their export stimulated growth and the massive liquidity in the Euromarkets. Yet the dependence of both Brazil and South Korea on exporting for their growth indicates the precariousness of their situation.

More important than the soundness of the debt, however, is the relation of debt to long-term growth. Where national growth is primarily trade related (e.g., as in Peru, South Korea, Mexico, Brazil, Chile, Zaire, the Philippines, Taiwan, Thailand, Turkey—accounting for 2/3 of all international debt), the debt/export ratio becomes key. Repayment of loans necessitates rapidly and consistently growing exports and the basis for reduction in current account deficits. The growth of protectionism in the advanced capitalist countries directly counters export growth. Internal markets in these countries are extremely bifurcated and limited. Thus, the Third-World debt problem is ultimately a trade problem, as Fishlow points out. A possible alternative strategy—pursued most consistently by Brazil, South Korea and Mexico—has been import substitution. Its success, however, reduced proportionately the exports from the advanced capitalist countries exactly in a period when exporters are competing fiercely for slow-growth markets. Ironically, this has led, in part, to a call for greater protectionism of the advanced capitalist countries' internal markets. But import substitution, too, depends on ultimate export to the advanced capitalist countries, creating the tendency for a vicious circle to be set up in periods of absolute or relative economic contraction. Thus, the champions of free trade and a return to a relatively liberal, open, international economic order have been the international banks—the holders of the debt—and the global corporations.

The domination of the international monetary system by private sector banks stands out as the debt/export ratio of all non-OPEC Third-World nations has grown from 66% in 1971 to 81% in 1977. It peaked at 108% in 1976.

As of March, 1977, commercial banks held $75 billion of a cumulative debt of Third World countries of about $180 billion; and the banks' share is increasing. Between 1971 through 1973 Third World countries borrowed $45 billion, about one-fifth supplied by banks. From 1974 through 1976 these countries borrowed $109 billion, of which banks supplied 42%. This rapid rise in borrowing from private commercial banks was an initial result of the oil price increases since the end of 1973, often needed to cover immediate current account deficits. Since 1975 loans have been of longer term and tied more closely to development projects rather than for financing current-account deficits. Nevertheless, indirectly the oil related current-account deficits affects these loans in as much as proportionately more exports are needed to finance the higher price of oil.

Given the uncertainties of the world economy, and specifically the difficulties in decreasing the debt/export ratio of the ten Third-World countries which hold the majority of Third-World debt, why have commercial banks been willing and anxious to loan massive amounts to these nations? The answer ties together some of the developments which have been outlined above, especially the growth of the Eurocurrency system and the related rise of U.S. commercial offshore banking in the Caribbean. In the Eurocurrency markets, bank branches and subsidiaries are not required to report to U.S. or any other authorities on their lending practices concerning maturity of loans and deposits, volume of business, interest charges and so on. It is probable that the banks make a larger profit on off-shore lending (whether to U.S. global corporations or to Third-World governments) than they would to U.S. domestic customers. The end result of the growth in offshore lending, especially since 1973, is to make the cost of money higher in the domestic U.S. market, as well as in the world market, particularly for Third-World loans. In turn this has enabled the U.S. banks to resist Federal Reserve pressures to cut the interest rates for their domestic operations.

Since the 1973 oil price increases the expansion of current account debts primarily of Third-World countries, but also of Italy and Great Britain, has caused a new demand for commercial bank lending. It is risky and unregulated since it is primarily run out of and has expanded the Eurocurrency markets. Further, the demand for loans has been stimulated by the ability of competing banks to sell their loans to various governments and private sector organizations. One important aspect of official borrowing by countries from banks involved in Eurocurrency operations is the apparent unlimited ability of the Eurocurrency market to meet any loan demand.

CONCLUSION

The breakdown of laissez-faire in the late 19th century brought the state to a new role: increasingly as centralizer and overseer/manager and/or planner in order to make monopoly capital economically and politically functional and legitimate, especially in response to demands placed on it by the organized working class and other reformist interests. The contemporary interventionist state has its roots in the social and political fabric of the nation-state. No such institution exists or shows signs for existing internationally. A supranational solution to the regulation and control of capital (even in its own interest) appears to be out of the question due to the inherent competition among different "denationalized" but still nationally-based capital units. The ability of advanced capitalist states to organize the world system in a coherent and stable manner also appears unlikely since the economic and political conditions in each country tend to demand different and often opposite imperatives. The inability to regulate the Eurocurrency system is indicative of this failure.

In pointing out the inflationary and destabilizing nature of these developments in the international monetary arrangement, a case is not being made for the primacy of monetary elements in world and/or domestic inflations. Rather, there is a complex cause/effect relationship which has yet to be fully understood and explained. Nevertheless, the breakdown of the international monetary system has contributed to the generation and especially to the international transmission of inflation.

Along with the managed float system, the increasingly important role of private banks in world reserve and credit creation adds not only to inflation but, and in the long run perhaps more importantly, to the instability of the system. Unregulated credit markets, in de Vries' words, ". . . have in the past led to cycles of boom and bust, which also seriously affect the banking institutions operating in them. That is the very reason why national banking regulations were developed. There is no good way of telling when the danger point is reached; it comes when confidence suddenly evaporates."[6] The IMF agreements of 1976 at Jamaica do nothing to deal with these central problems, thus giving a free hand to increased private sector expansion. The parallel with the condition of U.S. wildcat banks in the 1830s and 1840s becomes more exact as these developments continue. The crucial difference, as has been noted, is that while nations to a limited degree have been able to regulate banking institutions, there has been a total failure due to the nature of the situation to regulate internationally, even in the self-interests of capital. This is because of the inability of dominant capitalist countries, regardless of the party in power, to sacrifice their nationally-based accumulation and legitimation imperatives for international reasons of "stability." Underlying this is not only the necessary political fact of the nation state; but the fact that while the apparatus of capital is increasingly internationalized, its base remains overwhelmingly national. Therefore, capital of each nation competes frantically with capital from other nations in the world market. The greater monopolization of national capital operating internationally (e.g., France's attempts to forceably merge its key industries) means greater international competition. This in turn extenuates the anarchic aspects inherent in capital accumulation, only this time on an increasingly international scale and state. Laissez-faire reasserts itself, often even in spite of the expressed desires of corporate and banking capital which call for some sort of regulation. Yet, regulation does not exist on an international plane. The result is the increased instability of the world capitalist system.

NOTES

1. Andrew F. Brimmer and Frederick R. Dahl, "Growth of American International Banking: Implications for Public Policy," *The Journal of Finance* (May, 1975) p. 356.

2. U.S. House of Representatives, Committee on Banking, Currency and Housing, *Financial Institutions and the Nation's Economy, Compendium of Papers Prepared for the FINE Study*, 94 Congress, Second Session (June, 1976), Book II, Washington, D.C., pp. 205–207.

3. *Business Week* (August 21, 1978) p. 76.

4. George Ugeux, "The Rise of Disintermediation," *Euromoney* (June, 1977) p. 68.

5. *The New York Times* (May 9, 1977) p. 13.

6. Tom de Vries, "Jamaica, or the Non-Reform of the IMF," *Foreign Affairs* (April, 1976), p. 597.

18. The Dollar Standard

RICCARDO PARBONI

Riccardo Parboni examines the system of floating exchange rates that emerged after the collapse of the Bretton Woods monetary regime. Despite important differences, Parboni argues that the post-1945 fixed and floating exchange rate systems have functioned in generally similar ways. Both have allowed the United States to reap the benefits of seigniorage that accrue to the issuer of a widely used currency. Because the American dollar is used as the reserve currency of the international monetary system, the United States is less constrained by balance of payments concerns than other countries. By running current account deficits, the United States has been able to expropriate present and future assets at the expense of others. The problem of seigniorage has expanded during the 1970s, Parboni argues, with the growth of the Euromarkets. In a strong Realist argument emphasizing the pursuit of national interests, Parboni concludes that the United States has used seigniorage to "consolidate the power, competitivity, and predominance of the American economy throughout the world."

THE END OF BRETTON WOODS

Discussions of the problems of international finance commonly cite two dates, almost interchangeably, to mark the end of the Bretton Woods system: 15 August 1971 and 19 March 1973. It was in August 1971 that the United States, unilaterally withdrawing from commitments assumed under the Bretton Woods agreement, indefinitely suspended the convertibility of the dollar for gold and other reserve assets. In March 1973 the central banks of the major industrialized countries renounced their commitment to maintain the quotation of their respective currencies within a band of ±2.25% with respect to the dollar. Both these commitments—convertibility of the dollar for gold on the one hand and fixed exchange rates on the other—seemed equally essential characteristics of the old system; so much so that even after the dollar could no longer be converted for gold, many still insisted that the maintenance of fixed exchange rates was sufficient to keep the spirit of Bretton Woods alive.

With hindsight these events can be viewed with greater assurance. It now seems clear that the really essential characteristic of Bretton Woods was not the maintenance of parity but the convertibility of the dollar. Indeed, it is important to understand that exchange rates were not completely fixed even under the Bretton Woods system. Triffin has recently recalled that between 1948 and 1965 no less than ninety-four members of the International Monetary Fund altered the parity of their currencies—many more than once.[1] On the other hand, the present system of exchange rates does not absolutely reflect the rules of free fluctuation: after March 1973, the central banks rapidly discovered that it was simply not possible to abandon exchange rates to market forces completely.

FLEXIBLE EXCHANGE RATES

The reason for this lack of confidence on the part of the central banks lay in their observation that variations in exchange rates, far from correcting disequilibria in the balance of payments that cause them, could easily stimulate cumulative processes that would tend to aggravate these disequilibria. The sequence of events can be briefly outlined as follows. Trade flows, not to mention flows of many services, do not respond to variations in exchange rates very rapidly. The initial effect of a devaluation is therefore to reduce foreign-currency income, which exerts even greater downward pressure on the exchange rate. (Conversely, the initial effect of an upward revaluation is to augment the inflow of foreign currency, which tends to drive the exchange rate still higher.) The monetary authorities must then intervene to make sure that the cumulative effects of this process do not result in a rapid slide of the exchange rate in the event of a devaluation or an excessive skyrocketing of the rate in the event of a revaluation. Variations in exchange rates, however, do react on domestic price levels very rapidly. Depreciation of a currency accelerates inflation and thus reinforces the trend toward devaluation; appreciation of a currency contains the rise of prices and thus reinforces the tendency toward revaluation. When a national currency depreciates, the cost of imports, as measured in that currency, rises. If these imports consist of primary products or components, the increase in their prices is transmitted to the price of the finished products through increments in the cost of production. An increase in the prices of imported finished goods also produces a rise in price levels, because it 'raises the ceiling' of international competition and thereby enables domestic producers to raise the prices of their own products. The opposite effect pertains in cases of revaluation of a national currency.

A review of the available data seems to suggest that the speed at which prices respond to depreciation of national currencies is high; the effects on domestic price levels in the event of upward revaluation of the national currency, on the other hand, are relatively slight, because of the rigid price floors of modern economies, as a result of which corporations do *not* transmit decreases in the cost of imports in national currency to final products. Vicious circles are thus quite easily set in motion: devaluation leads to inflation, which leads in turn to further devaluation, and so on. Economies that get trapped in such circles find it quite difficult to break out of them. Virtuous circles are possible too, in principle: revaluation, followed by a slackening of price increases, followed by further revaluation, and so on. Except that since price levels respond less elastically to revaluations, virtuous circles require healthy doses of deflation in order to take hold. The existence of speculation, which can come into play at any point in either process, intensifying whichever inflection of exchange rates is under way, significantly increases the probability of vicious, and not virtuous, circles: the interaction between exchange rates and price levels ensures that speculation in currency markets acts almost exclusively as a destabilizing factor.

Currency authorities in national economies are therefore highly cautious in abandoning exchange rates to market forces. Obviously, this does not mean that devaluations and revaluations do not occur, but it does mean that the mechanism by which exchange rates vary is quite similar to the way official par values operated under the old system. Countries whose exchange rates are out of line—in other words, whose economies are no longer competitive—effect 'snap' devaluations, by abandoning efforts to support their currency on exchange markets and by playing on the differential of interest rates abroad in order to encourage withdrawals of short-term deposits. When the exchange rate has been depressed enough to render the economy competitive again, the authorities intervene massively on the market to defend the new 'par value' and prevent unwanted fluctuations.

This mode of operation of the currency system has been termed flexible, or floating, exchange rates. Now, it turns out that flexible exchange rates function so similarly to fixed exchange rates that reserve requirements have not even been reduced. On the contrary, the demand for international reserves on the part of the industrialized countries has even increased, because of the greater difficulty in stabilizing exchange rates in the absence of coordination with other countries.

There is, nevertheless, a profound difference between the systems of fixed and floating exchange rates: under the new system countries are much more willing to allow variations of the rate. This indulgence of variations is not the result of any neo-mercantilist attitude like that reflected in the 'beggar-thy-neighbour' policy applied in the thirties. Indeed, one of the greatest concerns of the founders of the Bretton Woods system was precisely to avoid any repetition of those policies. Today, however, the need to alter exchange rates arises in part from the desire to attenuate the varying impact of the rise in oil prices on rates of inflation, and therefore on competitivity, in the various economies. . . .

The trouble is that devaluations restore competitivity only temporarily, because of the effects on the rate of inflation described above. A country that wants to maintain a certain level of competitivity becomes enmeshed in a succession of devaluations, and pays the price of a very high inflation rate. In real terms, then, exchange rates have actually varied little, since the variations in nominal exchange rates for nearly all countries have been almost completely counterbalanced by increments in rates of inflation compared to the rest of the world. . . .

THE RISE OF DOLLAR HOLDINGS

The situation created once the dollar was no longer convertible for gold has been called the 'dollar standard'. This terminology seems entirely appropriate, although there has been no lack of critics who, emphasizing the literal significance of the word 'standard', deny that the term accurately describes the present international monetary situation. How can the dollar, whose value is constantly shifting, serve as the basis of a system of monetary relations? But the expression does capture one aspect of the situation rather well: the dollar may not be the reference point for other currencies, but it is surely the only point of reference for the dollar itself. Once the threat of the potential conversion of foreign-held dollars into gold had been eliminated, the limits to the injection of dollars into international circulation disappeared as well. After 1971 the world was flooded with dollars. This phenomenon was somewhat belatedly recognized by observers of the financial scene, who, with customary lexical resourcefulness, coined a succession of new expressions—first 'dollar glut', later 'dollar overhang'—during the first half of the past decade. The mass of dollars in international circulation has continued to rise since then, but no need has been felt to mint fresh terms with which to describe a situation that now borders on the absurd.

No one, it seems, thought it useful to employ the good old category of seigniorage to analyse the complex reality of today's international monetary system—perhaps because the word is now indelibly associated with De Gaulle's invective against the 'exorbitant privileges' of the United States. But these privileges were actually used with great moderation in the sixties; it would probably be natural to describe American behaviour toward the rest of the world today with more weighty terms perhaps more appropriate to court records than to international finance.

. . . During the nineteen years from 1951 to 1969 official US liabilities (meaning liabilities of foreign central banks and international institutions) rose by $12 thousand million, nearly all during the latter part of the 1960s. During the nine subsequent years the growth of this debt soared by $134 thousand million, which, even if inflation is taken into account, represents a very sizable increase compared with the previous period. World reserves also rose greatly during this period as a result of the American deficits, and the share of these reserves constituted by official US liabilities rose from 10% to 50%. Such statistics, which suggest a strong increase in American seigniorage, are on the contrary considered irrelevant by some financial commentators. In the highly qualified opinion of Michael W. Blumenthal, secretary of the treasury in the Carter administration, there is no longer any sense—if there ever was—in speaking of the privileges of the country that issues the reserve currency, for the following reasons: 'First, because with flexible exchange rates dollar accumulations by other countries are less an automatic result of the operation of the system and more a matter of discretion; second, because with the present large and open capital markets, onshore and off, many other deficit countries [other than the United States] can at any time be borrowing dollars in large amounts and putting them on the [currency] market—with the result that [official] borrowing to finance US deficits is not the major source of growth in the supply of dollars'.[2]

INTERPRETATIONS OF SEIGNIORAGE

Blumenthal's observations suggest that the American contention is that the link between private and official international liquidity makes it virtually impossible to ascribe seigniorage to any particular country. If we are to isolate the kernel of truth in this assertion, it is opportune to recall the meaning of 'seigniorage'. It refers to the profit that accrues to the country whose currency is used as an international means of payment, and it is equal, quantitatively, to the net amount of money this country places at the disposal of the rest of the world. This profit subsists whether the possession of reserve currency is voluntary, the fruit of an agreement between the issuing country and the others, or obligatory, as it is under the dollar standard. The advantage lies in the fact that the country that issues the reserve currency can finance its own deficits with payments in its own currency, without having to resort to financial assets abroad previously accumulated through foreign surpluses. In other

words, the country whose money serves as the reserve currency appropriates either real resources produced abroad (in the event that its
balance of payments deficit is a current-account deficit) or claims to
future use of these resources (if the deficit is a capital-account deficit. We
must also consider the particular case in which the capital-account deficit
is the result of an outflow of capital for direct investment abroad; then
the residents of the reserve-currency country acquire the right to use
foreign resources on foreign territory). It has been widely noted, of
course, that the deficits of the reserve-currency country may be caused
by this role itself. The reserve-currency country has to supply liquidity to
other countries, which need this liquidity in order to augment their own
reserves in proportion to the growth of trade. Nevertheless, it is
legitimate to regard as deficits induced by the issuing country's reserve-
currency role only those deficits that are clearly ascribable to some
initiative taken by the authorities in the countries that use the reserve
currency, either a bond issue or an effort by foreign governments or
their agents to raise funds on the financial markets of the reserve-
currency country. Naturally, if the reserve-currency country shows
deficits on other items, access to its capital market by other countries will
be proportionally reduced, and the other countries will then be in a
position to gather the reserves through a corresponding surplus. It is
therefore illegitimate to claim that the entire deficit of the reserve-
currency country is caused by the desire of other countries to accumulate reserves. It should also be noted that in the 1960s, when the United
States began to encounter balance of payments difficulties, restrictions
were imposed precisely on capital movements, going so far as to ration
official issues on the American market itself.

Nevertheless, so long as the reserve currency continues to be convertible for other assets (gold, for example), the country that issues this
currency does come under strong pressure to limit the quantity of its
money in circulation, in order to avert the threat of sudden massive
conversions into these other assets. In the literature, this is called the
'confidence problem'.

The confidence problem was one of the most hotly contested issues
throughout the 1960s, and led to the invention of numerous indices of
the international financial position of the United States, the deterioration of which would in practice act as an alarm signal that confidence in
the dollar was crumbling.

A restricted interpretation of 'seigniorage' has been evolving in
connection with the unfolding discussion of the confidence problem. On
this view seigniorage consists in the privilege of the reserve-currency
country to accumulate short-term debts in order to finance long-term
credits or investments abroad. At the root of this interpretation lies the
observation that *through the end of 1970* the United States registered no

trade deficits, and during the twenty years between 1950 and 1970 there were current-account deficits in only six years. Through the end of the sixties, then, American deficits could be attributed exclusively to capital movements, and in particular long-term capital movements and foreign investments. Indeed, the base balance (obtained by adding the balances of long-term capital flows and the current-account balance) was consistently in deficit from 1950 to 1970, except for one year, when the account balanced.

It thus seemed plausible to uphold an interpretation of seigniorage according to which the United States accumulates short-term debts by ceding dollars abroad destined to flow into the official reserves of foreign central banks, which would later redeposit them as short-term deposits in the US financial market. Parallel to these short-term foreign debts, the United States acquires long-term credits abroad, or makes direct investments. In other words, the United States acts as an investment bank whose balance-sheet would show short-term debits and non-liquid assets. Seigniorage was then said to consist in the ability to act as financial broker on a world scale, to command sweeping access to short-term credits from foreign countries. But the real gain for the reserve-currency country, namely its appropriation of foreign resources, was said to correspond merely to the difference between the debit and credit account, the equivalent of a bank's brokerage income. Seigniorage in this narrow sense is a patrimonial sort of concept referring to the international financial position of the centre-country, while seigniorage in the broader connotation is more properly a fluid concept relating to inflows and outflows in the balance of payments.

THE LINK BETWEEN PRIVATE AND OFFICIAL LIQUIDITY

Until the emergence of an international dollar market on a vast scale—the Eurodollar market—the seigniorage the United States derived year after year from its role as the reserve-currency country was uniquely determined by the American balance of payments on the basis of official settlements. Since the only dollars in circulation outside the United States were those held in the official reserves of central banks, this balance, measuring the variation in dollar reserves (that is, the variation in official US debt), automatically indicated how many dollars the American government had released into world circulation. Since the middle of the 1960s, the volume of dollars in circulation worldwide in the hands of private non-residents—called Eurodollars—has been rising. As has often been demonstrated, the mass of dollar-denominated deposits does not correspond exactly to any particular US balance of payments—nor, most important, does it equal the balance as computed on the basis of official settlements.

With the growth of the Eurodollar market there is no longer any equivalence, nor even functional relationship, between variations in official US liabilities and the total dollars held outside the United States. To begin with, an enormous volume of dollars are in private hands. Second, the dollar holdings of the central banks include not only assets deposited in the United States, but also dollar deposits held outside the United States, in Eurobanks. The variation in the volume of official dollar reserves has become greater than that of official US liabilities, the discrepancy caused by the intervention of the Eurodollar market. Through this market the central banks recycle dollars among themselves, increasing official dollar reserves without increasing official American liabilities. In addition, central banks can order dollar transfers 'through the back door', thus automatically diminishing both the volume of reserves and the volume of official American liabilities.

Moreover, since the Eurodollar market permits a genuine creation of deposits, similar to what occurs in a national banking system, it enables the central banks to create dollar deposits through operations with the Eurobanks; with these they can feed their own reserves, in addition to facilitating the recycling of the reserves of the central banks themselves, thus permitting a single deposit to function simultaneously as the reserve asset of two or more central banks.

There are now serious indications that the Euromarket coefficient has begun to exceed unity in recent years, thus causing a net creation of deposits. Finally, since the Eurodollar market is in direct communication with the American money market, the demand for funds on the part of central banks can be satisfied by drawing funds from the United States into the Eurodollar market. The loans issued by American banks to central banks through Euromarket banks increase the availability of world reserves, but they do not figure among official American debts, unless the central banks redeposit the funds in the American market. In sum, the existence of the Euromarket, with the interconnections it has woven between private and official liquidity, has vastly complicated the process of creation of reserves.

SEIGNIORAGE IN THE SEVENTIES

This phenomenon has important consequences for the analysis of seigniorage. As I have pointed out, so long as the only dollars in circulation outside the United States were those held by central banks, the size of seigniorage equalled the annual variations in official US liabilities. The existence of quantities of dollars in private hands, and the ability of central banks to resort to the market of these funds, makes the calculation of seigniorage much less straightforward. The variation of official debt is too narrow a measure, but the variation of official dollar reserves plus the variation of the Eurodollar market is too broad. In principle, it should be possible to calculate the scope of seigniorage even in the new situation. In practice, however, insuperable difficulties arise.

In sum, in the new situation created by the growth of private international liquidity and its inextricable link to official international liquidity, it becomes impossible accurately to determine the scope of American seigniorage. Variation in official US liabilities is only a faulty approximation of it. Nevertheless, even calculated in this manner, seigniorage was enormous during the 1970s and contributed more than in the past to the formation of reserves.

Some have maintained that the growth of international financial brokerage poses the question of whether there is any sense in continuing to try to define American seigniorage so punctiliously. We have seen that in the sixties some students, basing themselves on the fact that the American deficit resulted from capital outflows, had asserted that seigniorage consisted in the power to act as international financial intermediary, to gather funds in order to issue loans. By extension this interpretation gave rise to another, that seigniorage is merely the power to obtain credit from the rest of the world in order to finance one's own deficits. The expansion of international financial intermediation during the seventies allowed many countries enhanced access to foreign financing compared with the earlier period. According to this view, precisely because of the explosion of American deficits, seigniorage over the world money supply has now been extended to nearly all countries, which by resorting to international financial markets have been able to finance staggering deficits and to add to their own reserves not only assets deposited in the United States, but also a considerable volume of deposits in Eurocurrencies. In 1971 the central banks of the Group of Ten agreed not to deposit their own reserves in the Eurocurrency market, so the rise in official assets deposited in this market . . . , must be attributed almost entirely to developing countries, especially OPEC members. But the developed countries have also gained notable advantages from the existence of the Euromarkets, because they are able thus to obtain credits with which to finance their deficits. In other words, the Euromarkets have increased the speed of circulation of official reserves. In the end, since the existence of the Euromarkets (and to some extent the greater openness of national financial markets themselves) has increased the supply of official reserves and accelerated their rate of circulation, it has diminished the inherent privilege enjoyed by the United States as the reserve-currency country. This is the real meaning of the statement of former Treasury Secretary Blumenthal quoted earlier.

The genuinely greater recourse to international credit on the part of various countries encountering balance of payments difficulties, however, must not obscure the enormous difference that still separates the reserve-currency country from all the others. The reserve-currency country is able to tap the resources of the rest of the world virtually without restriction, simply by issuing its own currency. For countries that turn to international financial markets, however, credit is always limited and 'conditional'. In the case of loans issued by supranational bodies like the IMF, credit conditions are governed by norms and principles sanctioned by long practice. But even in the case of private credit, the country going into debt is compelled to settle its balance of payments and to accept certain norms of economic policy—otherwise the closure of bank credit is inevitable. Putting this reasoning in its simplest possible form, we may say that no country can allow itself to register negative current-account balances year after year without irremediably losing its credit worthiness. The United States, however, has not been subject to this constraint, . . . In the end, the dollar standard seems to have accentuated American seigniorage. As we shall soon see, unlimited exploitation of seigniorage by the United States could once again raise the confidence problem in relation to the dollar, and thus could encourage the rise of reserve assets alternative to the dollar. Before exploring these possibilities and considering what efforts the United States will make to prevent them from becoming reality, however, let us examine the consequences of the American deficits for world monetary and economic equilibrium.

THE AMERICAN PAYMENT DEFICITS

During the 1970s official American liabilities rose by about $15 thousand million a year, whereas the average annual increase during the previous twenty years had been about $600 million; the annual increase thus soared twenty-five fold. The seventies marked a new phase, both quantitatively and qualitatively, in the exercise of American seigniorage over the supply of reserves.

The post-war period can be conveniently divided into three phases, roughly corresponding to the three decades elapsed. During the first two phases—the fifties and sixties—the advantages that accrued to the United States consequent to its seigniorage were partially neutralized by the profits garnered by the rest of the world. As a recent taxonomy of systems of international economic organization put it, the United States exercised 'leadership' over the world economy. On the one hand, during the period 1950 to 1970 the US always maintained a current-account surplus, in particular in its trade balance. Moreover, the US authorities allowed this surplus to be less than it could have been, permitting their economic partners to devalue their own money relative to the dollar and to maintain discriminatory practices against American goods for long periods. On the other hand, during an initial phase the United States used this trade surplus, and in part its ability to issue international reserve money, to finance the accumulation of reserves by the rest of the world through a programme of transfers through aid and military assistance. In other words, the United States provided the world with the 'collective blessing' of economic stability while extracting no direct advantages for its own economy, but only indirect gains such as those produced by the general political reinforcement of the Western world made possible by the post-war economic boom and the development of trade on a grand scale. During a second phase, which began toward the end of the 1950s, the United States supplied the rest of the world with reserves no longer through transfers in the form of aid, but mainly through direct investment, the expansion of its own industry in foreign markets, especially Canada and the countries of Western Europe. During this second phase, American leadership, which had previously been based on consent, began to evolve into hegemony, and to provoke reactions from other countries that felt excluded from the benefits of seigniorage.

The third phase has been marked by a complete absence of any legitimation of American power. In reality, the United States no longer provides the collective blessing of world economic stability, but instead unhesitatingly pursues its own national interest, and has thus become the principal source of perturbation of the international economy. . . . During the first nine years of the 1970s, the United States ran up a current-account deficit of more than $30 thousand million. The current-account deficit depends essentially on the trade deficit, which reached the cumulative total of $70 thousand million, compared with a surplus of $40 thousand million over the preceding twenty years. . . .

In reality, the American deficits were caused by large and rising oil imports. In 1971, the United States, which until 1970 had been 90% self-sufficient in energy, began to increase its oil imports consequent to a decline in domestic production that lowered the percentage of total requirements met by national sources to slightly more than 50% by the end of the decade. American oil imports, . . . have risen continuously to attain the present figure of 8–9 million barrels a day, or 30% of total OPEC production, a total value of more than $40 thousand million in 1978. Because of their high oil exports, the producing countries are naturally able to sustain an enormous level of imports, of which the United States is the prime beneficiary. Indeed, the United States occupies first place in trade with the OPEC members, supplying something like 15% of their total imports. But despite this, the United States has not managed to cover the value of its oil imports and has thus incurred a large deficit with the OPEC countries. This, in large part, accounts for the overall trade deficit. . . .

The American trade deficit does not impel the world economy forward, but on the contrary is the direct cause of disorder in international financial relations, which in turn gives rise to the imbalance in economic relations and the recession now racking the world economy. Without the enormous US oil imports, the OPEC cartel would be unable to sustain itself. Now, the United States has little difficulty paying for oil imports on the order of $40 thousand million a year (or even more, as prices continue to rise), because it enjoys the privilege of paying for its imports in its own national currency: the United States is therefore not subject to balance of payments constraints. During the sixties, fear of the massive conversion of foreign dollar-holdings prevented the United States from taking advantage of this privilege. In the seventies, however, the introduction of the dollar standard allowed the United States to ignore foreign constraints completely. It is too early to tell whether fear of a possible currency crisis in the eighties triggered by a massive conversion of dollars into alternative reserve assets will once again place limits on the unbridled exercise of American seigniorage. . . .

The American deficits are not limited exclusively to items of trade, although the trade deficit probably has the greatest effects on the world economy, by propping up the high price of oil. . . .

There have also been rising deficits in capital flows for direct investment and in shifts of banking funds. Even though the influx of foreign capital to the United States has risen enormously (to the point that the stock of foreign investments, which had amounted to $13 thousand million in 1970, had risen to $40 thousand million by the end of 1978), the deficit in these capital flows in the 1970s approximately doubled compared with the average level of the 1960s. This testifies to a continuing expansion in American investment abroad. US capital, while continuing to flow toward its preferred destinations (Canada and Western Europe), is beginning massively to penetrate the manufacturing sector of those developing countries that have attained a certain degree of industrialization.

Finally, movements of bank capital, which were favourable to the United States during the sixties, partly because of the control system, showed a mounting negative balance in the seventies. This reflects the great foreign expansion of the American banking system. The ten largest US banks now derive more than 50% of their profits from international transactions. Since they are freely able to tap their own money markets in order to grant credit abroad, the American banks command a substantial edge over their competitors. US banks are now using this edge in an attempt to undermine London's role as the principal home of the Eurodollar. Indeed, for several years now the growth sector of the Euromarket has shifted to the 'offshore markets' in Caribbean islands created by subsidiaries of American banks. The scale of what is coming to be called the North American Eurocurrency market quadrupled between 1973 and 1978, while the size of the London market merely doubled during the same period. Because they have no difficulty supplying funds, the American banks are recovering their absolute supremacy in international financial brokerage, which had been threatened at the beginning of the seventies by the mounting self-assertion of Swiss and German banks, aided by the revaluation of their currency.

A careful reading of the evolution of American balance of payments statements allows us to reconstruct the manner in which seigniorage was unscrupulously exploited to consolidate the power, competitivity, and predominance of the American economy throughout the world. Had the United States been bound by the evolution of its balance of payments the way other countries are, its economy could not have been directed as it was. Solutions to American economic problems would have had to be sought through agreements with other countries in an effort to safeguard the interests of all members of the world community, as well as international economic and monetary equilibrium. To use Kindleberger's terminology, the present system of organization of international monetary relations can no longer be qualified as 'leadership', no matter how degenerate. The United States no longer supplies the collective blessing of economic stability, but instead appropriates the resources of the rest of the world and stands at the root of the imbalances in the world economy that have produced millions of unemployed and losses of accumulation. . . .

NOTES

1. ' "Europe and the Money Muddle" Revisited', Banca Nazionale del Lavoro, *Quarterly Review*, March 1978.
2. 'Remarks Before the International Monetary Conference—Mexico City, Mexico', *Department of the Treasury News*, 24 May 1978.

19. Third World Indebted Industrialization: International Finance and State Capitalism in Mexico, Brazil, Algeria, and South Korea

JEFF FRIEDEN

Jeff Frieden identifies and describes a recent strategy for Third World development, which he terms indebted industrialization. *Rather than reduce their international economic entanglements, some countries actively bind themselves to the international economy so as to exploit any opportunities for rapid development. The strategy of indebted industrialization called for massive foreign borrowing and enhanced the pivotal position of the state, the primary conduit for this flow of funds, in the development process. Frieden examines four cases and relates the changes in and success of development to the strategy of indebted industrialization. He concludes by drawing together the common experiences of the four cases and argues that indebted industrialization is a major component of a more general long-term transformation of the world economy in which production is increasingly shifted to the Third World. In this 1981 essay, he demonstrates the importance of international finance to patterns of production and trade within the international political economy.*

The past few years have seen an upsurge of interest in the debt owed by the less developed countries (LDCs) to commercial banks. Yet most scholars, bankers, policy-makers, and journalists have focused on only one aspect of LDC debt, its implications for the international financial system. There has been little investigation of the impact of recent trends in Third World borrowing on the borrowing LDCs themselves—quite unlike the post-World War II spread of multinational corporations into the LDCs, which provoked a substantial literature on the effects of foreign direct investment on developing countries. Yet LDC commercial bank debt is not simply an accumulation of numbers on bank balance sheets, a highly sophisticated form of electronic game; it represents the most rapid, most concentrated, most massive flow of investment capital to the Third World in history.

. . . In the case of Latin America, private financial institutions have displaced multinational corporations and official aid over the last fifteen years as the most important source of foreign capital available to Third World countries. In the 1960s, in fact, foreign direct investment accounted for some 30 percent of the total flow of external financial resources to Latin America, while bank loans and bonds provided only 10 percent. In the 1970s banks and bondholders were responsible for 57 percent of this flow—up from an annual average of $214 million in the 1960s to $6.5 billion in the 1970s—while the multinationals' share had dropped to about 20 percent.

Multinational corporations brought modern industrial production to the Third World and integrated it into the international capitalist system; but they also unleashed a torrent of nationalistic economic and political forces within the most rapidly industrializing LDCs. Multinational corporations contributed to the training and mobilization of technicians, economists, and development planners, and called forth a political reaction that demanded and obtained a governmental commitment to concerted national economic development in these dozen or so LDCs. In the late 1960s governments in such widely varied countries as Algeria, Brazil, Mexico, and South Korea—in partnership with and financed by the international banks in a pattern of foreign *indirect* investment—began the systematic construction of integrated domestic economic structures. These nationalistic state-capitalist regimes have joined with the internationalist finance-capitalists of the Euromarkets: the banks provide the capital, the state provides the muscle and brains to force-march the countries involved into the industrialized world. This paper will examine the rise of bank debt-financed, government-led industrialization in the LDCs. It will analyze the interplay of international finance, the state sector, and industrial growth in the four countries mentioned above, and will attempt to point out the implications of the process for the LDCs and for the international capitalist system.

THE GROWTH OF LDC COMMERCIAL BANK DEBT

In the past ten years the debt owed by the governments, government agencies, state-owned industries, and state-supported enterprises in the less developed countries has exploded. In 1970, according to the World

Bank, the LDCs owed $63.9 billion to foreign creditors; by the end of 1978 they owed $313.5 billion. With the general expansion of LDC external public debt[1] came a change in the composition of LDC borrowing: more and more loans came from private sources, especially from those banks active on the Eurocurrency market. While in 1970 $3.5 billion was committed to the LDCs by international financial markets (exclusive of suppliers' credits), 23 percent of total commitments, by 1978 $43.8 billion, 57 percent of the total, was so committed. Even allowing for the galloping inflation of the 1970s, the LDCs' debt to bondholders and private financial institutions nearly tripled between 1970 and 1976. The picture is quite clear: since the late 1960s LDCs have borrowed more heavily than ever before, and more of this borrowing has been done from private banks than anyone had imagined possible.

Some of the reasons for this enormous growth are clear, and have been amply treated by other authors. Crucial, of course, was the internationalization of banking and the concurrent rise of the Euromarkets, a vast quantity of capital controlled by a handful of international banks. Also important was the impressive economic growth of several LDCs in the 1960s, often fueled by foreign direct investment, which made them more attractive credit risks for the banks. The rapid increase in the price of oil late in 1973 gave a tremendous push to a process that was already in motion. . . . On the one hand, Middle Eastern oil exporters deposited huge sums in the international banks—$49 billion between 1974 and 1976. On the other hand, the oil price rise and the world recession raised the import bill of the LDCs at the same time as it reduced their exports to customers in the recession-ridden advanced capitalist countries. Thus, while in 1973 the nonoil LDCs covered some 85 percent of their imports with exports, by 1975 exports paid for only 67 percent of imports. It is well known that those LDCs with access to the international financial markets made up much of the difference by borrowing from the banks. Meanwhile, the 1974/75 recession in the advanced capitalist countries reduced loan demand there. The international banks, faced with a mountain of OPEC deposits and dwindling corporate demand, began pursuing the more credit-worthy LDCs (and even some entirely uncreditworthy ones) aggressively.

It is worthwhile here to make a few points about LDC borrowing from private financial markets. First, borrowing by less developed countries from private investors in the advanced capitalist countries is not new. Brazil floated its first "Eurobond" on the London market in 1824, and by 1960 Latin American governments owed some two billion dollars to foreign bondholders and financiers, an amount equal to about one-quarter of their debt to all creditors. . . . Private lenders (excluding suppliers) were owed $2.4 billion by the LDCs in 1960; this figure had more than doubled, to $5.3 billion, by 1965. Borrowing by LDC governments from private lenders is not a new phenomenon, but its proportions since the late 1960s have been so large as to transform what was formerly a fairly insignificant provider of funds to a few favored borrowers into the single most important source of foreign investment capital available to dozens of LDCs.

Secondly, even today the vast majority of private lending to the LDCs is concentrated at both ends: some twenty-five to thirty international banks do the lion's share of the lending, and some fifteen countries do the lion's share of borrowing. Indeed, . . . five OPEC members (Venezuela, Algeria, Iran, Indonesia, and the United Arab Emirates) and ten other LDCs (Mexico, Brazil, South Korea, Argentina, the Philippines, Morocco, Chile, Taiwan, Malaysia, and Peru) accounted for some four-fifths of all the publicly announced Eurocurrency bank credits to LDCs between 1976 and 1979, even though they had less than one-quarter of the Third World's population. In fact, in that four-year period, according to Morgan Guaranty Trust's authoritative *World Financial Markets*, five countries (Mexico, Brazil, Venezuela, South Korea, and Algeria) with one-tenth of the total population of the Third World accounted for over half of all LDC Eurobank loans.

Thirdly, most commercial bank lending to the Third World is in the form of loans made to or guaranteed by the public or state sector of the LDCs. A brief look at listings of Eurocurrency credits indicates who the major borrowers are: some 80 percent to 90 percent of these loans are to the public sector, with the remainder being guaranteed by the state. In the state sector major borrowers are, in varying proportions according to the country, the central government or central bank itself, state-owned industrial enterprises and public utilities, and national development banks. For example, in 1978 Mexican borrowers obtained some $6.5 billion in Eurocurrency credits and bonds. Of this amount 40 percent went to public development banks, 34 percent to state-owned utilities and industry, 12 percent to the central government, 11 percent to a number of private industrial companies, and 3 percent to a private bank. In all, some 86 percent of the borrowed funds went to public entities. Thus, investment capital is usually administered or allocated by public officials in the borrowing country.

Finally, borrowing by the state sector reflects growing developmentalist and nationalist demands in the LDCs. In virtually all of the heavy-borrowing countries economic development is highly politicized, and public opinion demands both economic growth and a measure of economic autonomy. No matter what the ideological bent of the regime and no matter what its form, from the one-party states of Algeria and Mexico to the military junta of Brazil and the police states of South

Korea, Taiwan, and the Philippines, the government must satisfy these demands for rapid economic expansion. But the earlier reliance on multinational corporations is no longer sufficient to fund the development of an integrated national economy. On the one hand, foreign corporations are often unwilling to invest in key heavy industrial sectors where capital requirements are high and rates of return low. On the other, there is generally a local consensus embracing technocrats, businessmen, military men, and labor that some industries are too politically sensitive or too important to national security to entrust to foreigners. Yet the only available alternative to foreign direct investment is foreign indirect investment, bank loans channeled through the public sector and used to establish or expand domestically controlled public or publicly-supported enterprises. If in the past many LDC governments encouraged foreign corporate investment to build up a modern industrial sector, today more and more are themselves the major force in initiating, financing or intermediating the financing of, and often even managing productive investment in modern industry. In the pursuit of local control over local investment, the state has taken over; yet, paradoxically, this state involvement in the economy has been based on borrowing from foreign banks. In short, the state sectors in these LDCs have in effect been mortgaged to the Eurobanks, and both the banks and their client states have staked their fortunes on rapid national economic development.

The Cases

A full appreciation of the background to and implications of LDC borrowing can only come from a detailed examination of the LDCs themselves. The great mystery of LDC debt, after all, is not why the banks lend; clearly they do it to make a profit, and the "supply side" of bank lending has been amply documented and dissected. The real questions that remain are why the LDCs borrow, where the money goes, and what the capital invested has created. My attempt to answer these questions led me to investigate four of the heaviest borrowers on the Euromarket. They are four widely varied cases: Mexico, Brazil, Algeria, and South Korea, by 1976 accounting for about half of all LDC debt to financial markets. . . .

In each case I shall summarize the general development strategies followed and the role of foreign borrowing in these strategies. Special attention will be paid to the interaction between the state sector, private foreign and domestic enterprises, foreign loans, and local national development strategies.

Mexico. As in many less developed countries, the dynamics of economic development in Mexico have been determined by two overriding facts: the legitimacy of the ruling elite has depended on rapid economic growth with a minimum of overt foreign involvement, yet there has been a chronic shortage of domestic investment capital to finance this growth. The legacy of the Revolution demanded Mexican control over the Mexican economy, and the regime of President Lázaro Cárdenas (1934–1940) spurred national economic development by nationalizing the petroleum industry and the railroads, and creating the Federal Electricity Commission and a series of national development banks of which *Nacional Financiera* (Nafinsa) was to become the most important.

It was the World War II-related isolation from traditional suppliers of manufactured goods that forced the Mexican state to play an active role in industrial development. Between 1941 and 1946 nearly 60 percent of all investment came from the public sector, and public-sector investment continued near this level after the war was over. Most of this public investment was in infrastructure and such strategic heavy industries as steel, petroleum, and fertilizers, and it was coupled with a policy of high tariffs on imported consumer goods. The goal of the policy was to promote the domestic production of consumer necessities, and it was quite successful: while one-third of all nondurable consumer goods were imported in 1929, this was down to 7 percent by 1950, and the proportion of imports to total consumption of all manufactured goods (that is, including consumer durables and capital goods) dropped from 52 percent in 1929 to 31 percent in 1950.

Yet this import-substituting industrial growth was achieved at great cost. Because Mexican capitalists were too few and Mexican taxpayers too poor to provide the large amounts of investment capital needed for industrial growth, and foreign investors were either preoccupied by the war or scared off by the nationalizations of the 1930s, the government was forced to fire up its printing presses to finance these enormous capital investments. Continual deficit financing of public-sector investments was highly inflationary: between 1948 and 1954 the wholesale price index rose 8.4 percent a year, well over four times the U.S. rate, and, given Mexico's economic weakness and close ties to the United States, this forced a series of devaluations that reduced the value of the peso from over twenty cents in 1948 to eight cents in 1954. By the mid 1950s the limits of what has been called "inflationary growth" had been reached, and the government adopted the so-called "stabilizing growth" strategy in effect until 1970.

The two pillars of Mexico's "stabilizing growth," as an American observer has noted, were "a substantial and dynamic public sector . . . and an equally dynamic and very profitable private sector." Indeed, government involvement in the economy grew steadily, especially in heavy industry and mining: government outlays went from 4.1 percent of Gross Domestic Product (GDP) in 1952 to over 13 percent in 1970. Perhaps even more important was the government's financing of the private sector: in the 1950s and 1960s Nafinsa alone accounted for one-third to one-half of all loans to private industry.

Government policy also encouraged private investment in manufacturing, especially by foreign corporations. The low levels of taxation and high level of effective protection of the domestic market for manufacturing—74 percent by 1960 as against 3.9 percent for agriculture—made it highly profitable for Mexican and foreign industrial corporations to expand local production, often as government-encouraged oligopolies. Net foreign direct investment grew steadily from one billion pesos in 1954 to 2.7 billion pesos in 1965; assets of U.S. corporations in Mexico quintupled in the 1960s, with most of this growth in manufacturing.

Rapid industrialization, however, was not without problems. The country's balance of payments deficit grew rapidly as Mexican and foreign-owned corporations imported capital goods to run the new factories. A large portion of these imports had been financed by agricultural exports of the United States, but by the late 1960s rapid population growth and slow growth in the rural sector reduced the surplus available for export. The simplest available alternative was to encourage more foreign investment. Yet rapid industrial growth had also strengthened the domestic industrialists, who began in the late 1950s to object to the competition that local subsidiaries of foreign corporations represented. Faced with a pressing need to attract foreign capital and powerful domestic demands to limit foreign investment, the government began to curb multinational corporations while attracting foreign investment in the form of bank loans and international bond issues.

It was during the administration of Gustavo Díaz Ordaz (1964–1970) that Mexico began to borrow from the banks in earnest. By 1966 the state was borrowing more from private sources than from official sources (AID, Eximbank, the World Bank group, the Inter-American Development Bank, etc.) and by 1967 the international banks alone were providing more than all official sources; between 1965 and 1970 public sources loaned $1.5 billion to Mexico, suppliers and others $675 million, and private financial institutions $2.3 billion.

The subsequent administration of Luís Echeverría (1970–1976) inherited the problems of the thirty-year emphasis on import substitution: chronic balance of payments deficits, a distorted domestic market and inefficient domestic industries, reliance on imports of capital equipment, and highly inequitable income distribution. In an attempt to satisfy increasing demands for social programs, government controls on foreign corporations, and state support for economic development, Echeverría embarked on a massive expansion of government involvement in the economy. Restraints on multinational corporations, stiffened in the early 1960s, were stiffened still further with the passage in 1973 of the Law to Promote Mexican Investment and Regulate Foreign Investment and the Law on Transfer of Technology. And, accelerating the process begun under Díaz Ordaz, the government financed its increased activities with foreign borrowing. . . .

Between 1971 and 1976 Mexico's federal government budget deficit went from 4.8 billion pesos (1% of GDP) to 57.4 billion pesos (3.8% of GDP); public-sector investment, expressed in 1960 prices, more than doubled during that period while private investment increased only 16 percent. The number of state-owned corporations jumped from 86 in 1970 to 740 in 1976; today the public enterprises dominate the oil, electricity, steel, petrochemicals, banking, transportation, and communications industries, and the public sector accounts for some 45 percent of GDP. Although Echeverría's successor, José López Portillo, has undertaken to moderate both public expenditures and foreign borrowing, the economy remains heavily dependent on a state intervention that remains in turn heavily dependent on foreign borrowing. Thus in 1978 the fiscal deficit of the public sector was 162 billion pesos, of which 69.7 billion (43%) was financed by borrowing abroad; in the parastatal sector, which includes most of the public industrial enterprises, 86.6 percent of financing came from abroad. By the end of 1979 the Mexican government reported that its external debt was nearly $30 billion, the vast majority owed to private sources.

By the end of Echeverría's administration international bankers had begun to worry about Mexico's creditworthiness, but these worries have dissolved as the state oil company, Pemex, has revealed and begun to exploit huge reserves of petroleum. Indeed, petroleum exports have gone from less than 5 percent of total exports in 1974 to nearly 45 percent in 1979. Despite the oil bonanza, the government has continued Echeverría's attempts to increase the export of manufactured goods, most successfully in the machinery and transport equipment sectors where exports rose from $250 million in 1974 to $725 million in 1978.

No discussion of the nexus between Mexican industrial growth, the state sector, and the international banks would be complete without a look at *Nacional Financiera,* or "Nafinsa." Founded in 1934 Nafinsa is by now, in the words of its 1974 charter, "the most important investment bank in the country," with capital resources of 77.6 billion pesos (over $6 billion) in 1974. As well as providing about one-third of all financing available to Mexican industry, it holds shares in ninety-eight enterprises in virtually every sector of the economy except agriculture. The sixty-seven industrial enterprises in which Nafinsa holds equity are concentrated in basic industry and include companies in steel, machinery, mining, fertilizers, pharmaceuticals, petrochemicals, pulp and paper, textiles, and food products.

It is not surprising, given the Mexican government's liberal use of foreign borrowing to finance industrial development, that two-thirds of Nafinsa's financial resources come from abroad, the bulk from private banks. Indeed, at the end of 1975 Nafinsa was the most important Mexican debtor, holding about one-third of Mexico's external public debt, a proportion that has since fallen as Pemex has borrowed ever more heavily. The case of Nafinsa is perhaps the archetype of foreign indirect investment in Mexico: the international banks make loans to Nafinsa, Nafinsa uses the loans to finance productive investment deemed essential to Mexican industrial development, the borrower invests the funds, earns a profit, repays the loan to Nafinsa, and Nafinsa repays the banks.

The beauty of the arrangement is obvious: it provides the Mexican government with funds to be disbursed to capital-hungry Mexican industrialists, it allows the state to mold the economy, and it avoids the political difficulties caused by the multinational corporations. The international banks get their profits, the Mexican capitalists get their investment capital, and the Mexican government preserves domestic legitimacy by providing funds for economic growth and protection from foreign corporations.

Brazil. In many ways the history of Brazil's industrial growth is very similar to that of Mexico's. As in Mexico, industrialization in Brazil began in the late 1930s and 1940s, and was based on import substitution and the creation of public corporations to provide basic inputs necessary for modern industry. In Brazil, the 1937–1945 Estado Novo government of Getúlio Vargas oversaw the process: during World War II the national steel corporation was founded and construction begun on Latin America's first integrated steel mill, and government mining, automotive, and caustic soda corporations were formed. Extremely high tariff barriers were erected, and by 1949 96.3 percent of all consumer nondurables were produced locally; by 1955 even consumer durables were 90 percent domestically manufactured.

Government intervention continued during Vargas's second administration in the early 1950s. In 1953 and 1954 the public development bank Banco Nacional de Desenvolvimento Economico (BNDE) and the national petroleum monopoly Petrobrás were created, along with a series of regional development banks and power companies. State-supported industrial growth picked up steam under Kubitschek (1956–1960), whose regime created a series of public enterprises in steel, electric power, and transportation. While in the early 1950s the public sector's share of gross fixed capital investment was 25 percent, Kubitschek's program of massive infrastructural construction increased this to 48 percent by 1960. At the same time, foreign manufacturing corporations were encouraged to establish subsidiaries, and $100 million a year in foreign direct investment entered the country, an amount equal to 10 percent of total investment. All the while, protectionism remained the rule; by 1966, before a liberalizing reform, effective protection of finished consumer goods averaged 190 percent.

As in Mexico, the result of government intervention, high tariff protection, and encouragement to foreign investors was rapid industrial growth: between 1949 and 1961 manufacturing output more than tripled, growing from 22 percent of GDP to 34 percent. Yet by the early 1960s import substitution was reaching its limits, as domestic producers supplied over 90 percent of all manufactured goods and even two-thirds of all capital goods by 1959. In addition, rapid economic growth had been financed by huge government deficits in a process similar to Mexico's "inflationary growth" of the early 1950s. The result was rampant inflation, which could not be controlled by the populist Goulart government (1961–1964). The economy stagnated from 1962 to 1968, and Brazil's economic problems contributed to the political turmoil of the early 1960s and to a right-wing reaction, which culminated in the military coup that overthrew Goulart in 1964.

The military government began almost immediately to orient the economy to the foreign sector. Coffee had always been the country's most important export, an important source of foreign exchange, while manufactured goods accounted for below 5 percent of total exports between 1946 and 1964. In order to make Brazilian manufactures more competitive on the world market, in 1967 the military regime reduced the effective protection of manufactured goods to half its former level, and in 1968 began to subsidize manufactured exports at a rate equal to between 19 percent and 30 percent of their value. Exports soared from $1.9 billion in 1968 to $2.7 billion in 1970 to $6.2 billion in 1973, and were $15.2 billion in 1979 of which industrial products constituted 56.2 percent.

In addition to the promotion of manufacturing for export, two essential components of the government's industrialization strategy were the encouragement of foreign direct investment, which averaged over one billion dollars a year in the past decade, and the rapid growth of the public sector, financed in large part by borrowing abroad. Total foreign direct investment is now about $15 billion, and foreign-owned corporations dominate the transport equipment, pharmaceutical, rubber product, and machinery sectors. Nevertheless, the relative importance of foreign corporations in the Brazilian economy has declined as the role of the state has grown and, in the words of a leading business weekly, "the government has in recent years thrown an increasing number of restrictions around foreign investment."

The Brazilian public sector is truly impressive. The twenty-five largest corporations in the country are stated-owned (number 26 is Mercedes-Benz of Brazil), and public enterprises accounted for 78 percent of the assets of the country's two hundred largest companies in 1978, up from 64 percent in 1972. The corresponding share of foreign corporations dropped from 20 percent to 9 percent in this period, while that of domestic private firms dropped from 16 percent to 13 percent. Of the 6,430 nonfinancial corporations included in this authoritative annual compilation of Brazil's largest firms, the 382 public enterprises accounted for 51 percent of assets, foreign firms for 11 percent, and private domestic firms for 38 percent.

The Brazilian government has also come to play the dominant role in domestic investment financing. In 1974 government sources, especially the Banco do Brasil and the BNDE, accounted for three-quarters of all investment capital provided to the private sector. In the words of Wilson Suzigan, a researcher at the government's Institute for Economic and Social Planning, "the State is directly or indirectly responsible for virtually all loans to the private sector for investment purposes."[2] All in all, the state now accounts for some 60 percent of all investments in the economy.

As in the case of Mexico, this massive government intervention has depended in large part on loans from the international banks. Borrowing on the Euromarkets has increased rapidly since 1969, both to finance major state-sector investments and to compensate for Brazil's post-oil-crisis balance of payments deficit. Since the late 1960s Brazil has alternated with Mexico as the most important LDC borrower on the Euromarket, with most of the loans going to Petrobrás, the public steel corporations, public utilities, and various development banks. In 1979 alone, Brazil raised some $5.8 billion in Eurocurrency bank loans and over $900 million in Eurobonds.

The story of Brazil's public external debt, then, is first and foremost—as in Mexico—the story of a steadily growing state sector in need of ever-larger sums of investment capital. Because our next case is Algeria, a nation with a radical ruling group, it is important to emphasize that in Brazil and Mexico the establishment and growth of the state sector was not an ideological but a pragmatic phenomenon. As Suzigan wrote of the Brazilian state sector, "its expansion had a very atypical 'ideology,' that of priority to growth, developing those sectors which private initiative was unable or unwilling to develop." The fact is simply that in Brazil and Mexico the political legitimacy of the regime has depended on the state's ensuring rapid economic growth. Since local businessmen are unwilling or unable to raise the capital necessary to develop heavy industries, and many of these sectors are not profitable enough or too politically sensitive to be left to the multinationals, the government has been virtually forced to play a leading role in basic industrial development. This role would be impossible without the huge sums provided by international financial markets.

Algeria. In Algeria the process of industrial investment carried out by the state with funds provided by international financiers is particularly clear. The Algerian state sector is all-encompassing, with domestic private enterprise permitted only in some portions of agriculture, trade, and light industry. The public corporations have borrowed extensively on the Euromarkets since 1970 to finance massive industrial investments. The nation's development strategy has been quite consistent since the mid 1960s, and it is based on the use of earnings from Algeria's petroleum and natural gas exports, supplemented by overseas borrowing, to build up modern hydrocarbons and basic industrial sectors. The goal is to create an integrated industrial system in order to guarantee economic independence.

The revolutionary regime of Ben Bella, which took power in 1962, inherited an economy decimated by colonialism, eight years of revolutionary war, counterrevolutionary sabotage, and the exodus of virtually all trained personnel and capital. The first few years of independence were dedicated primarily to reconstruction and were characterized by intense political struggles. In 1965 Colonel Houari Boumedienne overthrew Ben Bella and it was not until 1969 that Boumedienne consolidated his rule by defeating both rebellious tribal leaders and ultraleftist trade unionists and students.

The state began almost immediately to concentrate the commanding heights of the economy in its hands. In 1966 and 1967 mining, insurance, the local distribution networks of British Petroleum, Esso, and Mobil, and former colonial landholdings were nationalized, and three national deposit banks were created. In 1968 most remaining foreign-owned businesses were nationalized, state monopolies were established in the steel, chemicals, and textile industries, and the state navigation company began a program of rapid expansion. In 1970 the local holdings of Shell, Phillips, and two other foreign oil companies were nationalized; and in 1971 the two remaining French producers (CFP and ERAP) were taken over by the state hydrocarbons enterprise, SONATRACH, along with the country's pipelines and natural gas deposits. The government now controls every significant sector of the economy—even the most productive agricultural lands are in the public or "self-managed" sectors. The private sector is still important, accounting for 50 percent of agricultural production, 60 percent of construction, 65 percent of textile production, and 80 percent of commerce. Yet private business is almost exclusively to be found in farming, trade, and backward, labor-intensive light industries: with 40 percent of industrial-sector sales and 30 percent of industrial value-added in 1977, private businesses made less than 3 percent of the country's industrial investments and held less than 12 percent of industrial assets.

Virtually all industrial and even much agricultural investment, then, is made either by the central government or by the state enterprises, and public investment has emphasized industry—particularly heavy industry. In the 1967–1969 "pre-plan," which began industrial growth, 52 percent of government expenditures went to industry, of which 90 percent went to heavy industry, especially hydrocarbons and steel. But public investments began to soar with the first four-year plan (1970–1973), during which 27.9 billion dinars ($5.9 billion) were invested by the state, 44 percent in industry and 86 percent of this in heavy industry. The second four-year plan (1974–1977) was even more ambitious, and total expenditures were over 126 billion dinars (about $31 billion); again, 52 percent of this went to industry, 88 percent of this to heavy industry. Between 1970 and 1977, 270 new factories and 150 infrastructural projects were completed, and GDP went from $8.0 billion in 1973 to $21.8 billion in 1978. The hydrocarbons sector has predominated since the mid 1960s, and by 1977 it accounted for 29 percent of GDP. Meanwhile, industry and construction have grown rapidly; from below 15 percent of GDP in the early 1960s they have been around 25 percent since 1970. Manufacturing output, barely $300 million in 1967, was $2.2 billion in 1977, and this figure does not include hydrocarbons or construction. It is true that much of agriculture remains backward and much of industry inefficient, and that social welfare has been of lower priority than industrialization—which has led the post-Boumedienne government of Chadli Benjedid to place greater emphasis on agriculture and the production of consumer goods. Nevertheless it is beyond doubt that the Algerian economy sped towards industrial maturity in the 1970s.

This remarkable program of public investments and state-sector industrial growth was made possible primarily by Algeria's vast petroleum and natural gas reserves. Crude petroleum exports have been around fifty million tons a year for a decade, but the country's most important resource is natural gas, with the third largest estimated reserves in the world (three trillion cubic meters). Hydrocarbons account for over 90 percent of the country's exports, an estimated $10 billion in 1979. Still, the government's ambitious development plans have led it to the Euromarkets, and the international banks have been more than willing to make huge loans to a country with great exportable reserves of oil and gas. The government, for its part, has demonstrated a willingness to pursue productive investment seriously: for several years gross fixed investment has been over 50 percent of GDP, a figure that is probably without parallel anywhere in the world.

Since 1970 Algeria has borrowed massively from the international banks. The country's debt owed to financial markets went from $129 million in 1971 to just short of $2 billion in 1973, and borrowing has continued to climb. In 1978 and 1979 Algeria borrowed over five billion dollars in bank loans and bonds, and the current external public debt is about $19 billion. The most important Algerian borrower is SONA-TRACH, which needs enormous amounts of capital to finance the construction of new pipelines, refineries, and liquid natural gas plants. Other big borrowers are the national shipping company (CNAN), to expand the state's fleet; the national, foreign commerce, and consumer credit banks; and the state corporations in steel, hydraulic and construction material, electrical machinery, textiles, and chemical production.

In many ways the partnership between Algeria's regime and the banks is ironic. The Algerian government is one of the more radical in the Third World. Foreign direct investment is prohibited, although the state corporations eagerly solicit participation by foreign investors in joint ventures. And while the regime is strongly antiimperialist, and proclaims its chief domestic task to be the transition from the current state-capitalist system to socialism, it has recognized the utility of close economic relations with imperialist finance: as Boumedienne said in 1974, "the socialist countries have dealings with us on the basis of friendship. The capitalist countries have dealings with us on the basis of money."[3] The international bankers seem understanding, even appreciative: in the words of one candid banker, "We like Algeria because it's totalitarian and if the government says people will have to cut back consumption, they will."[4] The relationship, as in our previous examples, is symbiotic—although Algeria's hydrocarbons place it in a more favorable position than Brazil's. The banks make their profits on loans to the Algerian state sector and the regime relies on foreign financiers for about one-fifth of its investment capital. Between the two they are industrializing Algeria.

South Korea. Industrial growth in the Republic of Korea (South Korea) has been markedly different from that in our first three cases. In Korea, perhaps due to the need for a high level of ideological commitment to the letter if not the spirit of "free enterprise," government intervention in the economy has been less direct than in Brazil, Mexico, or Algeria. Secondly, Korean industrialization has been characterized by a single-minded and all-encompassing focus on the manufacture of industrial products for export, and the desire for more balanced industrial development has been subordinate to the incessant drive to export. Finally, while foreign capital has been crucial to the South Korean economy since World War II, the form of this capital inflow has been unusual, with a low level of foreign direct investment until recently, and very high levels of foreign aid due to the country's strategic importance to the United States and Japan.

The industrial development policy, such as it was, of the Syngman Rhee government of the 1950s emphasized the substitution of nondurable consumer goods. Economic development as a whole was entirely dependent on foreign aid, which financed three-quarters of total investment between 1953 and 1963. By the late 1950s the primitive import-substitution process had reached its limits, and economic stagnation set in. This, coupled with Rhee's legendary corruption and inefficiency, led to a student rebellion in May 1960, after which a civilian government came to power. Less than a year later Park Chung Hee led a military coup, and Park was officially "elected" President early in 1964. Throughout the 1960–1965 period, in the words of a western economist, "the entire orientation of trade and exchange-rate policy shifted. The Korean economy was restructured toward export promotion and away from the earlier emphasis on import substitution."[5]

The 1964–1966 period saw a series of major changes in economic policy: an income tax reform raised government revenues, interest rates were hiked to raise domestic saving, and a series of export incentives and subsidies was introduced. At the same time the normalization of relations with Japan in 1965, the passage of a new Foreign Capital Inducement Law in 1966, and government encouragement of overseas borrowing brought hundreds of millions of dollars in previously unavailable private commercial loans into the country. Net indebtedness went from $301 million in 1965 to $2.57 billion in 1970, and by the late 1960s two-thirds of the loans were from private sources, primarily as suppliers' credits. It has been estimated that without this massive influx of foreign capital in the 1960s, Korean output in 1971 would have been smaller by one-third.

As it was, streamlined domestic financial markets, state intervention, and foreign capital did the trick: Gross National Product (GNP, expressed in 1970 prices) grew from 1.5 trillion won in 1965 to 2.6 trillion won in 1970 to 4.1 trillion won in 1975. This growth was paced by manufacturing, which accounted for 40 percent of GNP growth while increasing its share of value-added from 14 percent in 1965 to 32 percent in 1976. Manufacturing growth in turn was due in large part to exports: the growth in exports was directly (i.e., without considering backward linkages or multiplier effects) responsible for 25 percent of manufacturing expansion. Exports, indeed, grew from $39 million in 1961 to $175 million in 1965, then $385 million in 1970, $5.08 billion in 1975, and some $15 billion in 1979. The composition of the country's exports also changed rapidly, from raw materials to light manufactures, and more recently towards heavy industrial products. In 1960 only 12.5 percent of exports were manufactured; by 1970 this proportion was up to 76 percent, and in 1978 they were 90 percent of all exports. In 1978 heavy industrial exports, insignificant before 1970, were 38.4 percent of all exports, and Korean firms sold 33,000 automobiles and $750 million worth of steel overseas in the year. The government's huge Pohang Iron and Steel Company now has a capacity of 5.5 million tons, making the Korean steel industry the world's twelfth largest; the Hyundai conglomerate, which is number ninety-eight on the *Fortune* list of the world's five hundred largest non-American industrial corporations, operates the world's largest corporate shipyard in Ulsan and is building the world's largest integrated machinery plant in Changwon.

Much of South Korea's industrial growth can be traced to the interaction of foreign capital inflows and government intervention, both direct and indirect. As we have noted, foreign direct investment was insignificant before 1965; by the end of 1978, as corporations took advantage of cheap labor, government incentives, and free-export zones, it was up to $940 million, and between 1970 and 1975 accounted for 17 percent of all manufacturing investment. Foreign corporate investments are primarily of Japanese origin and are concentrated in manufacturing, especially in chemicals, electronics, and textiles; by 1974 some 31 percent of manufactured exports were produced by subsidiaries of foreign firms. Nevertheless, foreign loans are a much more important source of investment capital: while foreign direct investment between 1970 and 1975 was $700 million, net borrowing was $3.7 billion. Foreign loans have been concentrated in some of the same export-oriented manufacturing sectors as foreign direct investment, as well as in nonmetallic minerals, steel, transport equipment, and petroleum. All in all, according to South Korea's Minister of Finance, foreign capital financed 40 percent of investment between 1962 and 1972.

The South Korean state has played a major role in spurring industrial development. For one thing, the government has encouraged economic concentration in the interests of export-competing efficiency and has close ties with the huge conglomerates that do the bulk of South Korea's manufacturing and exporting: Hyundai, Samsung, Daewoo, and their like. The conglomerates and their affiliated trading companies are enticed and persecuted into continually increasing exports, and, in the words of one business magazine, their "intimacy with government policymakers . . . makes 'Japan, Inc.' seem like economic anarchy."[6] In the 1970s direct and indirect subsidies, and tax and tariff incentives to exporters were equal to nearly one-quarter of the value of all exports, and the national medal of honor is awarded each year to the country's leading exporter. But the state's role goes beyond that of export incentives and encompasses the entire economy.

An exhaustive study of the Korean public sector published in 1975 concluded that "public enterprises clearly constituted a leading sector during the period of rapid Korean growth," and also noted that:

> the Korean public enterprises sector . . . [is] surprisingly large, considering the government's capitalistic ideological orientation. The inertia of historical antecedent can explain only a fraction of the paradox. Much more can be explained in terms of President Park's devotion to economic growth and the role of public ownership and control in overcoming various forms of private market imperfection. . . . [7]

The number of public enterprises grew rapidly in the late 1960s, from 59 in 1965 to 119 in 1969, while the value-added of the parastatal sector (in 1970 prices) grew from 90.6 billion won in 1964 to 271.7 billion won in 1972, from 6.8 percent of GDP to 10 percent. The public sector as a whole accounted for about 18 percent of GDP by 1972. State involvement was concentrated in manufacturing, finance, transportation and communications, and utilities. By 1972 Korea's public enterprises, both central government and parastatal, had 200,000 employees and an output of 870 billion won ($2.2 billion). All told, the Korean public sector is responsible for between one-third and one-half of all investments in the economy. Eurocurrency loans have been important in maintaining high levels of government investment, and among the public enterprises the utilities and the huge Pohang Iron and Steel Corporation have been major borrowers.

The Korean state's most important economic tool is in the realm of finance. Between 1963 and 1973 the government and its corporations accounted for around two-thirds of all financial intermediation. There is an extensive network of specialized state banks, with almost half of all loans outstanding in 1976; the Korean Development Bank (KDB) alone provides half of all financing to the country's capital goods industries. The specialized banks, especially the KDB and the Korean Exchange Bank, have borrowed extensively on the Euromarkets for relending to domestic businesses.

In order to expand production rapidly, the state has also actively encouraged private businesses to borrow heavily both at home and abroad. Indeed, Korea is unusual in that a good half of its external debt is owed by private firms; the public sector provides only a guarantee to the lender. As a result, Korean companies are among the most highly leveraged in the world, with debt-to-equity ratios of 5:1 and 6:1 not uncommon.

In brief, in South Korea, as in Algeria, Brazil, and Mexico, the government has served as an intermediary between international financial markets and local productive investment. As one Korean official put it, "the emphasis on increases in production and export have [sic] placed

almost all industries under the government's protection and support."
Whether its role has been to encourage foreign borrowing by private
firms, to borrow abroad itself for relending at home, or to have public
corporations borrow for capital investment, the South Korean state and
its foreign financiers have played a crucial role in pushing the economy
along the road of export-led industrialization at a dizzying pace.

CONCLUSIONS AND IMPLICATIONS

The experiences of industrial growth in our four cases are quite varied.
In Algeria and South Korea, the smallness of the local market led to a
heavy emphasis on exports—of hydrocarbons in the one and manufactures in the other—to fuel industrialization. Brazil and Mexico, with
larger domestic markets and more mature industrial structures, pursued
more balanced paths, although both have rapidly increased exports in
the process. Despite these differences a number of themes seem to be
common to all four examples of indebted industrialization.

In all four cases industrial production has grown by any measure very
rapidly. Output has expanded, the industrial structure has diversified,
and modern production techniques have been mastered.

Second, the relative importance of direct investment by multinational
corporations in these economies is on the decline. Foreign direct
investment provided a major impetus for industrial growth, and multinational corporations remain crucial in those very important sectors
where they have access to otherwise unavailable capital, technology,
expertise, and markets. Nevertheless, the process of industrialization,
which foreign corporations did much to initiate, has increased both the
desire for and the possibility of increased local private and public sector
participation in industrial growth. Furthermore, there is increasing
evidence that as local businessmen and technocrats increase their economic and political strength they favor tighter controls over foreign
corporations.

Third, the place of the multinational corporations as the main
provider of foreign capital has been taken by the international banks.
Each of the four countries is heavily dependent on foreign borrowing
for its economic growth.

Fourth, the central roles of overseer of industrial growth and intermediary between foreign financiers and domestic productive investment
have been played by the public sector. Under the pressure of local
demands for national economic development the state, allied with
foreign finance, has been the leading force in the economy.

In all cases the concurrent growth in industrial production and
external indebtedness has led to very rapid increases in exports—in all

but Algeria, of manufactured products, especially but not exclusively consumer goods.

The picture that emerges is clear. The dozen or so nations that have embarked to date on indebted industrialization have by so doing tied their fortunes more tightly than ever before to international trade, investment, and finance. Their state sectors have joined with the international financial empires to spur industrial growth and, in the process, increase their manufactured exports to the advanced capitalist countries. As these few select LDCs pile up industrial projects and bank debt the relative importance of multinational corporations has been reduced, although they still play a significant role in these rapidly industrializing economies.

Indebted industrialization is a major component of the more general long-term transformation of the world's economy. More and more manufacturing production is taking place in the Third World, and much of this increased manufacturing capacity is made possible, directly or indirectly, by increased manufactured exports to the Organization for Economic Cooperation and Development (OECD) area. We may take as exemplary the ten non-OPEC LDCs that have borrowed most heavily, and find that their exports soared from $820 million in 1965 to $24.4 *billion* in 1977. In 1965 these ten countries accounted for 32 percent of all LDC manufactured exports; by 1975 they accounted for 67 percent. By 1975 the Third World was responsible for about one-fifth of all the manufactured imports of the advanced capitalist countries, and in certain sectors the proportion was much higher; LDCs accounted for over 80 percent of all U.S. imports of clothing, 61 percent of footwear, 43 percent of textiles, and 42 percent of electrical machinery. Over half of the entire western European market (i.e., imports plus domestic production) for men's shirts is supplied by LDCs; about half of all radios and black and white television sets purchased by U.S. consumers are manufactured in the Third World.

In a general sense, OECD imports of manufactured products from the LDCs remain quite low, and nearly four-fifths of these imports are concentrated in just fifteen product lines—hardly a serious challenge to the industrial West. Yet in a more immediate sense, the growth in LDC manufactured exports comes at a time of, and has contributed to, stagnation in some of the corresponding industrial sectors in the OECD countries: textiles, clothing, footwear, electrical machinery, and, increasingly, steel. The heavily indebted, rapidly industrializing LDCs cannot service their debt without selling their manufactured products in OECD markets, but the uncompetitive manufacturers of these products in the OECD countries themselves cannot survive without excluding LDC exports. One or the other must cede: either the uncompetitive OECD producers in these sectors must resign themselves to a slow decline as the locus of production shifts, or they must erect ever-higher protectionist barriers to save their domestic markets, a choice that will almost certainly bring about economic disaster for their LDC competitors. Given the rising strength of protectionism in the advanced capitalist countries the latter course of events might seen inevitable; yet we should not forget that indebted industrialization is a two-sided affair, involving both debtors and creditors. The international banks have as much of a stake in LDC access to OECD markets as the LDCs themselves, for without this access the banks' clients cannot service their debt. The same holds true for those multinational corporations that have become truly international and rely heavily on the free flow of capital and commodities.

This conflict will be a major issue in the international economic disputes of the 1980s. For if the 1970s saw an industrialization of many LDCs predicated on free access to Northern markets, this very process gave impetus to forces that are fighting to limit access. Manufacturers in threatened sectors—and their allies in the labor movement—may succeed in protecting their markets, but such success will call into question both continued economic growth in the LDCs and stability in international financial markets. Alternatively, the international financiers and corporations, allied with their LDC clients, may succeed in preserving LDC access to markets in the advanced capitalist countries, but this success—while it may bring about a significant reordering of international trade and production—will be achieved at the expense of many traditional OECD industries. In either case—or in the event of some form of compromise between, on the one hand, LDC elites and international financiers who have staked their fortunes on rapid Third World industrialization and, on the other, threatened OECD manufacturers whose market shares and fortunes are equally at stake—the international economic and political system will have been transformed by the process of indebted industrialization.

NOTES

1. External public debt will be defined here as debt owed to foreign creditors payable in foreign currency, with a maturity of over one year, by governments, government agencies, public entities or private entities guaranteed for repayment by the government. Throughout this paper, the debt we are speaking of is of this kind—it does not include debts owed to domestic financial institutions (even when these are subsidiaries of foreign financial institutions), nor does it include debts owed by private sources not guaranteed by the government.

2. Wilson Suzigan, "As empresas do governo e o papel do estado na economia brasileira," in Fernando Rezende et al., Aspectos da participação do governo na economia (Rio de Janeiro: IPEA/INPES, 1976), pp. 113–15.

3. Quoted in *State Capitalism in Algeria* (Washington: MERIP, 1975), p. 8.

4. Quoted in "Algeria: The country that bankers love to hate," *Euromoney,* October 1977, p. 65.

5. Anne O. Krueger, *Studies in the Modernization of the Republic of Korea, 1945–1975: The Developmental Role of the Foreign Sector and Aid* (Cambridge: Harvard University Press, 1979), p. 82.

6. Harvey Shapiro, "Is South Korea's economic miracle in trouble?" *Institutional Investor International Edition*, May 1979, p. 122.

7. Leroy P. Jones, *Public Enterprise and Economic Development: The Korean Case* (Seoul: Korea Development Institute, 1975), p. 202.

20.   The International Organization of Third World Debt

CHARLES LIPSON

In this reading, originally published in 1981, Charles Lipson examines the international regime for Third World debt, which has thus far prompted debt service by countries even when they found it onerous to continue payments. Unlike other international regimes, the debt regime is composed not of sovereign nation-states, but of private commercial banks and the International Monetary Fund (IMF). The regime is extraordinarily effective in ensuring repayment of international loans by sovereign countries, Lipson argues, because of the "intrinsic sanction" available to the banks and IMF of denying access to further credit. The regime, in other words, is built "not on state power but on private sanctions and multilateral oversight." While beginning from the Realist perspective, Lipson generally agrees with the Liberals that within this issue area nation-states appear subordinate to the demands of the international market. Ongoing attempts to manage LDC debt have seen the IMF buffeted by pressure from international banks, their home governments, and debtor governments. The theoretical issues raised by Lipson are thus quite pertinent to current attempts to maintain a stable debt regime.

Throughout the 1970s Third World states borrowed heavily from international banks. Faced with sharply higher costs for energy and manufactured imports, many states aggressively entered the market for commercial loans. The most creditworthy, from Brazil to Korea and

Taiwan, have used these funds to offset their growing current-account deficits while maintaining relatively strong economic growth. But with the world economy sagging and interest payments rising, many less developed countries (LDCs) must cope with enormous debt burdens.

The size of these debts and the financial trouble they pose can be illustrated briefly. In 1970 the twelve largest nonoil LDC borrowers paid $1.1 billion in interest on their external debt, which amounted to slightly more than 6 percent of their export earnings. In 1980, by contrast, their interest payments totaled $18.4 billion and absorbed over 14 percent of export earnings. These still-mounting figures lead some economists to warn of serious debt problems as early as 1982 or 1983. Already some weaker economies, from Zaïre to Jamaica, have failed to meet repayment schedules; the largest recent case was Turkey, whose $3 billion debt had to be rescheduled in 1980. Overhanging all these cases are potential problems in much larger borrowers like Brazil, which owes over $60 billion and has interest payments equivalent to one-third of its exports. International lenders are beginning to feel nervous about debts like these and commercial banks, in particular, have substantial sums to worry about: over $170 billion in outstanding loans to oil-importing LDCs.

This mountain of debt was built mainly in the offshore capital markets. The astounding growth of these markets is one of the most striking developments in the modern world economy—barely noticeable in 1960, they had two decades later a gross size of nearly $1.5 *trillion*. Their rapid growth, which continues, began in the mid 1960s as depositors, borrowers, and major banks all learned to exploit their unique advantages. Their main advantage is lower cost, due mostly to less regulation. Domestic banks in the U.S.A., for instance, are required to hold some assets idle as reserves but their offshore branches and subsidiaries operate under no such restrictions. They can earn returns on all their assets. As a result, they can profitably offer higher deposit rates and slightly lower loan charges than their domestic counterparts. This near-absence of costly regulations has proved a powerful attraction to most large financial intermediaries and their customers.

By 1973—the year of OPEC's embargo—the offshore markets had already become a prominent component of world capital markets. Yet the embargo and subsequent oil price hike were to have a substantial impact on their growth: they stimulated the demand for payments financing and led to a much larger role for Third World borrowers.

Oil-importing states in the Third World faced immediate and severe balance-of-payments problems as soon as oil prices quadrupled. To elect to reduce imports swiftly by austerity measures was a politically unattractive strategy that implied sharply lower growth. Many LDCs, especially those with ambitious development programs, chose to adjust more slowly: they maintained industrial growth and financed the ensuing deficits in the lowest-cost credit markets. This basic policy choice, combined with a shortage of official financing for deficits, endowed the offshore markets with a critical role in balance-of-payments financing.

The huge payments imbalances of the mid 1970s and early 1980s meant, in effect, that oil producers had surplus revenues to invest abroad while oil consumers needed substantial financing. Between these surplus and deficit states stood the major commercial banks, operating in the virtually unregulated Euromarkets. By accepting massive short-term deposits (many from oil producers) and making medium-term loans (many to oil consumers), these banks "recycled petrodollar surpluses."

It was a booming business, and a quite profitable one. By the late 1970s the largest banks were deriving as much as half their operating earnings from international activities. When oil prices doubled again in 1979, the Eurobanks expanded their lending still further, although this time they acted more cautiously in recognition of the growing risks. Even so, it was commercial banks, not aid donors or official multilateral lenders, that performed the basic recycling function.

In only a few years, then, the Euromarkets had assumed a central role in mediating international capital flows and financing world trade. In the process, private banks had become major creditors of sovereign states, not only in the Third World but also in eastern and southern Europe.

The quality of these international loans has attracted increasing attention from borrowers, lenders, central bankers, and aid officials. Bank economists, in particular, have looked closely at borrowers' projected foreign-exchange earnings, at their debt ratios, and at other macroeconomic data. More globally, they have considered the growth of aggregate payment imbalances and the resulting demands on credit markets and foreign-exchange reserves. Their central aims are to forecast financing needs and debt-service capacity.

As important as these factors are, however, the soundness of international debt depends on more than the financial condition of the borrower—it depends equally on the willingness of sovereign states to repay. The debts, of course, are formal contractual obligations. But it is a commonplace to observe that in the international arena the performance of all obligations and the enforcement of all claims must be considered problematic. The reason is fundamentally Hobbesian. There is no overarching sovereignty, no sure enforcement of claims (judicial or otherwise), no "common power," as Hobbes observed, "to keep them all in awe." Yet the principle of self-help and the metaphor of anarchy, so often used to describe the underlying condition of international relations, should not be interpreted as an absence of structures that constrain state behavior and give rise to stable expectations. What must be explored in this particular case, then, is the character of the international political structures that have thus far prompted debt service by sovereigns, even when they have found it onerous to continue payments.

What is most compelling about these structures is that sovereigns are constrained less by other sovereigns than by sanctions and incentives organized primarily by multinational banks and official multilateral lenders. These structures include the deterrent threat of effective economic sanctions and the incentive of continued access to credit.

Commercial banks are crucial actors here. It is bank lending syndicates that are the source of powerful and virtually self-sufficient sanctions against default by solvent borrowers. Because syndicates are well-organized, with an agent bank primarily responsible for the loan's collection, and because there are extensive ties between syndicates, willful default threatens to cut off all sources of commercial credit. This implicit sanction stands behind all relations between Eurobanks and their Third World borrowers. Its implementation, it should be noted, depends upon the capacity of large numbers of independent banks to take concerted action.

When the problem stems from insolvency rather than unwillingness to pay, resolution may be more complicated. It may, for example, require substantial new credits plus fiscal and monetary restraints by the debtor. In such cases, market-based sanctions and incentives are typically supplemented by the International Monetary Fund. Besides providing technical advice and some financing, the Fund evaluates the debtor's proposed economic program and monitors its implementation. The usual result, worked out jointly by the debtor, the creditors, and the Fund, is a stabilization program and a "work-out" package for the debt, including a delayed repayment schedule and some new credit.

These structures of sanctions and incentives, built around nonstate actors, form the basis of stable expectations that debts are to be serviced promptly if there is any economic possibility of doing so. Debts are to be honored even if economic conditions are hard, even if the debts were incurred by defunct governments now held in disrepute.

This definition of obligations implies substantial constraints on state action: debts are to be assumed and serviced by incumbent governments, they are not to be repudiated (and they very seldom are). In practical terms, economic collapse by the debtor may require some readjustment of loan terms, and bargaining over the new terms may be very tough indeed. The norm in such cases is that renegotiations require mutual agreement; they are not to be set unilaterally by the debtor. The broad acceptance of this behavioral standard is demonstrated repeatedly in the careful statements of impoverished debtors and even revolutionary governments. Occasional exceptions, such as North Korea's unilateral suspension of debt service after the oil embargo, are quite rare. Much more common—and indicative of the strength of the debt regime—is the refusal of the Sandinistas to repudiate even the corrupt debts of Somoza. Iran under the ayatollah Khomeini is another compelling example of the strength and domain of these basic norms and related rules, and their backing by effective sanctions and incentives. According to the *New York Times*, "Many European bankers . . . argue that throughout the revolution, Iran has sought to meet its financial obligations, within the limits imposed by the Carter freeze." What is extraordinary is not that some Iranians wanted to disown the debts but that key financial officials did not. Their efforts to repay were made even though the debts were contracted under the shah, despite questions about their legality under local law, despite Islamic objections to interest payments, despite serious economic difficulties, and despite the obvious failure of state sanctions to secure Iran's compliance on other issues. The failure of state sanctions also suggests that the rewards and punishments related to debt service may not be organized by capital-exporting states but by the private creditors themselves.

Indeed, the most distinctive element of the regime is the peripheral role played by capital-exporting states. To understand this role, and its limits, one must distinguish clearly between the operation of offshore capital markets (which give rise to credit flows) and the supervision of outstanding debt (a stock problem).

Advanced capitalist states, where the major banks are headquartered, have unquestionably played a vital role in the growth of the Euro-markets. To begin with, their domestic regulations stimulated the Euromarket as a less costly source of funds. Moreover, as the market developed, monetary authorities in the United States generally avoided actions that might have stunted its growth. If the U.S. was concerned with its capital account, the British were concerned with London's role as an international financial center. They welcomed the Euromarket's development in the City. In these ways, state action and inaction shaped the institutional context of credit flows.

But aiding the development of the Euromarket, or even regulating the banks within it, is different from supervising Third World debt. That task has fallen largely to the commercial banks and the International Monetary Fund (IMF). Together they have developed informal but effective means of ensuring debt service—even when that involves domestic austerity or complex refinancing. These two nonstate actors have played the central roles in developing rules and procedures related to troubled debt. These arrangements, which currently center on ad hoc creditor conferences, are still relatively new. They are likely to evolve as the volume of debt grows, and they may be strained to the breaking point if prospective defaults are widespread. Still, they have developed over more than a decade and now comprise a coherent and distinctive regime for Third World debt. . . .

THE ROLE OF INTERNATIONAL BANKS IN DEBT CRISES

One of the most intriguing features of individual debt problems is the way in which the structure of international finance and the procedures of creditors combine to minimize the impact of crises on other debt. Acting in concert, lenders have compelled debt service when borrowers could pay and quietly reorganized obligations when they could not. In so doing, they have deterred defaults on financially sound loans while insulating their worldwide assets from crises that have occurred. There is, in other words, a political structure that undergirds international debt. Economic sanctions back its commercial security.

To understand this political structure one must first unravel a paradox. How can highly competitive commercial banks, operating in virtually unregulated capital markets, act cooperatively to prevent defaults? The central problem is collective action. To analyze it one must examine certain institutions and conventions of international banking, especially those that apply when default draws near.

While some major banks dominate their local markets, none controls the Euromarkets. In 1980, over sixty banks could claim they were lead managers for loans worth more than $1 billion. In a market this deep, no single bank or small group can determine interest spreads, loan maturities, or syndication fees. They are set competitively, in the context of overall market liquidity and specific borrower characteristics. But if Eurobanks are competitive deal-makers, how then do they manage to cooperate in crises? The answer lies in the formation of syndicates. Syndicate lending, and commercial lending more generally, involves considerable interdependence among banks. They have effective leadership in syndicate agents, ample incentives to cooperate to avert default, and relatively few incentives to cheat on collective arrangements.

To begin with, default on any syndicated loan involves a dozen or more syndicate members directly. Cross-default clauses affect still more banks. Written into all syndication agreements, these clauses give every syndicate discretionary power to call its loans in default even if all payments are current when another syndicate has called default. The immediate aim is to give each syndicate equal status in protecting its assets. The larger consequence is to deter capricious default by threatening to bankrupt the debtor. Since that entails losses for the creditors, too, cross-default clauses are at best a blunt and dangerous instrument.

Their mere presence draws lenders more deeply into each other's disputes, but they are involved only sparingly.

A more common approach is to reorganize troubled debt at creditor conferences. The syndicate structure, with agents responsible for each loan's administration, helps the numerous banks organize for debt restructuring. In 1978 negotiations with Peru, for instance, six large lenders from the U.S., Europe, Canada, and Japan represented the 84 banks involved. A subsequent agreement covered 283 banks.

Such tight interdependence does not imply that Eurobanks always agree on how to treat troubled debt.[1] There are some systematic differences among lenders, but formal and informal means have been devised to bridge these differences in order to act collectively. Ultimately, these arrangements are built on the structure of commercial lending itself: formal contractual arrangements, a dense network of interbank deposits, and reciprocal financial ties among the largest banks.

Differences regarding the treatment of debt can emerge within syndicates or between them. Syndicates with larger or worse arrears tend to favor more comprehensive refinancing. Within syndicates, large creditors often counsel patience as long as interest payments are nearly current. If arrearages become serious they prefer emergency refinancing to default. Banks with less at stake are less willing to provide time or money. For them, rescue operations may require undue managerial attention, or, in the case of smaller banks, an excessive share of capital. They may hope larger creditors will simply take over their portion of the loan. In any case, they are more inclined to declare default, recover what they can, and let the resulting damage stand as a warning to debtors.

Lenders resolve these divergent positions in two ways. First, all syndicate agreements have provisions that apply when the agent bank has difficulty collecting the loan. A few permit the agent bank to undertake its own initiatives, at least in limited fashion. Most require the agent to act on instructions from syndicate members, who vote in proportion to their share of the credit.[2] These provisions offer some contractual protection to minor creditors, although the protection can be very weak at times. The best-known example was in several Iranian loans where the largest New York banks simply overrode the minor creditors (European, Japanese, and regional American banks). This experience, and the litigation arising from it, should further clarify the role of syndicate agents and the rights of both participating banks and borrowers.

Besides these contractual provisions, informal ententes often prevail among overlapping syndicates. The danger is that once arrears are large, one or two syndicates might call a default rather than restructure the loan or accept slow payments. Since other creditors lack preferred status, they would have strong incentives to invoke cross-default clauses and claim what assets they could. Thus, a case of poorly performing loans could be transformed swiftly into a serious debt crisis, with some loss of bank assets certain. That prospect gives all banks pause, and it gives debtors some bargaining power. Furthermore, large creditors, bound together by joint lending and cross-depositing, may be reluctant to enforce isolated and contentious positions. The transcendent risk is that the code of cooperation and collective action will dissolve in other cases of troubled debt. This mutual but sometimes strained forebearance has characterized interbank relations in a number of cases, including debt renegotiations with Nicaragua and Zaïre.

To summarize, international banks have interlocked but not identical interests in crises, and they have syndicate agents to coordinate their actions. Equally important, if they do organize themselves, the prospect of their collective sanctions is almost certain to deter default among solvent borrowers. Such default—or debt renunciation, which is much more serious and much rarer—would deprive a debtor of virtually all international credit, except (perhaps) public aid from countries with overriding political concerns. Henry Wallich of the Federal Reserve Board emphasizes the grave consequences: "Unless [a country] were willing to undertake the political subservience of total dependence on another bloc," he says, "it would have to pay cash for every power station, every industrial project. That it could do so is beyond belief. Consequently, these countries have to continue to service their debts in whatever way they can."[3] Such severe sanctions, organized privately for the most part, have effectively deterred default by the solvent.

MANAGING DEBT CRISES: THE IMF AND CREDITOR CLUBS

As important as unified private sanctions are, they do not exhaust the problem of collective action in debt crisis. A borrower, fearing retribution, may not renounce its debt but still might not be able to pay. Nations can fall behind in servicing debts because of border wars, plummeting commodity prices, or simple economic mismanagement. As arrearages accumulate, the agenda is set for default or refinancing.

Refinancing is a complicated and difficult operation, involving not only the provision of external resources but the restructuring of domestic economic life. It is a politically delicate task that neither commercial banks nor government creditors can perform autonomously. The pivotal actor is the International Monetary Fund, which in the 1950s began playing a vital role in renegotiating debt and postponing default. Most significantly, the IMF provides the dominant institutional framework for the ongoing management of troubled debt, including the transfusion of new credit and the supervision of austerity policies. In the telling words of one prominent banker, the Fund plays the "vital 'syndicate leadership' role."[4]

The IMF's role in debt renegotiations has two phases. First, it assesses the relevant economic data and reaches agreement for a standby loan, subject to certain conditions. Second, it continuously monitors and evaluates the debtor's economic policies to ensure its adherence to the conditions.

Typically, an IMF loan agreement requires specific changes in economic policies and sets performance criteria. To guarantee that changes are made, the Fund provides credit in several stages as the borrower adapts to agreed stabilization guidelines. The guidelines are essentially stock recipes for improving current and capital accounts. The centerpieces are fiscal and monetary restraints, designed to lower demand for foreign goods without direct controls or other price distortions. Some public subsidies may be eliminated, and limits are typically placed on domestic credit expansion. Devaluation has long been standard, although the IMF is now reconsidering its priority because resistance has been so fierce. All these basic changes in national policy are masked by the dulling term "conditionality."

These stern conditions and the IMF's proven ability to oversee them form the basis for debt renegotiation. Both official and private lenders accept the IMF agreement as a signal that the debtor intends to crack down on its deficit. Lenders typically renegotiate their own claims on that condition: according to Anthony Solomon, who supervised international financial issues at the U.S. Treasury before his appointment to head the Federal Reserve Bank of New York, "Typically, when the Fund reaches an agreement with a country the banks—instead of rushing to ask for their own money . . . are willing to increase their lending because it has entered a period of stabilization under the tight controls of an IMF standby agreement."[5]

By providing resources for debtors on its own conservative terms, the Fund effectively provides public goods for creditors. The Fund acts directly on debtors: it helps organize official debt renegotiations, enforces conditionality, and audits stabilization programs. Indirectly, the Fund acts on creditors. By supervising the adjustment process, the IMF stiffens the resolve of creditors to provide more capital or at least more time. With the IMF monitoring a national program of economic discipline, private capital markets generally become more accessible and existing loans more secure. The Fund, in other words, permits the banks to act in their collective self-interest.

The IMF's involvement in debt negotiations does suggest an indirect role for advanced capitalist states. After all, they dominate the Fund's weighted voting and, as a rule, endorse its advice and surveillance. Still, the IMF should not be considered simply a cipher for state power. To begin with, it is a genuinely multilateral institution. If it generally represents the interests of major capital exporters in debt issues, those interests are at least highly aggregated. They are joint interests rather than those of a single state and general policy directions rather than specific instructions in most cases. The Fund's procedures are routinized and its professional staff is given considerable autonomy in individual negotiations. Ultimately, the Fund's role in these negotiations depends less on its financial resources and its general backing from advanced states than on the perceptions of other lenders. Their agreement that the IMF's advice is prudent combined with the Fund's unique capacity to monitor stabilization programs form the basis for its role in debt negotiations.

The debt negotiations themselves are now routinized. The debtor approaches the IMF or a major creditor seeking to reorganize its debt. The aim is to postpone impending repayments and secure new financing. As the IMF negotiates its standby agreement, private and official creditors conduct their own separate meetings. Using these informal club arrangements, they make complete inventories of external debts and gather other economic information. Their agreements, which presuppose an IMF standby arrangement, typically provide new financing and reschedule old debt. In the case of official debt, the multilateral agreement is not legally binding, but its recommendations form the basis of subsequent bilateral agreements. These ad hoc conferences are convened at the creditors' discretion and conform to the creditors' position that debt relief is an extreme event, forced by traumatic circumstances. Likewise, despite hard bargaining over the size of new credits and the ease of repayment terms, the agreements conform to the creditors' position that such extreme events are best handled by short-term, generally nonconcessionary, debt reorganization.

Whether the agreements involve public or private creditors, their most important convention deals with burden-sharing: creditors must be treated equally. Most-favored-nation clauses have eliminated side deals with minor creditors and have been extended to nonparticipants such as the Soviet Union.

These procedures developed incrementally in the 1950s and 1960s as official creditors (the so-called Paris Club) worked out joint approaches to debt rescheduling. Private creditor clubs (the London or New York Clubs) are a more recent development and their arrangements are therefore more tentative. While the groups meet separately, their deliberations are inevitably intertwined. Most notably, private lenders often strike bargains that closely resemble the official accords.

Despite these similarities, there are systematic differences between commercial and official debt negotiations. They typically involve complementary forms of debt consolidation: rescheduling and refinancing. Rescheduling, which normally applies to official debts, simply postpones the timetable for repayment. Refinancing replaces maturing debt with new obligations. Commercial banks prefer it because it avoids the implication that loan agreements have not been honored. At least formally it upholds the sanctity of contracts.

The reorganization of private debt is also less flexible since it is based on earlier syndication contracts and aims solely at averting private loan losses. Preserving the current discounted value of bank assets is the overriding goal. As a result, their agreements generally offer harder terms than official creditors. The official creditors have wider aims, more leeway, and more diverse policy instruments. Although they have traditionally favored hard terms and short reschedulings, they have recently been willing to soften their position in light of widespread payment problems in poor countries.

Whatever their differences, commercial and official debts are sometimes linked in renegotiations. The rescheduling of official debt is sometimes made contingent on the renegotiation of private debt. Bilateral agreements may also explicitly protect private debt, even if the lender's home government had not previously guaranteed it. Perhaps the most difficult issue is whether official creditors will insist on similar concessions from private lenders. The problem will grow as private debt accumulates and can create even sharper divisions if the banks and aid donors are from different countries. The political risk for aid donors is the charge, already raised in congressional hearings, that public funds might be used to bail out bank loans. The thorniest case arose in Zaïre when the Paris Club granted a three-year debt moratorium and rescheduled $1 billion in loans. The one hundred private creditors demanded tougher conditions, including continuing service on outstanding loans. "The Paris Club members," according to *Institutional Investor,* "were obviously distressed at this stubborness by the private sector. . . . But the private arrangements stuck."[6] Until now, such conflicts have been rare. Most governments have not been eager to push for comparability, perhaps out of solicitude for private capital flows, perhaps because it is very difficult to monitor.

These cross-cutting links between public and private debts are another way in which advanced states impinge on the international organization of Third World debt. Unlike domestic banking rules, which mainly affect Euromarket size, the Paris Club arrangements bear directly on individual private debts. But they appear considerably less important than the banks' autonomous procedures and those of the IMF. Still, as private debt continues to grow and as more parallel agreements are reached, ties between public and private lenders may be elaborated.

Formal ties and formal institutions are always possible, but they are unlikely at present. The ad hoc clubs have proved remarkably effective, at least as far as creditors are concerned. They have successfully resisted efforts to change their procedures, including the Group of 77's proposal at UNCTAD V to establish a permanent International Debt Commission.

The record shows why creditors prefer the status quo. Club arrangements isolate debtors while facilitating collective action by creditors. Since they are convened only in payments crises, debt relief cannot even be discussed except under extreme conditions. Indeed, that is one of the regime's well-established rules. Yet when emergencies do occur, the clubs can efficiently reschedule and refinance the debt.

This has not often been necessary. Of the countless billions loaned by governments and commercial banks between 1956 and 1978, only about $10 billion had to be rescheduled. Fifteen debtors were involved and a total of forty-two reschedulings were undertaken. The pace has since picked up slightly—from about two per year to five in 1979. Given the circumstances of the debtors, the terms seem to show the strength of the creditors' position. Until OECD donors eased some aid terms retroactively, interest payments had been forgiven only twice and no principal ever cancelled. Nor do the repeated reschedulings for some nations, India and Argentina for example, indicate that the first procedure failed. Rather, they suggest that the creditors were determined to keep the debtor on a short leash. By rescheduling only the debts falling due in one or two years, they kept a tight hold over payments financing and a close watch on the debtor's economic policies.

This kind of effective cooperation has made default prohibitively costly for any nation that can avoid it. A World Bank study of debt renegotiations underlines the point: "[R]ules of the game have emerged in the field of international finance. One such rule is that default by a debtor country is now excluded as a means of adjusting financial obligations to debt servicing capacity."[7]

NEW DEMANDS ON THE IMF

Although creditor clubs have successfully replaced unilateral default with multilateral debt consolidation, it should be stressed that the arrangements for private creditors are still new. So far, they have been involved in fewer than two dozen reschedulings. And sometimes the learning process can be difficult, as it was in Peru. Facing a payments crisis in 1976, the Morales government sought loans from U.S. banks as a substitute for IMF conditional credit. The banks agreed, accepting Peru's position that an IMF program would be politically destabilizing. The risk, for both the government and the banks, was a radical nationalist response. With the IMF on the sidelines, Citibank led a refinancing group and formed a steering committee to oversee economic retrenchment. But organizing for surveillance proved difficult, and the banks found themselves drawn deeply and visibly into Peruvian politics. They drew the lesson that commercial banks could not impose conditionality, only the IMF could. Since then, lenders have refused to depart from that practice.

To ensure that the IMF plays an effective role in the future, banks have proposed reforms for the Fund and additions to its lending resources. These proposals to strengthen the Fund have generally received support from the State Department and Treasury, and from other creditor states. Suggested changes range from Fund-sponsored insurance for private loans to IMF borrowing in commercial capital markets for relending purposes. Uniting these diverse proposals is the idea that the IMF and World Bank should bear more of the private lenders' risks and play a larger financing role.

Both the World Bank and the IMF are, in fact, seeking increases in their lendable resources. In addition, the World Bank has moved beyond its traditional "project" lending to support structural adjustment to higher energy prices. "In its new role," says *Business Week,* "the [World] bank will supplement the IMF in its efforts to recycle petrodollars and will help to provide a safety net under the commercial banks, which will continue to supply the bulk of balance-of-payments financing." The World Bank and BIS have also led efforts to provide more extensive and disaggregated information about debts. Finally, the World Bank has begun some cooperative financing with private lenders. Such a program potentially multiplies the Bank's resources while lowering commercial risks (by linking private assets to the inviolate claims of the World Bank). So far, the program has been limited in two ways. Its size remains small, and the World Bank refuses to insert an automatic cross-default clause to protect private lenders. Even so, cofinancing provides a near-guarantee for commercial loans.

Such arrangements linking public and private lenders are likely to grow, but they are limited by all lenders' demands for autonomy. Refinancing is an especially sensitive issue in that regard. Private lenders insist, for example, that in some critical cases a standby agreement with the IMF may still not be sufficient reason to extend new bank credits. Yet it seems clear from the course of debate and from the steps taken so far that more cooperation between Eurobanks and multilateral institutions is likely. Discussion has centered on the style and extent of cooperation, as well as the specific forms it should take, but not on its desirability: it can only diminish the risks of private foreign lending to the Third World.

Despite the importance of World Bank lending, reform proposals tend to focus on the IMF since it is not just a source of financing but of ongoing political supervision of debtors. Two issues dominate the various proposals: the level and form of IMF resources, and the political dilemmas of conditionality.

The Fund currently has substantial resources and it is relatively liquid. The Sixth General Review of Quotas increased resources by $12 billion. The Seventh General Review went much further, raising quotas by about $25 billion—a 50 percent increase. The Fund's newly inaugurated Witteveen facility has added another $10.5 billion. But another round of heavy borrowing is building, and that might require still larger increases in IMF resources.

Such increases face serious obstacles, mainly the connection between national voting weights and member contributions to general IMF resources. Acutely aware of this link, advanced states have pushed for various "special funds," since such funds can accept OPEC money without shifting the larger voting distribution. Ultimately, this arrangement depends on OPEC's acceptance—and there are some small signs of difficulty. In July 1980, Saudi Arabia raised the political price for its cooperation by demanding observer status for the Palestine Liberation Organization at both the IMF and the World Bank. After the U.S. blocked this move, the Saudis settled for a more conventional solution. They agreed to lend the Fund SDR 4 billion (about $4.9 billion) at market rates for each of the next two years and again in the third year if their payments position permits. The Fund's Board of Governors later announced that the Saudis had been permitted to nearly double their quota. With this increase, Saudi Arabia's share in total quotas rises to 3.5 percent (compared to over 19 percent for the United States), a quota that effectively guarantees the Saudis their own permanent member of the IMF Executive Board.

Despite this solution, the whole episode suggests the vulnerability of IMF funding procedures. The recognition of that vulnerability as well as the need for substantially more resources has led directly to the search for alternative funding procedures. The leading candidate is the World Bank's procedure: borrowing (for relending purposes) in international financial markets. By borrowing in the Eurocurrency markets, the Fund could simultaneously augment its resources, avoid making heavy demands on OPEC members, and lower its need for funding from a reluctant U.S. Congress. Moreover, the IMF already has the legal authority to undertake such borrowing. Its executive board urged consideration of this alternative in 1979, but so far the Fund has not acted. They may well within the next two years, but there are substantial problems in doing so. One is the Fund's lack of collateral. More important, an active program of borrowing would disrupt the tight links that now exist between each Fund member's quota payments, its voting rights, and its access to credit.

Of course, if the IMF's conditional lending is to have practical significance, it needs more than augmented resources. Borrowers must actually seek Fund aid. Conditionality is, after all, essentially contractual. It is the price of access to the IMF's higher credit tranches. Sovereign borrowers are increasingly reluctant to pay that price unless conditions are dire, and sometimes not even then. As a result, there are pressures to relax the IMF's tough lending standards.

Any shift in IMF standards poses a dilemma for creditors. If the IMF institutes more flexible conditions for its credit, more borrowers will turn to it. That is already the case with the IMF's special funds, which have fewer strings than regular borrowing. On the other hand, debtors often delay borrowing from regular credit tranches until the situation is critical. By weakening conditionality, the IMF is likely to play a larger role in payments financing and to become involved earlier with debtors' problems. For creditors, the price of such flexibility is that they can no longer consider the IMF's standards a proxy for their own. Private creditors, especially, have been perplexed by this dilemma and ambivalent about the choices it poses.

Meanwhile, the Fund has moved ahead and adopted new guidelines on conditionality. The change is gradual but not insignificant. Under Managing Director Jacques de Larosière, the IMF seems willing to extend larger credits, over longer periods, under somewhat less stringent conditions. The Fund's conditions are now limited to "macroeconomic variables," for example. This new position is evolving on a case-by-case basis and its impact on debt negotiations is still uncertain. It could weaken the now-close relationship between IMF standby agreements and private refinancing. On the other hand, a larger IMF role in debt management and an earlier involvement in problem cases could reduce the risks of commercial lending. Whatever the outcome, this new policy is not a dramatic change, and it will not drastically alter the Fund's impact on Third World debt. Rather, it will modify in an incremental way its already crucial role in dampening private risks.

CONCLUSION

This analysis of Third World debt suggests a novel and evolving relationship between private lenders and public institutions—a relationship that is at the heart of the debt regime. To understand that relationship, as well as the role played by capital-exporting states, one must distinguish clearly between the stock of debt and the flow of credit.

Demands for payments financing (indeed, for credit flows in general) arise from larger economic and political relationships—the openness of the international trade regime, supply and demand functions for traded goods, and the availability of nondebt financing such as foreign aid or direct foreign investments. Moreover, national economic policies are crucial in determining both the size of deficits and the means of financing them. The mediating role of offshore markets cannot be divorced from these political choices and commercial relationships or from the international political framework within which they take place. Here Gilpin's observation is quite pertinent: "What has to be explained are the economic and political circumstances that enable . . . transnational actors to play their semi-independent role in international affairs."[8]

In a general sense, the privatization of payments financing should be set in this larger context of state interaction. To the extent that the offshore markets are demand-driven, policy choices in oil-importing states are a significant source of market growth. More broadly, the markets' mediation between surplus and deficit states depends upon the configuration of current-account balances. . . .

. . . The supervision of debt has largely been a function of commercial banking arrangements and the IMF's conditional lending. The key procedure has been ad hoc creditor conferences, which began among aid donors in the mid 1950s, but is no longer limited to them. As the composition of capital flows changed, private banks developed a substantial stake and their own parallel creditor-club framework. As the problems of surveillance became clearer, first creditor states and later private banks demanded a role for the IMF in stabilization programs. The Fund's role is vital not because it provides capital but because it provides free collective goods and, indirectly, aids in creditor coordination. By signalling the creditworthiness of troubled debtors, it provides important information to all creditors. By monitoring its own conditional loans, it provides essential political surveillance. Private lenders, though they control the main spigots of international capital, cannot easily provide such collective goods for themselves.

As important as the IMF is in supervising debt crises, the coordination of private lenders is substantially a function of their own reciprocal relationships and the contractual character of their international lending. Most significantly, the vast majority of loans to Third World states are made through multinational banking syndicates, which have their own conventions and legal obligations. Relying on these contractual provisions and established procedures, agent banks then oversee the repayment of debt. If the loan is nonperforming, the agent is well placed to organize the syndicate for collective action.

In debt crises, these lending arrangements provide formal avenues for reconciling creditor preferences within syndicates. Should differences arise between syndicates, collective action is less certain but still common. Its basis is the far-reaching interdependence of the largest Eurobanks, with its implications of mutual support or retribution. Finally, should the informal codes of lender conduct fail, the debt's contractual character at least gives each bank some recourse in case of illegal usurpation by other banks. Together, these features of Eurocurrency lending markedly reduce the incentives for otherwise competitive banks to pursue beggar-my-neighbor policies in debt crises.

This political structure for collective action ensures that no state will default unless it is insolvent or is willing to accept a radical rupture with the capitalist world economy. The debts are politically secure because they are backed by a network of multilateral banks, private lenders, and (more marginally) advanced capitalist states. They are jointly capable of consolidating debt in emergencies and severely punishing those who default lightly.

The sanctions available to these institutions are powerful not only because they are coherent, but because of a basic structural feature of international finance: nations that expect to conduct multilateral trade require short- and medium-term financing plus other bank services. Thus, to deny access to credit is a powerful sanction. We might term it an "intrinsic sanction," since it is substantively related to the action being sanctioned and involves an issue-bounded relationship among the actors. Because debt sanctions are intrinsic and because they do not generally require creditors to inflict special costs on themselves, coordination problems are simplified. The close interdependence of international banks, their capacity to coordinate, and the IMF's permanent institutional framework virtually assure collective action in cases of impending default. Thus, there is an effective structure for the supervision of sovereign debt—a structure built not on state power but on private sanctions and multilateral oversight.

The strength of these arrangements lies in the capacity to isolate individual debt problems and, treating them in isolation, to resolve the discrete cases. That may also be the regime's greatest limitation. So far, ad hoc arrangements have been sufficient. But their scope is necessarily limited—too limited to anticipate and cope with a much larger agenda of troubled debt. There are no mechanisms to assure any given level of payments financing in the private markets. Nor do the IMF and World Bank have sufficient resources to offset any major change in the provision of private credit. As a result, a flurry of debt problems or, worse, a few major defaults could produce a self-defeating spiral of credit contraction. In such a risky environment, banks would be reluctant to lend freely so still more debt crises would emerge. The intervention of central banks would dampen some of the consequences. Lender-of-last-resort facilities might prevent illiquidity from spreading through the banking system, permitting some rollover credits for troubled debtors. Nothing, however, would ensure the provision of such credits on a substantial scale. None of this is meant as a forecast—rather, it is designed to show the institutional limits of the debt regime. So far, common action has been needed only to avoid very specific outcomes in a limited number of deviant cases. Perhaps as a result, the debt regime is poorly institutionalized. Certainly it is ill-equipped to cope with larger dilemmas in which the avoidance of default and the global provision of credit merge.

Whatever its limitations, the debt regime is surely distinctive. The configuration of nonstate actors seems to contravene Oran Young's claim that, "In formal terms, the members of international regimes are always sovereign states, though the parties carrying out the actions governed by international regimes are often private entities (for example, fishing companies, banks, or private airlines)."[9] For most issues, Young's statement holds. The state system does provide the basic framework for private economic transactions. It does so even in the case of offshore credit markets, as we have seen. But in the case of LDC debt, the central actors are the IMF and the major money-market banks, operating through integrated networks of foreign branches and subsidiaries. They not simply carrying out regime-governed actions, as Young would have it. Having become essential intermediaries in the international transmission of credit, they have also become the source of most regime rules, norms, and procedures.

Not only are these arrangements distinctive, they are relatively autonomous. That autonomy is striking because the debts themselves are so closely tied to other economic transactions. Yet shifts in larger political and economic relationships, even changes in closely related issues, do not seem to have diminished the security of Third World debts. The international monetary regime, for instance, has undergone profound and sometimes turbulent change since 1971. Likewise, the rules governing the treatment of foreign direct investment (the most obvious alternative to international lending as a source of long-term finance) have changed dramatically. While direct investment was increasingly subject to idiosyncratic national control, the debt regime has been characterized by coherent global rules and unified sanctions. Even the decline of hegemony has not weakened the political supervision of debt, although the ebbing of U.S. economic leadership has surely contributed to the relative decline of aid and the rise of offshore lending. All this suggests that the debt regime's structure and evolution do not coincide with developments in other issue-areas, even those that are closely related, or to broad changes in the international power distribution.

This does not imply that Eurolending and the allied structure of debt supervision could survive a traumatic rupture in international economic relationships. We have already indicated that the regime is premised on the rarity of debt problems, which are effectively insulated from the larger stock of global debts and treated as deviant cases. Within these limits, however, the debt regime has a singular issue structure and a relatively autonomous one. Although capital movements are partly a function of other economic flows, the international organization of debt is largely independent of these other issues. Its rules and procedures, its actors and their conventions, are all distinctive. Without relying on the diplomacy or military resources of advanced capitalist states, independent of hegemony or its gradual decline, they have provided solid political backing for foreign capital.

NOTES

1. Policy differences arose within lending syndicates in Indonesia, Turkey, Peru, Zaïre, and elsewhere. They are discussed by Jonathan Aronson in "The Politics of Private Bank Lending and Debt Renegotiation," in Aronson, ed., *Debt and the Less Developed Countries* (Boulder, Col.: Westview Press, 1979).

2. M. S. Mendelsohn, *Money on the Move* (New York: McGraw-Hill, 1980), p. 90.

3. U.S., Congress, Senate, Committee on Banking, Housing, and Urban Affairs, *Hearings on International Debt*, 95th Cong., 1st sess., 1977, p. 88.

4. Statement by Frederick Heldring, president, Philadelphia National Bank, in U.S., Congress, House, Committee on Banking, Finance, and Urban Affairs, *Hearings on U.S. Participation in the Supplementary Financing Facility of the International Monetary Fund*, 95th Cong., 1st sess., 1977, p. 142.

5. Ibid., p. 72.

6. Vivian Lewis, "Inside the Paris Club," *Institutional Investor/International Edition*, June 1980, p. 36.

7. IBRD, "Multilateral Debt Renegotiations: 1956–1968," unpublished, 11 April 1969, p. 39.

8. Robert Gilpin, *U.S. Power and the Multinational Corporation* (New York: Basic Books, 1975), p. 39.

9. Oran Young, "International Regimes: Problems of Concept Formation," *World Politics* 32 (April 1980), p. 333.

D. Trade

The international trade regime constructed under American leadership after the Second World War and embodied in the General Agreement on Tariffs and Trade (GATT) has facilitated the emergence of the most open international economy in modern history. After the Second World War, political leaders in the United States and many other advanced industrialized countries believed, on the basis of their experience during the Great Depression of the 1930s, that protectionism contributes to depressions, depressions magnify political instability, and protectionism therefore leads to war. Drawing upon these beliefs, the United States led the postwar fight for a new trade regime to be based upon the liberal principle of comparative advantage. Tariffs were to be lowered, and each country would specialize in those goods that it produced best—trading for the products of other countries as necessary. To the extent this goal was achieved, American decision makers and others believed that all countries would be better off and prosperity would be reinforced.

The American vision for the postwar trade regime was embodied in a plan for an International Trade Organization (ITO) to complement the International Monetary Fund. As originally presented in 1945, the American plan offered rules for all aspects of international trade relations. The Havana Charter creating the ITO was finally completed in 1947. A product of many international compromises, the Havana Charter was the subject of considerable domestic opposition within the United States. Republican protectionists opposed the treaty because it went too far. Free-trade groups failed to support it because it did not go far enough. President Harry Truman—knowing that it faced almost certain defeat—never submitted the Havana Charter to Congress for ratification. In the absence of American support, the nascent ITO died a quick and quiet death. The GATT was drawn up in 1947 to provide a basis for the trade negotiations then under way in Geneva. Intended merely as a temporary agreement to last only until the Havana Charter was fully implemented, the GATT became the principal basis for the international trade regime with the failure of the ITO.

Despite its supposedly temporary origins, the GATT has emerged as the most important international institution in the trade area. It is based upon four norms. First, all members of the GATT agree to extend unconditional most-favored-nation (MFN) status to one another. Under this agreement, no country will receive any preferential treatment not accorded to all other MFN countries. Additionally, any benefits acquired by one country are *automatically* extended to all MFN partners. The only exceptions to this rule are customs unions, such as the European Economic Community, and generalized systems of preferences, granted to many Third World countries in the 1970s.

Second, the GATT is based upon the norm of reciprocity, or the concept that any country that benefits from another's tariff reduction should reciprocate to an equivalent extent. This norm ensures "fair" and equitable tariff reductions by all countries. In conjunction with the MFN or nondiscrimination norm, it also serves to reinforce the downward spiral of tariffs initiated by the actions of any one country.

Third, "safeguards" or loopholes and exceptions to other norms are recognized as acceptable if they are temporary and imposed for short-term balance-of-payments reasons. Exceptions are also allowed for countries experiencing severe market disruptions from increased imports.

Fourth, in 1965, a development norm was added to the GATT that allowed (1) generalized systems of preferences (or unilateral and unreciprocated tariff reductions by developed countries on imports from their developing counterparts), (2) additional safeguards for "development" purposes, and (3) export subsidies by developing countries.

The GATT has been extremely successful in obtaining its declared goal of freer trade and lower tariffs. By the end of the Kennedy Round of the GATT in 1967, which was initiated by President John F. Kennedy in 1962, tariffs on dutiable nonagricultural items had declined to approximately ten percent in the advanced industrialized countries. In the Tokyo Round, concluded in 1979, tariffs in these same countries were reduced to approximately five percent. By the 1970s, tariffs were only a relatively minor impediment to trade. These significant reductions initiated an era of unprecedented growth in international trade; the two most rapidly increasing areas are the overlapping ones of trade between advanced industrialized countries and intrafirm trade (the exchange of goods within, rather than between, corporations).

At the same time that tariffs have been declining and trade increasing, new threats have emerged to the free-trade regime. With the success of the GATT, more and more industries have been exposed to increased international competition. Industry demands for some form of protection have increased in nearly all countries. Of particular concern is the growing use of voluntary export restraints, orderly marketing agreements, and other nontariff barriers to trade. The United States has been most successful at convincing other countries to voluntarily restrain their exports to its market. William Cline has recently estimated that voluntary export restraints and other nontariff barriers to trade imposed by the United States in the late 1970s and early 1980s affected nearly half of all manufactured goods imported into the United States.[1] Similarly, S. A. B. Page has found that 48 percent of the non-Communist world's trade was subject to some form of nonmarket control in 1980, up from 40 percent in 1974.[2] While the GATT regime has not been destroyed, it has certainly become weaker and more fragile.

Three questions concerning international trade in the postwar period are particularly important and are addressed in the following readings. How and why did a free-trade regime emerge after 1945? Why has protectionism enjoyed a resurgence since the early 1970s? Finally, what is the likely future of the international trade regime? Surprisingly, there is considerable agreement between Realists, such as David Calleo and Benjamin Rowland, and Stephen Krasner, and Liberals, on the importance of American leadership. Both ascribe the rise of free trade to the hegemonic position of the United States after World War II and the increasing protectionism of the 1970s to the declining position of the United States within the world economy. In the absence of a new hegemonic leader, Calleo and Rowland, and Krasner are relatively pessimistic on the future of the liberal international trade regime. G. K. Helleiner, focusing on the domestic sources of support for free trade, takes a different approach to explaining the postwar trade regime. Free trade, Helleiner argues, has generally been supported by the large multinational corporations, which require open international markets to take full advantage of their worldwide production capabilities. As capital has become internationalized, however, labor has increasingly turned toward protection in an effort to save jobs at home. Thus, trade politics has become increasingly class-based. Helleiner, nonetheless, remains more sanguine on the likely future of free trade. This section concludes with an essay by Joan Robinson on the special trade problems of the Third World, which has largely been left out of the postwar American-led international trade regime.

NOTES

1. William R. Cline, *Exports of Manufactures from Developing Countries* (Washington: Brookings, 1984).
2. S. A. B. Page, "The Revival of Protectionism and its Consequences for Europe," *Journal of Common Market Studies* 20 (September 1981).

21. Free Trade and the Atlantic Community

DAVID P. CALLEO AND
BENJAMIN M. ROWLAND

David Calleo and Benjamin Rowland examine the origins of America's post–World War II free-trade policy and the pressures that had beset it by the late 1960s. Initially, they focus on the ideology of Cordell Hull, President Franklin Roosevelt's secretary of state. They then discuss the conflicts with Europe after the war and emphasize the importance of the cold war in easing trade tensions between the United States and its NATO allies. Calleo and Rowland further argue that, by the late 1960s, the United States had become disillusioned with free trade. It had not strengthened the Atlantic alliance as promised by its advocates, and the trade balance of the United States was growing weaker. Free trade was being increasingly compromised as both Europe and the United States developed mutually exclusive regional trade blocs. Throughout this selection, Calleo and Rowland emphasize the close relationship between military and economic relations in the post–World War II era.

CORDELL HULL AND AMERICA'S LIBERAL VISION

. . . The great era of the American government's free-trade policy began in the 1930's, when Cordell Hull began his long tenure as Roosevelt's Secretary of State. Hull's vision of a new liberal world order dominated his policy. Indeed, his career strikingly illustrates what Halévy wrote of Bentham, the power of a man with one idea. Hull's free-trade convictions were, for the most part, based on traditional arguments. Specialization would maximize economic welfare, and hence promote that general world prosperity which was a precondition for peace. Universal access to foreign supplies, markets and investments would neutralize that competitive territorial imperative which lay at the base of the modern imperial scramble.

To the classic arguments, Hull added two with a particular American slant. Free trade would check domestic monopolies. And it would create a strong mutual interest between industrial and backward countries, the former afraid of overproduction and the latter starved for goods.

Throughout his long tenure, Hull had constantly to struggle not only against protectionist opposition, but against Roosevelt's ambiguous support. In the early New Deal, favored economists like Raymond Moley and George Peek advised Roosevelt toward a mercantilist policy of isolation, protection and preference. Thus Hull, his views ignored by Roosevelt, was powerless to act at the London Economic Conference of 1933, the conclave which confirmed the breakdown of the old liberal world system.

Nevertheless, in the fall of 1933, Hull scored a great success at the Montevideo Conference of American Nations. The Conference faithfully proclaimed the essentials of Hull's world vision: nonintervention, peaceful settlement of disputes and nondiscriminatory commerce. Thus fortified, Hull was able the following year to push through his masterstroke, the Trade Agreements Act. According to its provisions, the foundation of most American trade legislation ever since, all nonagricultural trade agreements were to be based on a reciprocal most-favored-nation principle. . . .

Once the War was under way, Hull saw his great chance to build a liberal order throughout the world. But the attempt, he realized, would bring him into direct conflict with those recent liberal apostates, the British. With his usual patient determination, Hull set out to destroy the British imperial preference system. Although Roosevelt gave him scant support in the beginning, Hull found the leverage he needed in Lend-Lease. In the agreement of 1942, the reluctant but desperate British "promised the elimination of all forms of discriminatory treatment in international commerce."[1] Before he finished, Hull used the same Lend-Lease Agreement to commit eleven other countries to his grand postwar vision. . . .

BRITAIN AND AMERICA IN ECONOMIC CONFLICT

As the War drew to a close, the tensions between Hull's American universalism and the interests of Britain and Russia grew more and more acute. Both Churchill and Stalin had quite different ideas about organizing the postwar world. Both shied away from the universal institutions where America's overwhelming power would predominate. Instead of American universalism, they preferred dividing the world into regional blocs.

Popular memory dwells upon the Cold War. But for a time, the financial struggle with Britain loomed as large in our policy. Churchill was determined to resist Hull's new order, which he, like de Gaulle, saw as a sign of a growing American taste for dominance. . . .

Under the Socialists, the Anglo-American quarrel soon encompassed not only Britain's external economic relations, but the policies for domestic reconstruction in Britain and Europe generally. The new Labour Government was determined to achieve a domestic economy based on full employment and the welfare state. Above all, it was determined not to return to the deflationary policies and massive unemployment of the interwar years. The British workingman, it was said, was no longer to be sacrificed to the interests of the City and the liberal international system. To maintain full employment, Labour was prepared to protect and control the British economy. Labour, moreover, was determined to preserve the imperial preference system as the device to stabilize British exports and currency. A modern form of mercantilism, by way of Keynesian economics, had come back into fashion.

There were, of course, urgently practical reasons for the Labour Government's view. To balance her payments, a Britain shorn of foreign assets and income had to increase prewar exports by some 50 percent, even if imports were kept stationary at the prewar level. It was difficult to imagine how the British might perform such a feat without strong import and financial controls. Britain, moreover, needed all the external support she could find—both from her traditional preferential trading system to help her exports and from a sterling bloc to tie up her huge wartime debts.

Such arrangements, however, were anathema to the votaries of multilateral free trade in the American State Department and Treasury. According to the prevalent State Department view, Europe's economic reconstruction depended essentially on a return to a liberal trading system as soon as possible. Doubtless some aid was necessary, but trade was to be Europe's chief restorative. Many Americans, moreover, feared a depression if no outlet were found for their country's greatly expanded productive capacity. The solution was to create as rapidly as possible an open liberal world, with sound convertible money and markets for our goods.

Europeans, too, feared a breakdown in the American economy. But the chief danger, they believed, came from American policies which were either naive and doctrinaire or short-sighted and greedy. If there was a slump, they believed, it would come from the mounting American trade and payments surplus and the accompanying dollar shortage in Europe. Without dollars, Europeans could not buy the goods to rebuild. Europe, therefore, needed a huge transfer of American funds, not lectures on the virtues of liberal free trade and convertibility. Europeans desperately wanted their old preferential markets while they were struggling to rebuild. Hull's liberal system seemed designed to consolidate a temporary American predominance into a permanent fact. . . .

The conflict between American plans and British interests was reflected in a series of strenuous negotiations—starting in 1944 with Bretton Woods, which established the IMF, and ending with the Geneva and Havana negotiations of 1947 and 1948, which finally failed to establish an International Trade Organization.

The Bretton Woods Conference was called to lay down the new international financial order. Commanding figures at the Conference were Britain's Lord Keynes and America's Harry Dexter White. At issue was the rigor and immediacy of the Fund's disciplinary action against a country in a balance-of-payments deficit. White, true to his liberal principles, insisted that countries in deficit be permitted only a minimum of restrictions on convertibility. To encourage monetary discipline, he also insisted on relatively limited credit to debtors. Keynes, concerned about full employment, insisted on a more forgiving system—with credits sufficiently ample to permit deficit countries to reach equilibrium without the traditional recourse to deflation and unemployment. The result was a compromise, heavily loaded toward the American position.

In any event, Bretton Woods proved only a declaration of principles, fated to remain mostly theoretical. No European currency was convertible at the time. The Americans, however, were determined to make the system operate as they wanted it.

Paradoxically, British weakness made it difficult either to meet or to resist American demands. The war had exhausted British economic power. To a considerable extent, the United States was responsible. Throughout the War, Hull, determined to break up the British bloc, had used the leverage of Lend-Lease skillfully and systematically to reduce Britain to a financial satellite. By 1945, British reserves and foreign investments were gone and Britain was begging a reluctant Congress for a massive American loan. Keynes arrived asking for a $6.6 billion grant. Aside from the U.S. Treasury's more sophisticated reservations, many in the Congress opposed aiding a socialist welfare state that seemed so busy assaulting the rights of private property. Keynes finally negotiated an offer of $3.75 billion. We used the opportunity to insist on various liberal conditions—chiefly, convertibility of the pound by 1947.

Meeting the requirement proved a disaster. Up to 1947, the British economy had done surprisingly well. In the second half of 1946, British exports were running at 111 percent of prewar, and imports had been reduced to 72.2 percent. Only one quarter of the American loan had actually been used up. But with convertibility came collapse. The trade account deteriorated rapidly—partly, it was felt, because foreign traders hoarded sterling to convert it into dollars. Since Britain had the only convertible currency in a Europe starved for dollars, the pressure on sterling proved immense. The whole operation, moreover, was not handled very well. Britain had not managed to fund her wartime indebtedness to the rest of the sterling bloc, and regulations to limit convertibility to transactions on current account proved ineffective. In any event, once the run on sterling began, the rest of the American loan quickly disappeared. The experiment in liberal economies was abandoned. Sterling was devalued and convertibility was not re-established until 1958.

The British henceforth took a tougher line. In the 1947 and 1948 negotiations to establish an International Trade Organization, Britain flatly refused to abandon imperial preferences. Hard bargaining ensued, with the British demanding genuine concessions that would help their trade, rather than specious declarations of principle. In the end, broad mutual reductions were negotiated, but the ITO that emerged was never put before Congress for a vote.

In any event, by the late forties, the whole climate was becoming more favorable to British and European interests and policies. To begin with, the principal American actors had changed. Hull and Morgenthau were gone and White was soon to be destroyed. Their immediate successors were mostly transitional figures, certainly less visionary. The new President had not yet completely found himself or his men. Through 1948, liberal initiatives were hobbled by a Republican Congress with strong protectionist and isolationist leanings.

By late 1947, moreover, even the most stubborn proponents of liberal multilateralism saw that America's postwar policy was failing to promote European recovery. Both America's trade surpluses and Europe's deficits had mounted higher each year. American policy, counting on free trade and convertibility, had grossly underestimated the task of European recovery. The existing institutions, policies and subventions were manifestly insufficient. The year 1948 saw a new American policy based on massive aid, and a discriminatory European bloc. Temporarily, Hull's universal vision was abandoned.

Over time, perhaps, the deflation and austerity envisaged in the IMF Charter might have brought recovery to Europe. But the new political climate did not seem to warrant the experiment. For 1947 was dominated by a new factor of surpassing significance, the Cold War with Russian communism.

THE COLD WAR RESOLUTION

America's euphoric sense of omnipotence and vast visions of a new international order had confronted, in Stalin's Russia and later Mao's China, obstacles infinitely more contrary than Attlee's Britain. The family quarrels over money were overtaken by the Cold War. The American liberal universe, discovering communism, became finite. The universalism of the UN and the IMF shrank to the Atlanticism of NATO and the OEEC. To be sure, the new anticommunist policy had something of the same tendency toward universalism that characterized the visions of Hull and Morgenthau. The Truman Doctrine was to defend "free peoples" everywhere. But the visions were nevertheless greatly scaled down from Hull's day. As the Third World proved increasingly intractable to any integrating order, the liberal system evolved more and more into an Atlantic bloc of the world's developed capitalist economies—a bloc justified not so much by the economic ideals of Cobden, Hull and Morgenthau as by the geopolitical visions of Mahan, Acheson and Dulles. For free trade was not the link which actually brought together postwar America and Europe. On the contrary, it was the issue that divided them. . . . The postwar Atlantic Community came into being only after the United States, prompted by its fear of Russian and domestic European communism, suppressed its liberal economic scruples in the interest of "mutual security" and Europe's rapid recovery. . . . Economics was subordinated to politics. Trade took directions from the flag. And America's hegemony over Europe took a more visible form than free-trade imperialism, and also a form more useful and acceptable to the Europeans.

To be sure, Hull's liberal lamp never went out, even if for some time it was obscured by the NATO shield. While the early 1950's were dominated by the politics of security, economic liberalism moved back to the center as the Cold War ebbed, Europe recovered, and the hegemonic Atlantic system, which was the Cold War's offspring, demanded a new pedigree. . . .

TRADE AND AMERICAN POSTWAR POLICY

In Hull's grand vision, as we have seen, free trade was expected to engage nations in peaceful and prosperous interdependence. Hull linked nearly everything else to his trade policy. The Axis powers were to be defeated because their economic policies meant a closed world of blocs. Our Allies were to be supported only if they renounced their preferential systems. Monetary systems were devised to facilitate trade; security systems to protect it. However lightly he was taken by Roosevelt and his contemporaries, Hull emerged as the figure who expressed most clearly the ideas that would dominate a good part of America's postwar policy.

In postwar America's Atlanticist vision, trade has in fact taken a central significance. Trade has been linked to the full complement of economic issues—including inflation, price stability, full employment and growth. Trade and growth are said to set up a "virtuous circle," the one stimulating the other. And, following Hull's prescription, trade has also been linked to a closely-knit Atlantic political system. Interdependence in trade is said to mean interdependence in foreign policy.

These two dimensions to trade policy, the economic and the political, have been mutually reinforcing. Assertions that trade policy injures domestic employment and production must contend with counter-assertions about trade's vital role in preserving international good will and "interdependence." Throughout the past decade, moreover, trade has grown more rather than less significant in American policy. On the one hand, as the immediate and obvious threats to Atlantic security have appeared to recede, and the American balance-of-payments difficulties grown more acute, economics increasingly has become the focus of international relations and the stuff of diplomacy. On the other, as security links have grown looser, promoters of Atlantic political unity have been inclined to rely all the more on transatlantic trade and economic connections in general. Thus for many in the Kennedy and Johnson Administrations, the Kennedy Round seemed no less important to the future of the Atlantic Community than NATO itself.

DISILLUSION WITH TRADE LIBERALIZATION

After a quarter of a century during which trade liberalization has commanded an almost religious deference from Western statesmen and economists alike, many signs now suggest a major shift, in the United States particularly. No new trading initiatives of significance have followed the Kennedy Round, completed in 1967, and indeed, Congress has only partly and conditionally accepted the fruits of those negotiations. In the early seventies, the American protectionist mood in general and the popularity of Nixon's trade measures in particular revealed a surprising fragility in the whole liberal trade policy—a fragility which suggests a certain erosion of its foundations and a growing disenchantment with its fundamental assumptions.

Several theories vie to explain why trade liberalization is now embattled. The most cheerful explanation sees the Kennedy Round so successful that nothing further remains to be done with tariffs. Trade liberalization now means the reduction of nontariff barriers, a complex task awaiting the development of new negotiating machinery.

The current militancy of protectionism in this country, however, threatens to undo more than the Kennedy Round and belies such facile optimism for the future. But nearly forty years after Hull's first trade legislation why should Americans be renouncing the Calico Goddess?

As the British experience suggests, free trade appeals most to those confident of their ability to compete in an open market. American goods, however, are growing less and less competitive; hence Americans are becoming more and more protectionist. Since 1971, the American balance of trade has officially fallen into deficit. While our exports have continued to grow, our imports have jumped at a substantially greater rate. Trade with Canada and Japan has shown the greatest and most rapidly increasing imbalance; but even the traditional surplus with the Common Market, while persisting through 1971, has shrunk. . . .

Explanations for the decline in America's trade balance and prescriptions for correcting it are both many and complex. Special factors like the Canadian-American Automobile Agreement may have sharply affected trade with particular countries. Special negotiations, it is hoped, will ultimately eliminate the deleterious effects of these special situations. More generally, the decline in our trade balance can be blamed on the peculiar American economic situation in recent years. The Vietnam war has placed extraordinary stress on the national economy, increasing imports, rendering exports less competitive, and setting off a spiralling inflation. Analysts hope that as an aberrant policy can be said to have caused the decline, a sane policy can reverse it. Phasing out the war, combined with internal correctives like wage and price controls, should end America's rapid inflation, restore price competitiveness to her products and hence rejuvenate the usual liberal trade constituency. Many analysts also expect much from the dollar's devaluation. As the key currency, the dollar has not been devalued since before World War II, whereas most of our major trading partners have devalued several times. An overvalued dollar has gradually sapped competitiveness, which, it is hoped, can now be restored.

Another set of explanations, however, sees America's trade balance declining less from short-term than from secular historical factors. Many Americans in the seventies like many British in the sixties, perceive a general decline in their society, or at least in those virtues most conductive to economic efficiency. Others see the gap between American and foreign wages not closing rapidly enough to compensate for a general loss of America's traditional advantages in management, technology and marketing. The loss of these advantages is often blamed on the overseas migration of so many American companies. To many with such views, restrictions on imports and foreign investments seem the obvious remedies.

Certain liberal analysts take a more hopeful view of the declining trade balance. The American economy is seen entering its mature phase. Hence manufacturing is a diminishing—and services are an increasing—constituent of GNP. In this view, all but the most advanced technological industries tend to move abroad. Regulations against pollution will hasten the migration. While the United States will thus earn less and less abroad from selling goods, more and more earnings will come from the sale of services and royalties. Above all, the steady stream of American investing overseas will yield a return to compensate for our trade deficit. Like Britain before World War I, the United States will be a rentier economy. Protectionism, therefore, is unwarranted and harmful to our own consumers.

This latter view, however cheerful and tidy it may seem to economists, appeals less to workers and those who represent them. Many of the arguments, moreover, are highly problematical. While manufacturing abroad may enhance a company's earnings, repatriated profits are scarcely as remunerative to American labor as domestic production. The assumption that new jobs can be created in "advanced" industries and services to compensate for a general decline in almost all the major manufacturing sectors seems highly questionable, even with "adjustment" assistance on a far more lavish scale than has ever been provided. Selling American services to foreigners on a scale to compensate for the dwindling exports of goods seems an equally uncertain prospect.

Under the circumstances, no one need wonder at the growing militancy of American protectionist forces and the uncertainty and disaffection among many who formerly supported trade liberalization. The whole policy, in fact, demands a fundamental re-evaluation, an inquiry conscious of the domestic costs as well as the benefits of trade liberalization.

An equally skeptical view seems imperative toward the political benefits which have been thought to accompany international trade liberalization. Even assuming that a more closely integrated pan-Atlantic economic and political community is a proper aim for American policy, and acceptable to Europe, is trade likely to promote that integration? Neither the trade figures themselves nor the recent experience of the Kennedy Round can confirm that trade promotes Atlantic integration.

To begin, it would be useful to consider the actual trading patterns of recent years. No one can deny that postwar transatlantic trade has grown significantly, or that the Atlantic countries as a whole have been trading more with each other than with third countries. From 1948 to 1970, this "Atlantic Trading Community" increased its share of total free-world exports from 62.5 percent to 70.6 percent, and its share of free-world imports from 62.2 percent to 70.9 percent. Between 1958 and 1970, the percentage of its members' exports to each other has increased from 61.5 percent to 72.8 percent of their total exports. . . . In other words, the Atlantic Community's share of world trade has been rising, and turning inward.

But these shifts can give only ambiguous support to partisans of transatlantic interdependence, for within these broad trends, trade has shifted significantly within the Atlantic Community itself—a shift which reflects a more self-sufficient Europe, relatively less involved in trade with America. The shift, of course, is only relative, and easy enough to lose sight of in the continuous growth of world trade. Nevertheless, the trends are significant and suggest that for both Europe and the United States, trade is centering itself increasingly within mutually exclusive regional blocs. . . .

NOTE

1. Cordell Hull, *Memoirs* Vol. 2 (New York: Macmillan, 1948), p. 976.

22. Transnational Enterprises and the New Political Economy of U.S. Trade Policy

G. K. HELLEINER

In this reading, G. K. Helleiner develops an interest-group–based explanation of recent American trade policy. He notes a number of changes in the contemporary political lineup within the United States on trade issues—labor has, for example, abandoned its traditional free-trade orientation—and proposes an explanation based on the rise of the multinational corporation. Multinational enterprises, Helleiner points out, have an interest in the freest possible movement of their goods, services, and capital across borders; they thus support economic openness both in their sectors and more generally. American labor, on the other hand, has been weakened by the rise of the multinational corporation and is attempting to protect itself with trade barriers. The two crucial interests in American trade policy disputes, then, are labor and multinational corporations; Helleiner generally regards the corporations as more likely to predominate in the conflict.

1. INTRODUCTION

Little of the orthodox literature of the theory of international trade addresses the question of the political sources of trade policies. The various arguments for the use of trade barriers are typically considered from the standpoint of 'the national interest' and, on the basis of conventional assumptions, the conclusion is reached that in all instances other than those where the terms of trade can be favourably altered, trade barriers are harmful to 'the nation' or are second-best means of attaining the stipulated 'national' objectives. The state is perceived as the representative of the collectivity of individuals and firms within the nation, for whom it (somehow) acts to maximize their collective welfare. There exists some discussion in this theoretical literature of the effects of trade barriers upon the distribution of the national income, but it is typically based upon crude two-factor assumptions which are not too illuminating for the understanding of empirically observable phenomena.

Among the few 'modern' trade economists who attempted, fairly early on, to explore the behaviour of the state with respect to international trade was Charles Kindleberger who, some 25 years ago, wrote a stimulating paper on group behaviour and trade policies in the late nineteenth century in such countries as Germany, Denmark, and the U.K. The state, he argued, was not 'neutral' and it, in effect, pursued the interests of powerful groups.[1] In recent years, these issues have been further explored in both theoretical and empirical terms with particular reference to the American context. This paper attempts to explore some of the roots of recent U.S. commercial policies and, in particular, to consider the implications of the rise of the U.S.-based multinational corporation for them. Implicit in the analysis which follows is a theory of the U.S. state which assumes that directly involved interests, of varying power and influence, bring pressure to bear upon the various institutions of government which form trade policy. The policy which results reflects the divergent strengths of these interests rather than the 'social welfare', however defined, of the United States.

2. THE STRUCTURE OF TRADE BARRIERS IN THE U.S.

. . . One observes, first of all, some major recent shifts in traditional U.S. political attitudes towards international trade and trade barriers:

1. U.S. organized labour (represented by the AFL–CIO) has shifted its over-all position from one of liberalism to one of protectionism.
2. The traditional trade policy stances of the major political parties

have been reversed; the Democratic Party has become more protectionist than the Republican Party.

3. Such representations as are made by business interests on the subjects of trade policy have become much more focused and industry-specific; pressures both for liberal trading policies and for protection are now more frequently offered by *particular* industry representatives rather than by broad-based cross-industry associations.

4. Labour and industry positions on trade policy *within the same industry* are now frequently at odds whereas traditionally they have typically been congruent.

Traditional studies of the politics of U.S. trade policies have concentrated on the functioning of lobbies, the attitudes of businessmen and politicians, the regional and/or sectional roots of the political parties and their consequent positions, and so forth. There have as yet been none which specifically take full account of the growing influence of the U.S.-based transnational enterprise. Yet, so far as an understanding of postwar U.S. international economic policy is concerned, the most significant new factor has been its rapid emergence, which has profoundly altered the structure of international exchange. The political changes described above can all be explained in terms of the rise of the U.S.-based transnational enterprise and the response of the U.S. labour movement to it. The next two sections outline the interests of these enterprises and of labour, respectively, in order to provide the background to such an explanation.

3. TRANSNATIONAL ENTERPRISES AND U.S. TRADE POLICY

There has recently been very rapid growth of 'international production' under the auspices of multinational firms; whereas in 1939 the value of international production made up only one-third of that of international trade, by 1970 the former exceeded the latter. A remarkably high proportion of international trade now takes place on an intrafirm basis in oligopolistically organized markets. The intrafirm trade is additional to the intra-industry trade which has also been widely remarked upon in recent years. The latter is the consequence primarily of differentiation in the final product and of inadequately detailed commodity classification systems. The intrafirm trade is, instead, associated with trade in intermediate products, technology gaps, and oligopoly. Intrafirm trade in intermediate goods and services stems from the fact that the markets for them are typically highly imperfect. In order to reduce search and transactions costs and to ensure their own maximum share of available quasi-rents, in these various imperfect markets, firms have every incentive to internalize transactions in them.

A detailed census for 1966 and a sample survey of 298 major U.S.-owned multinational firms (and their 5,237 majority-owned foreign affiliates) in 1970 have provided the first major compilation of data with respect to the dimensions and composition of U.S. international intrafirm trade.[2] These data indicate that in 1966, 66 per cent of total U.S. exports and 46 per cent of total U.S. imports were associated with U.S.-based transnational enterprises; these figures include transactions between U.S. residents who were not majority owners of overseas affiliates and U.S.-owned affiliates, and those between U.S. firms and foreigners who were not majority-owned affiliates. It seems reasonable to assume, however, that a considerable proportion of these latter transactions are, in fact, between enterprises with some form of link, e.g. minority ownership, licensing agreements, etc. An absolute lower bound on the relative dimensions of U.S. intrafirm trade is given by the proportions of total trade accounted for by trade between U.S. transnational enterprises and their own majority-owned affiliates: 21 per cent for exports and 16 per cent for imports in 1970.

Between 1966 and 1970, the trade associated with 298 multinational corporations (MNCs) which responded to the survey (and which accounted for over 70 per cent of total MNC-associated trade in 1966) rose more quickly than total U.S. trade—both in terms of export and import values. The trade between majority-owned foreign affiliates and U.S. parent firms grew most quickly of all. Between 1966 and 1970, while total U.S. imports grew by 56.3 per cent, imports by U.S. multinational firms from their own affiliates grew by 92.2 per cent in the manufacturing sector and by 81.9 per cent over all. (On the export side, the corresponding figures were: 43.3 per cent for total exports, 68.2 per cent for intrafirm manufacturing, and 71.2 per cent for intrafirm over all.) This relative increase in the importance of intrafirm and MNC-associated trade is found in both exports and imports. This suggests that intrafirm trade and the role of the transnational enterprise in trade is growing as part of a structural alteration in the mode of organizing the world's industry and not because of some chance correlation with industries experiencing particular characteristics.

Although transnational enterprises can be extremely adaptive and quick to respond to governmental policy shifts, they are none the less not without preferences of their own with respect to official policies. As powerful pressure groups they can be expected to seek to influence governmental policy in all the countries in which they operate, either through direct lobbying or through less direct means. U.S.-based multinational firms are sure to exert powerful influence upon the formation of U.S. commercial policy (as well as a wide range of other foreign economic and political policies). What, then, are these firms likely to want?

In their efforts to rationalize their world-wide activities and so maximize their long-run profits, national boundaries are decided nuisances to them. They involve the payment of customs duties, the meeting of various administrative requirements (particularly those relating to currency controls), frequent prohibitions or regulatory mechanisms, and the complications introduced by differential (and sometimes conflicting) tax and other legal stipulations. All of these impediments to the free flow of intrafirm resources can be regarded as analogous to transport costs for the purpose of optimizing a firm's world-wide operations. Like transport costs, these international barriers are less troublesome (and costly) when they are lower. One cannot therefore be surprised to find multinational firms acting as strong general advocates of freedom in international exchange and payments. Openness with respect to financial and human capital flows and technology trade is obviously no less important to them than free trade in goods and services. (As the U.S. shifts to the export of services, freedom in these respects will increasingly be in the U.S. national interest as well.) Indeed, the links between factor flows and goods flows are so close, in the context of a particular multinational firm's operations, as to be inseparable; the firm's decision as to whether to service a foreign market by exporting or producing abroad, for example, is largely a function of the barriers to goods, technology, and investment flows between the countries in question.

Still at the general level, firms with international interests have a further reason for opposing barriers to international flows imposed by the government of their own home country. Not only may these barriers impede their activities directly but, even where they do not, they may also stimulate foreign countries in which they are active to retaliatory action against either their exporting or investing activities (which may be in sectors unrelated to those in which the original action was taken). The survey already mentioned, of 298 of the biggest U.S.-based transnational manufacturing enterprises, found that on average, in 1970, they serviced foreign markets through overseas production to a (sales) value which was 2–3 times as large as that of their exports to these countries.[3] Thus their concerns with respect to retaliation are likely to be less focused upon trade than upon investment.

At a more specific level, what sort of trade policies should a particular transnational enterprise be most interested in? Above all, it seeks to avoid paying taxes or encountering other obstacles to intrafirm transactions. . . . One must therefore know what are the goods and services which are internationally traded by the firm in question. In general, it seems safe to say, primary inputs and intermediate products dominate intrafirm international trade. There is also evidence that products traded internationally within U.S.-based firms are relatively capital-intensive and research-intensive.

4. LABOUR AND U.S. TRADE POLICY

Were skilled and semi-skilled labour homogeneous and sold on perfect markets, it would always have made perfect sense for U.S. trade unions to seek to protect their members' income by restricting international exchange. They would gain both from the restriction of imports (and of labour itself) from countries in which labour is relatively more abundant, and from the restriction of outflows of capital and technology from the U.S. to such countries. This is because unskilled and semi-skilled labour is the relatively scarce factor in the U.S., or, in the context of a world of mobile capital and technology, because it is paid at very high rates by international standards. Their behaviour in recent years is thus fully in accord with the tenets of orthodox factor endowment theory, even though its assumptions are not, on the face of it, even approximately matched by the reality of either factor or product markets. It is not necessary to demonstrate . . . that the AFL–CIO is not representative of U.S. labour to explain its actions. What rather seems to require explanation is why the U.S. labour movement was previously so liberal in its approach to international trade.

One could postulate that U.S. labour was impressed by the exponents of the view that trade barriers caused or rendered more serious the depression of the 1930s, a repetition of which they wanted at all costs to avoid. An equally good explanation for earlier liberal positions could run in terms of the existence of non-competing groups—differentiated by skills, by industries, and by regions—which would render important the question of the representativeness of labour spokesmen. Bergsten's data show convincingly that a majority of the membership of the AFL–CIO is *not* in industries directly affected by international trade; 56 per cent of the membership is not even in manufacturing.[4] This fact alone could account for organized labour's prior opposition to protectionism.

If the latter explanation is correct, the recent alteration in position must derive from some *change* in the international environment since the composition of the membership has not recently altered significantly. Such a change is the emergence of the transnational enterprise, which has significantly weakened the position of the scarce factor labour, in every U.S. industry. . . . Labour is obviously particularly concerned with the implications of international trade in those firms and sectors in which there is little prospect of expanded intra-industry trade (notably where competing imports originate in less developed countries) and therefore employment gains to offset the possible job losses from imports.

5. THE NEW POLITICAL ECONOMY OF U.S. TRADE POLICY

The revised line-up of the two traditional political parties reflects the new elements of the political and economic scene. As the party of labour, the Democrats—despite their liberal traditions—have followed labour's shift toward protectionism. The business-oriented Republican party, now responsive to the needs of U.S.-based transnational enterprises, has become the party of liberalization in trade. . . . Both are highly receptive to the special cases made by particular industries; wherever labour and capital are still allied in seeking protection (wherever, that is, the firms in question have few international connections), both favour protection. Where in a particular industry, however, unions face a transnational enterprise, the conflict generally is resolved in favour of the latter.

U.S. trade policy is thus now being determined with reference to two main contributing thrusts: (1) that of organized labour which presses most vigorously for the maintenance or increase of protection in those industries in which labour is most vulnerable; (2) that of U.S.-based transnational enterprises, which press most vigorously for trade barrier reductions in those commodity classifications in which they themselves trade, and show no particular interest in those relatively labour-intensive and declining industries in which they are not directly involved. The result of these twin pressures, of which the latter is more powerful, is that particular combination of liberalization and protectionism which has, in fact, emerged.

This interpretation is supported by several pieces of suggestive evidence.

1. It is well known that import duties upon primary and intermediate products are typically lower than average duties on final products. Whether such products dominate intrafirm international trade because import duties on these products are typically lower or whether the duties are lower precisely because of the pressure from the producing firms to this effect cannot be firmly proven, but the presumption is usually that the causation runs in the latter direction. Only where there are already local producers of the inputs can there be any political pressure for duties or other protection on them; once they are imposed, the transnational enterprises are among those thereby stimulated to produce inputs locally rather than continuing to import or buying at arm's length from local suppliers, and if this local production is subsequently taken over by internationally-oriented firms, pressure for continued protection can be expected to decline.

2. This escalation in the tariff as one moves from primary to processing activities could also be interpreted more simply—as a reflection of
the frequent total absence of U.S. production of certain raw materials
and the consequent absence of protectionist pressures. But if the latter
simpler explanation is accepted, one still requires an explanation for the
usual continued escalation from semi-processed to processed and more
manufactured goods, for the semi-processed product can be, and
frequently is, made locally with imported (tariff-free) materials. One
would expect, other things being equal, political pressure from these
local producers to generate just as much protection as that achieved for
local raw materials or local final products. The fact that this is not, in
fact, typically found suggests that the pressures from the users are
relatively more effective than those from these particular producers.
Presumably, this is at least partially explained by the fact that these local
producers, particularly in the case of new products, are themselves often
vertically integrated with the eventual (often transnational) users, to
whom the duty on the input is of no protective significance. (In political
terms, one might also note the likelihood that using firms will be
considerably more geographically dispersed within the country, and
thereby able to influence more Congressional voters, than the original
semi-processing firm itself.) One can, then, explain this particular
escalation in terms of the political power of transnational enterprises the
bulk of whose intrafirm trade is in such intermediate products.

3. Since capital-intensity and research-intensity characterize the products which are traded across international borders within U.S.-based
firms, the facts that U.S. trade barriers are lower and Kennedy Round
reductions were greater in such products also support the view that
transnational enterprises have been influential in the determination of
the structure of U.S. trade barriers. U.S. production of labour-intensive
products in which these firms do not trade has clearly been relatively
well protected in consequence of unopposed labour pressure.

4. The creation of value added tariffs in the U.S. (duties levied upon
the difference between the gross value of the products concerned and
the value of inputs originating in the U.S., permitted under items 806.30
and 807.00 of the tariff schedule) reflects the same political pressures.
The only firms capable of employing such provisions are the
transnationally oriented ones, although in this case these include trading
firms as well as manufacturers. There has been a remarkably rapid rate
of growth in the use of the 807.00 provision, since its introduction in the
second half of the 1960s. Imports under the terms of item 807.00 have
risen fivefold from 1966 to 1974.[5] Even in the recession year 1974,
dutiable value under this item rose by 26 per cent. In 1974, fully 94 per
cent of this total dutiable value was found in the multinational-firm-
dominated metal products group (notably, motor vehicles, engines,

office machines, radio and television apparatus, semiconductors, air-craft, electronic memories, sewing machines, etc.). It is noteworthy that despite vigorous opposition to these provisions in the U.S. tariff on the part of the AFL–CIO they remain firmly in place. The presumption is that they do so because they generate substantial gains for politically powerful interests, the transnational enterprises, which more than offset these pressures from labour. At the industry level, where labour and capital are at odds in their approaches to the policymakers, so far, the preferences of the latter prevail.

5. A further striking example of the political strength of the transnational enterprise in the formation of U.S. (actually of North American) trade policy is the U.S.–Canadian auto agreement. While its origins lay in the desire of the Canadian Government to increase Canada's share of North American automobile production, the agreement reached was one peculiarly favourable to the transnational automobile industry. It provided for free trade in automobiles and automobile parts but, in the Canadian case, it was available *only to the producing firms* and not to Canadian consumers. (In the U.S. case, the deal actually required a special waiver from the provisions of the GATT because of its specific exclusion of third-country firms.) The agreement permitted a substantial rationalization of the North American automobile industry while offering significant continued price support for automobiles in Canada. Potential opposition from the labour movement in the U.S. (the UAW) was, in this case, bought off by a fairly liberal adjustment assistance programme, considerably more liberal in its effects than that developed for the Kennedy Round.

6. To some extent, the bias in trade barriers against products which are not traded by transnational enterprises extends to the trade in IOUs as well, that is, to capital markets. While the U.S. Government offers investment guarantees and insurance, and tax deferrals, for direct investors overseas, there are no corresponding encouragements to the importation by arm's-length U.S. investors of foreign bonds. (IBRD bonds seem to be the exception proving the rule.) To the contrary, there exists legislation in many states limiting or prohibiting the holding of foreign securities in the portfolios of banks, insurance companies, and pension funds. The effect is to discriminate in favour of capital flows which are intermediated by the transnational enterprise. . . .

CONCLUSION

This paper has been concerned to develop a pressure group approach to the understanding of recent U.S. trade policy. It has argued that the shift in the attitudes towards trade of the traditional political parties and the labour movement, and the increased differentiation of business attitudes thereto, are best interpreted as responses to the development of U.S.-based transnational enterprises in the postwar period. U.S. trade policy is now the product primarily of the political pressures from transnational enterprises on the one hand and organized labour on the other. Where these interests are in conflict in particular industries, the evidence suggests that the former will usually win out, and liberal trade policies will be pursued. Where U.S. firms are not internationally oriented, however, they are likely to ally with labour and to achieve some success in generating protection from competitive imports. Since the new political forces operative in the U.S. are likely to be replicated in other industrialized countries, the 'model' presented here may be of wider relevance.

NOTES

1. C. P. Kindleberger, 'Group behaviour and international trade', *Journal of Political Economy*, vol. 59, no. 1, Feb. 1951.

2. Betty L. Barker, 'U.S. foreign trade associated with U.S. multinational companies', *Survey of Current Business*, Dec. 1972. The data which follow are all taken from this source.

3. Ibid.

4. C. Fred Bergsten, 'The cost of import restrictions to American consumers', in Robert Baldwin and J. D. Ricardson (eds.), *International Trade and Finance* (Boston: Little, Brown, 1974), pp. 136–7.

5. These data were supplied by the U.S. International Trade Commission.

23. The Tokyo Round: Particularistic Interests and Prospects for Stability in the Global Trading System

STEPHEN D. KRASNER

Stephen Krasner applies Realist principles to the analysis of the international trading order. He argues that the general trend toward openness after World War II was a result of both United States hegemony and a corresponding ability on the part of the United States to lead the world toward reduced barriers to trade. This often required that the United States countenance trade restrictions by its allies, especially in Europe and Japan, in the interests of the stability of the international political and economic systems that the United States was rebuilding in the aftermath of World War II. Today, Krasner argues, a much less powerful United States is far less willing and able to sacrifice its short-term interests for long-term stability. American trade policy has thus come to look more like that of other developed nations, protecting and/or subsidizing many uncompetitive industries. Krasner believes that this change in international power relations has altered prospects for the openness of world trade; a move toward closure is more likely than it was during the era of United States hegemony, but 1930s-style trade wars are not inevitable.

INTRODUCTION

. . . The Tokyo Round of trade negotiations, more or less completed in April 1979, was heralded with the predictable hosannas. The agreements concluded at Geneva, which included tariff reductions, revisions of the General Agreement on Tariffs and Trade's (GATT) Articles of Agreement, several codes covering nontariff trade barriers (NTBs), and sectoral agreements for dairy products, meat, and aircraft, were described by GATT officials and national leaders as a triumph of free trade over rising protectionism. The codes dealing with NTBs were singled out because such issues had never been systematically confronted.

However, an examination of the provisions of the Tokyo Round suggests that the affirmation of liberality was not as unabashed as statements of political leaders suggest. The agreements hardly endorse protectionism, but they, like other international agreements of the 1970s, particularly the Jamaica accords revising the Articles of Agreement of the International Monetary Fund (IMF), at most legitimate a more differentiated international economic order. Rules and behavior have become more fragmented. Different countries and different sectors are treated in different ways.

The most important determinant of the Geneva accords was the particularistic calculations of interest undertaken by different states, often under pressure from national economic groups. Some of these groups, such as the agricultural industries of the EEC and Japan, unambiguously support restrictions. Others, such as high-technology industries and international banks, favor a liberal regime. Still others are so entangled in both exporting and importing that it is difficult for them to make any sensible calculation of their interests; they are carried by inertia. The summation of particularistic interests does not decisively favor either protectionism or free trade, but it does imply a more complicated trading regime.

Such a regime is not inherently unstable. Protectionism in some areas does not mean protectionism across the board. The extant international trading regime is, however, more fragile than the order that existed in the 1950s and 1960s, not because particular economic interests have changed, but because there has been a fundamental shift in the distribution of power in the international political system: The unique paramountcy enjoyed by the United States has come to an end.

Through the 1960s the United States was not only much larger than any other state in the Western bloc, it also enjoyed a commanding position in virtually åll issue areas. The United States facilitated the establishment and maintenance of an open trading regime by countering unexpected shocks and providing leadership. Furthermore, U.S. policy makers were prepared to sacrifice specific economic interests to long-term political goals; this led them to ease the burdens of an open regime for other countries by allowing them to discriminate against U.S. products. The United States no longer has the resources or the inclination to forego tangible material benefits for broad political objectives. While many sectors will continue to support an open regime, the absence of a hegemonic state willing and able to contain unexpected shocks leaves the regime more brittle. There is no internal dynamic leading to closure of the trading system, but collapse could occur nevertheless.

   This article first describes the central role played by the United States in the creation of the open trading regime of the post-World War II period. It then analyzes the particularistic calculus of interests that led to the tariff reductions and codes negotiated during the Tokyo Round. The concluding section assesses the prospects for stability and the dangers of a slide into a new protectionist era.

THE ROLE OF THE UNITED STATES

The United States played the leading role in the evolution of the postwar trading regime, a role that reflected its extraordinary position in the global political system. In terms of GNP, the simplest measure of international power, the United States at the end of World War II was three times larger than the Soviet Union, which was effectively isolated within its own bloc, and six times larger than its closest rival in the noncommunist world, Great Britain. Moreover, U.S. dominance encompassed a wide range of issue areas. The United States was the world's largest producer of food, petroleum, steel, and electricity. Its technological capabilities were unparalleled in established industries as well as in newer sectors such as computers and aircraft. It had the world's largest navy and a monopoly of nuclear weapons until 1949. Even into the 1960s the United States could counter an oil embargo by producing more oil. It could affect world sugar prices through its quota programs. It could promote European economic development with foreign aid. It could alter political developments in other countries through covert interventions. It could confront missile carrying freighters with a naval blockade. Policy makers had resources at their disposal which could be efficiently applied over a wide range of policy areas. They did not have to concern themselves with the fugacity of power resources because the variety of resources under their control was so extensive. This, as much as sheer size, was the distinguishing characteristic of U.S. power in the two decades after World War II.

   The United States used its power most forcefully to promote general political goals rather than specific economic interests. In the immediate aftermath of World War II U.S. leaders precipitously attempted to implement the letter of the Bretton Woods Accords, but with the collapse of Britain's effort at convertibility and the growing alarm about communism and the Soviet Union, they became more willing to compromise principles to strengthen their allies. They believed that greater trading opportunities would enhance economic reconstruction, and that economic reconstruction would make Europe and Japan less vulnerable to internal or external communist threats. In some issue areas, such as multilateral negotiations to lower tariffs, open trade was consistent with both liberal principles and specific U.S. economic interests. But in other areas the United States was prepared to allow discrimination against its own exports to alleviate the strain of involvement in international trade for its allies. Policies so permissive of violations of specific and identifiable economic interests can only be carried out by a state that is exceptionally strong, a state so powerful that it can focus on long-term, generally formulated goals only remotely tied to particular material objectives.

The willingness of the United States to sacrifice specific economic interests to long-term political goals was manifest in the active promotion of European integration and the toleration of discrimination against the United States by both Europe and Japan. It was believed that a unified Europe would integrate Germany and resist Soviet aggression and communist infiltration. Marshall Plan aid, disbursed through the Organization for European Economic Cooperation (OEEC), required joint arrangements. One of the provisions of the 1948 OEEC Charter called for the reduction of trade barriers within Europe. The 1950 OEEC Code of Liberalization was directed at the reduction of quantitative barriers to trade within Europe but not with the United States. The European Payments Union, for which the United States provided reserves, encouraged intra- rather than extra-European trade. The European Coal and Steel Community, which clearly violated a GATT requirement that customs unions cover virtually all products, received a waiver from the contracting parties to GATT because of U.S. backing. The Treaty of Rome was also vigorously supported by the United States, even though the establishment of associated states violated GATT articles and could only harm U.S. trading interests. As a result of the proliferation of regional integration schemes, the percentage of trade that took place under unconditional most favored nation (MFN) conditions fell from 90% in 1955 to 77% in 1970. While these blocs may have furthered global welfare through the creation of trade, they diverted trade from the United States.

The United States also tolerated Japanese protectionism to further political goals. By the late 1940s U.S. leaders, for reasons similar to those that led them to encourage European unification, had concluded that it was critical to rebuild the Japanese economy. Therefore, they accepted a high degree of economic protectionism in Japan during the 1950s and 1960s. The United States opened its market to Japanese goods while European countries continued discriminatory practices against Japan, even after it was admitted to GATT as a result of U.S. prodding in 1955. Only in the early 1970s did U.S. policy makers begin to push Europe to accept more Japanese goods. . . .

In sum, during the postwar period the United States did not try to fully exploit all of its commercial advantages. Free trade was accepted in areas where the United States did not have a comparative advantage and discrimination was tolerated where U.S. products did have an advantage. One study of the postwar trading system concludes "that postwar trade liberalization has been a beneficial exercise for America's trade partners, and that if any country could be said to have 'lost' within our given time-horizon it was the United States itself."[1]

The United States has now lost its unique paramountcy. This is reflected not so much in aggregate terms (GNP is still three times larger than that of its nearest noncommunist rival, Japan) as in specific issue areas. The U.S. share of world crude petroleum production has fallen from over 50% in the early 1950s to less than 15%, steel production from 45% to under 20%. In 1952 the United States held 68% of all international reserves; in 1962 it held 27%; and in 1977, only 6%. In 1947 the United States accounted for 32% of world exports; in 1957, 19%; in 1967, 15%; and in 1974, only 11%. In the 22 years between 1945 and 1968, the U.S. current account trade balance was in surplus 13 times; in the 11 years since 1967 it has been in surplus only once. The United States is still an exceptionally powerful country by any standard, but its position is far different from what it was in the late 1940s. Policy makers may be forced to use more expensive and dangerous resources in specific conflicts because more appropriate ones are not available. (Should the United States militarily occupy Arabian Gulf oil fields? Is it even capable of this?) While the United States will still prevail in disputes over many specific issues, it can no longer take the very farsighted view or muster the resources necessary to assure stability for various international regimes.

This change in the international position of the United States has two implications for the international trading system in general and the Tokyo Round in particular. First, U.S. central decision makers have more vigorously pursued national economic interests by protecting import-competing industries and promoting exports. In the past the United States has acted to shield many industries threatened by imports: the dairy industry beginning in 1954, the petroleum and textile industries in the late 1950s, and the steel industry in 1967. While the level of protection has varied, the fragmented nature of the U.S. political system has made it impossible for central decision makers to ignore interest group pressures. The scope and depth of such protection has, however, increased in the 1970s as more sectors have been subject to foreign competition. Existing laws have been enforced more vigorously. The professional staff dealing with anti-dumping cases was increased from 5 in 1968 to 41 in 1972. From 1960 through 1968 there were 11 positive determinations of injury under the Anti-Dumping Act; from 1969 through 1977, there were 65 positive determinations.

The United States has also begun to press more vigorously for greater export opportunities. Policy makers were not oblivious to such matters in the past, but concern has markedly increased. . . . For both exports and imports there is now more willingness on the part of decision makers in the executive branch to press for clearly defined economic objectives, whereas in the 1950s and 1960s protectionist actions by the United States were virtually always the result of popular initiatives projected through Congress.

The agenda of the Tokyo Round reflected the new U.S. concern for specific and precise issues. Earlier trade negotiations were more circumscribed. The only nontariff measures negotiated during the Kennedy Round were the American Selling Price (ASP) for customs valuations of some chemicals, the antidumping code, some European user taxes on automobiles, and Swiss regulations affecting canned fruit imports. The ASP issues were forced on the United States by Europe and the agreement reached at Geneva was ultimately rejected by the Congress. The antidumping code was gutted by a congressional provision that U.S. law would take precedence over the code. The Tokyo Round had a much broader agenda and most of the issues were raised by the United States. Two matters, commercial aircraft and counterfeit goods, were introduced at U.S. insistence in the summer of 1978. While U.S. policy makers had negotiated vigorously on tariff questions during the earlier rounds of multilateral trade negotiations, they were prepared to ignore other practices that damaged U.S. trade. This, as the broad agenda of the Tokyo Round indicates, is no longer true.

The second consequence of the decline in U.S. power for the trading regime is that the United States is no longer as concerned with preserving international norms if they conflict with specific U.S. interests. The clearest example of this shift is the program announced in August 1971. In the Tokyo Round the willingness to compromise established principle is reflected in departures from nondiscrimination, reciprocity, and market determination of economic activity. Nondiscrimination in particular was a central precept of the postwar trading regime. It had been endorsed by U.S. leaders not simply because of their adherence to classical economic doctrines, but also because they believed that selective discrimination encouraged economic and political blocs which exacerbated international tensions. Yet in the Tokyo Round departures from unconditional MFN treatment are embodied in the government procurement, subsidy, and proposed safeguard codes, and in revisions of GATT. In the past the principle of unconditional MFN treatment was often honored in the breach; in the Tokyo Round it was directly compromised.

PARTICULARISTIC INTERESTS

Because the United States is now behaving more like an ordinary power, the policies of all major trading countries have become more alike. They are driven by specific economic interests rather than general long-term visions of how the international system should be ordered. These interests can be of two kinds: macroeconomic and sectoral. Both macroeconomic and sectoral considerations can provide an impetus toward either openness or closure in the international trading regime.

From a macroeconomic perspective an open system offers the benefits of lower inflation rates and greater welfare. There have been examples of countries that have reduced trade barriers to lessen price increases. Germany unilaterally lowered tariffs in 1956 and 1957. Argentina, Iceland, Canada, Ireland, and Switzerland implemented their Kennedy Round tariff cuts ahead of schedule to alleviate inflation. While the anti-inflation effects of openness are greater for smaller countries, there is some benefit for large countries as well.

These macroeconomic benefits cannot, however, be exaggerated. If they were the critical determinants of international economic policy, trade barriers would have been eliminated long ago. Most recent studies of what has come to be called the political business cycle suggest that politicians find it more attractive to pump up the economy, particularly before elections, than to control inflation. . . .

The following argument assumes that macroeconomic performance is held constant. Sectoral interests have had an important impact on international trade policy. Most of the exceptions to the liberal trading regime of the postwar period involve specific sectors such as steel and textiles. A sectoral perspective is biased toward protectionism because groups suffering immediate losses are likely to act more vigorously than groups contemplating future gains. Under present conditions, however, the consequences of this asymmetry should not be exaggerated. The range of interests enjoying benefits from the present international economic regime has grown prodigiously as a result of three decades of increasing openness. Of U.S. manufacturing jobs, 12% now produce for export; of U.S. farm acreage, 33% (of gross sales, 25%) rely on foreign buyers; and of the profits of U.S. corporations, 33% are generated by overseas activities. In addition, U.S. banks have dramatically increased their foreign lending. One simple overall measure of involvement in the world economy is the ratio of trade (exports plus imports) to GNP. This ratio rose during most of the nineteenth century, fell during the interwar period, and recovered in the postwar period, with a particularly rapid rate of increase since 1970. . . .

These aggregate figures obscure a further consideration that undercuts sectoral pressures for protectionism: Many industries confront crosscutting pressures. They are involved in both exporting and importing. . . .

The number of sectors experiencing crosscutting pressures is much greater in the United States and Europe than it is in Japan. . . .

The high level of crosscutting pressures in the United States and Europe is further highlighted if sectoral trade balances are broken down on a regional basis. . . . These figures show a striking degree of balance in European and American trade in manufactures. . . . Given this situation of relative trade balance within particular sectors, it would be surprising to find any definitive pressure for stifling trade in manufactures between the United States and the EEC. For food, however, the EEC has a large deficit with the United States and produces many of the products that it imports, a situation highly conducive to restrictive practices. . . .

Trade with Japan is much more susceptible to protectionist pressures, particularly from Europe. With the exception of chemicals and textiles, Europe has a negative trade balance with Japan in all of its manufacturing sectors. . . . Furthermore, Europe has few primary product sectors with much interest in exporting to Japan. In 1976 primary product exports accounted for 16% of European exports to Japan. If restrictions that Europe has already imposed on Japan were eliminated, the trading pattern would be even more skewed.

In the case of U.S. trade with Japan, sectoral interests are not so overwhelmingly biased toward restrictive policies. There are no crosscutting pressures within sectors of the kind so prevalent in European-American trade, but there are primary commodity sectors with very strong interests in the Japanese market. In 1976 raw materials exports accounted for more than 60% of U.S. exports to Japan. These sectors can provide countervailing pressure against restrictionist sentiments from manufacturing sectors.

Trading relations between industrialized areas and newly industrializing countries (NICs) are also typified by countervailing but not crosscutting, inter- but not intrasectoral, pressures. While some industries in wealthier countries are experiencing strong competition from NICs, others are expanding their markets in these countries. This is true even in the textiles sector. . . . In this industry industrialized countries sell the factors of production (raw materials and machinery) to developing countries which do the processing (making clothing).

This analysis of regional sectoral trade can be summarized in four general patterns, which are presented in order of increasing propensity toward protectionism.

(1) *No Pressures.* There are few import-competing sectors in either trading area. The clearest example is European and Japanese

trade with Third World countries that export raw materials and do not have significant manufacturing sectors.

(2) *Crosscutting Pressures.* There is high intrasectoral trade. The best example is manufacturing trade between the United States and Europe. Even with a very open system, industries may not be able to classify themselves as import competing or export oriented. Such confusion is even more likely if there is a high degree of multinational investment in a sector. Since most sectors experiencing crosscutting pressures are heavily involved in world trade, they are likely to favor liberal policies.

(3) *Countervailing Pressures.* There are identifiable export-oriented and import-competing sectors. Some groups would benefit from protectionism, but some would benefit from continued openness. The clearest examples are trade between the United States and Japan, between the United States and copper- and sugar-exporting LDCs, and between the industrialized areas and the NICs of the Third World. The impact of a trade policy is determined by the relative political power of export-oriented and import-competing sectors.

(4) *Negative Pressures.* One partner has only import-competing industries. The clearest example is European trade with Japan.

This array of trading patterns does not suggest that sectoral interests will generate any decisive movement toward protectionism, but it does suggest a propensity in the United States and Europe to apply selective restrictions against particular products and countries.

THE TOKYO ROUND

Differentiated treatment of products and countries was manifest in the Tokyo Round, which led to the following accords:

(1) A series of tariff cuts.

(2) Revisions of GATT related to dispute settlement, differential treatment for LDCs, and trade restrictions for balance of payments reasons.

(3) Five codes to liberalize nontariff barriers. The codes deal with: (a) subsidies and countervailing duties, (b) customs valuation, (c) government procurement, (d) technical barriers and standards, and (e) import licensing procedures. In addition, negotiations are continuing for codes on safeguards and trade in counterfeit products. The antidumping code concluded during the Tokyo Round was slightly revised.

(4) A sectoral agreement for trade in civil aircraft.

(5) Essentially consultative arrangements for trade in dairy and bovine meat products.

How do these agreements relate to the liberal ideal of nondiscriminatory trade expansion dictated by market principles, which is enshrined in GATT, and to the pattern of particularistic interests described in the previous section? They can be divided into three groups:

(1) The tariff reductions, Agreement on Trade in Civil Aircraft, and the codes concerning customs valuation, technical barriers, and import licensing closely conform with classical liberal principles. They are a manifestation of generally high involvement in the world economy and trading relations in which import-competing industries are absent or in which trading sectors experience crosscutting cleavages (trading patterns 1 and 2). These measures will increase trade on a nondiscriminatory basis and reduce state intervention.

(2) The codes related to government procurement and subsidies will have mixed results: They will increase the level of international transactions and the range of decisions influenced by market forces, but they will enhance the possibility of discriminatory treatment. These codes reflect trade patterns in which there are crosscutting pressures within sectors or countervailing pressures across sectors, with export-oriented groups holding the weight of power (trading patterns 2 and 3). There is a general desire to increase trade but also to protect particular import-competing sectors.

(3) The agreements related to agriculture, special and differential treatment for LDCs (in the revisions of the GATT and NTB codes), and the safeguards code (if it is finally approved) are farthest from the liberal ideal. They will not do much to increase trade, since they tacitly endorse discriminatory treatment and state interference in the allocation of resources. They reflect trading relationships in which the weight of countervailing pressures is on the side of protectionist groups or in which one trading partner has only import-competing industries (trading patterns 3 and 4). In addition, the effort to secure special and differential treatment not so much manifests existing trade patterns as the Third World's desire to legitimate a new trading order, one in which developing countries would be exempted from the obligation to offer reciprocal treatment.

In all aspects of the negotiations the positions of the major actors—the United States, the EEC, Japan, and the LDCs—were determined by their particularistic interests. Basically the United States, which wanted to change nontariff practices that were impeding its trade, and the LDCs, which wanted special and differential treatment, were the demanders in the negotiations. The Tokyo Round for the EEC was an exercise in damage limitation, attempting to give up as little as possible without alienating the United States and thus threatening the trading system as a whole. For the Japanese, with their large positive trade balance, the problem was not to open markets for more exports but to fend off demands for greater access to the Japanese market and forestall more protectionist policies against Japanese goods. The guiding principle for all participants was the classical mercantilist dictum urging an increase in trade surpluses, rather than the neoliberal prescript of maximizing aggregate welfare. Gone are the 1950s when the United States actually encouraged discrimination against its own exports. . . .

. . . The outcome of the Tokyo Round does not accord with any general principle. In some areas the agreements closely conform with liberal ideals of increasing trade, enhancing the autonomy of the market, and upholding nondiscrimination. In other areas the agreements fail to expand trade, legitimate state intervention, and endorse discriminatory practices. The underlying rationale for this outcome was not general principle but particularistic interests. In areas where there are no significant import-competing industries or where there are crosscutting cleavages within sectors, steps were taken which move the international trading system closer to the liberal ideal. In areas where import-competing industries dominate national political decisions, the MTN agreements endorse existing discriminatory and restrictive practices.

PROSPECTS FOR STABILITY

Can such a fragmented order be stable? The prevailing answer is no. Most policy makers and analysts in the United States see international trade as a disequilibrium system in which failure to sustain movement toward greater openness precipitates a descent along the slippery slope to rampant protectionism. The essence of the slippery-slope view of international trade is that within countries capitulation to protectionist pressures in one industry leads to capitulation in other sectors. Between countries increased protectionist actions lead to retaliation. . . .

The postwar regime does not offer much support for the slippery-slope position. The regime has been peppered with exceptions to liberal principles in agriculture, textiles, and in the protectionism of Japan and the EEC. There is no logically necessary relationship between protection in one sector and protection in another at the national or international level. Within a country appeals for protection based on government consistency are only one of many variables affecting an industry's position. Virtually all empirical investigations indicate that other factors, such as size, employment level, geographic concentration, and political organization are far more important.

In the international economic system the ability to retaliate against protectionist measures depends on the relative opportunity costs of change for the parties involved. Those countries that are now most likely to be targets of protectionism—Japan and industrializing LDCs—are not in a position to retaliate because the consequences of a trade war would be more damaging to them than to importing countries. The opportunity costs for the United States and Europe of producing manufactured products that they now import from Japan and the NICs would be small compared to the costs these countries would encounter as a result of shifting factors and finding new markets. Thus neither empirical evidence nor opportunity cost comparisons suggest that the international trading order is a disequilibrium system in which restrictions in one area invariably lead to restrictions in others.

The possibility of collapse is, however, immanent in the present situation. It comes not from the internal dynamics of the trading system (the spread of protectionism across sectors and between countries), but from the changing distribution of power in the international system. An international regime can have many sources of support—economic, ideological, and political. In the 1950s the international trading regime was able to draw upon all three of these factors. Economically, a generally open system with the United States tacitly accepting many restrictions was attractive to all of the major trading areas. Ideologically the "lessons" of the 1930s had been learned firsthand by most of the world's leaders: A closed regime led to economic difficulties, trading blocs, political antagonisms, and war. Politically, the United States had the power and the commitment to support the regime.

In the present period clearly defined economic interests have become the dominant force sustaining the regime. Ideological considerations, though weak, cannot be dismissed, if only because there has been no convincing alternative to a liberal order presented in the United States. In Britain a group of academics known as the Cambridge Group have advocated more restrictive policies and have gotten a wide hearing in the press and government circles. The French have never been enamored of the principle of free trade. And the LDCs reject altogether the principle that all states should be treated alike. Thus, ideological commitments to a liberal international trading order have eroded.

The most important change affecting the prospects for stability of the international trading system has, however, been the decline of American power. Particularistic calculations of interest can impart considerable inertia. A regime that is already open is likely to stay open. Inertia cannot, however, maintain the course of a regime that is buffeted by external shocks. This task is most effectively performed by a hegemonic power. In the 1950s and 1960s U.S. policy makers had the resources to counter shocks in virtually any issue area. This is no longer true. Contrast the U.S. surplus oil capacity in 1967, when the Arab exporting states attempted an embargo, to U.S. dependence on imports in 1973; or the U.S. ability to effect regime changes in Iran in 1953 to relations with Khomeini in 1979. In a multipolar world, even if all major actors support an open system, they may not be able to achieve the level of policy coordination necessary to generate the resources needed to preserve stability. Thus, the international trading system may go on, but it may also radically change. In a multipolar world the importance of *fortuna* of unanticipated shocks increases, for there is no hegemonic state to provide *virtu*.

NOTE

1. Curzon, G. and V. Curzon (1976) "The management of trade relations in the GATT," in A. Shonfield (ed.) *International Economic Relations of the Western World 1959–1971*. London: Oxford Univ. Press, p. 200.

24. Trade in Primary Commodities

JOAN ROBINSON

Well-known Marxist economist Joan Robinson explores here the constraints that developing countries face in a world market they have little control over. She asserts that a variety of economic and noneconomic factors place the developing nations in a subordinate position in the international trading system. For Robinson, unlike for Liberals, foreign trade has a very mixed impact on the development process, and may indeed serve to disrupt Third World economies. Robinson's view is representative of that of Marxists and others who believe that international capitalism, and world trade in particular, is structured to ensure the maintenance of the Third World in economic and political subordination to the developed countries.

The Third-World countries of today were drawn into the capitalist world market, under regimes of formal and informal colonialism, as appendages of the metropolitan nations to supply raw materials and exotic commodities to the industrial centre. These may be divided into broad types, though there are important variations within each type. Minerals had to be produced where the deposits were found. Animal products required vacant land for ranching. The tropical belt around the world provided facilities for vegetable products, some, such as rubber, transplanted from west to east; some, such as coffee, from east to west. These provide the basis for consumption-goods industries, especially some fruits, tea, coffee and chocolate, and for some industrial raw materials including rubber and natural fibres. They now provide the basis for export earnings which are potentially valuable for development, but their distribution amongst the territories of modern states is completely arbitary, depending upon accidents of economic geography and of their history in colonial and neo-colonial times.

This raises once more the question of what constitutes a national economic entity. The sources of raw materials which were developed by investment from the metropolitan countries are largely still owned and controlled by capitalist corporations. Mining companies in Africa, for instance, employ local labour and have been induced to train local personnel for the lower rungs of management but policy is still in the hands of the overseas headquarters and is administered on the spot by expatriates whose loyalty is to the corporation rather than to the country where they are working. The policy is directed towards making profits for the corporation as a whole. When a single corporation operates in many countries and in many activities—for instance fabricating metal as well as mining ore, the amount of profit attributable to any one activity can be manipulated, by the prices at which products are transferred from one branch to another, to suit the convenience of the corporation, not the needs of the country where the activity is carried out.

The share in proceeds that the local government obtains as royalties and taxes depends upon the relative economic power and negotiating ability of the parties when an agreement between the corporation and a newly-independent government was drawn up. . . .

There is nothing in economic theory to say what is a fair return on natural resources. A corporation can claim that a country within whose boundaries ore happens to have been discovered had neither the finance nor the know-how to develop for itself. Only investment and management by the corporation have turned it into economic wealth. The spokesman for the country can reply that without access to its soil no wealth could have been created. Here there is a sharp clash of interests which cannot be settled by appeal to any accepted rules.

To keep up supplies to the industrialised countries will require new investments, and the Third World countries may be able to demand stiffer terms in the future. Then the interests of the industrial nations will be involved and the outcome will depend upon the balance of power in the world market, not upon any economic principle. . . .

TERMS OF TRADE

There has been much discussion of the overall terms of trade between primary and manufactured products and much complaint from spokesmen for the Third World that the world market system operates unfavourably for them. . . .

In the Third World countries, the level of wages on plantations and mines is kept low by a massive reserve of unemployed labour and the absence of strong trade unions. Where comparable commodities are produced in the West as well as in the Third World (say, sugar in Australia) output per head is generally much lower in the Third World (because of the high investment that has taken place in the West) but wage rates are lower in a greater proportion, so that the Third World countries are low-cost producers. Does this give them an advantage in trade?

Where there is direct competition between natural commodities and synthetics performing the same function—for instance fibres and rubber—low wages have proved an advantage in a defensive sense, for if costs had been higher those products might have been wiped out altogether. In many lines, however, while it is true that the lowest-cost producer has a competitive advantage, this is only an advantage over other producers of the same commodity. For all of them together, demand at any moment is rigid and does not vary much with prices. One can take the market away from another and so appear to gain from being able to sell at a lower price, but the total demand for the commodity as a whole is not increased.

Competition between rival producers, say of tea or oil seeds, may shift demand from one to another but it does not bring about an increase in total receipts for all the competitors taken together. Indeed, when demand is 'inelastic' to price, a reduction in selling price increases the amount bought, if at all, less than in proportion to the fall in price, so that total receipts for all the sellers of the commodity taken together are reduced. This situation is sadly common in the market for primary commodities.

For this reason, the favourite remedy of the IMF for a trade deficit—depreciation of the exchange rate—is often disastrous. Devaluation by a country which is an important source for a commodity precipitates a fall in its price and reduces export earnings all round.

Many countries, each anxious for exports, can produce the same or closely similar commodities; they keep prices low for each other by causing supply to run ahead of demand. Thus, the entry of East Africa into the production of tea and coffee has been a disadvantage to India and Brazil. All three southern continents compete with each other in many tropical specialities. Each can gain an advantage in competition with the others but the result is to keep down the gains from trade for the Third World as a whole. . . .

MONOPSONY

Unfavourable terms of trade emerge in a more or less competitive world market; they are also influenced by the inequality of the commercial and financial power of the parties concerned.

Even in competitive conditions, there is a large gap between the sales value of a raw material at the point of export and at its final destination, which covers transport and handling costs and the profits of dealers. Freight rates are kept at a level that makes shipping profitable. For the workers employed in transport and commerce, wage rates are generally much higher than those in the producing country, and dealers' profits have to be high enough to cover the risks (from their point of view) created by fluctuating prices. Furthermore, nowadays the world market is far from competitive. For most raw materials, the fabricators have open or tacit cartel arrangements to limit competition amongst themselves, while they are buying from weak, scattered and competitive sellers.

The trade in tropical foodstuffs has been to a large extent taken over by a few large transnational corporations, who evidently do not compete keenly with each other but agree in keeping down purchase prices.

This phenomenon is strikingly illustrated by the trade in bananas. Two corporations, with another smaller one, dominate sales in USA, West Europe and Japan, and dominate purchasing in the producing countries, particularly in Central America. The formation of a union of banana exporting countries (UBEC) precipitated a trade war in 1974 in which the buyers penalised countries which tried to impose an export tax by refusing to buy, stopping production on their plantations, and physically destroying boxes of bananas at the ports. The buyers won, and the taxes were withdrawn.

The break-down of the final price in 1971 was such that the gross return to growers was 11.5 per cent of proceeds. The retailers' gross margin was 31.9 per cent. The rest was costs and profits on transport and handling. Formerly shipping and ripening were provided by separate companies. Now the great corporations are integrating these stages of the business, presumably saving costs and increasing their own profit margins.

Technical changes, such as disease resistant breeds, irrigation and improvements in packing and transport have lowered costs. The benefit was partially passed on to consumers but not at all to the primary producers.

The inability of countries competing with each other for exports to restrict supply has led to a continuous deterioration of the terms of trade for the sellers of bananas.

The corporations pass a part of the surplus that they extract from the Third World to the rich countries in taxation (though they are experts at evasion), to rentiers, and in the salaries of their personnel (some of whom may be nationals of poor countries by origin); the rest they amass as finance to increase their own operations.

The consumers in the rich countries have the advantage of secure supplies and guaranteed quality, as well as of the low cost at point of origin (though this makes only a small difference to the final price). It is in this sense that workers in the rich countries, as well as capitalists, are benefiting from the exploitation of the poor countries.

This story is typical of many food products supplied to Western consumers by the great monopsonistic buyers from the Third World.

INSTABILITY

The greatest drawback of depending upon primary commodities for export earnings is the unpredictability of the market. The agricultural sector within an industrial economy usually has enough political leverage to see that it is sheltered in one way or another from the worst effects of instability, while strong capitalist firms in extractive industries can form protective rings for themselves. The Third World countries which import such commodities must pay the protected prices, while their own products, for the most part, are left to the mercy of the laws of supply and demand.

Instability is at three levels. For particular commodities, changes in technology, in consumers' habits or in prices of complementary or substitutable commodities, from time to time cause unforeseeable long-run changes in conditions of demand. These may go either way; for instance, the demand for natural fibres was first devastated by synthetics and then revived by the rise in price of oil that made them expensive. As the rich countries grow, demand sometimes runs ahead of potential supply, so that one commodity or another enjoys a seller's market for a time. This very fact encourages both substitution and a search for new sources of supply so that the advantage of scarcity is soon lost. There is likely to be a general long-run tendency to check the growth of demand relatively to supply; the great versatility of modern technology and the malleability of consumption at a high standard of life mean that no individual natural commodities are indispensable. In spite of all the anxiety nowadays about exhaustible resources, it seems likely that the central buyer will continue to have the whip hand over the peripheral seller for a long time still.

Changes on the side of production also create instability. Crop failure in one region gives a sudden bonus to rival producers in others, or the opening up of a new source of supply is a disaster for the old ones.

Such accidents affect particular commodities. General and chronic instability is transmitted to the market as a whole from the instability of the industrial capitalist economy. The rise and fall of activity in booms and slumps at the centre affects all the countries of the periphery, and the ebb and flow of military expenditure affects very many.

On top of the large swings in demand are superimposed continuous day-to-day oscillations in prices. Direct purchase by the great corporations bypasses the organised produce exchanges, but they still have an important sphere of operation in the trade in many commodities. The business of dealers is to bridge the gap both in time and space between producers and purchasers. They invest finance in buying commodities from the original producers and pass them on to the buyers as required.

The opportunity to make profits by this use of finance arises from the shortage of finance that usually besets the sellers, particularly of seasonal crops. The working capital of a producer is absorbed in a season's output and he needs to sell in order to replenish it and start the next cycle of production. The dealer can buy when price is at its lowest, hold stocks and feed supplies out to the market as prices rise. The inability of the producers to hold back sales to wait for a rise of price is most pronounced for small peasants, but even institutions such as a marketing board may be pressed for cash. Moreover, to hold stocks is to take a risk. Apart from more or less predictable seasonal swings, movements in commodity prices are continually being brought about by changes in the relations of supply and demand. The dealers have to be better informed about market conditions than the producers and, indeed, part of their business is to make profits out of superior knowledge and successful guess-work.

This business is necessarily speculative in the sense that it depends upon taking a view of what will happen next. According to textbook theory, dealers perform a service to the economy by buying in stocks when prices are tending to fall and selling out when prices are tending to rise, thus stabilising prices through time. But guess-work is not always stabilising. Since each watches the others to try to divine how their guesses are going, there is a natural tendency for movements of opinion to set up perverse reactions. A rise in price, instead of restraining demand, as in the textbook theory, increases buying in expectation of a further rise and a fall in price increases sales. Thus, the dealers may themselves bring about the fluctuations that it is supposed to be their function to mitigate.

In popular language 'speculation' is a bad word, and certainly vicious manipulations of the market do occur, but in the general way this kind of speculation cannot be regarded as vicious for it is a normal and inevitable result of playing the game according to the rules of the free market system.

These three layers of instability—long-run shifts in demand, cyclical swings and speculative oscillations interact with each other, and for countries which depend on the world market for their export earnings, make coherent economic policy difficult and turn long-range planning into a dubious gamble.

STABILISATION SCHEMES

The unsatisfactory operation of the market for commodities has long been recognised and spokesmen for the Third World are now urgently demanding reform. They hope to find means, within the world market system, to improve their terms of trade, and to mitigate the nuisance of instability, which works against their interests far more than in their favour.

In principle, the price of a commodity can be kept within a certain range by holding supplies off the market when demand is falling and releasing them when it is rising. This can be done through the operation of a buffer stock, buying and selling the commodity, or by an agreement among producers to restrict output when price has reached a lower limit and to permit sales to expand when price reaches an upper limit; or by some combination of these two principles.

There has been a great deal of talk about the advantages of schemes to stabilise prices but in practice very little has been done. . . . This arises from the fact that the main advantage of stabilisation is to the sellers, who are weak and disorganised, while finance and economic power belong to the buyers—traders and manufacturers in the industrial countries.

The instability of primary product prices is a nuisance for buyers as well as for sellers, but the problem is much more urgent for the sellers than for the buyers. The cost of materials plays a small part in the total trade of the industrialised economies and a still smaller part in their total income, while for many Third World countries receipts from sales of a single commodity, or two or three, dominate their export earnings, and export earnings have a strong influence over the prosperity of their whole economy. From a national point of view, the rise of prices is far less damaging to the buyers than a fall to the sellers, while from the point of view of the traders and manufacturers concerned, in the industrial country, most of a rise in costs is passed on in prices to their own customers. The buyers, therefore, have much less at stake than the sellers. Moreover, the ideology of a capitalist democracy permits government interference with the free play of market forces to favour interests in the home country (for instance by support prices or protection) but is extremely reluctant to admit any responsibility for the effects of home policies upon interests abroad.

If the problem were merely fluctuations of prices about a predictable trend, the operation of a buffer stock would clearly be profitable and capitalist finance would be devoted to stabilisation. But a trend is something that statisticians can perceive over a run of years in the past. It cannot be perceived in advance, particularly in the present age of drastic political and technological discontinuities in the evolution of patterns of supply and demand.

The buyers have generally found that a period of scarcity and high prices for a particular raw material leads before long to a shift in demand (say, the substitution of a synthetic for a natural product) and calls into being fresh sources of supply, so that a brief seller's market is followed by a prolonged buyer's market. (This is just what the spokesmen for the sellers complain of.) The free market system hitherto has suited the interests of the buyers on the whole and they do not encourage plans to interfere with it.

On the side of the sellers, there is a general interest in stabilisation and improvement in their terms of trade, but there are conflicts of interest amongst themselves. The basic mechanism of stabilisation is to withold supplies from a falling market, but for any one seller it is better to get something than nothing. There is always a temptation to sell, although at the expense of another supplier's market, and the temptation is all the stronger when a scheme to raise prices is getting under way. Restriction requires the imposition of discipline over individual interests in a common cause. This means that there must be an authority in each country where the commodity is produced to regulate output, for instance by a system of central procurement or by the allocation of quotas; there must be an agreement amongst the countries on the distribution of the burden amongst them and there must be mutual confidence that it is being fairly carried out.

Furthermore, there are great technical difficulties in arriving at an agreed formula for dealing, for instance, with the relative prices of varieties and grades, for what goes under the name of any single commodity is by no means homogeneous, either technically or commercially. A scheme which has to cover a number of sources of supply involves conflicts of interest amongst them; there is a general conflict between new entrants to the market who want to be allowed to expand their share in output and the old producers who want to restrict it; and there are innumerable minor conflicts over details in any scheme, which make it hard to find a formula which all parties will, first, agree to accept and, second, abide by in face of change. When the buyers are not particularly keen on supporting an agreement, they have ample opportunity to play upon the conflicts within the group of sellers.

Over and above all these difficulties, the sellers lack the finance required to set a scheme afloat. . . .

MONOPOLY POWER

There is one notable case in which a group of sellers were able to use the laws of the market in their own favour—that is the rise in the price of oil in 1973. The Organisation of the Petroleum Exporting Countries was founded in 1960. It arose out of conversations between Venezuela and Iran with the Arab League about the possibility of defending the oil exporters against reductions in the price being imposed upon them by the international oil companies. A secretariat was set up, and all the exporters made gains from their improved bargaining position.

For the Arab League, oil had always had a strategic and political importance. In support of the October War with Israel in 1973, a boycott was instituted against Israel, the USA and Holland. (The distributing companies went through the motions of implementing it while seeing that none of their customers were effectively deprived of supplies.)

This experience made the Arabs realise the potential monopoly power of the oil producers and OPEC imposed a quadrupled price of oil. This was implemented by the distributors, who made enormous profits for themselves.

The success of OPEC has inspired the idea that other groups—for instance, the sellers of bauxite—might also exercise monopoly power to improve their proceeds from sales, but it is unlikely that any general solution to the problem of the weakness of Third World exports could be reached by this means.

There were certain unique features about the case of oil. First, the whole pattern of development in industry had grown round cheap oil from the Middle East, so that demand was inelastic and could not quickly be shifted; secondly, the main producers were bound together by a political motive and had no difficulty in carrying the smaller ones with them; thirdly, the largest producers were in the unusual position of having a sparse population (as well as preserving a highly unequal distribution of income) so that the only imports they required were luxury goods, prestigious buildings and armaments. They had no urgent need for any more export earnings than they were receiving already, and so they did not have the usual reluctance to restrict output in order to maintain the level of prices for the group as a whole. Finally, the distributors were ready to play along with the producers, and, indeed, made huge profits for themselves in the process. This concatenation of circumstances in unlikely to be repeated.

The spokesmen for the industrialised nations appeared to be deeply shocked by the whole affair, but, though OPEC states regard themselves, formally, as part of the Third World, it is only natural that their sudden wealth should incline them towards playing the financial game according to the rich countries' rules.

WORLD INFLATION

One of the complaints made by spokesmen for the Third World is that the purchasing power of their exports is constantly being eroded by inflation in the industrial countries raising the prices of the products that they want to buy.

In the capitalist world today, there are two separate systems of price formation, which can be broadly distinguished, though there is some overlap between them.

For primary products, as we have seen, prices oscillate with the relations of demand to supply; for manufactures, a system of cost-plus prevails; that is to say that the business concerned form selling prices by adding a gross margin to direct running costs (wages, materials and power) calculated to cover overhead costs at some normal level of operation, plus an allowance for net profit.

There are great differences in the power of different types of business to control the prices at which they sell, but monopoly does not necessarily mean restricting output to keep profits high, for the great corporations compete with each other, continually expanding into new markets. The general rule that movements of prices are governed by movements of costs applies to them as much as to small competitive producers.

The main element in costs in industry as a whole is the cost of labour. The price level for manufactures in general is therefore governed by the relation of money-wage rates to productivity. The level of wage rates, in turn, is determined by the fortunes of the class war, that is the struggle of organised labour to maintain its share in the proceeds of industry.

During the long run of expansion and prosperity (interrupted only by minor recessions) for a quarter of a century after the end of the second world war, real-wage rates were rising in all the Western countries, though, as we have seen, their fortunes were not all alike. The continuous rise of money wage rates, necessary to keep the share of real wages from falling, had a tendency to overshoot, so that money wages rose faster than productivity, bringing about a rise in the level of prices; thus, what now seems a mild degree of inflation became chronic.

During this period, various commodities experienced different movements but, on the whole, growth of supply kept ahead of demand and the terms of trade, overall, moved in favour of manufactures. This contributed to the rise of real-wage rates and to some extent to allay inflation in the Western countries. But foodgrains were an exception. The growth of prosperity, particularly in the Soviet sphere, was increasing the consumption of meat and deflecting grain into feeding livestock.

In the 1970s a strong boom developed, particularly in the United States, and the prices of materials shot up. The rise in the price of oil in 1973 exaggerated a movement that was already taking place. In industry, a rise in the cost of materials raises prices relatively to money-wage rates, and therefore generates a demand for a compensating rise in money wages.

Thus the Western world experienced an alarming increase in the rate of inflation, which coincided with a serious slump in activity; the slump brought a fall in the prices of industrial materials (except for oil) but inflation in the West continued and, with rising unemployment, the class struggle became all the more embittered. This experience has brought about a new phase in capitalist development. Western governments are now more anxious to check inflation than to preserve employment. (The neo-neoclassical economists have obligingly come forward with a new theory that inflation is due to a decline in unemployment below its 'natural level'.)

Now as soon as an upswing in industrial activity causes material prices to begin to rise, fear of inflation puts a brake on revival. The new international economic order which is evolving in this situation does not seem to be propitious to meeting the demands of the Third World to an improvement in their share in the benefits of international trade. . . .

IV. CURRENT PROBLEMS IN INTERNATIONAL POLITICAL ECONOMY

The 1980s have been turbulent years in the international economy. Among the complex economic and political issues of the decade, three broad problems stand out: trade and monetary relations between the United States, Japan, and Western Europe; developing-country debt; and widespread poverty in Africa, Asia, and Latin America. The readings in Part IV address these topics.

In the 1970s, an international monetary system based on a gold-backed dollar and generally fixed exchange rates gave way to a system of floating rates in which currency values are determined on private markets. In the meantime, international inflation rates rose, and the dollar's value relative to other major currencies dropped. In 1979, American monetary policy began to concentrate on fighting inflation. The result was a worldwide rise in interest rates, followed rapidly by a deep recession, a reduction in inflation, and a dramatic rise in the dollar's value. Although inflation was brought down, the strong dollar wreaked havoc with many American industries' ability to compete internationally. The American trade deficit grew to well above $100 billion, even as the United States government financed large portions of its growing budget deficit by borrowing from foreigners. In 1986, the dollar dropped back to its lowest levels in nearly forty years. Yet, the underlying uncertainty about international trade and monetary trends remains. Currencies fluctuate widely, many of the world's major nations are experiencing unprecedented trade surpluses or deficits, and capital flows across borders in enormous quantities. In Reading 25, Lester Thurow discusses some of the issues raised by these developments.

One major imbalance of the unsettled 1980s was the financial crisis that affected many heavily indebted developing nations. After 1981, dozens of less developed countries, which owe hundreds of billions of dollars to private banks and Western governments, were unable to maintain payments on their debts and were forced to reschedule their obligations. The debt crisis led to economic and political instability in many major debtors, and to fears of an international banking crisis that would have had serious repercussions for the industrial countries. As

Richard E. Feinberg demonstrates, the crisis has been managed by a mix of government intervention and public-private cooperation, yet the problem is clearly not resolved.

In the background of many discussions of contemporary international economic problems is the desperate plight of the hundreds of millions of people who live in abject poverty in the less developed countries. The world's attention was drawn to Third World poverty most graphically by a wave of famines that swept Africa in the 1980s, but the ranks of the impoverished, the malnourished, and the uneducated are growing all over the Third World; and, in some regions, especially sub-Saharan Africa, living conditions have probably deteriorated substantially since 1970. The solutions to this pressing human problem are hotly debated. While some believe that capitalism is incapable of alleviating poverty in Latin America, Africa, and Asia, A. W. Clausen, former president of the World Bank, argues strongly that market forces represent the best hope for the masses of the developing world.

25. America, Europe and Japan: A Time to Dismantle the World Economy

LESTER THUROW

In this reading, Lester Thurow examines the principal problems facing the United States, Europe, and Japan within the contemporary international political economy. For Thurow, America's low productivity growth rates, Europe's consistently high unemployment, and Japan's rising export surpluses all threaten the current international trading system. Pessimistic about the possibilities of multilateral policy coordination, Thurow concludes with a plea for renewed American leadership.

From 1962 to 1984 the world's exports rose from 12% to 22% of total output. Even in the United States, which has not traditionally been heavily dependent on international trade, exports rose from 6% of GNP in 1962 to 13% of GNP in 1981 before retreating in the face of an overvalued dollar. With exports rising as a fraction of GNP, the world was effectively becoming more and more economically integrated.

Will this postwar trend continue? I believe not. The world economy is in fact at a turning point, and the next ten years are likely to witness a lessening of economic integration.

The reasons for this belief are simple. First, the current degree of economic integration has outrun the world's collective political willingness to manage it. To make today's world economy work, the major industrial countries would have to be willing to co-ordinate their monetary and fiscal policies and to limit movements in exchange rates between major currencies. While both are within the realm of economic feasibility, neither seems within the realm of political feasibility. In the end the national instabilities produced by this collective management

385

failure will force countries to reduce their involvement in the world economy.

Second, within the economies of each of the three major industrial actors—Japan, Europe and the United States—there are unsolved domestic economic problems that can most easily be solved by isolating oneself from world trade.

America faces a productivity problem. To be competitive on world markets at current wage rates it must accelerate its rate of productivity growth. If it cannot, it is likely to withdraw from international competition and retreat into protection.

Europe faces an employment problem. If it cannot begin to generate jobs in the framework of an open economy, it must retreat to a closed economy where it can generate jobs.

Japan faces a trade imbalance problem. Japan relies on exports to lead its domestic growth; but, given the structure of the Japanese economy, the rate at which exports must grow to maintain prosperity far exceeds the rate at which imports will grow without major structural changes. If Japan cannot make the structural adjustments necessary to make imports grow as fast as exports, the rest of the world will gradually exclude Japan from their domestic markets and force Japan to reduce its dependency on world trade.

While each of these problems has a feasible local solution, the local solutions are politically difficult and unlikely to be put in place. To solve their local problems, all of the three major actors will find themselves forced partly to dismantle the current world economy.

THE AMERICAN PROBLEM

America faces a problem that is simply put. The huge technological edge enjoyed by Americans in the 1950s and 1960s has disappeared. Whereas America once had effortless economic superiority, it is now faced with competitors who have matched its economic achievements and may be in the process of moving ahead of it. What is worst, at precisely the moment when America's effortless superiority has vanished, the American economy has been absorbed into a world economy. For most goods there is now a world market, not just an American market. Competition is worldwide, not just American. As a result, America faces the difficult task of learning to compete in a new world economy just at the point when America's relative economic strength is weaker than it has been at any time since the second world war. . . .

While America's previous position of economic superiority has clearly ended, its current position is probably not one of inferiority . . . . [T]he rest of the world has caught up with the United States but is not yet ahead. America's competitive position is one of "an equal among equals."

There is a real danger, however, that America is falling from parity to inferiority if one examines comparative rates of growth of productivity. American productivity growth rates have been below those of Europe and Japan ever since the war, but more importantly they are still below those of Europe and Japan even though these countries have now essentially caught up. In the years from 1977 to 1983, productivity grew at the rate of 1.2% per year in American manufacturing: one-half Germany's growth rate (2.5%), one-third the French rate (3.5%), and less than one-third the Japanese rate (3.9%). Manufacturing is also a relatively bright spot in the American productivity picture. Since the war, productivity growth in the private economy has steadily fallen from 3.3% (1947–65) to 1% (1977–84) . . . .

If such differences in growth rates continue to exist for very long, substantial inferiority cannot be far away.

To outsiders there are simple solutions for America's productivity problems. Nobody can build a high-quality economy out of low-quality inputs just as nobody can build a high-quality product out of low-quality components. Yet whenever the basic inputs—capital, labour, management, labour-management relations—going into the American economy are compared with those of the competition they just don't seem to measure up.

In America's large cities 8% of those entering the workforce test out as functionally illiterate (ie, they cannot read at a fifth-grade level). The average American 17-year-old knows half as much mathematics as the average Japanese 17-year-old. Given such science and maths scores it should come as no surprise that Japan produces twice as many engineers per capita as the United States and that with twice as many engineers on the payroll Japanese products seem to be a little better engineered. In America, test scores both for those leaving high school and going on to college and for those leaving college and going on to graduate school have fallen 10% in the past 15 years. Where America once had a labour force with educational abilities equal to that of the best, it no longer does.

In 1984, America's gross fixed investment (a measure that includes investment in housing) was 16% of GNP. At the same time the Germans were investing 20% and the Japanese 28%. If America were to have kept up with the Japanese in terms of plant and equipment investment per worker (and in the long run it must), it would have had to have essentially doubled its investment to 30% of GNP because of its more rapidly growing labour force. In any one year such gaps make little difference, but compounded over a few decades they spell the difference between success and failure.

America's personal savings rate, 5% in 1983, was the lowest in the industrial world by a factor of almost three. Our neighbours the Canadians saved 13%, the West Germans 14%, the Japanese 21% and the Italians 23%. It does not take a genius to know that Americans cannot compete on world markets saving less than their competitors.

America invests less in civilian research and development than any of its major industrial competitors. American civilian R&D spending runs at about 1.5% of GNP while our competitors are spending 2%. Americans aren't smarter than the Germans or French. German scientists with money will beat American scientists without money most of the time. In the 1950s and 1960s America spent more, not less, on civilian research and development than its competitors.

While it is harder to quantify, American management cannot escape its share of the blame. American firms have undeniable problems with quality control. When asked to rate the quality of their cars, buyers listed only two American-built cars among the top ten. Management is responsible for quality control. If American products are shoddily built, the American management is shoddy.

On that famous bottom line, each major input into the economy will have to be as good as those of the competition if America is to be competitive. A world-class economy demands world-class inputs. Converting existing American inputs into world-class inputs is not technically hard. But doing so is politically difficult. It is not easy to tighten up a school system or reduce consumption.

A far easier solution will be to extend protection to non-competitive industries and gradually reduce America's involvement in international trade. The social changes necessary to meet foreign competition with superior products and productivity are difficult to accomplish while the laws necessary to keep the rest of the world out of the American market are easy to pass.

THE EUROPEAN PROBLEM

In Europe the problem is a lack of jobs. Unemployment has risen every year for more than a decade and is now well into the double-digit range. In some countries unemployment exceeds the levels seen in the Great Depression. No set of democracies can tolerate such a situation for long. Europe's current slow withdrawal from the world economy will eventually become a flight into protection to create jobs unless the employment problem can be turned around.

While on a net basis there have been no new jobs generated in Europe since 1970, the American economy has in the same period of time generated more than 30m; more than 4m in 1984 alone. If one looks at the reasons for the differences between the United States and Europe, it is a good illustration of how it is easy to solve the problems of others while remaining unable to solve one's own problems.

The European problem begins with macro-economic co-ordination. President Reagan proved that Keynesian economics still works, but President Mitterrand also proved that no country in Europe is big enough to practise it alone. If demand is to be expanded, all will have to expand simultaneously. If such co-ordination cannot be arranged, the European common market simply isn't viable.

While America and Europe are often seen as similar, their labour markets are in fact very different. Relative to the price of capital, American wages were 37% lower in 1983 than they were in 1972. This has not happened in Europe. Wages have risen relative to the price of capital until very recently.

The relative price of capital and labour provides a key signal for capitalists making investment decisions. In Europe, where labour costs were rising relative to the cost of capital, firms were told to substitute capital equipment for workers wherever possible. Workers were becoming more expensive relative to machinery. Firms responded as they should to these signals, and the European capital-labour ratio rose 3% per year in the decade ending in 1983. Firms, however, only add employees if their sales growth exceeds their productivity growth. Combine high-productivity growth with governments generally unwilling to pump aggregate demand into the system and European firms could meet their markets with the same or smaller labour forces. The net result was good productivity growth but bad employment growth.

In the United States the capitalists got a very different signal. With labour costs falling relative to the cost of capital, firms were told to substitute workers for capital equipment wherever possible.

The relative movements in average wages also underestimate the real differences between the two economies. Legally-mandated and socially-expected fringe benefits are much larger in Europe than in America. By law, workers in Belgium get a six-week vacation. By law, nobody gets any vacation in the United States and two weeks is the accepted social norm.

There is also less variance in wages in Europe than in America. Minimum wages are much closer to average wages in Europe than they are in America where the legal minimum wage is just 40% of the average hourly wage and largely unenforced (8% of the American workforce works at less than the legally mandated minimum wage). In the recession of 1982 only 43% of those unemployed received any unemployment insurance payments whatsoever and among those who did receive payments it replaced 40% of what they had previously earned. As a result, industries can thrive in the United States paying low wages whereas they could not pay low wages and survive in Europe. Much of

America's employment gain has in fact been in low-wage jobs which the average European worker would reject as unacceptable.

It is easy for an American to tell Europeans to lower their wages, reduce fringe benefits, and relax legal minimum wages, but it is politically hard to do so. No one wants to give up those long vacations and generous fringe benefits.

Europeans are often envious of the rapid growth of new firms in Silicon Valley in California. Their response has tended to focus on subsidies for research and development and the need for a European venture capital industry to help new start-ups. Such activities are unlikely to solve the European jobs problems. What is needed is different forms of social organisation.

New start-ups have one great advantage in America. Firms can easily fire unneeded workers. Advance notice need not be given; severance pay need not be paid. Firms simply do not need to carry unneeded workers if demand is not what was expected. Workers can be hired with the knowledge that if they are not needed they can be quickly fired.

In Europe firings range from difficult and expensive to impossible. This makes it much riskier and more expensive to go into business. What is a reasonable risk in America where labour is a variable cost becomes an unreasonable risk in Europe where labour is an overhead fixed cost.

I am not recommending the American solution to the European job problem. It would be far better to create labour market flexibility with a variable bonus such as that of the Japanese, but if Europe is not able to adopt some solution to its labour market rigidities it will have to close its economy and reflate to create jobs. If one looks at what has happened to unemployment rates in the past decade (up from 2% to more than 11%) under the current system it is difficult to imagine that the current system can continue.

THE JAPANESE PROBLEM

Japan relies on exports to keep its economy running. When the multiplier effects are included, exports accounted for all of Japan's growth in 1983 and two-thirds of its growth in 1984. In 1981 and 1982 there were quarters when domestic Japanese sales were falling but the economy was still growing. Exports were providing more than 100% of the net growth in Japan. When these exports hit the American and European economies, however, they cut local sales and produce unemployment. The unemployment that would normally flow from a stagnant Japanese domestic economy was essentially being exported.

America's trading deficit with Japan, $37 billion in 1984 and likely to be much higher in 1985, is economically and politically unacceptable.

Within the United States, the trade imbalance leads to irresistible political pressures to retreat into ever-widening circles of protection.

Americans have to take some of the blame for the trade deficit with Japan. American firms have refused to design products explicitly for the Japanese market, have refused to learn the Japanese language and customs, have demanded instant success, and have often acted as if it is the duty of Japan to run its economy precisely as the American economy is run. The American government has contributed to the problem by letting the dollar-yen exchange rate rise until it is simply impossible for any American manufacturer to compete.

The origins of Japan's trade surplus are easy to find. Both after the Meiji restoration and the second world war Japan was a poor country desperately anxious to catch up. Its limited foreign exchange earnings had to be devoted to buying foreign technology and machinery that Japan could not produce for itself. To meet this need the whole economy was organised to minimise imports of non-essential goods. If a firm wanted to expand, for example, it had to find ways to expand that did not require foreign goods.

In a western country, that legitimate national need would have taken the form of (easily dismantlable?) legal rules and regulations. In Japan's non-legal consensus society they took the form of social norms and social organisation. How does a foreign firm break in as a new supplier of industrial components, for example, when Japanese firms place a premium on maintaining long-term intimate supply relationships with nearby suppliers in the just-in-time inventory system?

Japan now has an industrial structure that does not absorb imports just when it needs to buy imports to hold markets open for its exports. To change that internal structure, however, involves major industrial shifts that are politically no easier to accomplish in Japan than they would be in the United States or Europe.

There are essentially two options. Japan could practise domestic Keynesian economics to keep demand growing and change the structures of its economy and culture so that imports grow in pace with exports, or Japan could find itself systematically kept out of foreign markets to hold its exports down. From the point of view of a world economy the first option is far better since it leads to an expansion rather than a contraction of world trade and economic integration. But the second option is by far the more likely.

MACRO-ECONOMIC CO-OPERATION

In the recovery from the 1981–82 recession the Reagan administration proved that Keynesian aggregate demand policies still work and that the

United States is still strong enough to use Keynesian policies to restart the world's economic engines. What is not clear, however, is how long the United States can pull the resultant load.

Of the 3m jobs lost in the 1984 trade deficit of $123 billion, Japan, Europe plus Canada, and the rest of the world each received the gift of about 1m American jobs if bilateral deficits are examined. The OECD estimates that one-third of the growth in Western Europe in 1984 could be traced to the American recovery and the high value dollar. Despite this external impetus to their economic growth, most of the rest of the world was still caught up in slow growth in 1985. Most industrial countries had positive growth rates, but few countries outside of the United States had growth rates strong enough to reduce unemployment. And without those millions of jobs from America most of the rest of the world would still have been buried in the recession that began in 1981. . . .

The current situation comes about for a simple reason. While the United States has been pursuing an expansionary fiscal policy of large and rising federal deficits, the rest of the industrial world has been pursuing exactly the opposite policy. America expanded its structural budget deficit from 1980 to 1984, but the rest of the industrial world contracted theirs. Conversely the rest of the world has run a low-interest-rate policy while the United States was running a high-interest-rate policy. The net result has been a rapid recovery in the United States which fuelled a weak recovery in the rest of the industrial world. Abroad, the positive demand effects from the American trade deficit more than offset the negative demand effects from falling foreign government deficits. But unless one believes that the United States can forever run a large trade deficit the macro-economic underpinnings of the current recovery are unsustainable. Whenever the dollar falls and the American trade deficit unwinds, the recovery in the rest of the world stops.

Given the current degree of world integration, it is no longer possible to have unco-ordinated national economic policies where countries attempt to go it alone. Yet co-ordination has repeatedly proven to be beyond reach at the annual economic summits of the industrial powers. This leaves those powers with no option but to sharply reduce the current degree of economic integration and return to the era when it was possible to have viable national economic policies.

At the moment, the world is on this track—moving towards less economic integration and more viable national economic policies. The process is already under way as industry after industry—steel, shipbuilding, cars, consumer electronics—is withdrawn from real international trade and becomes a "managed" industry with formal or informal quotas or other government marketing arrangements. Protection will provide the vehicle for disintegrating the world economy and making national economic policies once again viable, but at an enormous economic and political price.

CO-ORDINATING EXCHANGE RATES

Co-ordinating monetary and fiscal policies would remove some of the violent swings in exchange rates, but not all. Flexible exchange rates are an area where the economics profession was simply wrong. Back in 1971, when the world went on to the current system of flexible exchange rates, economists were sure that it would be impossible to have large fluctuations in exchange rates between major countries over short periods of time or to have currencies that were fundamentally over or undervalued. Yet in the past decade both have occurred.

If changes in productivity, inflation and nominal exchange rates are added together, the real dollar-yen exchange rate rose an amazing 70% over a few months in the early 1980s.

With such violent swings in exchange rates, it simply isn't possible to run efficient economies. Nobody knows where economic activity should be located; nobody knows the cheapest source of supplies; wherever economic activities are located they will be located in the wrong place much of the time. The result is a needless increase in risk and uncertainty, rising instability from protectionism, a shortening of time horizons as firms seek to limit risk and uncertainty by avoiding making long-term commitments, reductions in major new long-term invest-ments, large adjustment costs as production is moved back and forth to the cheapest locations, the expectation of future inflationary shocks, with consequent instability in interest rates . . . .

To correct the situation one need not go back to fixed exchange rates—that is neither possible nor desirable—but it does mean an international agreement to dampen wild fluctuations. The obvious answer is some system of crawling pegs where an attempt is made to isolate the changes needed in foreign exchange rates to accommodate changes in countries' long-term competitiveness—their relative rates of inflation and productivity—from the temporary factors that cause cap-ital flows from one country to another. Nobody can make these judg-ments perfectly but, as the European monetary system demonstrates, it is possible to dampen wild fluctuations

This is unlikely to occur, however. Intellectual fashions often domi-nate current events and the present intellectual fashion favours non-intervention. But with non-intervention and wild currency fluctuations in what is in fact the world's reserve currency, the current world economic system cannot work. Eventually nations will revert to more workable, even if less desirable, national solutions. . . .

NEEDED: AN INTERNATIONAL MANAGER

As it is now structured the international trading system is not working. Most of the world is still experiencing stagnation with rising unemployment. That can only continue with the current pattern of monetary and fiscal policies. America's productivity, Europe's employment, and Japan's export surpluses all threaten the system. Every year the number of products subject to formal or informal restrictions gets larger.

Structural changes will be required to make the world trading system work. This, in turn, requires management. For unless there is a manager actively concerned about the future of the international trading system, the system will simply disappear in a sea of protection.

While the United States is no longer strong enough to dictate economically to the rest of the world, as it did immediately after the war, it is still the strongest country in the industrial world. In the next 20 years the manager's job is going to be one of seeking consensus and making compromises—not giving orders. Only the United States is capable of filling this frustrating role. Unfortunately America has abdicated this responsibility. It needs to take it up again.

26. LDC Debt and the Public-Sector Rescue

RICHARD E. FEINBERG

Richard E. Feinberg surveys both public and private actions in the 1982–1984 debt crisis. While rhetorically opposed to government intervention in the economy, the Reagan administration, according to Feinberg, acted quickly and pragmatically to halt the crisis. It organized rescue packages, expanded the role of the International Monetary Fund, and rescheduled private debt. Feinberg argues that the debt problem demands continued pragmatic adjustments in relations between government and the private financial sector.

In times of crisis, the public sector often intervenes to stabilize shaky private markets and to protect the national interest. Even conservative politicians then set aside their philosophical preference for market mechanisms in favor of government action. Responding to the global recession and the Third World debt crisis, public-sector institutions—including governments in industrial and developing countries and multilateral agencies—have become increasingly active in international credit and investment markets, even when those in power have been ideologically disinclined to do so.

When the deterioration in the creditworthiness of many Third World nations generated a near-panic among international banks, the task fell to official agencies to contain the crisis. Reluctantly but ineluctably, the Reagan Administration contained its hostility toward multilateral financial institutions and approved the doubling of the resources available to the International Monetary Fund. It supported the initiatives of two men of impeccably conservative credentials—Paul Volcker and IMF Managing Director Jacques de Larosière—as they impinged upon the management prerogatives of the commercial banks by indicating how much they should lend to which developing countries. In addition, contrary to its general policy of "getting government off the backs of the people," the Administration worked with Congress to increase the authority of those regulatory agencies that oversee international banking. . . .

Similarly, Third World governments of diverse ideological stripes intervened more heavily in the allocation of foreign exchange and domestic credit in the 1980s. Pursuing countercyclical fiscal policies, many ran budget deficits that absorbed a rising share of available domestic credit in order to cover recession-driven revenue shortfalls. Under pressure from the debt crisis to husband scarce financial resources, governments also stepped in to determine the distribution of foreign exchange. For its part, the indigenous private sector in many developing countries contracted relative to the public sector, a result of scarce, expensive credit and generally adverse business conditions that led to widespread bankruptcies.

The story told here is not intended to suggest that the public sector has or should take control of international finance and investment. Rather, the purpose is to demonstrate that in these spheres, as elsewhere in the global economy, public and private actors can have vital, complementary roles and that, particularly during crises, an assertive public sector can serve the general welfare and save the private sector from its own structural weaknesses.

THE PUBLIC SECTOR'S INVOLVEMENT IN RESCHEDULING

Voluntary private lending to many developing countries came to a screeching halt in mid-1982. The credit markets suddenly found themselves mired in a deteriorated global economy. The length and depth of the global recession, the steep descent in commodity prices, and the new and persistent reality of high interest rates transformed seemingly creditworthy countries into dubious risks. Frightened, many banks closed their windows to new loans and tried to shorten or reduce existing exposure.

To forestall a collapse of private markets, governments had to act. The Reagan Administration took steps in several areas, including the following.

Rescue Packages

When the Mexican government was forced to suspend debt payments in 1982, the U.S. government demonstrated that it could act quickly and decisively. In a few intense days, the Administration pasted together an emergency package of over $8 billion. The official sources were multiple: short-term "swap" lines of credit from the Federal Reserve System and the Treasury Department's Exchange Stabilization Fund (often through the Bank for International Settlements), the Commodity Credit Corporation, and the U.S. Strategic Petroleum Reserve (for advance payments on oil purchases). In addition to the immediate relief, the IMF soon agreed to put up nearly $4 billion over three years. The U.S. government and the IMF also acted to block the banks' flight from Mexico. They supported Mexico's request for rolling over debts due in the near term. In separate addresses, de Larosière and Volcker urged the banks to continue new lending. This sharp departure from the traditional "arm's-length" relationship between the regulators and the international banks established a pattern—repeated for Argentina, Brazil, Chile, Yugoslavia, and other countries—in which official agencies, generally led by the IMF, would seek to overcome the anarchic, self-destructive tendencies of panicky credit markets by bringing all the banks together to persuade them to act in their collective self-interest. Official agencies would indicate both how much credit they could provide and the gap the private sector would have to fill for the debtor country to meet its external obligations, including debt service. Having provided the analysis of the debtor country's earning and financing needs, and sometimes actually assembling hundreds of concerned bankers, officials left it to the banks to divide the burden among themselves.

To keep banks lending to key debtors, officials used a combination of positive and negative inducements. The "carrots" consisted of official credits, an IMF-monitored economic stabilization program, and favorable treatment of new loans by the regulators. The "sticks" included the withholding of IMF and other official loans until the banks agreed to lend new money and, reportedly, exhortations by the regulators— especially toward the smaller, more reluctant regional banks—to play ball. This mix persuaded the banks that their self-interest lay in orderly retrenchment rather than disorganized retreat. Banks would just have to live with most of their existing exposure and even extend some new loans, albeit in amounts considerably below the levels of the "go-go" years.

The IMF's New Roles

Initially, the Reagan Administration was unenthusiastic about increasing IMF resources, but the near-collapse of the private capital markets reversed its position and drove it to support an accelerated and substantial increase in quotas. As a result, resources potentially available to the IMF were approximately doubled. This filled some of the gap being left by reluctant private lenders. IMF lending jumped from an amount equal to less than 1 percent of commercial bank lending in 1979 to over 50 percent in 1983. . . .

Increased resources enhanced the IMF's ability to perform its traditional role of providing policy advice to member governments. But in response to the crisis in the private financial markets, the IMF took on additional roles, assisting the industrial-country governments and banks in formulating and coordinating their policies toward the Third World.

As already noted, the Fund's coordination of policies extended to persuading and coercing the banks to continue modest lending. It helped to impose discipline on markets whose boom—and now bust—mentality had threatened to destabilize the international financial system and their clients' economies. Finally, it worked to coordinate the activities of other lenders, public and private, to increase their collective leverage over borrowers. Commercial banks, government agencies, and often the World Bank waited to approve new credits until the IMF gave the signal that the debtor government had agreed to the appropriate stabilization measures. The U.S. government did occasionally give priority to perceived diplomatic interests, providing new loans in the absence of an IMF agreement (as in Honduras, El Salvador, and Israel). But more often the Administration joined commercial banks to starve recalcitrant debtors of desperately needed credits until they bowed to IMF prescriptions. Conversely, the IMF reinforced the banks' bargaining strength by leaving the impression that it would withhold credits should debtors default on commercial obligations.

Taking on the multiple roles of economic forecaster, policy planner, market disciplinarian, gatekeeper of access to new credits, and police officer for financial norms and obligations, the International Monetary Fund boldly reorganized international credit markets during their worst moments since the Great Depression.

Co-financing

The IMF was not alone in seeking to stimulate new bank lending to developing countries. With the support of the Reagan Administration, the World Bank and the U.S. Export-Import Bank (Eximbank) also attempted, with partial success, to catalyze private finance through various "co-financing" and guarantee schemes.

Instead of financing entire projects by itself, the World Bank has since the mid-1970s sometimes delegated a portion to private lenders. During fiscal 1980–84, World Bank co-financing operations involved an annual average of $1.4 billion in private credits. The Bank noted with disappointment in its 1984 annual report that its co-financing program was being retarded by the shortage of World Bank-style investment projects in recession-ridden developing countries; nevertheless, it expressed satisfaction that the nine "B-loans" completed or substantially completed during fiscal 1984, totaling $1.1 billion, covered a substantial portion of the estimated $5 billion in new commercial bank loans extended during the first nine months of its 1984 fiscal year (July 1983 to March 1984). The Reagan Administration also looked to the Eximbank to stimulate new credits by covering some of the political and commercial risks incurred by banks and suppliers that provide trade finance. The Administration supported increases in Eximbank guarantees and insurance, which reached $8.5 billion in fiscal 1983 (while showing less enthusiasm for the Eximbank's own direct-credit program). The Administration also prompted the Eximbank to open special guarantee and insurance lines of $1.5 billion for Brazil and $500 million for Mexico. Finally, the Foreign Credit Insurance Association (FCIA)—an amalgam of private insurance companies created as an Eximbank affiliate to issue commercial- and political-risk insurance—nearly collapsed as a result of losses incurred in the global recession; the Eximbank was forced to agree to underwrite all of the risk covered by FCIA insurance policies, making the FCIA merely its agent. In effect, the retreat of the private-sector insurers compelled the public sector to step in and absorb the entire risk in insuring private trade finance.

The co-financing schemes of the Eximbank and the World Bank might have been more effective were it not for institutional constraints. Facing record losses in the Third World, the Eximbank became more cautious in some markets. The World Bank refused to grant banks a mandatory cross-default clause that would force its own loan into default if a member government defaulted against the co-financed commercial loan. The overall budgetary ceilings that the Reagan Administration was imposing on the World Bank were less binding than the reticence of the commercial banks and the recession-induced shortage of new projects, but such caps could slow the growth of co-financing in the future.

Despite these limitations, a rising proportion of new loans being made to developing countries were associated with World Bank co-financing as well as co-financing and insurance from export-credit agencies—or were part of IMF-coordinated loan packages. Less willing than before to act alone, the alarmed private sector increasingly sought the clasp of the visible hand of government before risking capital in uncertain Third World markets.

Commercial Debt Rescheduling

The banks' biggest challenge has been to protect their existing exposure, endangered by the deteriorated international environment. Since most developing countries clearly could not meet the schedule for repayment of principal, debts had to be restructured. Whereas official creditors had their "Paris Club," no formal creditor-debtor framework existed for conducting negotiations on commercial bank debt when the crisis broke in 1982. In helping to design and manage the process whereby commercial bank debts could be restructured, official agencies played a major role in at least six ways.

First, the IMF calculated the debtor nations' financing needs. These projections informed official and private creditors about the amount of debt that could be served and how much needed a new repayment timetable, as well as how much new lending would be needed.

Second, and more generally, the IMF served as a conduit of information between the debtor countries and their creditors. It provided detailed data on the current and probable future state of the debtors' economies and in some cases also sought, with varying degrees of success, to organize debt-information systems. The banks were thereby in a position to make more informed and rational decisions.

Third, IMF stabilization programs tried to begin to restore some confidence in the debtor nations' creditworthiness. The banks generally made reschedulings contingent upon the signing of an IMF stand-by arrangement. As the IMF noted in 1983, "negotiations with the banks and the Fund often took place simultaneously and in some of the major cases, their successful conclusions were closely interrelated."

Fourth, official agencies in some cases provided "bridge" financing during the renegotiation period. Pending agreement on a medium-term financial package, central banks in the industrial countries sometimes provided short-term injections of liquidity to prevent an interruption in the developing countries' external payments. As the case of Mexico illustrated, the Federal Reserve Board and the U.S. Treasury worked with the commercial banks to stitch together the rescue package.

Fifth, acting in defense of the long-term economic and political interests of the banks themselves as well as U.S. diplomatic interests, officials urged banks to reduce interest spreads and fees—advice that the banks began to heed in 1984. (Congress had reinforced this advice in 1983 when it reduced the incentives to charge high fees, legislating that any loan fee exceeding the administrative cost of making a loan would have to be amortized over the life of the loan rather than taken in full up front.)

Sixth, public officials nudged banks to abandon their traditional preference for "short-leash" reschedulings and undertake major, multi-year debt restructurings. The communiqué issued by the heads of state of the seven leading industrial nations at their June 1984 summit in London forcefully encouraged "more extended multi-year rescheduling of commercial debts." Shortly after the London summit, the commercial banks and Mexico set the new pattern by agreeing to reschedule some $50 billion in principal payments falling due through 1990.

Thus official agencies have become deeply involved in many facets of the rescheduling process. Some bankers were annoyed at these interventions, viewing them as usurpations of their managerial prerogatives, but many recognized that they might not have survived otherwise. . . .

GOVERNMENT EXPANSION IN DEVELOPING COUNTRIES

The same forces that drove the Reagan Administration to intervene in financial markets forced governments in the Third World to intrude more deeply into their own domestic economies. In many countries, governments became voracious consumers of credit. Their deficits widened: spending expanded to offset the decline in private-sector employment and consumption, and revenues fell as the tax base contracted. The average ratio of government expenditure to gross domestic product for all developing countries rose, according to the IMF, from 25.8 percent in 1979–81 to 27.8 percent in 1982 and 28.4 percent in 1983. To finance this relative increase in the size of the public sector, governments had to soak up a rising share of available credit, at the expense of the private sector. (Some of the resources captured by governments were used to meet service on the external debt. In that sense, governments gave preference to external creditors as against domestic borrowers. In this conflict of interest between the international banks and the indigenous private sector, Third World entrepreneurs lost out. At the same time, governments increasingly assumed some responsibility for the external debts of private borrowers.) The public sector's absorption of domestic credit in Brazil rose from 12 percent in 1979 to 45 percent in 1983; in Kenya, from 27 to 38 percent; and in Sri Lanka, from 36 to 42 percent.

Many governments also slapped on exchange controls and imposed administrative mechanisms for determining trade flows. In some cases, as in Brazil, Chile, and Mexico, the crisis even forced governments to abandon efforts at trade or exchange liberalization. The IMF commented that "in developing countries, measures to restrict imports and current payments have increasingly been the response to severe balance-of-payments problems." While pointing to certain trends toward liberalization in some countries, the IMF found "a general reversion to exchange controls" in developing countries experiencing balance-of-payments difficulties as well as the increased use of other restrictive practices, including the widespread build-up of arrears on debt-service obligations, the control of invisibles (such as personal travel allowances), and the use of administered, multiple-currency arrangements.

The private sector was most severely wounded in Latin America. As sales revenues slumped and debt-service costs rose sharply, profits fell, cash flows contracted, and bankruptcies multiplied. In Brazil, for example, business failures hit record levels. Severe recession also brought disaster to some domestic financial sectors. The Mexican government at one blow nationalized a banking sector reeling from massive devaluations, burdensome foreign debts, and capital flight. The debt crisis hurt private firms in another way: governments that controlled foreign-exchange allocation tended to give preference to debts owed by public-sector institutions. Private firms had to stand at the end of the queue, and some were forced to liquidate assets being held abroad in order to honor their debt-service obligations.

To be sure, there were some contrary trends in China and elsewhere in Asia, Hungary, and some Latin American and sub-Saharan African countries. For the most part, however, efforts at denationalization were incipient and halting, facing the political constraints of vested interests and the financial thinness of private capital markets. In any case, these counter-trends should not blind us to the impressive shift of relative power and resources to the public sector that occurred in many Third World countries. . . .

PRAGMATISM IS STILL NEEDED

Rhetoric and reality can be far apart. Over the last four years, the U.S. government combined passionate faith in the free market with international financial policies that relied heavily on official action. Public-sector institutions mobilized their own resources and sought to coordinate private markets in order to manage a global financial crisis. This increased public-sector activity was required to steady credit markets and to reduce the costs of a deep economic recession. Similarly, governments in many developing countries intervened more decisively in their own credit and foreign-exchange markets.

In managing the debt crisis, public-sector institutions demonstrated their capacity to act quickly and effectively. Despite the tremendous size and complexity of the international financial markets, their workings proved not to be beyond the understanding or reach of wise functionaries. Their masterful crisis management enabled the commercial banks to avoid catastrophic losses, although some write-offs were experienced in 1984 and more can be expected in the future. (The amelioration of the debt crisis in 1983–84 was also the result of economic recovery in the United States, itself the product of government action: the strong fiscal stimulus from the Administration's programmed budget deficit.)

Some of the reforms have created new structures that ought to be institutionalized and strengthened. Through their inclusion in the IMF's General Arrangements to Borrow and their use of central-bank swap lines of credit, the developing countries have been more fully integrated into the international financial system. New mechanisms and modalities have been created for the rescheduling of commercial debt. In the

United States, as in other industrial countries, regulatory agencies have been permanently empowered to supervise international lending with greater vigor.

Other reforms that responded to the more momentary aspects of the crisis are unlikely to endure. The banks are anxious to make IMF-managed lending a matter of memory and to resume voluntary market decisions. But the creation by the banks of their own Institute for International Finance—to gather data on debtors' economies and debt positions and to discuss bankers' lending strategies—suggests a hesitancy to return completely to the decentralized market of the past. It remains to be seen whether the new private Institute will be able to perform some of the functions of the IMF adequately.

As developing countries adjust their economies to the new global realities, IMF stabilization programs will gradually end and the IMF will become a net recipient of capital flows from the Third World. Both the Reagan Administration and many developing countries favor such a withdrawal. The Administration wants to limit the IMF to emergency, short-term lending. At the same time, the IMF's stringent stabilization programs have won it few new friends in the developing countries; despite its role in preventing a financial collapse that would have caused great damage to creditors and debtors alike, it is widely perceived as having captured a global adjustment process that provided the Third World with little voice and a disproportionate burden.

Although considerable progress has been made, it would be a grave mistake to imagine that the debt problem has been definitively solved. Many debtor nations have only begun to readjust their development strategies; their debt-service ratios remain very high; and their ability to sustain rapid export expansion depends on many unknowns, including growth rates and trade policies in the industrial countries. Popular demand for relief from austerity could still interrupt debt service or jeopardize export growth. Moreover, the sharp contraction in both private credit and investment flows that has occurred over the last three years has deprived developing nations of needed capital and delayed their recovery. The commercial banks continue to behave with extreme caution, and net lending to the non-oil developing countries dropped to near zero during the first half of 1984. Even if direct investment becomes more robust, it will certainly not expand rapidly enough to offset the reduction in bank flows. Developing countries will have to struggle to raise internal savings rates to offset the reduced availability of external capital. . . .

The key to the successful management of these problems can be found in the lesson of the recent past: changing circumstances demand a pragmatic adjustment in the relations between the public and private sectors.

27. Poverty in the Developing Countries

A. W. CLAUSEN

In this address, A. W. Clausen, then President of the International Bank for Reconstruction and Development (World Bank), set forth a classically Liberal view of the economic and social problems of the Third World. For Clausen, freer international trade and payments represent the brightest hope for economic development, just as the domestic market mechanism provides the best manner of achieving more social equity for the people of the Third World. Clausen does see a proper role for government intervention, especially in the provision of basic human services and infrastructure. Nonetheless, he regards the market as the most efficient provider of economic well-being to the impoverished peoples of the less developed countries.

. . . Some people imagine that poverty in developing countries is a hopeless situation, that progress is impossible. This image of the world is demonstrably false. But our survey of poverty in 1985 does not give us any cause for complacency either.

The situation is most bleak in Sub-Saharan Africa. In nearly all the nations of Africa, one-half to three-fourths of the population subsist in absolute poverty. Statistics about the number of people in absolute poverty can be only very approximate. But the poverty is no less deadly because we cannot measure it precisely:

In Gambia, for example, over half of all rural children die by age five.
In Guinea-Bissau, almost the entire population suffers from malaria and diarrhea. Sixty percent of the people in Guinea-Bissau suffer from respiratory infections.
Even in Nigeria, with one of the highest per capita income levels of Sub-Saharan Africa, over a third of urban families and over half of rural families are unable to obtain a calorie-adequate diet.

For Sub-Saharan Africa as a whole, life expectancy at birth is 49 years, compared with 75 years in the world's industrial countries. There is still only one nurse for every 3,000 Africans, one doctor for every 21,000

Africans; here in the United States, we have one nurse for every 140 persons, one doctor for every 520. Of the school-age children in Africa, one in five is not enrolled in school.

As low as these indicators of health and education in Africa are, they were much lower only two or three decades ago. The number of doctors and nurses in proportion to population has doubled since 1960. The proportion of children in school has also doubled since 1960.

But in the early 1970s, average income began falling in the poorest countries of Africa. Food production fell behind population growth. Today, even if all the food available in Africa, including imports, were divided equally, it would not be enough to meet even minimum per capita calorie requirements.

Population growth in Africa is higher than anywhere else in the world—and it is accelerating. The efficiency of investment in Africa is lower than anywhere in the world—and it is declining.

Economic malaise has contributed to mounting political instability. Violence within and between nations has increased, and, mainly as a result, one in 200 Africans today is a refugee.

The global recession has accelerated the process of economic decay in Africa. Some African governments are not able to provide the most basic services such as road maintenance anymore or, for that matter, even pay their own employees regularly.

Then, in addition to all these other problems, drought struck much of Africa beginning in 1982. . . .

. . . Leaders of the relief effort will be the first to insist that emergency relief is not enough. We must act with equal vigor to tackle Africa's long-term development problems. Otherwise, we are bound to see deepening poverty—mass starvation again and again—in Sub-Saharan Africa.

By contrast, let me turn now to two developing regions of the world that have been making impressive progress against poverty: East Asia, including China, and the Mediterranean countries. Not so long ago, these regions were characterized by widespread, miserable poverty. But now the bulk of the people in these regions have enough to eat, substantial improvements have been made in infant mortality and life expectancy, and virtually all children go to school. Poverty is still pervasive only in remote areas, such as the two Yemens, or in countries scarred by war, such as those of Indochina.

China is a special case. It is much poorer than the rest of East Asia, but China, too, has eliminated the worst aspects of poverty. Notwithstanding much progress, the government of China still considers about one-fifth of China's population to be unacceptably poor. And we in the Bank concur with that judgment.

Redistribution of wealth has helped to reduce poverty in several countries—including China, of course, but also including a country as capitalistic as the Republic of Korea. Most of the developing countries of East Asia and the Mediterranean have also made special efforts to help the poor on an ongoing basis—through the expansion of public education, for example. But it is no coincidence that these regions have also been characterized by economic success generally. Rapid and sustained economic growth has been basic to the reduction of poverty in East Asia and the Mediterranean.

Most of the developing countries in East Asia and the Mediterranean have maintained special efforts to reduce poverty throughout the recent recession. Now that their economies are growing again, we can expect them to make further progress in reducing poverty.

The world can also take encouragement from the development saga of South Asia. Only twenty years ago, the prospects for South Asia looked as dismal as the prospects for Africa seem right now. Yet South Asia has made considerable progress against poverty.

In the 1960s, India and its neighbors were forced to import massive amounts of food, especially in years of bad weather. There was every reason to be concerned that population would continue to increase faster than food production. We had visions of endemic famine and violence in South Asia. But most of South Asia has now achieved food security through the Green Revolution. Economic growth has more than kept pace with population growth, and India and Pakistan have managed to establish large industrial sectors in the process of that economic growth.

Pakistan is the only country in the region that actually reduced the number of its citizens in poverty during the 1970s. India reduced the proportion of its population in poverty, but, because of population growth, the number of poor people actually increased. Sri Lanka has long scored relatively high on indicators of social welfare, but at the other extreme is Bangladesh—where more than three-quarters of the population remain trapped in absolute poverty.

South Asia still includes at least half of the world's poorest people. Yet the heroic efforts of the past twenty years have averted what could have been a nightmare, and significant parts of South Asia have demonstrated economic promise.

Average per capita income in Latin America is higher than in the developing countries of East Asia. Yet the incidence of absolute poverty in Latin America remains disproportionately high. There is little absolute poverty in countries such as Argentina or Costa Rica. But poverty is still a serious problem in most of Latin America, and the region includes countries such as Bolivia and Haiti where the extent of poverty is not much different from that found in Sub-Saharan Africa.

Latin America was dealt a body blow by the international debt crisis.

In Mexico, for example, real wages fell 25 percent between 1981 and 1983. In Chile, urban unemployment reached 30 percent. The nations with the biggest debts have now all adopted economic adjustment programs and have arranged to reschedule significant portions of their debts, but some of the smaller countries seem to be floundering and are still looking for ways to deal with their economic and social problems. Poverty has become more severe and widespread throughout Latin America and the Caribbean, and the prospects are grim in those countries that cannot settle on reasonable programs of adjustment.

In sum, the historical record shows that progress against poverty is possible. But progress is probably more difficult as we enter 1985 than it has been for decades. . . .

Let me make an important point: commitment to the poor need not imply a bias against the private sector. . . . There is no more powerful force for progress against poverty than the initiative and ingenuity of poor people themselves.

But selective government intervention is necessary, too. Public education, especially elementary education, yields very high economic returns in developing countries. Government action is also needed to improve and extend health and family planning services more widely. There are an estimated 65 million couples in developing countries who do not want more children but still do not use contraception, often for lack of access to effective contraceptives.

We have not found very effective ways to raise the productivity of the poorest 10 to 20 percent of the population—landless laborers, for example. Some of the very poorest people in any society are sick or handicapped and will always need help from relatives or from society as a whole. But by and large our experience has confirmed that the goals of economic growth and poverty reduction can be entirely complementary to each other.

But then came the worst recession in more than forty years. Most developing countries have been confronted with severe balance of payments problems. Average per capita income has stagnated, and in many countries it has actually declined.

For most developing countries, regaining financial stability and then reviving economic growth have become urgent priorities. For poor people too—perhaps especially for poor people—financial and economic recovery is vital. Poor people suffer terribly under conditions of general economic decline.

The nations of the world are all knit together through international trade, capital flows, and transfers of technology. So revival of economic growth in the developing countries depends partly on the economic policies of the world's industrial countries. If the industrial countries manage to maintain their own economic expansion and resist the pressures for protectionism, the developing countries will be able to increase their export earnings. There is no one factor which is more important to Third World growth than export earnings. Lower interest rates are also of vital concern to the heavily indebted countries. In addition, the industrial countries can help by encouraging a revival of international investment—by commercial banks and private corporations, and also through official channels such as the World Bank.

And, of course—perhaps most important—economic growth in the developing countries depends very much on their own efforts too. On the whole, the developing countries have adjusted to recession and the debt crisis remarkably well. They were forced to cut back drastically on imports and incomes, but many countries have managed to cut back in an orderly way and, therefore, reduce the destructive impact of the crisis.

Some countries have, simultaneously, eliminated long-standing inefficiencies in their economies and shifted resources into export products. Such adjustments in economic structure may add to the short-term hurt, but they do help to rekindle growth in the long term. In many of the most hard-pressed developing countries, such structural adjustment is necessary to renewed economic growth—and renewed economic growth is absolutely essential for progress against poverty in the years ahead. . . .

. . . Progress against poverty in the years ahead will also depend on economic adjustment policies within the developing countries—policies designed to distribute the costs and benefits of adjustment fairly.

Some governments have taken steps to protect the poor in the process of adjustment. In Brazil, for example, while wage increases have generally been held down below the rate of inflation, wages at the lower end of the scale have been allowed to keep pace with inflation. In Indonesia, the government has needed to reduce its public investment program dramatically, but it has given high priority to public investments that are important to the poor—in agriculture, for example.

Programs to improve education, health, agricultural productivity, and municipal services among the absolute poor are difficult to get under way. If a government dismantles them in a budget-cutting exercise today, it will take years to build them up again.

It is possible, in designing adjustment programs, to identify policy reforms that will accelerate growth and, at the same time, concentrate the increase in incomes among the poor. Liberalizing trade encourages efficiency and growth, but it especially encourages labor-intensive industry in the developing countries and, therefore, more jobs for the poor. Raising agricultural prices stimulates increased production and, at the same time, benefits smallholder farmers. When government subsidies go mainly to relatively well-off people in the cities, cutting back will make the economy more efficient and, at the same time, reduce the tax burden on poor farmers.

The government of Zambia is pursuing a package of reforms that includes price decontrol, a more realistic exchange rate, wage restraint, and the reduction of subsidies. While these reforms have lowered the real incomes of some Zambians, especially in the urban areas and the formal sector, the majority of Zambians, who live and work in the rural areas, are benefiting from higher agricultural prices. As part of the adjustment package, the government has also managed to increase spending on health and education and on public investment in agriculture.

The government of China has also let agricultural prices rise, and China's peasants now have more scope for private production. These reforms have led to a bonanza of increased agricultural production, and they have raised the incomes of most of China's poorest people by at least 50 percent over the past five years.

Progress against poverty in the world has suffered a setback in the 1980s. But we now know from experience that progress is possible and that focused efforts to foster growth among the poor are workable. . . .

It is hard to believe now, but only a generation ago the prospects of Korea were regarded as dismal. The Koreans have proven the experts to be dead wrong.

Twenty years ago, recurrent famine and increasing violence in South Asia seemed all too likely. But India and Pakistan have achieved food security for hundreds of millions of the world's poorest people.

So now is the time to dream of an Ethiopia where people are well fed from their own production. Now is the time to dream of a Gambia in which children will live to realize their genetic potential.

I am not, by nature, a dreamer. I am a banker.

But the developing countries have already shown that mass, abject poverty can be eliminated. With redoubled efforts on their part, with continued assistance from us in the industrial countries, the elimination of absolute poverty in this world of ours is a feasible project. . . .

Acknowledgments (continued from p. iv)

December 1979, with permission of the International Studies Association, Byrnes International Center, University of South Carolina, Columbia, SC 29208. © 1979 International Studies Association.

Robert Kudrle, "The Several Faces of the Multinational Corporation: Political Reaction and Policy Response," from *An International Political Economy*, ed., W. Ladd Hollist and F. La Mond Tullis (Boulder: Westview, 1985), pp. 175–197.

David A. Lake, "International Economic Structures and American Foreign Economic Policy, 1887–1934," *World Politics* 35, no. 4 (July 1983). Copyright © 1983 by Princeton University Press. Reprinted with permission of Princeton University Press.

Stanley Lebergott, "The Returns to U.S. Imperialism, 1890–1919," *The Journal of Economic History* 40, 2 (June 1980). Reprinted with permission of The Economic History Association and the author.

V. I. Lenin, *Imperialism: The Highest Stage of Capitalism*, selected passages. © 1939, Ren. 1967. Reprinted by permission of International Publishers Co., Inc., New York.

Charles Lipson, "The International Organization of Third World Debt," *International Organization* 35, 1 (1981). Reprinted by permission of The MIT Press, Cambridge, Massachusetts, and The University of Wisconsin Board of Regents.

Riccardo Parboni, "The Dollar Standard," from *The Dollar and Its Rivals* (London: Verso, 1981). Reprinted by permission.

Edith Penrose, "The State and the Multinational Enterprise in Less Developed Countries," from *The Multinational Enterprise*, John H. Dunning. Reprinted by permission of George Allen & Unwin.

Joan Robinson, "Trade in Primary Commodities," © Cambridge University Press. Reprinted with permission of Cambridge University Press.

B. Rowthorn, "Imperialism in the Seventies: Unity or Rivalry?" from *New Left Review* 69, Sept./Oct. 1971. Reprinted with permission by Verso NLB.

Richard L. Sklar, "Postimperialism: A Class Analysis of Multinational Corporate Expansion," *Comparative Politics*, 9 (October 1976), 75–92. © The City University of New York.

Lester Thurow, "America, Europe and Japan: A Time to Dismantle the World Economy," *The Economist*, November 9, 1985, pp. 21–26. Reprinted with permission by The New York Times Syndication Sales Corporation.

Raymond Vernon, "International Investment and International Trade in the Product Cycle," Reprinted from *Quarterly Journal of Economics*, vol. 80, no. 2, 1966 with permission of author.

Jacob Viner, "Power Versus Plenty as Objectives of Foreign Policy in the Seventeenth and Eighteenth Centuries," *World Politics* 1, no. 1 (Oct. 1948). Published by Princeton University Press.

Index

411